Goa & Mumbai

Panaji & Central Goa
p78

Mumbai
(Bombay)
● p38

☐ Goa

South Goa
p159

THIS EDITION WRITTEN AND RESEARCHED BY

Paul Harding

Abigail Blasi, Trent Holden, Iain Stewart

Contents

ASHIYANA RETREAT
CENTRE, MANDREM P152

PALOLEM P183

Contents

CHURCH OF OUR LADY OF THE
IMMACULATE CONCEPTION, PANAJI P79

Welcome to Goa & Mumbai

Pint-sized Goa is more than beaches and trance parties. A blend of Indian and Portuguese cultures, sweetened with sun, sea, sand, seafood and spirituality, there's nowhere in India quite like it.

Beach Bounty

Goa's biggest draw is undoubtedly its virtually uninterrupted string of golden-sand beaches. This shimmering strand of sand stretches along the Arabian Sea from the tip to the toe of the state, and each of the various beaches have developed their own personalities and reputations since the hippie days of the '60s. They cater to every tropical whim: choose from backpacker Arambol or bolder, brasher Baga; from the palm-fringed sands of Palolem to hippie market bliss at Anjuna or lovely, laid-back Mandrem; from expansive groomed sands in front of fancy five-star resorts or hidden crescent coves, where the only footprints will be the scuttling crabs and your own.

Spiritual Sanctuary

Want to top up your Zen as well as your tan? Welcome to winter in Goa where yoga is king and the crop of spiritual activities grows more bountiful each year: sunrise t'ai chi sessions, reiki healing courses, meditation and just about every other form of spiritual exploration are practised freely. Many travellers come here for a serious yoga experience and you'll find everything from drop-in classes to teacher training courses and spiritual retreats.

Spice of Life

Food is enjoyed fully in Goa and Mumbai (Bombay), as it is throughout India. The scents, spices and flavours of Goa's cuisine will surprise and tantalise even seasoned travellers: whether it's a classic fish curry rice, a morning *bhaji-pau* (bread roll dipped in curry), a piquant vindaloo, with its infusions of wine vinegar and garlic, or a spicy *xacuti* (coconut and chilli) sauce, the Indo-Portuguese influence is a treat for the tastebuds. While you're here, visit a backcountry spice farm to learn why the Portuguese were so excited about Goa.

Colonial Heritage

Both Goa and Mumbai stand out in India for their extraordinary colonial-era architecture and heritage. Mumbai's British legacy of gaudy Gothic and Indo-Saracenic buildings is an architectural feast not to be missed. The Portuguese arrived in Goa in 1510, lured by the exotic East and the promise of lucrative spice routes. Their indelible mark is still evident in the state's baroque architecture, whitewashed churches, crumbling forts, colourful Catholic ceremonies, mournful fado music and the stunning cathedrals of Old Goa.

Why I Love Goa & Mumbai

By Paul Harding, Writer

My first visit to Goa, in the late '90s, was also my first visit to India. After travelling overland from Delhi through central India and Mumbai, Goa – with its beaches, all-night parties and laid-back tropical vibe – was a blissful surprise. I've been back many times and while some things may have changed, the essence remains the same. I love hanging around by the beach, cruising through impossibly green countryside on two wheels, and the evening ritual of watching the sun melt into the Arabian Sea with a cold beer and a plate of spicy prawns. And I love the Goan people – hard-working, optimistic, quick with a smile and always happy to chat.

For more about our writers, see page 256

Above: Hindu temple, Goa

Goa & Mumbai

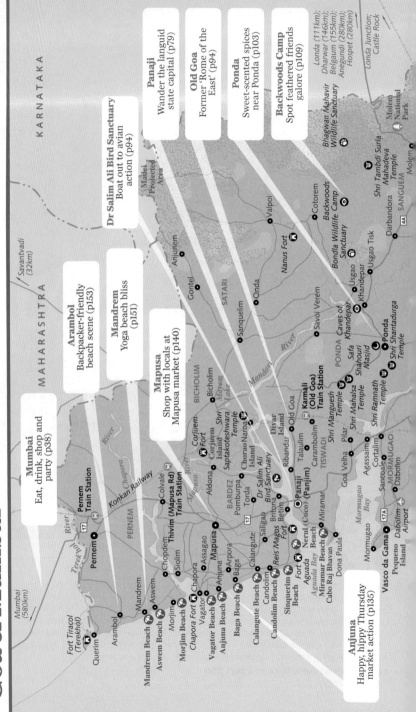

Mumbai
Eat, drink, shop and party (p38)

Arambol
Backpacker-friendly beach scene (p153)

Mandrem
Yoga beach bliss (p151)

Dr Salim Ali Bird Sanctuary
Boat out to avian action (p94)

Panaji
Wander the languid state capital (p79)

Old Goa
Former 'Rome of the East' (p94)

Ponda
Sweet-scented spices near Ponda (p103)

Backwoods Camp
Spot feathered friends galore (p109)

Mapusa
Shop with locals at Mapusa market (p140)

Anjuna
Happy, hippy Thursday market action (p135)

MAHARASHTRA

KARNATAKA

Mumbai
(580km)

Savantvadi
(32km)

Londa (111km);
Dharwar (146km);
Belgaum (155km);
Anegundi (280km);
Hospet (280km)

Londa Junction;
Castle Rock

0   10 km
0   5 miles

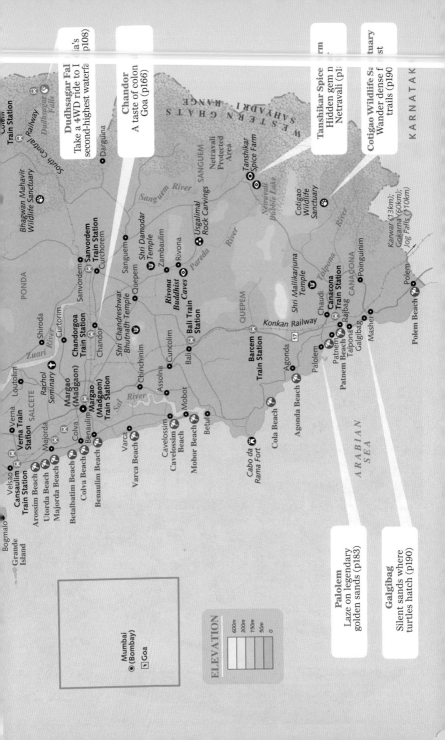

Dudhsagar Fal...
Take a 4WD ride to I...ia's (p108)
second-highest waterfa...

Chandor
A taste of colon...
Goa (p166)

Tanshikar Spice...rm
Hidden gem n...
Netravali (pl...

Cotigao Wildlife Sa...tuary
Wander dense f... st
trails (p190)

KARNATAK...

Palolem
Laze on legendary
golden sands (p183)

Galgibag
Silent sands where
turtles hatch (p190)

Mumbai
◉ (Bombay)
▽ Goa

ELEVATION

600m
300m
150m
50m
0

Goa & Mumbai's
Top 12

Palolem Beach

balmy seas, gently swaying palm trees, good food, beach huts galore and a colourful backpacker-oriented beach-bar scene make Palolem (p183) a favourite with travellers from across the globe. Even Matt Damon went for a run here in *The Bourne Supremacy*. Though some say it's too crowded in high season, there are few better all-round beaches in Goa for yoga, kayaking, swimming or just lazing in your beachfront hammock, and the quieter beaches of Patnem and Agonda are just a short ride away.

Panaji (Panjim)

Slung along the banks of the broad easy, breezy city with the delightful old Portuguese-era districts of Fontainhas and Sao Tomé the perfect setting for a lazy afternoon of wandering. Sip firewater feni with locals in a hole-in-the-wall bar, gamble the night away on a floating luxury casino, clamber up to the wedding-cake-white Church of Our Lady of the Immaculate Conception or poke about in boutiques and book shops. You'll probably find you're not missing the beach one bit.

Anjuna Market

3 Whether you're in the market for some serious souvenirs or simply looking for an injection of local life, Goa's many markets are the place to be. The most famous is Anjuna's flea market (p135), held every Wednesday in high season since the 1970s. It's a curious blend of traders and stalls from all over India, backpackers, day trippers and the odd dreadlocked hippie, but it's not to be missed. For more local flavour, head to Mapusa (p140) for its mammoth Friday market day, where you'll find fresh produce, spices and textiles in tightly packed stalls thronging with locals.

Mumbai's Colonial-Era Architecture

4 Mumbai (Bombay) is not all eating, shopping and Bollywood. After you've had your fill of all three, take time to explore the city's Victorian colonial-era architecture (p41), with a stroll past the Gateway of India, the 1848-built High Court, the University of Mumbai and the extravaganza that is Chhatrapati Shivaji Terminus (Victoria Terminus) train station. You can even take up residence at the heritage Taj Mahal Palace Hotel, Mumbai, gazing over Mumbai's harbour, for that most Raj-era of city retreats.

Gateway of India (p42) and Taj Mahal Palace Hotel (p41)

Mellow Mandrem

5 Downward-dog the days away in lovely, laid-back Mandrem (p151), where an early morning yoga class, followed by a refreshing swim, an afternoon on a sun lounge with a good book and perhaps an ayurvedic massage is perfect for your spiritual soul. This is one of Goa's prettiest beach strips and an ideal base for accessing Aswem and Morjim to the south and backpacker-friendly Arambol to the north – all with their own impressive beach huts and activities from surfing to paragliding. Ashiyana Retreat Centre (p152)

Spice Farms

6 South Indian spices were a major attraction for the seafaring Portuguese and today one of the best day trips away from the beach is to one of several commercial spice plantations (p105) orbiting around Ponda. They can be a little touristy but the plantation tours are fascinating and aromatic. Most offer a delicious buffet thali lunch served up on a banana leaf, and some farms have a resident elephant or two for rides and bathing. If you're in the south, visit the remote and virtually tourist-free Tanshikar Spice Farm (p188). Tropical Spice Plantation (p105), Ponda

Old Goa

7 The 17th-century Portuguese capital of Goa (p94) once rivalled Lisbon and London in size and importance and was widely known as the 'Rome of the East'. Today all that remains of the once-great city is a handful of amazingly well-preserved churches and cathedrals – but what a sight they are! Basilica of Bom Jesus contains the grizzly 'incorrupt' body of St Francis Xavier, while Se Cathedral is the largest in Asia. Stop by for Mass on a Sunday morning, marvel at the intricately carved alters, and imagine religious life here four centuries ago. Sé Cathedral (p97)

AMAR GROVER/GETTY IMAGES ©

Cruising the Backroads

8 Cruising Goa's back lanes and beach villages on two-wheels is practically *de rigueur* in Goa and is a great way to get around. For just a few dollars a day you can hire a moped or Royal Enfield motorbike at any of Goa's beach resorts, and head out into the hinterland to experience a slower, pastoral pace of life in the clean, green Goan countryside. Cruise out to villages such as Chandor (p166) and Quepem (p168), protected forest areas such as Netravali and cross rivers on old flat-bottomed vehicle ferries to see how rural Goans really live. Enfield motorbike, Anjuna Flea Market (p138)

Watching Wildlife

9 Goa's forests and wildlife reserves offer plenty for nature lovers. Avid birdwatchers will be in heaven spotting local species in the Dr Salim Ali Bird Sanctuary (p94), Bondla Wildlife Sanctuary (p107) or Goa's many other prime locations. Mingle with monkeys at Cotigao Wildlife Sanctuary (p190), watch baby olive ridley turtles hatch beneath a full moon at Galgibag beach (p190) or hole up in the hinterland at bird-abundant Backwoods Camp (p109). Boat trips are another highlight, where you can spot dolphins playing offshore or mugger crocodiles basking in the river estuaries. Black-crowned night heron, Dr Salim Ali Bird Sanctuary (p94)

Mumbai to Goa by Train

10 The Konkan Railway (p234), linking Mumbai with Mangaluru (Mangalore) and passing through Goa, is one of India's great railway journeys. Construction of the railway was a mammoth infrastructure challenge only completed in 1998. Today it crosses rivers and valleys with some 2000 bridges and more than 90 tunnels. Whether you're riding in a second-class sleeper or fancy air con carriage, on the 12-hour Konkan Kanya Express or nine-hour Jan Shatabdi Express, make sure you sit near the window to watch the best show in town roll past. Konkan Railway (p234)

Fabulous Festivals

Dudhsagar Falls

11 the calendar here is packed with cultural events, religious feasts, street parades and music festivals. Among the biggest Catholic festivals are Panaji's Carnival in February and the Feast of St Francis Xavier in Old Goa in December. Major Hindu festivals include Shantadurga in January and Diwali in October. India's biggest international film festival is held in Panaji in November. And what would Goa be without a big dance party? Sunburn Goa is a four-day music fest in Vagator between Christmas and New Year – a time when all of Goa parties hard! Holi festival (Shigmotsav; p18), Arambol

12 frothy Dudhsagar (p108) is the second-highest waterfall in India (after Jog Falls in Karnataka) and a great day-trip adventure. Located deep in the Western Ghats on Goa's central border with Karnataka, the 300m-high tiered waterfall can be reach from Colem by a bumpy 4WD ride through stunning jungle scenery. Take a dip in the soothing pool or climb the rocky path to the head of the falls for great views.

NISCHI/LEO/GETTY IMAGES ©

14

Need to Know

For more information, see Survival Guide (p221)

Currency
Indian rupee (₹)

Languages
Konkani is the Goan language; English is widely spoken, along with Hindi and Portuguese. Menus are often in Cyrillic.

Visas
For most nationalities 30-day electronic visas are available. For longer stays, apply for a six-month tourist visa.

Money
ATMs available in towns and at beach resorts. Credit cards accepted at travel agents, in some midrange hotels and all top-end places.

Mobile Phones
Local SIM cards can be used on most smart phones, or phones can be set to (expensive) roaming.

Time
Indian Standard Time (GMT/UTC plus 5½ hours).

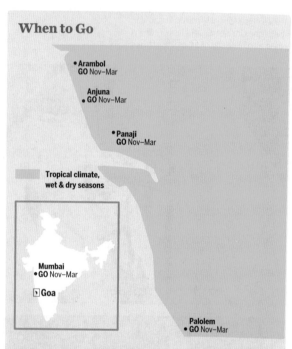

When to Go

- Arambol
  GO Nov–Mar

Anjuna
- **GO** Nov–Mar

- Panaji
  GO Nov–Mar

Tropical climate, wet & dry seasons

Mumbai
- **GO** Nov–Mar

⬧ Goa

Palolem
- **GO** Nov–Mar

High Season
(Nov–Mar)

➡ Warm, sunny weather, with balmy but cool evenings.

➡ Calm seas perfect for diving, boat trips and swimming.

➡ Peak tourist numbers and prices, especially over frenetic Christmas and New Year.

Shoulder Season (Apr, Oct)

➡ Quiet beaches, hotel bargains, but just a few beach shack restaurants and huts open.

➡ Seas may be too rough for swimming or boat trips.

➡ April can be hot and very humid.

Low Season
(May–Sep)

➡ Most tourist operations close.

➡ The monsoon brings rain, humidity, green countryside and local celebrations.

➡ Fewer tourists so the perfect time to experience 'real' Goan life.

Useful Websites

planet.com/india/goa) A great first go-to point for information.

Goa Tourism (www.goa-tourism.com) Goa's state tourism body.

Time Out Mumbai (www.time outmumbai.net) Daily listings and reviews.

Goacom (www.goacom.com) Listings, information and recipes.

Planet Goa (www.planet-goa.com) Online magazine.

What's Up Goa (www.what supgoa.com) Listings, events and more.

Important Numbers

From outside India, dial the international access code (☑00), India's country code (☑91), then the number you want, minus the initial '0'.

Country code	☑91
Police	☑100
Fire	☑101
Ambulance	☑102
General emergencies	☑108

Exchange Rates

Australia	A$1	₹51
Canada	C$1	₹53
Euro zone	€1	₹72
Japan	¥100	₹53
New Zealand	NZ$1	₹47
UK	UK£1	₹100
US	US$1	₹64

For current exchange rates see www.xe.com

Daily Costs

Budget:
Less than ₹1500

➡ Stay in beach huts at backpacker-favoured beaches

➡ Eat at local joints and self-cater at markets

➡ Buy alcohol at liquor stores or supermarkets

➡ Travel on local buses

Midrange: ₹1500–7000

➡ Combine traveller-oriented beach restaurants with local eateries

➡ Rent a scooter; take an auto-rickshaw or taxi for short trips

➡ Stay in higher-end beach huts or air-con guesthouses

➡ Sunset drinks in shacks or bars

Top End: More than ₹7000

➡ Stay in boutique heritage hotels or the best beach huts

➡ Rent a car, or travel by taxi

➡ Dine opulently, but don't miss meals at local hang-outs

➡ Indulge in ayurvedic massage and yoga retreats

Opening Hours

Outside high season (November to March) many tourist-oriented shops, restaurants and services may be closed completely. Some businesses may close for an hour or two in the afternoon or have reduced services during the low season (May to September). Hours provided are for high season.

Banks 10am to 2pm Monday to Friday, to noon Saturday

Bars noon to midnight

Clubs 10pm to 5am

Restaurants & Cafes 8am to 11pm

Shops 10am to 6pm

Arriving in Goa

Dabolim Airport, Goa (p233)

destinations; many hotels offer pick up.

Madgaon Railway Station, Margao (p166) Main stop on Konkan Railway; prepaid taxi booth to all Goan destinations.

Karmali Railway Station, Old Goa (p92) Closest to Panaji; reservations at Panaji Kadamba Bus Stand.

Kadamba Bus Stand, Panaji (p92) Long-distance and local buses; private long-distance bus companies have ticket booths here, but depart from the inter-state bus stand.

Thivim Station (p143) and **Mapusa Bus Stand (p143)** Closest rail and bus services to Calangute and Anjuna.

Getting Around

Car & Motorcycle Many travellers hire a scooter or motorbike for their trip; self-drive cars are less common but car and driver services are affordable for a group.

Taxi & autorickshaw Good for short hops around and between towns and beach resorts. Taxis will also take you on longer trips – agree on a fare beforehand.

Bus Extremely cheap, slow but fun local way of getting between towns and villages.

Train There are two rail lines in the state but it's not a particularly quick or convenient way of getting around.

For much more on **getting around**, see p235

If You Like...

Good Food

No matter what your culinary persuasion, you'll satisfy your cravings in Goa and Mumbai. From street vendors dishing up superb snacks to fine candlelit dining on the shores of the Arabian Sea, the crucial thing is to arrive hungry.

Mumbai A city of spectacular eateries, from the humblest *bhelpuri* street stall to the fanciest Mughal feast. (p63)

Candolim, Calangute & Baga Dress up (or down) and head to one of the many sophisticated world cuisine restaurants on this epic resort strip. (p124)

Cooking courses Learn to cook like a local with professionally run courses at Siolim, Arpora or Palolem. (p32)

Panaji Enjoy local food – Indian and Goan – in the fabulously atmospheric Old Quarter or animated city centre of the mellow state capital. (p87)

Pampering

Luxury is done well in Goa but the best of the spas are housed in boutique hotels and five-star resorts and come with a healthy price tag. You can enjoy a traditional ayurvedic massage at many places for around

₹1000, a Thai foot massage in Calangute or Candolim for around the same, or a full-day spa treatment for up to US$600.

Sereno Spa The spa at the Park Hyatt in Arossim is one of Goa's best. (p172)

Hummingbird The place for pampering on Palolem Beach is this spa at Ciaran's. (p185)

Quan Spa Deluxe pampering at the Goa Marriott in Miramar. (p92)

Nilaya Hermitage Boutique luxury in Arpora. (p131)

Rejuve Spa At Rajbag's Lalit Golf & Spa Resort. (p190)

Shopping

Goa's shops, markets and street stalls are full of handicrafts and souvenirs from all over India. Local stuff includes bottles of feni, decorative textiles, painted tiles and silver jewellery.

Mumbai Whether it's antiques, clothes, handicrafts or meandering through markets that gets your retail juices flowing, Mumbai has India's best shopping. (p72)

Anjuna Market The place to be on a Wednesday is hanging out with backpackers, hippies and package tourists at this

venerable open-air market institution. (p138)

Golden Heart Emporium Vending classics, new releases and harder-to-find Goan titles, this well-stocked Margao book store is a treasure trove for bibliophiles. (p165)

Mapusa Market Browse fresh produce, spices, clothes and knick-knacks with droves of locals at Mapusa's Friday market. (p142)

Nightlife & Drinking

Goa is notorious for a good party: dance to trance or simply enjoy a cold beer at any beach shack or local bar.

Anjuna's Beach Bars Anjuna knows how to party, especially at the southern end of the beach where Curlies, Cafe Lilliput and Shiva Valley regularly fire up. (p138)

Tito's Lane Baga's original clubbing strip gets lively with Club Mambo and Cafe San Francisco among the best. (p133)

LPK Waterfront This giant club looking over the Nerul River across to Candolim is whimsical in design and pumping in attitude. (p126)

Floating Casinos, Panaji The luxury casino boats on the

Mandovi River offer an entertaining night out with free drinks, buffet dinner and floor shows, and gambling of course. (p89)

Silent Discos, Palolem Dance the night away in outward silence at one of Palolem's headphone parties. (p187)

Mumbai Hip, minimalist clubs, grungy backstreet bars, cool jazz joints, '80s-music dives: only in Mumbai. (p67)

PLAN YOUR TRIP IF YOU LIKE...

History & Architecture

Goa's colonial heritage is probably most visible in its Portuguese-style mansions, churches and forts, allowing you to peel away the years and glimpse a much older Goa.

Basilica of Bom Jesus, Old Goa Visit a saint's desiccated relics at this splendid laterite basilica dripping with silver stars and ecclesiastical glory. (p96)

Church of Our Lady of the Immaculate Conception Clamber the steps to Panaji's wedding cake of a church, where sailors once stopped to thank the heavens for their safe arrival from Portugal. (p79)

Braganza House, Chandor One of few mansions open to the public, the split-personality Braganza House is a fascinating insight into how the aristocratic Goan other half once lived. (p167)

Palaćio do Deão, Quepem A labour of love for its owners – you can take tea on the terrace of this stunning *palaćio,* marvelling at the wealth of painstakingly renovated detail. (p168)

Goan forts The Goan coastline is dotted with the atmospheric remnants of a once mighty seafaring nation: the best are Reis Magos, Cabo de Rama and Fort Aguada. (p178)

Top: Mapusa Market (p142)
Bottom: Ayurvedic massage by the beach, Goa

Month by Month

January

The prime time for visiting Goa, post-Christmas and New Year January means blue skies and warm weather, making it perfect for hitting the beach but not too hot for getting to grips with the state's cities and wildlife sanctuaries.

☆ Banganga Festival

A two-day classical-music festival held at the Banganga Tank in Mumbai (Bombay), in musical tribute to the Lord Ram, who, legend has it, once stopped over here and provided locals with water direct from the holy Ganges.

☆ Reis Magos Festival

Held at Reis Magos, Chandor and Cansaulim on 6 January, this festival sees a re-enactment of the journey of the Three Wise Men to Bethlehem, with young boys playing the Magi.

★ Shantadurga

Also known as the 'Procession of the Umbrellas', this is one of Goa's most attended festivals, wherein a solid silver statue of Hindu goddess Shantadurga is carried between the villages of Fatorpa and Cuncolim, fronted by 12 umbrella-carrying young men.

★ Festa das Bandeiras

Migrant working men return home to Divar Island in mid-January to celebrate their local saint's day by waving the flags of the countries in which they're currently working and, more bizarrely, firing dozens of peashooters at each other.

★ Republic Day

The celebration of India's 1950 establishment as a republic is a public holiday, held every 26 January.

February

Another reliably warm and sunny month for lazing on the beach or seeing the sights, February sees fewer crowds than January and a procession of festivals.

☆ Elephanta Festival

Classical music and dance performances are held under starry night skies on Mumbai's Elephanta Island.

☆ Kala Ghoda Arts Festival

This two-week-long festival in Mumbai has a packed program of arts performances and exhibitions from the first Saturday in February. See www.kalaghodaassociation.com.

★ Shigmotsav (Shigmo)

Goa's take on the Hindu festival of Holi marks the onset of spring over the full moon period with statewide parades, processions, and revellers flinging huge quantities of water and coloured tikka powder with wild abandon.

✲✲ Carnival

mayhem characterise the annual Carnival in Panaji (Panjim), held on the three days prior to Lent. Festivities come to a head on Sabado Gordo (Fat Saturday), when you'll see a procession of floats through the city's packed streets.

✲✲ Hanuman Festival

Ten days in February see the Hindu monkey god Hanuman celebrated at Panaji's Maruti Temple.

✲✲ Shivratri

To celebrate the traditional anniversary of the God Shiva's wedding day, large-scale religious celebrations are held at the many Shiva temples across Goa on the 14th (moonless) night of the new moon, in the Hindu month of Phalgun, which falls in either February or March.

March

Things are starting to heat up considerably by now, but it's still high season in Goa – good for beach lounging, swimming and Easter celebrations.

✲✲ Procession of All Saints

Held in Goa Velha on the fifth Monday during Lent, this is the only procession of its sort outside Rome, where dozens of huge statues of the saints are paraded throughout the village.

✲✲ Easter

Churches fill up statewide over the Christian festival of Easter, with plenty of solemn High Masses and family feasting. The biggest church services are held in

April

Most tourists have departed Goa, and temperatures begin rising in anticipation of the monsoon, still over a month away. If you can stand the heat, it's quiet and calm, with great deals on accommodation.

✲✲ Feast of Our Lady of Miracles

Held in Mapusa 16 days after Easter, this cheerful festival, also known as a *tamasha,* is famously celebrated by both Hindus and Christians at Mapusa's Church of Our Lady of Miracles.

May

May is perhaps the most uncomfortable month in Goa, with heat and humidity, and everyone awaiting the coming of the rains. Most tourist operators have closed for the season.

✲✲ Igitun Chalne

One of Goa's most distinctive festivals, specific to the temple in Sirigao (near Corjuem Fort). *Igitun chalne* means 'fire-walking', and

the high point comes when devotees of the goddess [...] traverse a pit of burning coals to prove their devotion.

June

It's here! The monsoon's arrival sparks a host of celebrations, and the land turns miraculously green overnight. Water buffalo bask, children dance in the showers, and frogs croak out elated choruses.

✲✲ Feast of St Anthony

This feast on 13 June in honour of Portugal's patron saint takes on particular significance if the monsoon is late in appearing, whereupon each Goan family must lower a statue of the saint into its family well to hasten the onset of the rains and pray for bountiful crops.

✲✲ Sanjuan

The Feast of St John (Sanjuan) on 24 June sees young men diving dangerously into wells to celebrate the monsoon's arrival, and torching straw dummies of the saint himself, to represent John's baptism and, consequently, the death of sin.

LUNAR CALENDAR

Many festivals follow the Indian lunar calendar (a complex system based on astrology) or the Islamic calendar (which falls about 11 days earlier each year), and therefore change annually relative to the Gregorian calendar. Contact local tourist offices for exact festival dates.

Sangodd

The annual Feast of St Peter and St Paul on 29 June marks another monsoonal celebration, and is particularly ebullient in Candolim, where boats are tied together to form floating stages and costumed actors play out *tiatrs* (Konkani dramas) to vast crowds.

July

Ramadan

Falling either at the end of June or early July, 30 days of dawn-to-dusk fasting mark the ninth month of the Islamic calendar. Muslims traditionally turn their attention to God, with a focus on prayer, purification and charitable giving.

Eid al-Fitr

Muslims celebrate the end of Ramadan with three days of festivities, beginning 30 days after the start of the fast.

August

Though the monsoon is slowly receding, the rains are still a-coming; fisherfolk await calmer waters and local life goes on, almost tourist-free.

Nariyal Poornima

In both Goa and Mumbai, a coconut offering is made to Lord Varuna, god of the sea, to mark the start of the postmonsoon fishing season; fishermen pray for a bountiful harvest before hitting the first choppy waves of the August seas.

Independence Day

India's 1947 independence from Britain is celebrated with an annual public holiday on 15 August.

Feast of the Chapel

Coastal Cabo Raj Bhavan draws scores of visitors each 15 August to a special church service in honour of its 500-year-old chapel's feast day, which long predates Independence Day.

Bonderam

Celebrated annually on the fourth Saturday in August on sleepy Divar Island. Locals take part in processions and mock battles to commemorate historical disputes that took place over island property.

September

The rains have all but subsided, leaving a scoured, green Goa just ripe for the upcoming tourist season. Local businesses begin building the season's first beach shacks. Popular time for domestic tourists.

Ganesh Chaturthi

Mumbai's biggest annual festival – a 10-day event in celebration of the elephant-headed Ganesh – sweeps up the whole city: the 10th day, which sees millions descend on Mumbai's Girguam Chowpatty to submerge the largest statues, is particularly ecstatic.

October

Though not all beach businesses are in full swing, October's warm days tempt a trickle of in-the-know travellers, who benefit from the widest choice in long-stay accommodation.

Gandhi's Birthday

The national holiday of Gandhi Jayanti is a solemn celebration of Mohandas Gandhi's birth, on 2 October.

Feast of the Menino Jesus

On October's second Sunday, coastal Colva's village church sees its small and allegedly miracle-working statue of the Infant Jesus dressed up and paraded before scores of devoted pilgrims at this important village festival.

Dusshera

This nine-day Hindu festival celebrates the god Rama's victory over Ravana in the Hindu epic Ramayana, and the goddess Durga's victory over Mahishasura. It's celebrated with bonfires and school-children's performances of scenes from the life of Rama.

Diwali

A five-day Hindu 'festival of lights', this beautifully illuminated festival celebrates the victory of good over evil with the lighting of oil and butter lamps around the home, lots of family celebration and loads of firecrackers.

November

High season really kicks off in November, when the countryside remains post-monsoon green, and Goans gear up for the tourist onslaught. This, along with February, is perhaps the best time to visit.

Feast of Our Lady of Livrament

Each mid-November sees a cheerful saint's day street fair set up in Panaji, outside the tiny Chapel of St Sebastian, in the Goan capital's atmospheric old Portuguese-infused Fontainhas district.

☆ International Film Festival of India

This annual film festival (www.iffi.gov.in) – the country's largest – graces Panaji's big screens with a gaggle of Bollywood's finest glitterati jetting in for premieres, parties, ceremonies and screenings.

December

Packed with parties, December is the wildest, busiest and most expensive month to be in Goa, especially between Christmas and New Year.

Seek out trance parties, Christmas parades and feasting

☆ Goa Arts & Literary Festival

Inaugurated in 2010, this is South India's premier literary and arts festival (www.goaartlitfest.com), attracting writers, poets, artists, musicians, speakers and performers to Panaji over four days in early December.

Feast of St Francis Xavier

Thousands upon thousands of pilgrims file past the shrivelled old remains of St Francis Xavier in Old Goa every 3 December, kicking off a week-long festival and fair, complete with large-scale open-air Masses.

Feast of Our Lady of the Immaculate Conception

Panaji's wedding-cake Church of Our Lady of the Immaculate Conception plays host to this feast and large, joyful fair on 8 December.

Liberation Day

This unusually sober celebration on 17 December marks Goa's 'liberation' from Portugal by India in 1961 with military parades.

☆ Sunburn Goa

'Asia's biggest music festi-dolim to Vagator and offers a four-day extravaganza of dance music between Christmas and New Year.

☆ VH1 Supersonic

New five-day EDM festival held in Candolim from December 26.

Christmas

Midnight Masses abound in Goa on 24 December, traditionally known as *Misa de Galo* (Cock's Crow) since they often stretch on far into the wee hours, while the following Christmas Day is celebrated with feasting, fireworks and festivities.

☆ Siolim Zagor

Siolim's multifaith Zagor, which takes place on the first Sunday after Christmas, involves a procession culminating in folk plays, music and celebrations.

☆ New Year's Eve

This is the party night many travellers have been waiting for. Fireworks displays erupt up and down the coast and dance parties take over the beaches. Book ahead for dining or club venues.

Itineraries

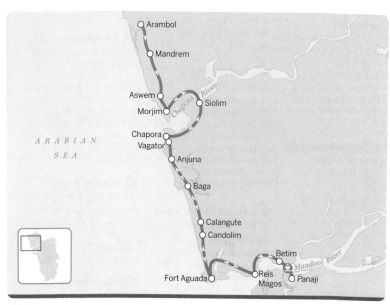

Arambol

Mandrem

Aswem

Siolim

Morjim

Chapora River

Chapora

Vagator

ARABIAN SEA

Anjuna

Baga

Calangute

Candolim

Betim

Mandovi River

Reis Magos

Panaji

Fort Aguada

2 WEEKS Northern Beaches

For travellers zipping south from Mumbai, the northern beaches encompass a little of everything that's great about Goa – fine beaches, forts, rivers, lively resorts, yoga and nightlife.

Start by taking the short cut across the Mandovi River by vehicle ferry from **Panaji** to **Betim** and pay a visit to refurbished **Reis Magos Fort** before taking in the views from hilltop **Fort Aguada**. The beaches of **Candolim**, **Calangute** and **Baga** make up Goa's busiest resort strip so there's always plenty to do here, from water sports to nightclubs and beach shacks to fine dining. Head north of the Baga River to **Anjuna**, where the hippie trance days all began. It's a good place to join a yoga class, party at one of the beachfront clubs or browse the Wednesday flea market. Nearby, **Vagator** and **Chapora** are easygoing villages with a relaxed party vibe: climb Chapora Fort for great sunset views or dine on the clifftop at Thalassa. Across the Chapora River is Russian-flavoured **Morjim**, mellow **Aswem** and **Mandrem**, with upmarket hut villages, a lovely clean beach and good yoga retreats. Then it's on to **Arambol**, a popular backpacker beach with a Bob Marley vibe and paragliding from the northern headland.

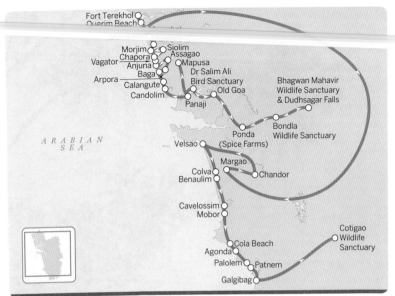

Goa in a Nutshell

4 WEEKS

Start in the state capital, **Panaji**, where you can easily spend a few days staying in heritage accommodation, cruising the Mandovi River and eating well at Goan restaurants. Following the Mandovi eastwards, birdwatchers will enjoy taking the ferry over to Chorao Island for a visit to the mangroves of the **Dr Salim Ali Bird Sanctuary**. Otherwise continue to Goa's greatest historic site – the churches and cathedrals of **Old Goa**.

The next day head further east to visit the Hindu temples around **Ponda**, spending the afternoon having lunch and taking a plantation tour at a spice farm. Further on nature lovers will enjoy Goa's smallest wildlife sanctuary, **Bondla**, and its largest, **Bhagwan Mahavir**, or a trip to **Dudhsagar Falls**.

Returning to Panaji, it's time to hit the beach. For beaches north of the Baga River, head straight up the NH66 to **Mapusa** and continue from there. Otherwise take the free ferry across the Mandovi and follow the back road over the Nerul River and along Fort Aguada Rd, exploring crowded **Candolim**, **Calangute** and **Baga** beaches. Cross the Baga River to **Arpora** – if it's a Saturday, don't miss one of the night markets at Baga or Arpora. Continue north to the village of **Assagao** to sample some of Goa's best yoga retreats.

From here you can explore the coast from the hippie, party beaches of **Anjuna** and **Vagator**, and the boutique hotels of **Siolim** to the northern beaches of **Morjim**, **Aswem**, **Mandrem** and **Arambol**. Further north is secluded **Querim Beach**, from where you can take the vehicle ferry across the Terekhol River to **Terekhol Fort**, Goa's most northerly point.

Now head south down the NH66 to **Margao**, a good base from which to explore the traditional villages around **Chandor**, or hit the beaches which stretch roughly from **Velsao** south to **Colva**, **Benaulim**, **Cavelossim** and **Mobor**. South of the Sal River, it's a beautiful coastal drive to isolated **Cola Beach**, laid-back **Agonda**, then onto the palm-fringed southern jewel of **Palolem**. There's plenty to do here, from lazing with a book to exploring **Patnem** and **Galgibag** beaches and **Cotigao Wildlife Sanctuary**.

Top: Palolem (p183)

Bottom: Cabo da Rama (p180)

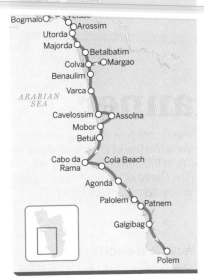

Southern Sun
2 WEEKS

Back-Country Trips
5 DAYS

South Goa is as much about lazing on the beaches as the north, but there are some interesting inland adventures here too. Start in busy **Margao**, where you can browse the market and grab a bite to eat at Ruta's World Cafe or Longhuino's.

The beach at **Colva** is just 6km west of Margao and stretches up and down the coast. If you're into scuba diving, head north to **Bogmalo**, via pretty **Utorda** and **Velsao** beaches, or make you way south to **Benaulim** (visit Goa Chitra museum here) through five-star territory at **Varca** and **Cavelossim** to the lovely spit of land at **Mobor**, where you can stop for lunch at the Blue Whale shack near the mouth of the Sal River.

Follow the coastal road through bucolic Betul to lovely **Agonda**, calling in at **Cabo de Rama fort** and secluded **Cola Beach**.

The final coastal stretch leads to Goa's little paradise beach at **Palolem**, great for swimming, yoga, cooking courses and beach huts. **Patnem** is a little more peaceful. Intrepid travellers should hire a bike and explore further south to **Galgibag** and **Polem** beaches.

Take a few days to get off the beaten track.

From **Panaji**, start out early to Colem for **Dudhsagar Falls**. On the way back stop at Tambdi Surla for **Shri Mahadeva Temple**, the elephant camp at **Jungle Book** or some birdwatching at **Backwoods Camp**. Another excellent self-drive day trip from Panaji is to take a picturesque circuit from **Old Goa**, to serene **Divar Island** (via a ferry), catch another ferry to **Naroa**, where you can take in **Mayem Lake**, **Corjuem Fort** and **Aldona**. Return to Panaji via **Torda**, visiting the Houses of Goa museum.

Head south to Margao, from where you can explore the villages of **Chandor**, with one of Goa's grandest Portuguese mansions, **Quepem**, **Loutolim** and the ancient **Rivona Buddhist caves** and prehistoric **Usgalimal rock carvings**.

Continue on to Palolem or Patnem, from where you can head inland through forest and farmland to the **Netravali Protected Area** to discover the mysterious 'bubble lake', the **Tanshikar Spice Farm** and jungle treks to remote **waterfalls**.

Plan Your Trip
Beach Planner

With more than 100km of sand-fringed coastline shelving into the Arabian Sea, Goa's beaches can exude the feel of a tropical island and at times it's easy to forget you're in India. Whether laying out your sarong or just lazing about in the shade of a palm-thatch beach shack while nursing a cold beer, the question is: which beach?

Best for...

Partying
Calangute and Baga (p127), Anjuna and Vagator (p135), Candolim (p119), Palolem (p183)

Families
Palolem (p183), Patnem (p188), Mandrem (p151), Aswem (p150), Arambol (p153), Vagator (p143)

Peace
Agonda (p181), Cola and Khancola (p180), Mandrem (p151), Polem (p191), Querim (Keri; p154)

Water Sports
Candolim and Sinquerim (p119), Calangute and Baga (p127), Colva (p174), Benaulim (p176), Arambol (p153)

Which Beach?

When deciding which Goan beach to visit, the decision shouldn't be made on just the aesthetics of sand and sea: it's about choosing the beach community that suits your style of travel and sense of place. The villages and resorts vary in character, depending on the types of tourists and travellers who congregate there, the standards of accommodation, restaurants, nightlife and activities on offer.

Locating the perfect beach is the secret to making the most of your stay. It could be backpacker beach huts; book-friendly, people-free sands; yoga shalas or the party crowd. Goa is small enough that you can jump on a scooter or in a taxi and explore.

Best Beaches for...
Swimming & Water Sports

Most of Goa's beaches offer water sports seasonally – parasailing, jet skis and speedboats. Swimming is safest at patrolled beaches.

➡ Palolem (p183) Calm waters offer the safest ocean swimming in Goa. Also the best place for kayaking and stand-up paddleboarding.

➡ Calangute (p127) & Candolim (p119) Several water-sports operators offer a full range of activities on Goa's busiest beach strip. Also has scuba-diving outfits.

➡ Arambol (p153) Another gentle beach for ~~... with a surf club~~ and paragliding.

➡ Colva (p174) & Benaulim (p176) ... as Calangute but all of the adrenalin sports are on offer at respective beach entrances; Colva is popular with domestic tourists.

➡ Aswem (p150) A good choice mainly for its excellent surfing and kite-surfing school and kayaking on the river.

➡ Bogmalo (p170) Notable mainly for its scuba-diving school and access to Grande Island.

Family Fun

Families will find a lot to like about Goa's beaches.

➡ Vagator (p143) Rock pools and calm waters make Vagator's three little bays great for kids. Food and drink vendors gather at the entrance.

➡ Palolem (p183) One of the best all-round beaches for families with plenty of activities, safe swimming and beach-facing huts.

➡ Patnem (p188) Similar to Palolem but smaller and quieter, Patnem is very family-friendly with a large expat community, and schools and kindergartens nearby.

➡ Arambol (p153) A popular beach with long-staying families, Arambol has a relaxed backpacker vibe, good budget accommodation and relatively safe waters.

Partying & Drinking

Goa loves to party and there's a liberal attitude to drinking, but it's not quite Ibiza on the subcontinent. The all-night trance parties on beaches and in coconut groves are largely consigned to history but EDM parties, raves, dance festivals and night-clubs still happen in season.

➡ Anjuna (p135) Late-night parties are legendary at Anjuna's southern beach shacks, especially popular Curlies.

➡ Baga (p133) Tito's Lane is the place of choice for many young Indians on a weekend away from their IT jobs, as well as package tourists staying in the area.

➡ Vagator (p143) Some traces of Goa trance and hippie heyday remain in Vagator and Chapora.

➡ Candolim (p119) Two of Goa's most upmarket nightclubs are found here, along with busy bar-restaurants along Fort Aguada Rd.

➡ Palolem (p183) Silent headphone parties happen most nights and Leopard Valley is nearby, on the way to Agonda.

SAFE SWIMMING

One of the most ... in Goa is to be found right in front of you. The Arabian Sea, with its strong currents, often steeply shelving sands and dangerous undertows, claims lives each year. Goa's main beaches are patrolled by lifeguards during 'swimming season' (November to March). Be vigilant with children, avoid swimming after drinking alcohol and don't even consider swimming during the monsoon.

Relaxing with a Good Book

➡ Mandrem (p151) Along with Aswem and Morjim, this broad, hassle-free beach is ideal for lounging, with just a scattering of beach shacks.

➡ Patnem (p188) Not crowded like its popular neighbour, peaceful Patnem will re-energise your soul.

➡ Benaulim (p176) With just a few beach shacks and most accommodation back in the village, you'll find plenty of quiet spots on Benaulim and Sernabatim beaches.

➡ Polem (p191) Goa's southernmost beach has just one basic place to stay so don't come looking for action.

➡ Querim (Keri; p154) Near the Terekhol River, this empty northern beach feels remote but is just around the headland from Arambol.

Backpackers & Budget Travellers

➡ Arambol (p153) Huts and rooms along the clifftop path remain some of the cheapest in Goa, making this popular with backpackers.

➡ Anjuna (p135) A wide range of accommodation, two backpacker hostels, good cafes and plenty of bikes to rent for commuting to neighbouring beaches.

➡ Vagator & Chapora (p143) Picturesque beach, cool fort; these laid-back villages attract budget travellers who like to chill and party.

➡ Palolem (p183) & Patnem (p188) There's a hut to suit all tastes and budgets here, along with a genuine traveller vibe.

➡ Benaulim (p176) Cheap rooms in village houses, though it may be a little quiet for some.

BEACH SHACKS

One of the distinguishing features of Goa's beaches are the seasonal restaurant shacks that line the sands on just about every beach. Of the 350 shacks erected in 2014/15, some 200 were along the megabusy Candolim–Calangute–Baga beach strip. Other beaches, especially in the south, might have just one or two shacks.

Depending on the granting of licenses, the lateness of the monsoon or availability of materials, shacks start to go up in early October (some are not built until November) and are dismantled again in late April. Goan tourism department licensing regulations are quite strict on size, location and ownership (foreigners are not permitted to own or work in the shacks). They're usually constructed from timber and bamboo with palm-thatch roofing and sand floors but some are rather more sophisticated and all are required to have electricity, refrigeration, effective sewerage and waste systems and (since 2014) CCTV. Most also offer free wi-fi to customers.

As for food and drink, fresh fish and seafood is usually bought from local markets or fishing boats each day, but there's also a lengthy menu of Indian, Goan and Western dishes, including breakfast, usually printed in English and Russian Cyrillic.

Yoga & Spirituality

➡ Anjuna (p135) This is the closest beach to the retreats at Assagao and there are frequent drop-in classes and courses in Anjuna itself.

➡ Mandrem (p151) & Aswem (p150) A number of reputable yoga schools and spiritual retreats call Mandrem home in season and there's a good ayurvedic massage centre.

➡ Palolem (p183) & Patnem (p188) Some interesting new yoga outfits have set up at these perennially popular beaches.

➡ Arambol (p153) Popular Iyengar yoga school and numerous drop-in classes and retreats.

Five-Star Treatment

Goa has more five-star resorts and boutique hotels per square kilometre than anywhere else in India. Even if you're not staying, you can almost always book a table at a fancy in-house restaurant, an afternoon at a spa or even pay to use the pool.

➡ Varca, Cavelossim & Mobor (p179) South Goa's five-star strip includes the Leela, Holiday Inn and Radisson Blu.

➡ Candolim & Sinquerim (p119) Two sprawling Taj Vivanta resorts plus some fine boutique hotels such as Aashyana Lakhanpal.

➡ Mandrem (p151) & Aswem (p150) The high standard of beach-hut operations has turned Mandrem and Aswem into one of the classiest beach strips in the north.

➡ Rajbag (p189) Dominated by the five-star Lalit Golf & Spa Resort, complete with championship nine-hole golf course.

➡ Arossim (p171) & Majorda (p173) Resorts such as Park Hyatt, Kenilworth and boutique Vivenda Dos Palhacos make this an upmarket strip with mostly quiet beaches.

Nature

➡ Talpona & Galgibag (p190) The beach strip between the Talpona and Galgibag rivers is wonderfully deserted, backed by pines and with protected olive ridley turtle nesting sites.

➡ Cola (p180) With its lagoon and pair of swimming beaches this is one of the prettiest spots on the coast and you'll often see langur monkeys in the trees.

➡ Morjim (p149) Very popular with long-staying Russian visitors, this is also a protected turtle-nesting site where the Chapora River meets the sea.

Beach Huts

➡ Palolem (p183) Where the beach-hut craze really took off – Palolem still has some of the best in Goa.

➡ Agonda (p181) Beach hut design is taken to another level at some of Agonda's mini-resorts.

➡ Patnem (p188) A smaller version of Palolem with some nice, laid-back hut villages.

➡ Mandrem (p151) Fabulous hut resorts connected to the beach by bamboo bridges make Mandrem a popular choice.

➡ Arambol (p153) Backpacker-friendly Arambol has a string of beach-facing huts on the main strip and around the cliff-tops.

Plan Your Trip
Yoga & Activities

India is widely regarded as the birthplace of yoga and Goa is the place that many teachers and practitioners set up for the winter season. From your open-air beachfront or jungle yoga shala, there are few better places to downward dog or salute to the sun.

Yoga

The best time to visit is mid-November to early April, when all outfits or retreats are open and courses are in full swing. A handful of smaller classes operate year-round, so it's still possible to get your yoga fix, even during the monsoon.

Palolem, Agonda and Patnem in the south of the state, and Arambol, Mandrem, Anjuna and Assagao in the north, are particularly great places to take classes or longer courses. At most beach centres you'll find no shortage of morning and afternoon classes.

Teachers and practitioners are largely an ever-changing parade of foreigners or Indian teachers who set up shop in Goa as soon as the monsoon subsides. Peruse hotel, restaurant or cafe notice boards for current and upcoming courses.

Ayurveda

Goa offers plenty of opportunities to explore ayurvedic treatments. Briefly defined as an ancient science of plant-based medicine, ayurveda's Sanskrit name comes from a combination of *ayu* (life) and *veda* (knowledge); ancient ayurveda resources described 2000 species of plants, of which at least 550 are still in use today. Illness, in the doctrine of ayurveda, comes from a loss of internal balance, which can be restored through a regime of massage and *panchakarma* ('five therapies' internal purification).

Which Yoga Class?

Ashtanga
Often referred to as 'power yoga', it's active and physically demanding, good for some serious toning.

Bikram
Also known as 'hot yoga', with a focus on correct alignment, Bikram's 26 poses are performed at 105°F (41°C) and 40% humidity – not hard to achieve on a Goan April day.

Hatha
Covers a whole gamut of styles, but generally refers to yoga focused on breath work (*pranayama*), and slow, gentle stretching, making it good for beginners.

Iyengar
Slow and steady, often using 'props', in the form of blocks, balls and straps.

Kundalini
Aims to free the base of the spine, to unleash energy hidden there, and usually involves lots of core, spine and sitting work.

Vinyasa
An active, fluid series of changing poses characterises Vinyasa, sometimes called 'flow yoga'.

The first part of this regime (and without doubt the most popular) comprises an hour-long massage with warm medicated oils, followed by a cleansing steam bath. Other treatments include aromatherapy and *shirodhara* (pouring of warm oil on the forehead).

The second part of the full regime, the internal purification, takes longer and most people opt for a fortnight's course of treatment and strict diet in order to feel its full advantages.

Ayurvedic therapy treatments can be found at most beach villages, but ask around for personal recommendations and ensure that a massage is conducted by a female if you're a woman and a male if you're a man. Another option is to head to one of the spas at a five-star hotel. It won't be cheap but you can be certain of well-trained staff and superluxurious treatments.

GOA'S YOGA CENTRES

Scattered across Goa are a number of respected options for yoga classes, courses, retreats and teacher certification.

➡ Ashiyana Retreat Centre (p152), Mandrem

➡ Bamboo Yoga Retreat (p189), Patnem

➡ Brahmani Yoga (p135), Anjuna

➡ Himalayan Iyengar Yoga Centre (p153), Arambol

➡ Himalaya Yoga Valley (p152), Mandrem

➡ Oceanic Yoga (p152), Mandrem

➡ Purple Valley Yoga Retreat (p142), Assagao

➡ Shamana Retreat (☑07507715975; www.shamanaretreats.com; Sadolxem Village; yoga classes ₹500; ☺9.30am & 4pm Mon-Fri), Patnem

➡ Space Goa (p186), Palolem

➡ Sushumna Yoga (p142), Assagao

➡ Swan Yoga Retreat (p142), Assagao

➡ Yoga Magic (p142), Anjuna

➡ Yoga Village (☑0832-2244546; www.yogavillage.org; 2-week retreat €800), Morjim

Outdoor Activities

Goa has plenty to keep you active once you tire of the horizontal approach to its great outdoors, from impromptu cricket and beach volleyball matches to hilltop paragliding. You'll find plenty of seasonal eco-slanted activities on offer: nature walks and day trips, river cruises, birdwatching and guided hikes through the state's national parks. As with most Goan activities, outfits change regularly and it's best to check noticeboards in hotels, restaurants and cafes for up-to-the-minute offerings.

Diving

Although Goa is not internationally renowned as a diving destination, its waters are regarded as the third-best spot for diving in India (after the Andaman and Lakshadweep Islands).

The shallow waters off the coast are ideal for less-experienced divers; typical dives are at depths of 10m to 12m, with abundant marine life to be seen. The main problem is that visibility is unpredictable and is adversely affected by the Mandovi and Zuari rivers; on some days it's 30m, on others it's closer to 2m, so it's best to check daily before deciding to go out. A Discover Scuba course costs around ₹5000 and a four-day PADI open-water course starts from ₹20,000. For certified divers, one dive costs ₹3000, two dives cost ₹5000. The dive season runs from late October to April.

The highlights of diving in Goa are the wreck dives – there are hundreds of wrecks along Goa's coastline, including Portuguese and Spanish galleons and more recent wrecks of merchant and naval ships. It's said that vast quantities of treasure still lie on its ocean beds, remnants from the wrecks carrying wealthy Portuguese traders.

Popular dive sites include Grande Island and St George's Island, while south of Goa, Devbagh Island (near Karwar) and Pigeon Island off the Karnataka coast are also frequently used. Professional Association of Dive Instructors (PADI) accredited operations in Goa include:

➡ Barracuda Diving (p129)

➡ Dive Goa (p93)

➡ Goa Aquatics (p127)

➡ Goa Diving (p171)

Wildlife guide, photographer, snake handler, writer, there
are few people in Goa better equipped to lead you into the wilds than Rahul
Alvares. His most unusual tour is 'Snake Watch', a two-hour morning or afternoon trip
(₹2100 per person) to see, photograph and learn about native snakes in the wild.

Also popular are his expert four- to six-hour birdwatching trips (₹2300 to ₹2700),
three-day photography workshops (₹9000) and jungle camping trips (from ₹3300
per person). Rahul will also customise trips.

He's the author of *The Call of the Snake* and co-author of *Birds of Goa*. Check his
website at www.rahulalvares.com to see his sublime wildlife photography and to
contact him regarding tour bookings.

Water Sports

Most water-sports outfits are run on a
seasonal, itinerant basis, and it's enough to
turn up at a beach and look around for a
shack offering your activity of choice. Calangute and Colva are the busiest beaches
for water sports. Activities include jet skiing, parasailing, wake-boarding, kayaking,
surfing and kitesurfing. Paragliding is
popular from the cliffs at Arambol. The best
places for kayaking are Palolem's calm bay
or the state's numerous rivers and estuaries.

Wildlife Watching

Goa's hinterland is great for spotting wildlife, from the blazing kingfishers that fleck
the coastal strip's luminescent paddy fields,
to the water buffalo that wander home
come sunset after a hard day's wallowing.

Goa's wildlife sanctuaries host hard-to-
spot wonders such as gaurs (Indian bison),
porcupines, wild boar and the occasional
pangolin (scaly anteater) or leopard. A loud
rustle in the leaves overhead often signals
the arrival of a troop of langur monkeys.

Taking a riverine trip inland, you might
be rewarded with sightings of crocodiles,
otters, and yet more birdlife: just try spotting a Ceylon frogmouth or a fairy bluebird
without at least the hint of a satisfied smile.

Best for Birds

➡ Backwoods Camp (p109)
➡ Dr Salim Ali Bird Sanctuary (p94)
➡ Bondla Wildlife Sanctuary (p107)
➡ Divar Island (p101)

Best for Beasts

➡ Cotigao Wildlife Sanctuary (p190)
➡ Bondla Wildlife Sanctuary (p107)

➡ Bhagwan Mahavir Wildlife Sanctuary (p108)
➡ Jungle Book (p109)

Day Trips & Tours

A great way to see more of Goa, especially
if time is tight, is to sign up for a day trip
or two. Travel agents and taxi drivers at
any beach resort can organise tours, offering visits to otherwise hard-to-reach
sights, including river cruises and Keralan-
style houseboat stays.

➡ **Goa Tourism** (www.goa-tourism.com) A
surprisingly good range of bus- and boat-based
day trips, taking in an astonishing number of
sights in a single day.

➡ **KOKOindia** (☑9637224112; www.
kokoindia.com) This expat tour agent is based in
Patnem and offers bespoke tours all over India
but also some interesting day trips from Palolem
and Patnem, including a lunch trip to Quepem
and custom river trips.

➡ Betty's Place Boat Trips (p179)
➡ Canopy Ecotours (p163)
➡ Day Tripper (p129)
➡ John's Boat Tours (p121)
➡ Jungle Book (p109)
➡ Spice Plantations (p105)

Volunteering

Many travellers to Goa are keen to give
something back to this beautiful, but
sometimes vulnerable, state. One great
way to do this is to spend part of your stay
volunteering: whether it's a few hours,
days or weeks working with stray animals
or disadvantaged people, there are some
rewarding opportunities.

COOKING CLASSES

Cooking classes are gaining popularity in Goa. Some of the best:

➡ Siolim House, Siolim (p149)

➡ Mukti Kitchen, Arpora (p135)

➡ Rahul's Cooking Class, Palolem (p183)

➡ Masala Kitchen, Palolem (p183)

➡ Spicy Mama's, Assagao (p141)

➡ Holiday on the Menu (www.holiday-onthemenu.com; courses from US$169), Betim

Planning

Most of Goa's volunteering options require a little advance planning, and it pays to be in touch with nonprofit organisations well before you depart home. Check any organisations out thoroughly before you offer your time – the website www.ethicalvolunteering.org has some useful tips. To legally work with a registered charity in India, even as a volunteer, you must technically have an employment visa. Moreover, working with children requires criminal record background checks, so it takes a few months to organise. Minimum placements are usually one month but can be as long as one year.

A number of charity organisations offer volunteer placements, often with accommodation and meals included for a fee, and they can usually organise the necessary paperwork for visas.

Some local animal-related organisations are happy to receive casual visitors to play with the animals or help with walking, cleaning and feeding, but you may need evidence of a recent rabies vaccination – drop in or call ahead.

Getting Involved

There are a number of reputable charities and international organisations offering placements in Goa, but Lonely Planet does not endorse any organisations that we do not work with directly, so it is essential that you do your own thorough research before agreeing to volunteer with any organisation. Volunteering opportunities include animal welfare, orphanages and women's shelters.

➡ **El Shaddai** (p141) This British-founded charity aids impoverished and homeless children throughout Goa, running a number of day and night shelters, an open school and children's homes throughout the state. Volunteers are also welcomed for fund-raising activities, or to visit one of the Assagao schools between 4.30pm and 6.30pm (call ahead). For more information, they operate a stall at the Anjuna flea market.

➡ **Mango Tree Goa** (☑9881261886; www.mangotreegoa.org; The Mango House, 148/3 near Vrundavan Hospital, Karaswada, Mapusa, Goa) This UK-registered organisation helps Goa's disadvantaged children by providing daycare centres, medical, educational, nutritional and other essential aid. Volunteers can fill a variety of roles, as teachers, childcare assistants and outreach workers, while there are also positions available for qualified doctors and nurses.

➡ **Goa Animal Welfare Trust** (☑9763681525, 0832-2653677; www.gawt.org; Curchorem; ⊙9am-5.30pm Mon-Sat, 10am-1pm & 2.30-5pm Sun) Based in South Goa, this trust operates an animal shelter at Curchorem helping sick, stray and injured dogs, cats and even a calf or two. Volunteers are welcome, if only for a few spare hours to walk or play with the dogs. GAWT also operates a **shop** (☑0832-2653677; www.gawt.org; ⊙9.30am-1pm & 4-7pm Mon-Sat) and information centre in Colva.

➡ **International Animal Rescue** (Animal Tracks; ☑0832-2268272; internationalanimalrescuegoa.org.in; Madungo Vaddo, Assagao; ⊙9am-4pm) An internationally active charity operating Animal Tracks rescue facility in Assagao. Visitors and volunteers (both short and long term) are always welcome, though rabies vaccination is expected.

➡ **Animal Rescue Centre** (☑0832-2644171; Chapolim; ⊙10am-1pm & 2.30-5pm Mon-Sat) About 3km from Palolem this centre takes in sick, injured or stray animals.

➡ **Primate Trust India** (www.primatetrustindia.org; Camurlim) This rehabilitation centre cares for orphaned and injured monkeys or rescued illegal pets. Volunteer placements are available for a minimum one-month stay if you book in advance and obtain the necessary visa.

➡ **Bethesda Life Centre** (☑0832-245 9962; www.blcgoa.com; Bambolim Complex, Alto Santa Cruz, Tiswadi) This Goan charity supports shelters for disadvantaged women and children, including HIV sufferers. Volunteer placements are available; see the website for details.

Plan Your Trip

Travel with Children

Goa is the most family-friendly state in India. What could be better than taking the kids to the beach...every day? Goa excels as a holiday destination on many fronts: its short travel distances, wide range of foods for all tastes, reliable climate, and a range of activities for kids of all ages...even away from the beach.

Goa for Kids

Though India's sensory overload may at first prove overwhelming for younger kids, the colours, scents, sights and sounds of Goa more than compensate by setting young imaginations ablaze. With a little planning and an open mind, travelling with children will open up a whole new world for you too.

Goa's beaches are excellent for playing in the sand with a bucket and spade, and for paddling and water sports, though strong currents make swimming at most beaches risky, even for adults. Beaches are patrolled but children may feel safer swimming at a hotel pool or water park.

At the busiest beaches you'll be surprised by how many kids and families are around – mostly Indian families holidaying from outside Goa. Foreign children, especially fair-haired ones, can be quite a novel attraction. Don't be surprised if groups of people ask to pose for photographs with your child. Generally it's good-natured attention but if it gets too much, offer a polite 'no'.

Away from the beach, kids should enjoy boat trips on calm local rivers, trips to spice farms and wildlife sanctuaries, shopping at markets or a day at the movies.

Best Beaches for Kids

Goa's beaches are all a little different in character and some are more family-friendly than others. All have seasonal beach shacks with cold drinks, child-friendly food and often free wi-fi, and many have water sports including (for older kids) banana boat rides, jet skis and tandem parasailing.

Palolem

The calm, shallow waters in this bay (p183) are the safest for swimming in all of Goa. There are a few families among the backpackers. You can hire kayaks and paddleboards, or go on a sunset boat trip.

Patnem

Good paddling on calm days, Patnem (p188) has fewer people than Palolem and a more relaxed vibe, as well as great drop-in kindergartens and schools.

Baga & Calangute

Goa's busiest beach strip (p127) has lots of bucket-and-spade vendors, water sports and plenty of other children to make friends with.

Arambol

There are shallow seas popular with long-stayers, safe swimming in Sweetwater Lake and paragliding from the hilltop (p153).

Mandrem & Aswem

Lovely beaches with few hawkers, sophisticated hut accommodation and a surf shop (p151).

WHAT TO PACK

Most things you will need can be bought locally, usually for much cheaper prices than you would see at home. Disposable nappies (diapers) are widely available but relatively expensive. The environmentally-friendly move may be to switch to cloth nappies; any hotel can arrange laundry for you. Formula is available in Goa in local and Nestlé brands.

Essentials Hat, sunscreen and tropical-strength mosquito repellent.

First-aid kit Heat-rash cream, plasters, antiseptic, paracetamol etc.

Lightweight portacot These are hard to find in Goa.

Baby or child carrier Or do as locals do and carry your baby front-side in a sarong. Prams are a pain but a lightweight stroller can be useful for tired toddlers.

Electronic distractions For teenage kids, a tablet or smartphone loaded with apps and music can be a godsend and free wi-fi is common in hotels and cafes.

Beach-Free Highlights

Splashdown Water Park (p135) Water slides, pools, fountains and waterfalls to entertain everyone from toddlers to adults.

Spice Farms (p105) Central Goa's commercial spice farms are a surprisingly entertaining family day out: spice plantation tours, thali lunch and an optional elephant bath.

Dolphin-Spotting Trips Charter an outrigger fishing boat and spot dolphins on trips from Candolim, Coco, Baga or Palolem.

Jungle Book (p109) This eco elephant park is a good place to ride, feed and bathe with elephants in a jungle setting.

Goa Science Centre & Planetarium (p92) Most kids will enjoy the planetarium and simple science exhibits on a rainy day.

Track II Go Karting (☏0832-24914526; Calangute-Anjuna Rd, Arpora; 10 laps ₹250; ⊙4-10pm Tue-Sun) Older children with some driving experience might want to have a go at this exciting Arpora track.

INOX Cinema (p90) Panaji's modern cinema shows mainstream Hollywood (as well as Bollywood) films. Check website.

Caculo Mall (p90) Timezone arcade, 7D cinema, play centre, bowling alley, fast food and boutique fashion stores.

Cooking classes (p32) Get the kids involved in a spicy cooking class.

Planning

➡ Ask your local doctor or travel clinic about immunisations and antimalarials. See p238.

➡ Pack loose-fitting clothing (with long sleeves and pants) for evening mosquito protection.

➡ Most hotels and guesthouses are child-friendly and will supply a mattress or have a family room.

➡ If you've got fussy eaters, don't fret. Beach shacks and restaurants can prepare nonspicy pizzas, pancakes, toast, eggs or tasty rice and dahl. Supermarkets in Candolim, Panaji and Anjuna stock all sorts of Western foods.

➡ There are loads of taxis for day trips around Goa (none have child seats) but families should consider using the women's taxi service (p236).

School & Kindergarten

With lots of long-staying foreigners, Goa has a number of seasonal child-care centres; Anjuna and Arambol are good places to check out in the north, while Palolem and Patnem, with large expat communities, have recommended schools.

Vrindhavan Kindergarten (☏8007322583; www.vrindhavan-kindergarten.de; Patnem; ⊙8.30am-3pm Mon-Fri) For kids aged two to six years, this expat-run kinder has daily activities and learning for walk-ins (₹900 per day) or longer term (₹9000 per month).

Vidya Aranya School (☏7767832283; www.vidyaaranya.com; Palolem) Has an after-school kids club where drop-ins are welcome, as well as regular classes (in English) for children from six years of age.

Paradise School Goa (☏8806383011; www.paradiseschoolgoa.com; Pansulem; ⊙9am-3pm Mon-Fri) This international community school near Patnem welcomes children aged five to 11 for a term or a full year.

Regions at a Glance

Though Goa is a relatively small state, the differences in character between the regions, villages and beach enclaves are surprisingly pronounced.

Central Goa is home to the capital, Panaji (Panjim), an unmissable example of Goa's Portuguese heritage, as well as the state's biggest historical attraction in nearby Old Goa. Rather than enjoying beaches, this is the place to explore history, culture, architecture, wildlife parks and authentic Goan life away from the coastal strip.

North Goa's buzzing resorts offer plenty of nightlife, shopping, yoga retreats and fine dining, with just a few patches of quiet sands but plenty of action. Goa's busiest beach strip is between Candolim and Baga and the state's most famous traveller scenes – Anjuna, Vagator and Arambol – are perennially popular with long-staying visitors.

South Goa is more serene, with a largely laid-back traveller vibe, Goa's biggest five-star resorts and its most picturesque beach community at busy little Palolem. Don't miss some inland exploration here, from traditional villages to wildlife sanctuaries.

One of India's most dynamic cities, Mumbai (Bombay) is a popular gateway to India and a stepping stone to Goa. The city is an assault on the senses, but there are few better places in India for shopping, dining, architecture and experiencing cosmopolitan city life.

Mumbai (Bombay)

Food
Architecture
Shopping

Indian Cuisine

Indulge all your foodie fantasies in this city of superlative cuisines from across India. Munch Mughlai kebabs and Punjabi banquets, but leave space for Mumbai's delectable street-food snacks.

Colonial-Era Architecture

Mumbai's colonial-era architecture is some of the country's finest, with iconic sights such as the Gateway of India, High Court, Taj Mahal Palace, Mumbai, and Chhatrapati Shivaji Terminus (Victoria Terminus) dominating the skyline.

Diverse Shopping

Teeming bazaars, high fashion from Indian designers, quality handicrafts, antiques and bric-a-brac in abundance make Mumbai a fabulous place to throw caution to your luggage allowance. Mutton St is the place to discern a real antique from a fake, while Crawford Market is the spot to mingle with grocery-shopping locals.

p38

Panaji & Central Goa

History
Wildlife
Temples

Fascinating History

Picturesque Portuguese-era homes and historic riverside buildings are a highlight in the relaxed state capital of Panaji. Not far away, Old Goa's glorious cathedrals once earned it the title 'Rome of the East'.

Birdwatching & Elephants

Dr Salim Ali Bird Sanctuary, on lovely Chorao Island, makes for a leisurely spot of birdwatching beside the river. Further afield are Bondla and Bhagwan Mahavir Wildlife Sanctuaries. Backwoods Camp is an ornithologist's dream while Jungle Book is the place to commune with elephants.

Hindu Temples

Temples abound around Ponda, where the Shri Manguesh and Shri Laxmi Narasimha temples are especially worth a visit. Further east, Tambdi Surla is home to an interesting little 12th-century temple, which has survived centuries of conquerors and temple demolitions.

p78

North Goa

Nightlife
Yoga
Beaches

Vibrant Nightlife

North Goa is the place to party. Calangute, Baga and Candolim are popular for clubs and live music, while Anjuna and Vagator pull out the stops with late-night rave parties.

Yoga Retreats

Yoga and spirituality are big business with dozens of retreats, courses and drop-in classes setting up for the winter, especially in Anjuna, Assagao, Mandrem and Arambol.

Beaches for All

From the boisterous beaches of Baga to the relatively empty white sand at Mandrem, there's a beach to fit every inclination in North Goa. Arambol, Vagator and Anjuna's beaches are popular with backpackers; Calangute, Candolim and Sinquerim are the places to head for water sports; while Arambol is best for paragliding.

p118

South Goa

Beaches
Luxury
Exploration

Laid-Back Beaches

South Goa has some of India's finest beaches and with its chilled-out vibe this is the place to find a patch of peaceful paradise. An almost uninterrupted strip of sand stretches from Velsao to Mobor via Colva and Benaulim, but in the far south Palolem, Patnem, Agonda and tiny Cola show off Goa's coastline at its best.

Luxury Resorts

The south has a string of five-star, beachfront resorts, from the Leela in Mobor to the Lalit in Rajbag, with golf courses, spas and all-round pampering.

Get Off the Beaten Track

Getting off the beaten track is easy in South Goa, where tiny coastal villages invite exploration by scooter, motorbike or rental car. Trips to Usgalimal, Netravali and Cotigao are adventurous. The ride down the coast from the Sal River to Agonda is one of the prettiest in the state.

p159

On the Road

Mumbai (Bombay)

☎ 022 / POP 21.1 MILLION

Best Places to Eat

➡ Peshawri (p67)

➡ Revival (p64)

➡ Dakshinayan (p66)

➡ Koh (p65)

➡ La Folie (p64)

Best Places to Stay

➡ Taj Mahal Palace, Mumbai (p60)

➡ Residency Hotel (p61)

➡ Abode Bombay (p60)

➡ Sea Shore Hotel (p59)

➡ Juhu Residency (p62)

Why Go?

Mumbai is big. It's full of dreamers and hard-labourers, star-lets and gangsters, stray dogs and exotic birds, artists and servants, fisherfolk and *crorepatis* (millionaires) – and lots of people. It has India's most prolific film industry, some of Asia's biggest slums (as well as the world's most expensive home) and the largest tropical forest in an urban zone. Mumbai is India's financial powerhouse, fashion epicentre and a pulse point of religious tension. It's even evolved its own language, Bambaiyya Hindi, which is a mix of...everything.

If Mumbai is your introduction to India, prepare yourself. The city isn't a threatening place but its furious energy, limited public transport and punishing pollution makes it challenging for visitors. The heart of the city contains some of the grandest colonial-era architecture on the planet but explore a little more and you'll uncover unique bazaars, hidden temples, hipster enclaves and India's premier restaurants and nightlife.

When to Go
Mumbai (Bombay)

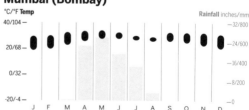

Dec & Jan The very best, least sticky weather.

Aug & Sep Mumbai goes crazy for Ganesh during its most exciting festival, Ganesh Chaturthi.

Oct–Apr There's very little rain, post-monsoon; the best time of year for festivals.

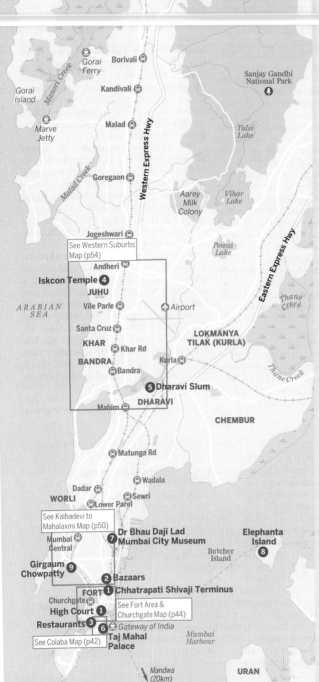

Mumbai Highlights

the magnificence of Mumbai's colonial-era architecture: **Chhatrapati Shivaji Terminus** (p43), **High Court** (p47) and **Gateway of India** (p42)

❷ Investigating the labyrinthine lanes and stalls in Mumbai's ancient **bazaar district** (p73)

❸ Dining like a maharaja at one of India's best restaurants such as **Indigo** (p63)

❹ Feeling the love with the Krishna crowd at the unique **Iskcon Temple** (p53)

❺ Exploring the self-sufficient world of Asia's largest shantytown, **Dharavi Slum** (p59)

❻ Sleeping at the **Taj Mahal Palace, Mumbai** (p60), one of the world's iconic hotels, or having a drink at its bar, Mumbai's first

❼ Ogling the gorgeous Renaissance revival interiors of the **Dr Bhau Daji Lad Mumbai City Museum** (p49)

❽ Beholding the commanding triple-headed Shiva at **Elephanta Island** (p55)

❾ Catching the city's sea breeze among playing kids, big balloons and a hot-pink sunset at **Girgaum Chowpatty** (p49)

History

Koli fisherfolk have inhabited the seven islands that form Mumbai from as far back as the 2nd century BC. Remnants of this culture remain huddled along the city shoreline today. A succession of Hindu dynasties held sway over the islands from the 6th century AD until the Muslim Sultans of Gujarat annexed the area in the 14th century, eventually ceding it to Portugal in 1534. The only memorable contribution the Portuguese made to the area was christening it Bom Bahai. They handed control to the English government in 1665, which leased the islands to the East India Company.

Bombay flourished as a trading port. The city's fort was completed in the 1720s, and a century later ambitious land reclamation projects joined the islands into today's single landmass. The city continued to grow, and in the 19th century the fort walls were dismantled and massive building works transformed the city in grand colonial style. When Bombay became the principal supplier of cotton to Britain during the American Civil War, the population soared and trade boomed as money flooded into the city.

Bombay was a major player in the Independence movement, and the Quit India campaign was launched here in 1942 by Mahatma Gandhi. The city became capital of the Bombay presidency after Independence, but in 1960 Maharashtra and Gujarat were divided along linguistic lines – and Bombay became the capital of Maharashtra.

The rise of the pro-Marathi, pro-Hindu regionalist movement in the 1980s, spearheaded by the Shiv Sena (literally 'Shivaji's Army'), shattered the city's multicultural mould by actively discriminating against Muslims and non-Maharashtrians. Communalist tensions increased, and the city's cosmopolitan self-image took a battering when 900 people, mostly Muslims, were killed in riots in late 1992 and 1993. The riots were followed by a dozen retaliatory bombings which killed 257 people and damaged the Bombay Stock Exchange.

Shiv Sena's influence saw the names of many streets and public buildings – as well as the city itself – changed from their colonial monikers. In 1996 the city officially became Mumbai (derived from the Hindu goddess Mumba). The airport, Victoria Terminus and Prince of Wales Museum were all renamed after Chhatrapati Shivaji, the great Maratha leader.

Religious tensions deepened and became intertwined with national religious conflicts and India's relations with Pakistan. A series of bomb attacks on trains killed over 200 in July 2006. Then, in November 2008, a coordinated series of devastating attacks (by Pakistani militants) targeted landmark buildings across the city, as the Taj Mahal Palace hotel burned, passengers were gunned down inside the Chhatrapati Shivaji train station and 10 killed inside the Leopold Cafe backpacker haunt.

MUMBAI IN...

Two Days

Begin at one of the city's architectural masterpieces, the **Chhatrapati Shivaji Maharaj Vastu Sangrahalaya museum** (p46), before grabbing a drink in **Pantry** (p64) and exploring the galleries and scene in the bohemian Kala Ghoda district. Lunch Gujarati-style at **Samrat** (p64).

In the afternoon continue admiring Mumbai's marvellous buildings around the Oval Maiden and Marine Drive before heading to Colaba, the heart of the city. Tour the city's iconic sights, the **Gateway of India** (p42) and **Taj Mahal Palace hotel** (p60) around sunset, and be sure to have a drink at the **Harbour Bar** (p68). In the evening either fine dine at **Indigo** (p63) or chow down at **Bademiya** (p63), followed by (for those with the stamina) a nightcap at sky bar **Aer** (p69).

The next day, head to the granddaddy of Mumbai's colonial-era giants, the old Victoria Terminus train station, **Chhatrapati Shivaji Terminus** (p43). Then investigate **Crawford Market** (p73) and its maze of bazaars, hidden temples and unique street life. Lunch at **Revival** (p64). Make your way over to **Mani Bhavan** (p49), the museum dedicated to Gandhi, and finish the day wandering the tiny lanes of **Khotachiwadi** (p49) followed by a beach sunset and *bhelpuri* at **Girgaum Chowpatty** (p49). In the evening head to hip nightlife hub **Bluefrog** (p70) for dinner, and then bop to a band or DJ.

TOP FESTIVALS IN MUMBAI

Mumbai Sanskruti (⊘Jan) This free, two-day celebration of Hindustani classical music is held on the steps of the gorgeous Asiatic Society Library in the Fort area.

Kala Ghoda Festival (www.kalaghodaassociation.com; ⊘Feb) Getting bigger and more sophisticated each year, this two-week-long art fest held in Kala Ghoda and the Fort area sees tons of performances and exhibitions.

Elephanta Festival (www.maharashtratourism.gov.in; ⊘Mar) This classical music and dance festival takes place on the waterfront Apollo Bunder at the Gateway of India.

Nariyal Poornima (⊘Aug) This Koli celebration in Colaba marks the start of the fishing season and the retreat of monsoon winds.

Ganesh Chaturthi (⊘Aug/Sep) Mumbai gets totally swept up by this 10- to 12-day celebration of the Hindu god Ganesh. On the festival's first, third, fifth, seventh and 11th days, families and communities take their Ganesh statues to the seashore at Chowpatty and Juhu beaches and auspiciously submerge them.

Mumbai Film Festival (MFF; www.mumbaifilmfest.org; ⊘Oct) New films from the subcontinent and beyond are screened at the weeklong MFF at cinemas across Mumbai.

In late 2012, when the Sena's charismatic founder Bal Thackeray died (500,000 attended his funeral), the Shiv Sena mission begin to falter, and in the 2014 assembly elections, President Modi's BJP became the largest party in Mumbai.

Despite recent troubles Mumbaikars are a resilient bunch. Increased security is very much part of everyday life today and the city's status as the engine room of the Indian economy remains unchallenged. However, the Mumbai politicians certainly have their work cut out, with the megacity's feeble public transport, gridlocked streets, pollution and housing crisis all in desperate need of attention.

◉ Sights

Mumbai is an island connected by bridges to the mainland. The city's commercial and cultural centre is at the southern, claw-shaped end of the island known as South Mumbai. The southernmost peninsula is Colaba, traditionally the travellers' nerve centre, with many of the major attractions.

Directly north of Colaba is the busy commercial area known as Fort, where the British fort once stood. This part of the city is bordered on the west by a series of interconnected grassy areas known as maidans (pronounced may-*dahns*).

Continuing north you enter 'the suburbs' which contain the airport and many of Mumbai's best restaurants, shopping and nightspots. The upmarket districts of Bandra, Juhu and Lower Parel are key areas.

◎ Colaba

Along the city's southernmost peninsula, Colaba is a bustling district packed with elegant art deco and colonial-era mansions, budget-to-midrange lodgings, bars and restaurants, street stalls and a fisherman's quarter. Colaba Causeway (Shahid Bhagat Singh Marg) dissects the district.

If you're here in August, look out for the Koli festival Nariyal Poornima, which is big in Colaba.

★**Taj Mahal Palace, Mumbai** LANDMARK
(Map p42; Apollo Bunder) Mumbai's most famous landmark, this stunning hotel is a fairy-tale blend of Islamic and Renaissance styles, and India's second-most photographed monument. It was built in 1903 by the Parsi industrialist JN Tata, supposedly after he was refused entry to one of the European hotels on account of being 'a native'. Dozens were killed inside the hotel when it was targeted during the 2008 terrorist attacks, and images of its burning facade were beamed across the world. The fully restored hotel reopened on Independence Day 2010.

Much more than an iconic building, the Taj's history is intrinsically linked with the nation: it was the first hotel in India to employ women, the first to have electricity (and fans), and it also housed freedom-fighters (for no charge) during the struggle for independence.

Colaba

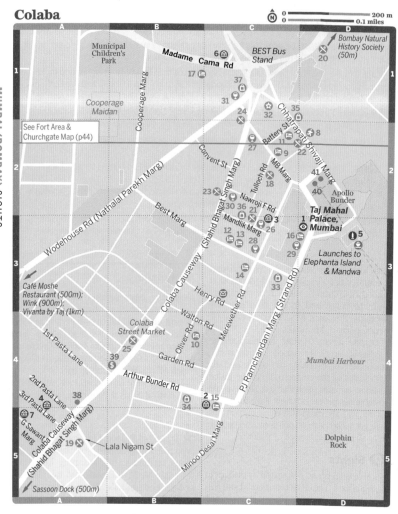

Today the Taj fronts the harbour and Gateway to India, but it was originally designed to face the city (the entrance has been changed).

Gateway of India
MONUMENT

(Map p42) This bold basalt arch of colonial-era triumph faces out to Mumbai Harbour from the tip of Apollo Bunder. Incorporating Islamic styles of 16th-century Gujarat, it was built to commemorate the 1911 royal visit of King George V, but wasn't completed until 1924. Ironically, the British builders of the gateway used it just 24 years later to parade the last British regiment as India marched towards independence. These days, the gateway is a favourite gathering spot for locals and a top place for people-watching. Giant-balloon sellers, photographers, vendors making *bhelpuri* (thin fried rounds of dough with rice, lentils, lemon juice, onion, herbs and chutney) and touts rub shoulders with locals and tourists, creating all the hubbub of a bazaar. In March, they are joined by classical dancers and musicians who perform during the Elephanta Festival (p41).

Boats depart from the gateway's wharfs for Elephanta Island.

Sassoon Dock   WATERFRONT
Sassoon Dock is a scene of intense and pungent activity at dawn (around 5am) when colourfully clad Koli fisher-folk sort the catch unloaded from fishing boats at the quay. The fish drying in the sun are *bombil*, used in the dish Bombay duck. Photography at the dock is prohibited.

◉ Fort Area & Churchgate

Lined up in a row and vying for your attention with aristocratic pomp, many of Mumbai's majestic Victorian buildings pose on the edge of Oval Maidan. This land, and the Cross and Azad Maidans immediately to the north, was on the oceanfront in those days, and this series of grandiose structures faced west directly to the Arabian Sea.

Kala Ghoda, or 'Black Horse', is a hip, atmospheric subneighbourhood of Fort just north of Colaba. It contains many of Mumbai's museums and galleries alongside a wealth of colonial-era buildings and some of the city's best restaurants and cafes.

★ **Chhatrapati Shivaji Terminus**   HISTORIC BUILDING
(Victoria Terminus; Map p44) Imposing, exuberant and overflowing with people, this monumental train station is the city's most extravagant Gothic building and an aphorism for colonial-ear India. It's a meringue of Victorian, Hindu and Islamic styles whipped into an imposing Daliesque structure of buttresses, domes, turrets, spires and stained-glass. As historian Christopher London put it, 'the Victoria Terminus is to the British Raj what the Taj Mahal is to the Mughal empire'.

Some of the architectural detail is incredible, with dog-faced gargoyles adorning the magnificent central tower and peacock-filled windows above the central courtyard. Designed by Frederick Stevens, it was completed in 1887, 34 years after the first train in India left this site.

Fort Area & Churchgate

Girgaum
Chowpatty
(1.5km)

Metro Big
(100m)

41

Bombay
Hospital

New Marine Lines
(Sir Vithaldas Thackersey Rd)

Maharshi Karve (MK) Rd

Marine Dr

Mahatma Gandhi (MG) Rd

Master Rd

24
14
49
33
31
39 27 26 29
3 45
7
K Dubash Marg
Dr VB Gandhi Marg
46
15

Enlargement

44

D Rd
38
C Rd
Churchgate
Train Station

CHURCHGATE
B Rd

Back Bay

28
A Rd

E Rd

Indiatourism

Western
Railways
Reservation
Office

13

Veer Nariman Rd

40

Brabourne
Stadium

Dinsha Wachha Marg

35

J Tata Rd

37

Maharshi Karve Rd

Oval
Maidan

Air India

56

Madame Cama Rd

8

19

Barrister Rajni Patel Marg

Jet
Airways

See Colaba Map (p42)

Municipal
Children's
Park

NARIMAN
POINT

42

43

55

36

J Bajaj Marg

59

57

Cooperage
Maidan

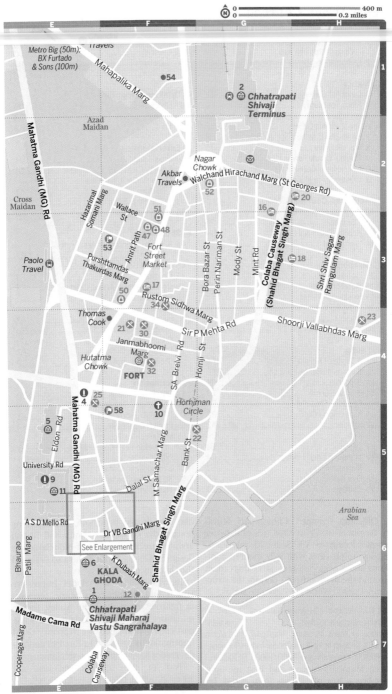

0 _____ 400 m
0 _____ 0.2 miles

E   F   G   H

Metro Big (50m);
BX Furtado
& Sons (100m)

Travels

Mahapalika Marg

● 54

2
Chhatrapati
Shivaji
Terminus

Azad
Maidan

Nagar
Chowk

Akbar
Travels

Walchand Hirachand Marg (St Georges Rd)

52

Cross
Maidan

Mahatma Gandhi (MG) Rd

Hazarimal
Somani Marg

Wallace
St

51

16

20

Colaba Causeway
(Shahid Bhagat Singh Marg)

Shri Shiv Sagar
Ramgulam Marg

47   48

Amrit Path

53

Fort
Street
Market

Bora Bazar St

Perin Nariman St

Mody St

Mint Rd

18

Paolo
Travel

Purshttamdas
Thakurdas Marg

50

17

Rustom Sidhwa Marg

34

Thomas
Cook

21   30

Sir P Mehta Rd

Shoorji Vallabhdas Marg

23

Janmabhoomi
Marg

32

SA Brelvi Rd

Homji St

Hutatma
Chowk

FORT

4   25

58

10

Hornjman
Circle

5

Eldon Rd

22

University Rd

9

11

Dalal St

M Samachar Marg

Bank St

Arabian
Sea

A S D Mello Rd

Dr VB Gandhi Marg

See Enlargement

Bhaurao
Patil Marg

6

K Dubash Marg

Shahid Bhagat Singh Marg

KALA
GHODA

1

12

Chhatrapati
Shivaji Maharaj
Vastu Sangrahalaya

Madame Cama Rd

Cooperage Marg

Colaba
Causeway

E   F   G   H

Fort Area & Churchgate

Officially renamed Chhatrapati Shivaji Terminus (CST) in 1998, it's still better known locally as VT. Sadly, its interior is far less impressive, with ugly modern additions and a neglected air – stray dogs roam around the ticket offices – despite the structure's Unesco World Heritage Site status.

★Chhatrapati Shivaji Maharaj
Vastu Sangrahalaya   MUSEUM
(Prince of Wales Museum; Map p44; http://csm vs.in; K Dubash Marg, Kala Ghoda; Indian/foreigner ₹50/300, camera/video ₹200/1000; ☺10.15am-6pm) Mumbai's biggest and best museum displays a mix of exhibits from across In-

dia. The domed behemoth, an intriguing hodgepodge of Islamic, Hindu and British architecture, is a flamboyant Indo-Saracenic design by George Wittet (who also designed the Gateway of India).

Its vast collection includes impressive Hindu and Buddhist sculpture, terracotta figurines from the Indus Valley, Indian miniature paintings, porcelain and some particularly vicious-looking weaponry. Good information is provided in English, and audio guides are available in seven languages.

Two of the upstairs galleries are air-conditioned, offering a welcome relief to

THE ART DISTRICT

Delhi, is the centre of the action. A slew of galleries are showing incredible work in some gorgeous spaces across the city.

Kala Ghoda hosts a wonderful two-week festival (p41) each February, with some great exhibitions (as well as music, theatre, dance and literary events).

Year-round, the second Thursday of each month is 'Art Night Thursday', when galleries stay open late and the vibe is social. Gallery crawls are sometimes organised; check **Mumbai Boss** (www.mumbaiboss.com) for the latest or the free fold-up *Mumbai Art Map*, available at galleries and bookstores. To go more in depth, check out the magazine *Art India*, available at most English-language bookshops, which has news, background and criticism on work from across the country.

Or, just read nothing and go see pretty things on your own: many galleries are within walking distance of one another in Colaba and Fort. If street art is more your thing, don't miss the Great Wall of Mumbai (p53).

Chatterjee & Lal (Map p42; www.chatterjeeandlal.com; 1st fl, Kamal Mansion, Arthur Bunder Rd, Colaba; ⊙11am-7pm Tue-Sat) Work by emerging artists and historical material.

Galerie Mirchandani + Steinruecke (Map p42; www.galeriems.com; 1st fl, Sunny House, 16/18 Mereweather Rd, Colaba; ⊙11am-7pm Tue-Sat) Contemporary Indian art and sculpture; the gallery is just behind the Taj Mahal Palace hotel.

Gallery Maskara (Map p42; www.gallerymaskara.com; 6/7 3rd Pasta Lane, Colaba; ⊙11am-7pm Tue-Sat) This Colaba gallery showcases exciting contemporary art.

Jhaveri Contemporary (www.jhavericontemporary.com; Krishna Niwas, 58A Walkeshwar Rd, Walkeshwar, Malabar Hill; ⊙11am-6pm Tue-Sat) Cutting-edge photography and art from Indian and overseas artists.

Project 88 (Map p42; www.project88.in; BMP Building, NA Sawant Marg, Colaba; ⊙11am-7pm Tue-Sat) Well established gallery which features leading Indian artists.

the summer heat. There's a fine cafeteria at the entrance and the museum shop is also excellent.

Marine Drive PROMENADE
(Map p44; Netaji Subhashchandra Bose Rd) Built on reclaimed land in 1920, Marine Dr arcs along the shore of the Arabian Sea from Nariman Point past Girgaum Chowpatty and continues to the foot of Malabar Hill. Lined with flaking art deco apartments, it's one of Mumbai's most popular promenades and sunset-watching spots. Its twinkling nighttime lights earned it the nickname 'the Queen's Necklace'.

Hundreds gather on the promenade around Nariman Point in the early evening to snack and chat, when it's a good place to meet Mumbaikars.

University of Mumbai HISTORIC BUILDING
(Bombay University; Map p44; Bhaurao Patil Marg) Looking like a 15th-century French-Gothic mansion plopped incongruously among Mumbai's palm trees, this structure was designed by Gilbert Scott of London's St Pan-

cras train station fame. There's an exquisite **University Library** and **Convocation Hall**, as well as the 80m-high **Rajabai Clock Tower** (Map p44), decorated with detailed carvings. Since the 2008 terror attacks, there's no public access to the grounds but it's still well worth admiring from the street.

High Court HISTORIC BUILDING
(Map p44; Eldon Rd; ⊙10.45am-2pm & 2.45-5pm Mon-Fri) A hive of daily activity, packed with judges, barristers and other cogs in the Indian justice system, the High Court is an elegant 1848 neo-Gothic building. The design was inspired by a German castle and was obviously intended to dispel any doubts about the authority of the justice dispensed inside.

Visitors are permitted to explore the building and attend cases. Inside it's quite a spectacle, with court officials kitted out in starched white tunics offset with red cummerbunds and scarlet berets, while robed barristers strut about with their chests puffed out.

No photography is permitted; cameras have to be left with guards at the entrance.

Keneseth Eliyahoo Synagogue   SYNAGOGUE
(Map p44; www.jacobsassoon.org; Dr VB Gandhi Marg, Kala Ghoda; camera/video ₹100/500; ☺ 11am-6pm Mon-Sat, 1-6pm Sun) Built in 1884, this unmistakable sky-blue synagogue still functions and is tenderly maintained by the city's dwindling Jewish community. It's protected by very heavy security, but the caretaker is welcoming (and will point out a photo of Madonna, who dropped by in 2008).

St Thomas' Cathedral   CHURCH
(Map p44; Veer Nariman Rd; ☺ 7am-6pm) This charming cathedral, begun in 1672 and finished in 1718, is the oldest British-era building standing in Mumbai: it was once the eastern gateway of the East India Company's fort (the 'Churchgate'). The cathedral is a marriage of Byzantine and colonial-era architecture, and its airy interior is full of grandiose colonial-era memorials.

Jehangir Art Gallery   ART GALLERY
(Map p44; www.jehangirartgallery.com; 161B MG Rd, Kala Ghoda; ☺ 11am-7pm) FREE Recently renovated, this excellent gallery hosts shows by local artists and the occasional big name; it's also home to Samovar Café (p65).

National Gallery of Modern Art   MUSEUM
(NGMA; Map p42; www.ngmaindia.gov.in; MG Rd; Indian/foreigner ₹10/150; ☺ 11am-6pm Tue-Sun)

DHARAVI SLUM

Mumbaikars were ambivalent about the stereotypes in 2008's *Slumdog Millionaire*, but slums are very much a part of – some would say the foundation of – Mumbai city life. An astonishing 60% of Mumbai's population lives in slums, and one of the city's largest slums is Dharavi. Originally inhabited by fisher-folk when the area was still creeks, swamps and islands, it became attractive to migrant workers from South Mumbai and beyond when the swamp began to fill in due to natural and artificial causes. It now incorporates 2.2 sq km of land sandwiched between Mumbai's two major railway lines, and is home to perhaps as many as a million people.

While it may look a bit shambolic from the outside, the maze of dusty alleys and sewer-lined streets of this city-within-a-city are actually a collection of abutting settlements. Some parts of Dharavi have mixed populations, but in other parts inhabitants from different parts of India, and with different trades, have set up homes and tiny factories. Potters from Saurashtra (Gujarati) live in one area, Muslim tanners in another; embroidery workers from Uttar Pradesh work alongside metalsmiths; while other workers recycle plastics as women dry pappadams in the searing sun. Some of these thriving industries, as many as 20,000 in all, export their wares, and the annual turnover of business from Dharavi is thought to exceed US$700 million.

Up close, life in the slums is fascinating to witness. Residents pay rent, most houses have kitchens and electricity, and building materials range from flimsy corrugated-iron shacks to permanent multistorey concrete structures. Perhaps the biggest issue facing Dharavi residents is sanitation, as water supply is irregular – every household has a 200L drum for water storage. Very few dwellings have a private toilet or bathroom, so some neighbourhoods have constructed their own (to which every resident must contribute financially) while other residents are forced to use rundown public facilities.

Many families have been here for generations, and education achievements are higher than in many rural areas: around 15% of children complete a higher education and find white-collar jobs. Many choose to stay, though, in the neighbourhood they grew up in.

Slum tourism is a polarising subject, so you'll have to decide for yourself. If you opt to visit, Reality Tours & Travel (p59) does a illuminating tour, and puts a percentage of profits back into Dharavi. Some tourists opt to visit on their own, which is OK as well – just don't take photos. Take the train from Churchgate station to Mahim, exit on the west side and cross the bridge into Dharavi.

To learn more about Mumbai's slums, check out Katherine Boo's 2012 book *Behind the Beautiful Forevers*, about life in Annawadi, a slum near the airport, and *Rediscovering Dharavi*, Kalpana Sharma's sensitive and engrossing history of Dharavi's people, culture and industry.

KHOTACHIWADI

life as it was before high-rises. A Christian enclave of elegant two-storey wooden mansions, it's 500m northeast of Girgaum Chowpatty, lying amid Mumbai's predominantly Hindu and Muslim neighbourhoods. These winding lanes allow a wonderful glimpse into a quiet(ish) life free of rickshaws and taxis. It's not large, but you can spend a little while wandering the alleyways and admiring the old homes and, around Christmas, their decorations.

To find Khotachiwadi, aim for **St Teresa's Church** (Map p50), on the corner of Jagannath Shankarsheth Marg (JSS Marg) and Rajarammohan Roy Marg (RR Rd/Charni Rd), then head directly opposite the church on JSS Marg and duck down the second and third lanes on your left.

MUMBAI (BOMBAY) SIGHTS

Well-curated shows of Indian and international artists in a bright and spacious exhibition space.

Delhi Art Gallery
ART GALLERY

(Map p44; www.delhiartgallery.com; 58 VB Gandhi Marg, Kala Ghoda; ⊙11am-7pm) **FREE** Spread over four floors of a beautifully restored cream colonial-era structure. Showcases important modern Indian art from its extensive collection and well-curated exhibitions.

◉ Kalbadevi to Mahalaxmi

★ Dr Bhau Daji Lad Mumbai City Museum
MUSEUM

(Map p50; www.bdlmuseum.org; Dr Babasaheb Ambedkar Rd; Indian/foreigner ₹10/100; ⊙10am-6pm Thu-Tue) This gorgeous museum, built in Renaissance revival style in 1872 as the Victoria & Albert Museum, contains 3500-plus objects relating to Mumbai's history – photography and maps, textiles, books and manuscripts, *bidriware*, laquerware, weaponry and exquisite pottery.

The landmark building was renovated in 2008, with its Minton tile floors, gilded ceiling mouldings, ornate columns, chandeliers and staircases all restored to their former glory. Contemporary music, dance and drama feature in the new Plaza area, where there's a cafe and shop.

The museum is located in the lush gardens of Jijamata Udyan; skip the zoo.

Mani Bhavan
MUSEUM

(Map p50; ☑23805864; www.gandhi-manibhavan.org; 19 Laburnum Rd, Gamdevi; donation appreciated; ⊙9.30am-6pm) As poignant as it is tiny, this museum is in the building where Mahatma Gandhi stayed during visits to Bombay from 1917 to 1934. The leader formulated his philosophy of satyagraha (nonviolent protest) and launched the 1932 Civil Disobedience campaign from here. Exhibitions include a photographic record of his life, along with dioramas and documents, such as letters he wrote to Adolf Hitler and Franklin D Roosevelt and tributes from Ho Chi Minh and Einstein.

Girgaum Chowpatty
BEACH

(Map p50) This city beach is a favourite evening spot for courting couples, families, political rallies and anyone out to enjoy what passes for fresh air. Evening *bhelpuri* at the throng of stalls at the beach's southern end is an essential part of the Mumbai experience. Forget about taking a dip: the water's toxic.

On the 10th day of the Ganesh Chaturthi festival (p41), in August or September, millions flock here to submerge huge Ganesh statues: it's joyful mayhem.

Mumba Devi Temple
HINDU TEMPLE

(Map p50; Bhuleshwar) Pay a visit to the city's patron goddess at this 18th-century temple, about 1km north of Chhatrapati Shivaji Terminus. Among the deities in residence is Bahuchar Maa, goddess of the transgender *hijras*, and *puja* (prayer) is held here several times a day.

Haji Ali Dargah
MOSQUE

(Map p50; www.hajialidargah.in; off V Desai Chowk) Floating like a sacred mirage off the coast, this Indo-Islamic shrine located on an offshore inlet is a striking sight. Built in the 19th century, it contains the tomb of the Muslim saint Pir Haji Ali Shah Bukhari. Legend has it that Haji Ali died while on a pilgrimage to Mecca and his casket miraculously floated back to this spot.

Kalbadevi to Mahalaxmi

800 m
0.5 miles

Arabian Sea

Patanwala Marg

Dr Bhau Daji Lad Mumbai City Museum 🏛 1

Victoria Gardens (Veermata Jijabai Bhonsle Udyan)

Victoria Rd

BYCULLA

Byculla Train Station

S Balwant Singh Rd

J Jiijibhoy Rd

Clare Rd

Bapurao Jagtap Marg

Maulana Azad Rd

Morland Rd

🌸 12

14 🌸

Mahalaxmi Train Station

6 ⊚

Mumbai Central Bus Terminal

J Boman Behram Marg

Foras Rd

Bluefrog (1km); Aer (1.1km); Canvas Laugh (1.5km); Cathay Pacific (1.6km); Comedy Store (2km)

22 🍴

National CTC

Mumbai Central Train Station

Falkland Rd

Tardeo Rd

Mahalaxmi Racecourse

Willingdon Sports Club Golf Course

Nehru Centre (200m)

Lala Lajpat Rai Rd

17 ✕

21 🍺

Japanese Consulate

TARDEO

Altamount Rd

G Deshmukh Rd (Peddar Rd)

Kemp's Corner

4 ⊚

20 Vatsalabai Desai Chowk

7 ⛩

29 🍴

Bhulabhai Desai Rd (Warden Rd)

CUMBALLA HILL

Breach Candy Hospital

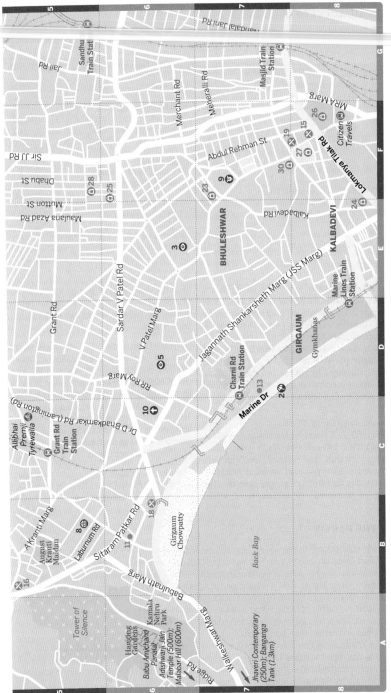

Kalbadevi to Mahalaxmi

It's only possible to visit the shrine at low tide, via a long causeway (check tide times locally). Thousands of pilgrims, especially on Thursday and Friday (when there may be *qawwali*, devotional singing), cross it daily, many donating to beggars who line the way.

Sadly parts of the shrine are in a poor state, damaged by storms and the saline air, though a renovation plan exists. It's visited by people of all faiths.

Mahalaxmi Dhobi Ghat   GHAT
(Map p50; Dr E Moses Rd, Mahalaxmi; ⊙4.30am-dusk) This 140-year-old dhobi ghat (place where clothes are washed) is Mumbai's biggest human-powered washing machine: every day hundreds of people beat the dirt out of thousands of kilograms of soiled

Mumbai clothes and linen in 1026 open-air troughs. The best view is from the bridge across the railway tracks near Mahalaxmi train station.

Bombay Panjrapole   ANIMAL SHELTER
(Map p50; www.bombaypanjrapole.org.in; Panjrapole Marg, Bhuleshwar; ⊙11am-6pm) In the middle of bustling Bhuleshwar market is, of all things, this shelter for 300 homeless cows. Donkeys, goats, birds, dogs and ducks are also looked after. You can wander around and pet the cows and calves and, for a small donation, feed them fresh greens. It's near Madhav Baug Post Office.

Mahalaxmi Temple   HINDU TEMPLE
(Map p50; off V Desai Chowk) It's only fitting that in money-mad Mumbai one of the busiest

THE PARSIS

Mumbai is home to the world's largest surviving community of Parsis, people of the ancient Zoroastrian faith, who fled Iran in the 10th century to escape religious persecution from invading Muslims. 'Parsi' literally means Perisan. Zoroastrians believe in a single deity, Ahura Mazda, who is worshipped at *agiaries* (fire temples) across Mumbai, which non-Parsis are forbidden to enter. Parsi funeral rites are unique: the dead are laid out on open-air platforms to be picked over by vultures. The most renowned of these, the **Tower of Silence**, is located below the Hanging Gardens in Malabar Hill, yet screened by trees and hidden from public view.

The Mumbai Parsi community is extremely influential and successful, with a 98.6% literacy rate (the highest in the city). Famous Parsis include the Tata family (India's foremost industrialists), author Rohinton Mistry and Queen singer Freddie Mercury. If you want to try Parsi cuisine, head to Brittania restaurant (p65).

WORTH A TRIP

THE GREAT WALL OF MUMBAI

Starting as an initiative by artists to add colour to a suburban street in Bandra, the Wall Project (www.thewallproject.com) has introduced vibrant public art, murals and graffiti across the city. There's no official membership, and the art has been created by both amateurs and professionals.

The guidelines are that no advertising, political statements, religious content or obscene messaging should be used. Social messaging that's too preachy is not encouraged either.

Hundreds of individuals have joined the project, with most murals dealing with personal stories: their dreams, desire for change, criticisms and frustrations.

Perhaps the most spectacular stretch is a 2km canvas along Senapati Bapat Marg (Tulsi Pipe Rd), between the train stations of Mahim and Dadar on the Western Line, where the art parallels the tracks. It's a very thought-provoking and enriching experience to take in; allow an hour and a half to explore.

This particular wall had long been coveted by the Wall Project founders, but they expected firm opposition from the authorities. Instead they were actually approached by the city's Municipal Commissioner, who invited them to create something. Around 400 people contributed.

Many murals on Senapati Bapat Marg have a theme that's relevant to India and Mumbai such as the environment, pollution and pressures of metropolitan life. One mural of a Mumbai cityscape simply says 'Chaos is our Paradise'.

Bandra is another area rich in street art, where many walls and bridges have been customised: Chapel Lane is a good place to start investigating.

and most colourful temples is dedicated to Mahalaxmi, the goddess of wealth. Perched on a headland, it is the focus for Mumbai's Navratri (Festival of Nine Nights) celebrations in September/October.

Babu Amichand Panalal Adishwarji Jain Temple JAIN TEMPLE
(Walkeshwar Marg, Malabar Hill; ⊙ 5am-9pm) This temple is renowned among Jains for its beauty – given how beautiful Jain temples are, that's saying a lot. Check out the paintings and especially the ecstatically colourful zodiac dome ceiling. It's a small, actively used temple; visitors should be sensitive and dress modestly.

Nehru Centre CULTURAL COMPLEX
(⌨ 24964676, 24964680; www.nehru-centre. org; Dr Annie Besant Rd, Worli; Discovery of India admission free, planetarium adult/child ₹50/25; ⊙ 10am-6pm Tue-Sun, Discovery of India 11am-5pm, planetarium English show 3pm) The Nehru Centre is a cultural complex that includes a planetarium, theatre, gallery and an interesting history exhibition, Discovery of India. The architecture is striking: the tower looks like a giant cylindrical pineapple, the planetarium like a UFO. High-quality dance, drama and live music events are held here.

The complex is just inland from Lala Lajpat Rai Rd.

Malabar Hill AREA
(around BG Kher Marg) Mumbai's most exclusive neighbourhood, at the northern end of Back Bay, surprisingly contains one of Mumbai's most sacred oases. Concealed between apartment blocks is Banganga Tank, an enclave of serene temples, bathing pilgrims, meandering, traffic-free streets and picturesque old *dharamsalas* (pilgrims' rest houses). According to Hindu legend, Lord Ram created this tank by piercing the earth with his arrow. For some of the best views of Chowpatty, about 600m west, and the graceful arc of Marine Dr, visit Kamala Nehru Park.

⦿ Western Suburbs

★ Iskcon Temple HINDU TEMPLE
(Map p54; www.iskconmumbai.com; Juhu Church Rd, Juhu; ⊙ 4.30am-1pm & 4-9pm) A focus for intense, celebratory worship in the sedate suburbs, this temple is a compelling place to visit. Iskcon Juhu has a key part in the Hare Krishna story, as founder AC Bhaktivedanta Swami Prabhupada spent extended periods here (you can visit his modest living

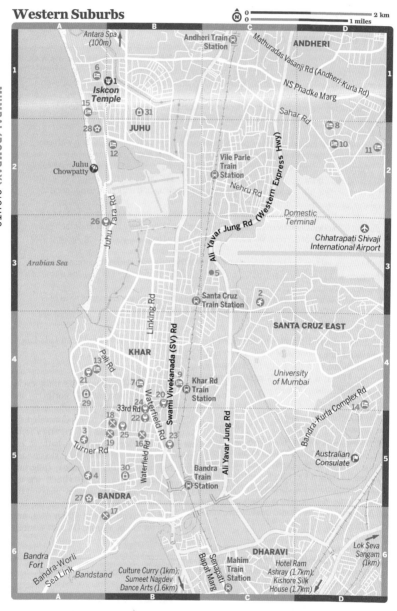

quarters in the adjacent building). The temple compound comes alive during prayer time as the faithful whip themselves into a devotional frenzy of joy, with *kirtan* dancing accompanied by crashing hand symbols and drumbeats.

Murals that are dotted around the compound detail the Hare Krishna narrative. The Iskcon (p62) hotel that is located here is also recommended, as is the canteen (meals ₹70).

Western Suburbs

◎ Gorai Island

Global Pagoda   BUDDHIST TEMPLE
(www.globalpagoda.org; Gorai; ⊘ 9am-7pm, meditation classes 10am-6pm) Rising up like a mirage from polluted Gorai Creek is this breathtaking, golden 96m-high stupa modelled on Myanmar's Shwedagon Pagoda. Its dome, which houses relics of Buddha, was built entirely without supports using an ancient technique of interlocking stones, and the meditation hall beneath it seats 8000.

There's a museum dedicated to the life of the Buddha and his teaching, and 20-minute meditation classes are offered daily; an on-site meditation centre also offers 10-day courses.

To get here, take a train from Churchgate to Borivali (exit the station at the 'West' side), then take bus 294 (₹5) or an autorickshaw (₹40) to the ferry landing, where Esselworld ferries (return ₹50) depart every 30 minutes. The last ferry to the pagoda is at 5.30pm.

◎ Elephanta Island

★**Elephanta Island**   HINDU TEMPLE
(Gharapuri; Indian/foreigner ₹10/250; ⊘ caves 9am-5pm Tue-Sun) Northeast of the Gateway of India in Mumbai Harbour, the rock-cut temples on Gharapuri, better known as Elephanta Island, are a Unesco World Heritage Site. Created between AD 450 and 750, the labyrinth of cave temples represent some of India's most impressive temple carving. The main Shiva-dedicated temple is an intriguing latticework of courtyards, halls, pillars and shrines; its magnum opus is a 6m-tall statue of Sadhashiva, depicting a three-faced Shiva as the destroyer, creator and preserver of the universe, his eyes closed in eternal contemplation.

It was the Portuguese who dubbed the island Elephanta because of a large stone elephant near the shore (this collapsed in 1814 and was moved by the British to Mumbai's Jijamata Udyan). There's a small museum on-site, with informative pictorial panels on the origin of the caves.

Pushy, expensive guides are available – but you don't really need one as Pramod Chandra's *A Guide to the Elephanta Caves,* widely for sale, is more than sufficient.

Launches (Map p42) head to Gharapuri from the Gateway of India every half-hour from 9am to 3.30pm. Buy tickets (economy/deluxe ₹130/160) at the booths lining Apollo Bunder. The voyage takes about an hour.

The ferries dock at the end of a concrete pier, from where you can walk or take the miniature train (₹10) to the stairway (admission ₹10) leading up to the caves. It's lined with souvenir stalls and patrolled by pesky monkeys. Wear good shoes.

Activities

Mumbai has surprisingly good butterfly- and birdwatching opportunities. Sanjay Gandhi National Park is popular for woodland birds, while the mangroves of Godrej (13km east of Bandra) are rich in waders. The **Bombay Natural History Society** (BNHS; Map p44; ☑ 22821811; www.bnhs.org; Hornbill House, Shahid Bhagat Singh Marg; ⊙9am-5.30pm Mon-Fri) runs excellent trips every weekend.

Outbound Adventure   OUTDOOR ADVENTURE
(☑26315019;   www.outboundadventure.com)
This outfit runs one-day rafting trips on the Ulhas River from July to early September (₹2000 per person). After a good rain, rapids can get up to Grade III+, though usually the rafting is calmer. Also organises camping (from ₹1500 per person per day) and canoeing trips.

MUMBAI FOR CHILDREN

Kidzania (www.kidzania.in; 3rd flr, R City, LBS Marg, Ghatkopar West; ⊙child/adult Tue-Fri ₹950/500, Sat & Sun ₹950/700) is Mumbai's latest attraction, an educational activity centre where kids can learn all about piloting a plane, fighting fires, policing and get stuck into lots of art- and craft-making. It's on the outskirts on the city, 10km northeast of the Bandra Kurla Complex.

Little tykes with energy to burn will love the Gorai Island amusement parks, **Esselworld** (www.esselworld.in; adult/child ₹790/490; ⊙11am-7pm, from 10am weekends) and **Water Kingdom** (www.waterkingdom.in; adult/child ₹690/490; ⊙11am-7pm, from 10am weekends). Both have lots of rides, slides and shade. Combined tickets are ₹1190/990 (adult/child).

The free **Hanging Gardens**, in Malabar Hill, have animal topiaries, swings in the shade and coconut-wallahs. **Kamala Nehru Park**, across the street, has a two-storey 'boot house'. Bombay Natural History Society (p56) also conducts nature trips for kids.

Wild Escapes   TREKKING
(☑66635228; www.wild-escapes.com; treks from ₹780) Weekend trekking trips to forts, valleys and waterfalls around Maharashtra.

Yoga House   YOGA
(Map p54; ☑65545001; www.yogahouse.in; 53 Chimbai Rd, Bandra; class ₹700; ⊙8am-10pm) A variety of yoga traditions are taught at this homey, Western-style yoga centre, housed in a Portuguese-style bungalow by the sea. There's also a charming cafe.

Yoga Cara   YOGA, MASSAGE
(Map p54; ☑022-26511464; www.yogacara.in; 1st fl, SBI Bldg, 18A New Kant Wadi Rd, Bandra; ⊙yoga per class/week ₹600/1500) Classic hatha and iyengar yoga institute. Massages (from ₹1850 per hour) and treatments are excellent here; the SoHum rejuvenating massage is recommended. Ayurvedic cooking classes are also offered.

Antara Spa   SPA
(☑022-66939999; www.theclubmumbai.com; 197 DN Nagar, Andheri West; 1hr massage from ₹2450; ⊙10am-10pm) Luxury spa with skilled therapists offering a range of therapies and treatments, including Swedish, Thai and hot-stone massages.

Palm Spa   SPA
(Map p42; ☑022-66349898; www.thepalms spaindia.com; Chhatrapati Shivaji Marg, Colaba; 1hr massage from ₹3200; ⊙9.30am-10.30pm) Indulge in a rub, scrub or tub at this renowned Colaba spa. The exfoliating lemongrass and green-tea scrub is ₹2500.

Child Rights & You   VOLUNTEERING
(CRY; Map p50; ☑23096845; www.cry.org; 89A Anand Estate, Sane Guruji Marg, Mahalaxmi) Raises funds for marginalised children. Volunteers can assist with campaigns (online and on the ground), research, surveys and media, as well as occasional fieldwork. A four-week commitment is required.

Lok Seva Sangam   VOLUNTEERING
(☑022-24070718; http://loksevasangam.word press.com; D/1, Everard Nagar Eastern Express Hwy, Sion) Works to improve lives in the city's slums. Medical staff who can speak Hindi/Marathi or those with fundraising skills are needed.

Vatsalya Foundation   VOLUNTEERING
(Map p50; ☑24962115; www.thevatsalyafoun dation.org; Anand Niketan, King George V Memorial, Dr E Moses Rd, Mahalaxmi) Works with

SANJAY GANDHI NATIONAL PARK

It's hard to believe that within 1½ hours of the teeming metropolis you can be surrounded by a 104-sq-km protected tropical forest. At **Sanjay Gandhi National Park** (☎28866449; Borivali; adult/child ₹30/15, vehicle ₹100, safari admission ₹50; ⊙7.30am-6pm Tue-Sun, last entry 4pm) bright flora, birds, butterflies and elusive wild leopards replace pollution and concrete, all surrounded by forested hills on the city's northern edge. Urban development has muscled in on the fringes, but the heart of the park is still very peaceful.

A trekking ban is in force to protect wildlife, but you can still walk in the woods if you go with Bombay Natural History Society. On your own, you can cycle (hire bikes cost ₹20 per hour, ₹200 deposit) or take the shuttle to the Shilonda Waterfall, Vihar and Tulsi Lakes (where there's boating) and the most intriguing option, the **Kanheri Caves** (Indian/foreigner ₹5/100), a set of 109 dwellings and monastic structures for Buddhist monks 6km inside the park. The caves, not all of which are accessible, were developed over 1000 years, beginning in the 1st century BC, as part of a sprawling monastic university complex. Avoid the zoo-like lion and tiger 'safari' as the animals are in cages and enclosures.

Inside the park's main northern entrance is an information centre with a small exhibition on the park's wildlife. The best time to see birds is October to April and butterflies August to November.

The nearest station is Borivali, served by trains on the Western Railway line from Churchgate station (30 minutes, frequent).

Mumbai's street children. There are long- and short-term opportunities in teaching English, computer skills and sports activities.

Welfare of Stray Dogs VOLUNTEERING
(Map p44; ☎64222838; www.wsdindia.org; Yeshwant Chambers, B Bharucha Rd, Kala Ghoda) Operates sterilisation and antirabies programs. Volunteers can walk dogs, treat street dogs, manage stores, educate kids in school programs or fundraise.

🎓 Courses

★ Yoga Institute YOGA
(Map p54; ☎26122185; www.theyogainstitute. org; Shri Yogendra Marg, Prabhat Colony, Santa Cruz East; per 1st/2nd month ₹650/450) At its peaceful leafy campus near Santa Cruz, the respected Yoga Institute has daily classes as well as weekend and weeklong programs, and longer residential courses including teacher training (with the seven-day course a prerequisite).

Kaivalyadhama Ishwardas Yogic Health Centre YOGA
(Map p50; ☎22818417; www.kdhammumbai.org; 43 Marine Dr; ⊙6am-7pm Mon-Sat) Several daily yoga classes as well as workshops; fees include a ₹800 monthly membership fee and a ₹600 admission fee.

★ Bharatiya Vidya Bhavan LANGUAGE COURSE, MUSIC
(Map p50; ☎23871860; www.bhavans.info; 2nd fl, cnr KM Munshi Marg & Ramabai Rd, Girgaum; per hour ₹500; ⊙4-8pm) Excellent private Hindi, Marathi, Gujarati and Sanskrit language classes. Contact Professor Ghosh (a Grammy Award–winning composer and musician) for lessons in tabla, vocals, sitar or classical dance.

Sumeet Nagdev Dance Arts DANCE
(SNDA; ☎24366777; www.sumeetnagdevdance arts.in; Silver Cascade Bldg, SB Marg, Dadar West; 1hr class ₹450) SNDA offers tons of dance classes, from samba and ballet to 'Indian Folk Bollywood'. Classes are also held at a **Chowpatty location** (Studio Balance, Krishna Kunj, 29/30 KM Munshi Marg).

🧭 Tours

Fiona Fernandez' *Ten Heritage Walks of Mumbai* (₹395) has walking tours of the city, with fascinating historical background. The Government of India tourist office can provide a list of approved multilingual guides; most charge ₹750/1000 per half-/full day.

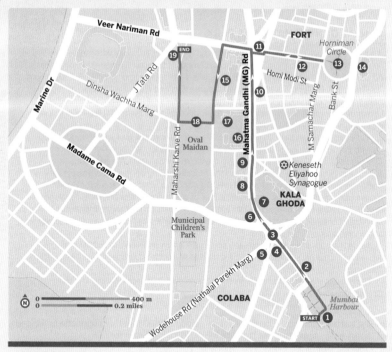

City Walk
Architectural Mumbai

START GATEWAY OF INDIA
END EROS CINEMA
LENGTH 2.5KM; 1½ HOURS

Mumbai's defining feature is its distinctive mix of colonial-era and art deco architecture. Starting from the ❶ **Gateway of India** (p42), walk up Chhatrapati Shivaji Marg past the art deco residential and commercial complex ❷ **Dhunraj Mahal**, towards ❸ **Regal Circle**. Walk the circle for views of the surrounding buildings – including the art deco ❹ **Regal cinema** (p72) and the ❺ **Majestic Hotel**, now the Sahakari Bhandar cooperative store. Continue up MG Rd, past the beautifully restored facade of the ❻ **National Gallery of Modern Art** (p48). Opposite is the landmark ❼ **Chhatrapati Shivaji Maharaj Vastu Sangrahalaya** (p46) built in glorious Indo-Saracenic style. Back across the road is the 'Romanesque Transitional' ❽ **Elphinstone College** and the ❾ **Sassoon Library & Reading Room**, where members escape the afternoon heat

lazing on planters' chairs on the upper balcony. Continue north to admire the vertical art deco stylings of the ❿ **New India Assurance Company Building**. On an island ahead lies ⓫ **Flora Fountain**, depicting the Roman goddess of flowers. Turn east down Veer Nariman Rd, walking towards ⓬ **St Thomas' Cathedral** (p48). Ahead lies the stately ⓭ **Horniman Circle**, an arcaded ring of buildings laid out in the 1860s around a beautifully kept botanical garden. It's overlooked from the east by the neoclassical ⓮ **Town Hall**, home to the Asiatic Society library. Backtrack to Flora Fountain, continuing west and turning south onto Bhaurao Patil Marg to see the august ⓯ **High Court** (p47) and the ornate ⓰ **University of Mumbai** (p47). The university's 80m-high ⓱ **Rajabai Clock Tower** (p47) is best observed from within the ⓲ **Oval Maidan**. Turn around to compare the colonial-era edifices lining Maharshi Karve (MK) Rd, with the row of art deco beauties culminating in the wedding-cake tower of the classic ⓳ **Eros Cinema** (p72).

A **cruise** on Mumbai Harbour is a good way to see the Gateway of India and Colaba harbourfont from the sea. Half-hour ferry rides (₹80) depart from the Gateway of India; tickets are sold on-site.

★**Reality Tours & Travel**   SLUM TOUR
(Map p44; ☑9820822253; www.realitytour sandtravel.com; 1/26, Unique Business Service Centre, Akber House, Nowroji Fardonji Rd; most tours ₹750-1500) ✐ Compelling tours of the Dharavi slum, with 80% of post-tax profits going to the agency's own NGO, **Reality Gives** (www.realitygives.org). Street food, market, bicycle and Night Mumbai tours are also excellent.

Bombay Heritage Walks   WALKING TOUR
(☑23690992, 9821887321; www.bombayherit agewalks.com; per 2hr tour from ₹2500, for up to 5 people) Run by two enthusiastic architects, BHW has terrific tours of heritage neighbourhoods.

Mumbai Magic Tours   CITY TOUR
(☑9867707414; www.mumbaimagic.com; 2hr tour per person from ₹1750) Designed by the authors of the fabulous **Mumbai Magic blog** (www.mumbai-magic.blogspot.com), these city tours focus on food markets, traditional dance and music, and Jewish heritage, among others.

Nilambari Bus Tours   BUS TOUR
(MTDC; ☑020-22845678; www.maharashtratour ism.gov.in; 1hr tour lower/upper deck ₹60/180; ⊙7pm & 8.15pm Sat & Sun) Maharashtra Tourism runs open-deck bus tours of illuminated heritage buildings on weekends. Buses depart from and can be booked at both the **MTDC booth** (Map p42) and the **MTDC office** (☑22841877; www.maharashtra tourism.gov.in; Madame Cama Rd, Nariman Point; ⊙9.45am-5.30pm Mon-Sat).

🛏 Sleeping

Mumbai has the most expensive accommodation in India, and you'll never quite feel like you're getting your money's worth. Welcome to Mumbai real estate!

Colaba is compact, has the liveliest tourist scene and many budget and midrange options. The neighbouring Fort area is convenient for the main train stations (CST and Churchgate). Most of the top-end places are dotted along Marine Dr and out in the suburbs. Note that although there are very few hotels in the cosmopolitan areas of Juhu

SLEEPING PRICE RANGES

The following price ranges refer to a double room and are inclusive of tax:

$ less than ₹2500
$$ ₹2500 to ₹6000
$$$ more than ₹6000

and Bandra, many airport hotels are only a 15-minute taxi ride away.

No matter where you stay, always book ahead.

🛏 Colaba

★**Sea Shore Hotel**   GUESTHOUSE $
(Map p42; ☑22874237; 4th fl, 1-49 Kamal Mansion, Arthur Bunder Rd; s/d without bathroom ₹700/1100; 🛜) This place is really making an effort, with small but immaculately clean and inviting rooms, all with flat-screen TVs, set off a railway-carriage-style corridor. Half the rooms even have harbour views (the others don't have a window). The modish communal bathrooms are well-scrubbed and have a little gleam and sparkle. Wi-fi in the reception area only.

Carlton Hotel   HOTEL $
(Map p42; ☑22020642; 1st fl, Florence House, Mereweather Rd; s/d/tr without bathroom from ₹1050/1550/2300, s/d with AC ₹2900/3200; 🌀) Rooms here are a fair deal for the location, with original floor tiles, high ceilings, a contemporary touch or two, and some boasting balconies with colonial-era Colaba views; however, many lack private bathrooms. The building itself is rundown and staff could be more eager to please.

Bentley's Hotel   HOTEL $
(Map p42; ☑22841474; www.bentleyshotel.com; 17 Oliver Rd; r incl breakfast ₹1740-2490; 🌀🛜) A welcoming Parsi-owned place in the heart of Colaba which travellers either love or hate, depending on which of the five apartment buildings they end up in. First choice are the spacious, colonial-style rooms in the main building; avoid Henry Rd and JA Allana Marg. Air-conditioning is ₹315 extra, wi-fi is reception-only.

India Guest House   GUESTHOUSE $
(Map p42; ☑22833769; 3rd fl, 1/49 Kamal Mansion, Arthur Bunder Rd; s/d without bathroom

from ₹400/500; 📞) Run by the same people as the excellent Sea Shore Hotel, this overflow place is not as attractive but its boxrooms (some with partial sea views) are cheap as chapatis and enjoy a fine location. However, the design (partition walls, shared bathrooms at one end of the corridor) means that it feels more student house than hotel.

Salvation Army Red Shield
Guest House
GUESTHOUSE $

(Map p42; ☑22841824; red_shield@vsnl.net; 30 Mereweather Rd; dm incl breakfast ₹350, d with fan/AC incl breakfast ₹1100/1500; ❄@) A Mumbai institution popular with rupee-pinching travellers. Accommodation is very spartan (and a little grubby) but doable for a night or so. Dorms cannot be reserved in advance: come just after the 9am kickout to ensure a spot. Curfew is midnight.

★ YWCA
GUESTHOUSE $$

(Map p42; ☑22025053; www.ywcaic.info; 18 Madame Cama Rd; s/d/tr with AC incl breakfast & dinner ₹2400/3640/5450; ❄@📶) Efficiently managed, and within walking distance of all the sights in Coloba and Fort, the YMCA is a good deal and justifiably popular. The spacious, well-maintained rooms boast desks and wardrobes and multichanelled TVs (though wi-fi is restricted to the lobby). Tariffs include a buffet breakfast, dinner and a daily newspaper.

Hotel Suba Palace
HOTEL $$

(Map p42; ☑22020636, 22020639; www.hotelsubapalace.com; Battery St; s/d with AC incl breakfast ₹5520/6340; ❄📶) 'Palace' is pushing it a little but this modern, brilliantly located little place is certainly verging on boutique hotel territory with its contemporary decor: neutral tones are offset with zebra-print quilted headboards in the tasteful rooms. There's a good in-house restaurant and free wi-fi.

Regent Hotel
HOTEL $$

(Map p42; ☑22021518; 8 Best Marg; s/d with AC incl breakfast ₹3920-4910; ❄@📶) A dependable choice where staff go the extra mile to help out guests. Located just off Coloba's main drag and has well-furnished rooms with good-quality mattresses and modern marble-floored bathrooms.

Hotel Moti
GUESTHOUSE $$

(Map p42; ☑22025714; hotelmotiinternational @yahoo.co.in; 10 Best Marg; d/tr with AC ₹3300/4500; ❄@📶) A gracefully crumbling, co-

lonial-era building in prime Colaba, where owner Raj is generous with advice about the city. Rooms are simply furnished (many have some period charm, like ornate stucco ceilings), but all could be better maintained.

★ Taj Mahal Palace,
Mumbai
HERITAGE HOTEL $$$

(Map p42; ☑66653366; www.tajhotels.com; Apollo Bunder; s/d tower from ₹15,800/17,620, palace from ₹23,530, 25,990; ❄@📶🏊) The grand dame of Mumbai is one of the world's most iconic hotels and has hosted a roster of presidents and royalty. Sweeping arches, staircases and domes and a glorious garden and pool ensure an unforgettable stay. Rooms in the adjacent tower lack the period details of the palace itself, but many have spectacular, full-frontal views of the Gateway to India.

With a myriad of excellent in-house eating and drinking options, plus spa and leisure facilities, it can be a wrench to leave the hotel premises. All guests are entitled to an exceptional guided tour, which provides illuminating context about the hotel's role in the city's history.

★ Abode Bombay
BOUTIQUE HOTEL $$$

(Map p42; ☑8080234066; www.abodebou tiquehotels.com; 1st fl, Lansdowne House, MB Marg; r with AC incl breakfast ₹5850-14,400; ❄📶) Terrific new hip hotel, stylishly designed using colonial-era and art deco furniture, reclaimed teak flooring and original artwork; the luxury rooms have glorious free-standing bath tubs. Staff are very switched on to travellers' needs, and breakfast is excellent with fresh juice and delicious local and international choices. A little tricky to find, it's located behind the Regal Cinema.

Vivanta by Taj
HOTEL $$$

(☑022-66650808; www.vivantabytaj.com; 90 Cuffe Pde; s/d from ₹8050/9230; ❄📶🏊) In a quiet, leafy neighbourhood 1.5km south of the Gateway, this towering hotel has relatively modest rates (for Mumbai!), considering its excellent facilities which include a large pool, excellent gym, lounge bar and lots of good dining choices.

Gordon House Hotel
HOTEL $$$

(Map p42; ☑22894400; www.ghhotel.com; 5 Battery St; r incl breakfast ₹7700; ❄📶) Light, airy, spacious and well-equipped rooms a stone's throw south of the Gateway to India. Design-wise each floor is themed: the decor

GROWING PAINS

Shoehorned into a narrow peninsula that juts into the Arabian Sea, Mumbai is one of the world's most congested and densely populated megacities. The numbers are startling: over 22 million live in the Mumbai conurbation and around 60% of these live in slums.

While the city is blessed with sea to the west and a large bay to the east, it's also cursed by the narrowness of the spit of land it calls home. Every day over six million commuters from the outer suburbs attempt to reach their workplaces in the south of the city via a network of antiquated suburban trains and buses. A desperately needed metro link to the heart of the city is planned (but not scheduled to be completed until at least 2020, if on time). For years the city planners invested in an ever-increasing number of flyovers, as car ownership has grown by 58% since 2000, while failing to build a single bus lane or cycle path. Gridlock is the norm and the pollution is punishing, with particulate and nitric oxide levels way above WHO danger levels.

The future of the city is in the balance. Mumbai is one of the least green cities on earth, with open spaces, parks and recreation grounds accounting for only 2.5% of its total area (Delhi has 20%, Chandigarh 35%). Yet on the eastern side of town, stretching north from the shoreline of Colaba, is a vast area of decaying docklands which has been long-slated for redevelopment. Will it be set aside for green space, parks and leisure facilities or luxury housing and concrete?

ranges Mediterranean (think terracotta tiles, bold colours), Scandinavian (blond wood, clean lines) and Country (er...patchwork quilts?). There's a good Asian restaurant on the ground floor.

Fort Area & Churchgate

Traveller's Inn HOTEL **$**
(Map p44; ☎22644685; 26 Adi Marzban Path; dm/d ₹630/1880, d with AC incl breakfast ₹2550; ✹@☎) On a quiet, tree-lined street, this small hotel is a very sound choice with clean, if tiny, rooms with cable TV that represent good value. The three (fan-cooled) dorms can get Hades-hot in summer but are a steal for Mumbai – bring your own ice pack (and exorcist). The location's excellent, staff are helpful and there's free wi-fi in the lobby.

Hotel Lawrence GUESTHOUSE **$**
(Map p44; ☎22843618; 3rd fl, ITTS House, 33 Sai Baba Marg, Kala Ghoda; s/d/tr without bathroom incl breakfast ₹850/950/1500) Run by kindly folk, this venerable place has been hosting shoestring travellers for years. Rooms are certainly basic but kept pretty tidy, as are the communal bathrooms. Boasts an excellent Kala Ghoda location, on a quiet little lane accessed by a ramshackle old lift.

Hotel Oasis HOTEL **$**
(Map p44; ☎30227886, 30227889; www.hotel oasisindia.in; 276 Shahid Bhagat Singh Marg; r ₹1620-3050; ✹☎) Hotel Oasis enjoys a convenient location near the CST and offers decent accommodation for the modest rates asked. Rooms are smallish, and some are low on natural light, but they have flat-screen TVs and in-room wi-fi.

★Residency Hotel HOTEL **$$**
(Map p44; ☎22625525; www.residencyhotel.com; 26 Rustom Sidhwa Marg, Fort; s/d with AC incl breakfast from ₹4430/4670; ✹@☎) The best-run midranger in Mumbai, the Residency is the kind of dependable place where you can breathe a sigh of relief after a long journey and be certain you'll be looked after well. It's fine value too, with contemporary rooms that boast mood lighting, fridges, flat-screens and hip en suite bathrooms. Its Fort location is excellent and you'll find some fascinating books to browse over breakfast in the pleasant cafe. For the best rates, always book via the hotel's own website.

Welcome Hotel HOTEL **$$**
(Map p44; ☎6631488; welcomehotel@gmail.com; 257 Shahid Bhagat Singh Marg; s/d incl breakfast from ₹3280/3890, without bathroom from ₹1810/2020; ✹☎) Service is a little hit 'n' miss but rooms here are simple and comfortable, and shared bathrooms are well kept. Top-floor executive rooms are more boutique than midrange.

Trident HOTEL **$$$**
(Oberoi Hotel; Map p44; ☑66324343; www.
tridenthotels.com; Marine Dr; s/d from
₹15,300/17,000; ❇@🌐🏊) This Marine Dr
landmark is part of the Oberoi Hotel com-
plex, but offers better value and a pleasing
contemporary look in its restaurants, bars
and pool area. Upper-floor ocean-view
rooms offer truly spectacular vistas of the
Queen's Necklace. Wi-fi, surprisingly, costs
extra.

📷 Western & Northern Suburbs

★ **Juhu Residency** BOUTIQUE HOTEL **$$**
(Map p54; ☑67834949; www.juhuresidency.com;
148B Juhu Tara Rd, Juhu; s/d with AC incl breakfast &
wi-fi from ₹5850; ❇@🌐) Essential oil aromas
greet you in the lobby at this excellent boutique hotel with an inviting, relaxing atmosphere (and a fine location, five minutes' walk
from Juhu beach). The chocolate-and-coffee
colour scheme in the modish rooms works
well, each boasting marble floors, dark
woods, artful bedspreads and flat-screen TVs.
There are three restaurants – good ones –
for just 18 rooms.

To top it all, free airport pick-ups are
included.

Hotel Oriental Aster HOTEL **$$**
(Map p54; ☑022-28232323; http://theorien
talaster.com; 45 Tarun Bharat Society, Dr Karanjiya
Road; r with AC & breakfast from ₹4700; ❇🌐) An
efficiently run airport hotel with attractive
modern rooms that have space and a splash
of art on show; bathrooms are small but per-
fectly formed. There's 24-hour room service,
and free wi-fi and airport transportation.

Anand Hotel HOTEL **$$**
(Map p54; ☑26203372; anandhote@yahoo.
co.in; Gandhigram Rd, Juhu; s/d with AC from
₹2580/4230; ❇🌐) Yes, the decor's in 50
shades of beige but the Anand's rooms are
comfortable, spacious and represent decent
value, considering the prime location on a
quiet street next to Juhu beach. The excellent in-house Dakshinayan restaurant (p66)
scores highly for authentic, inexpensive
meals too. It's a particularly good deal for
solo travellers.

Hotel Regal Enclave HOTEL **$$**
(Map p54; ☑67261111; www.regalenclave.com; 4th
Rd, Khar West; r with AC incl breakfast from ₹6000;
❇🌐) Enjoys a stellar location in an exceed-
ingly leafy part of Khar, right near the sta-
tion (some rooms have railway views) and

close to all of Bandra's best eating, drinking
and shopping. Rooms are spacious and com-
fortable, with pleasant if unoriginal decor.
Rates include airport pick-up.

Iskcon GUESTHOUSE **$$**
(Map p54; ☑26206860; www.iskconmumbai.
com/guest-house; Juhu Church Rd, Juhu; s/d
₹3100/3500, with AC ₹3400/4000; ❇@🌐) An
intriguing place to stay inside Juhu's lively
Iskcon complex. Though the hotel building
is a slightly soulless concrete block, some
rooms enjoy vistas over the Hare Krishna
temple compound. Spartan decor is offset by
the odd decorative flourish such as Gujarati
sankheda (lacquered country wood) furniture, and staff are very welcoming.

Hotel Neelkanth HOTEL **$$**
(Map p54; ☑26495566, 26495569; 354 Linking
Rd, Khar West; s/d from ₹2460/3380; ❇🌐)
Rooms at the friendly Neelkanth are in-
advertently retro, with lots of marble and
chrome-trimmed wooden furniture; check
out the sublimely mod logo too. Yes, it's
old-fashioned, but it's also decent value for
this neighbourhood with great shopping
nearby.

Hotel Suba International BOUTIQUE HOTEL **$$**
(Map p54; ☑67076707; www.hotelsubainter
national.com; Sahar Rd, Andheri East; r with AC
incl breakfast from ₹6400; ❇🌐) A 'boutique
business' hotel that's very close to the airport (free transfers are included) and boasts
modish rooms with clean lines and stylish
touches.

Le Sutra BOUTIQUE HOTEL **$$$**
(Map p54; ☑022-66420025; www.lesutra.in; 14
Union Park, Khar West; s/d incl breakfast from
₹7900/10,450; ❇🌐) This hip hotel in the
happening Khar area blends contemporary
chic with traditional artefacts (textiles and
hand-carved chairs) and some statement art
in its lovely rooms. The in-house gallery, spa,
cafe and restaurants (Out of the Blue and
Olive) seal the deal. Check the website for
special offers that include dinner or a spa
treatment.

Sofitel Mumbai BKC HOTEL **$$$**
(Map p54; ☑022-61175000; www.sofitel-mum
bai-bkc.com; C-57, Bandra Kurla Complex Rd; s/d
from ₹7720/8500; ❇🌐🏊) Located in Mumbai's BKC business district, which is handy
for the airport and close enough to Bandra,
the Sofitel offers commodious comfort levels. Rooms have a mod-Indian design and

facilities are excellent, with great restaurants and one of the best breakfast buffets in the city.

ITC Maratha HOTEL $$$
(Map p54; 28303030; www.itchotels.in; Sahar Rd, Andheri East; s/d incl breakfast from ₹16,450/19,200; ❄@🛜🏊) The five-star hotel with the most luxurious Indian character, from the Rajasthani-style lattice windows around the atrium, to the rooms with their silk throw pillows and lush raspberry-and-grey colour schemes. Peshawri (p67), one of Mumbai's best restaurants, is located here.

Sun-n-Sand HOTEL $$$
(Map p54; 66938888; www.sunnsandhotel.com; 39 Juhu Chowpatty; r with AC from ₹10,000; ❄@🛜🏊) A beachfront institution with well-maintained if slightly dated rooms that are big on browns and beiges. Rates (add ₹1000 or so for a sea view) are competitive given the location in exclusive Juhu and free airport transfers. Staff are eager to please.

🍴 Eating

Flavours from all over India collide with international trends and taste buds in Mumbai. Colaba is home to most of the cheap tourist haunts, while Fort and Churchgate are more upscale, a trend that continues as you head north to Mahalaxmi and the western suburbs, where you'll find Mumbai's most international and expensive restaurants.

Sample Gujarati or Keralan thalis (all-you-can-eat meals), Mughlai kebabs, Goan vindaloo and Mangalorean seafood. And don't forget, if you see Bombay duck on a menu, it's actually *bombil* (fish dried in the sun and deep-fried).

🍴 Colaba

Bademiya MUGHLAI, FAST FOOD $
(Map p42; Tulloch Rd; light meals ₹60-150; ❷8pm-1.30am) Formerly a tiny, outrageously popular late-night street stall, Bademiya now encompasses a (dingy) seating area too. Yes, prices have risen, but it remains a key Colaba hang-out for its trademark buzz and bustle, plus its delicious meat-heavy menu. Expect spicy, fresh-grilled kebabs, mutton and chicken curries, and tikka rolls.

Olympia INDIAN $
(Map p42; Rahim Mansion, 1 Shahid Bhagat Singh Marg; meals ₹80-140; ❷7am-midnight) While we didn't encounter any athletes at the Olympia, its *masala kheema* (spicy minced meat; ₹40) is certainly a breakfast of champions when munched with a couple of roti. A simple place renowned for its pocket-friendly meat dishes; the seekh kebab and chicken butter fry masala (₹80) are also great.

Hotel OCH INDIAN $
(Map p42; Shahid Bhagat Singh Marg; mains ₹50-150; ❷7am-10.30pm) A good Colaba cheapie, with decent lunch thalis and lots of Punjabi dishes in a large, cafeteria-like setting. Popular with families and cops working next door.

Sufra MIDDLE EASTERN $$
(Map p42; 16A Cusrow Baug, Shahid Bhagat Singh Rd; meals ₹120-250; ❷11am-11.45pm) Serves up excellent Arab dishes such as *kibbeh* (chicken, burgul and mint bites), falafel, shwarma, kebabs and fresh juices at very reasonable rates. It's a tiny place with just a few tables so best for a hit and run or takeaway.

⭐Indigo FUSION, CONTINENTAL $$$
(Map p42; 66368980; www.foodindigo.com; 4 Mandlik Marg; mains ₹780-1250; ❷noon-3pm & 6.30pm-midnight; 🛜) This incredibly classy

STREET FOOD

Mumbai's street cuisine is vaster than many Western culinary traditions. Stalls tend to get started in late afternoon, when chai complements much of the fried deliciousness; items are ₹10 to ₹25.

Most street food is vegetarian. Chowpatty Beach is a great place to try Mumbai's famous *bhelpuri*. Stalls offering samosas, *pav bhaji* (spiced vegetables and bread), *vada pav* (deep-fried spiced lentil-ball sandwich), *bhurji pav* (scrambled eggs and bread) and *dabeli* (a mixture of potatoes, spices, peanuts and pomegranate, also on bread) are spread through the city.

For a meaty meal, Mohammed Ali and Merchant Rds in Kalbadevi are famous for kebabs. In Colaba, Bademiya is a late-night Mumbai rite of passage, renowned for its chicken tikka rolls.

The office workers' district on the north side of Kala Ghoda is another good hunting ground for street snacks.

MUMBAI (BOMBAY) EATING

Colaba institution is a colonial-era property converted into a temple of fine dining. Serves inventive, expensive European and Asian cuisine and offers a long wine list, sleek ambience and a gorgeous rooftop deck. Favourites include the pulled duck tortellini, Kochi oysters, and pork belly with maple-glazed apple. Reserve ahead.

Indigo Delicatessen   CAFE $$$
(Map p42; www.indigodeli.com; Pheroze Bldg, Chhatrapati Shivaji Marg; snacks/mains from ₹320/470; ⊙8.30am-midnight; 🔊) Bustling and fashionable cafe-restaurant with cool tunes and massive wooden tables. The menu includes all-day breakfasts (₹155 to ₹385) and international classics such as pork ribs, thin-crust pizza and inventive sandwiches. It's busy so service can be stretched.

Self-Catering
Colaba Market   MARKET
(Map p42; Lala Nigam St; ⊙7am-5pm) The Colaba market has fresh fruit and vegetables.

Saharkari Bhandar Supermarket   SUPERMARKET
(Map p42; ☑22022248; cnr Colaba Causeway & Wodehouse Rd; ⊙10am-8.30pm) Well-stocked for self-caterers.

🍴 Fort Area & Churchgate

Pradeep Gomantak Bhojanalaya   MAHARASHTRIAN $
(Map p44; Sheri House, Rustom Sidhwa Marg; mains ₹60-150; ⊙11am-4pm & 7.30-10pm) A simple but satisfying place that serves Malvani cuisine and gets very busy at lunchtime. Its *bombil* rice plate (₹70) and crab masala (₹65) are very flavoursome and prepared with real care and attention. Wash your meal down with *sol kadhi* (a soothing, spicy drink of coconut milk and kokum).

Badshah Snacks & Drinks   INDIAN $
(Map p50; Lokmanya Tilak Rd; snacks & drinks ₹40-120; ⊙7am-12.30am) Opposite Crawford Market, Badshah's been serving snacks, fruit juices and its famous *falooda* (rose-flavoured drink made with milk, cream, nuts and vermicelli) to hungry bargain-hunters for more than 100 years.

★ La Folie   CAFE $$
(Map p44; Ropewalk Lane, Kala Ghoda; croissants/cakes from ₹110/220; ⊙noon-11pm) Chocoholics and cake fetishistas look no further, this minuscule Kala Ghoda place will satisfy your cravings, and then some. Owner Sanjana Patel spent seven years in France studying the art (addiction?) of pastry- and chocolate-making, which was obviously time well spent. Try the delectable Madagascar cake (chocolate with raspberry mousse) with a latte (₹130) or the 70% cocoa Venezuelan-sourced chocolates.

Frankly, wherever you are dining in South Mumbai skip the dessert menu and head here instead.

★ Revival   INDIAN $$
(Map p50; www.revivalindianthali.com; 361 Sheikh Memon St, Kalbadevi, opp Mangaldas market; mains ₹200-360, thali from ₹350; ⊙noon-4pm & 7.30-10.30pm, lunch only Sun; ❄🍴) Thali mecca near Crawford Market where waiters in silken dhoti come one after another to fill your plates with dozens of delectable (veg-only) curries, sides, chutneys, rotis and rice dishes in an all-you-can-eat gastro onslaught. The thali menu changes daily and the premises are air-conditioned.

Pantry   CAFE $$
(Map p44; www.thepantry.in; B Bharucha Rd; snacks/meals from ₹200/270; ⊙8.30am-11pm; 🔊) Pantry is a bakery-cafe that offers a choice of fine pies and pastries, soups and sandwiches plus delicious mains (such as curry leaf chicken with burgal pilaf). Breakfasts are legendary: try the tomato scrambled eggs with parmesan and rosti, or some organic-flour waffles with fruit. The elegantly restored historic premises are also perfect for a coffee and slab of cake.

Samrat   GUJARATI $$
(Map p44; ☑42135401; www.prashantcaterers.com; Prem Ct, J Tata Rd; thali ₹400, mains ₹160-290; ⊙noon-11pm; ❄) Samrat has an à la carte menu but most rightly opt for the famous Gujarati thali – a cavalcade of taste and texture, sweetness and spice that includes four curries, three chutneys, curd, rotis and other bits and pieces. Beer is available.

Oye Kake   NORTH INDIAN $$
(Map p44; 13C Cawasji Patel St; mains ₹120-180; ⊙11am-4pm & 7-11pm) Intimate all-veg Punjabi place where the daily thali (₹170) is widly popular with local office workers and renowned for its authenticity. Signature dishes include the panner tikka masala, *sarson da saag* (mustard leaf curry) and the *parathas;* lassis are excellent too. Prepare to have to wait for a table.

DABBA-WALLAHS

A small miracle of logistics, Mumbai's 5000 *dabba-wallahs* (literally 'food container person'; also called tiffin-wallahs) work tirelessly to deliver hot lunches to office workers throughout the city.

Lunch boxes are picked up each day from restaurants and homes and carried on heads, bicycles and trains to a centralised sorting station. A sophisticated system of numbers and colours (many wallahs don't read) identifies the destination of each lunch. More than 200,000 meals are delivered – always on time, come (monsoon) rain or (searing) shine. This system has been used for over a century and there's only about one mistake per six million deliveries. (In a 2002 analysis, *Forbes Magazine* found that the *dabba-wallahs* had a six-sigma, or 99.99966%, reliability rating.)

Look for these master messengers midmorning at Churchgate and CST stations.

A Taste of Kerala
KERALAN $$
(Map p44; Prospect Chambers Annex, Pitha St, Fort; mains ₹70-170, thali from ₹110; ⊙6am-midnight) Inexpensive Keralan eatery with lots of coconut and southern goodness on the menu; try a thali (served on a banana leaf) or one of the seafood specials like the prawn pepper masala. It also serves Punjabi and meat dishes. Staff are very welcoming, and there's an air-conditioned dining room.

Café Moshe
CAFE $$
(Map p42; www.moshes.in; Chhatrapati Shivaji Marg; light meals ₹200-380; ⊙9am-midnight; ☎) Moshe's menu has more than a nod to the Middle East, with excellent mezze, pita bread sandwiches and wraps, salads and outstanding hummus bowls (₹250 to ₹280) that have a choice of toppings. Desserts, juices and coffee also score highly.

Other outlets, all serving the same great food, include the flagship restaurant (7 Minoo Manor, Cuffe Pde; ⊙9am-midnight), in a heritage building, and the bookstore cafe (Map p50; Crossword, NS Patkar Marg) at Kemp's Corner.

Bademiya Restaurant
NORTH INDIAN $$
(Map p44; ☎22655657; Botawala Bldg, Horniman Circle; mains ₹110-220; ⊙11am-1am) The grown-up, sit-down version of Bademiya's legendary Colaba street-side stand (p63) has the classic rolls and rotis, plus biryanis, tikka masalas and dhals. Delivers.

Kala Ghoda Café
CAFE $$
(Map p44; www.kgcafe.in; 10 Ropewalk Lane, Kala Ghoda; light meal ₹100-280, dinner ₹380-530; ⊙8.30am-11.45pm; ☎) ✐ Tiny boho cafe with a handful of tables that's a favourite with creative types. There's usually interesting art or photography. Serves organic coffee and tea, sandwiches, salads and breakfasts.

Suzette
FRENCH $$
(Map p44; www.suzette.in; Atlanta Bldg, Vinayak K Shah Marg, Nariman Point; meals ₹300-450; ⊙9am-11pm Mon-Sat; ☎) This relaxed Parisian-style place with delectable crêpes, croques, salads, pasta and loungy music. On the crêpe front, sweet tooths should try the jaggery and butter; for a savoury flavour, order an *italie* (with pesto, mozzarella and mushrooms). The Bandra branch (Map p54; St John's St, Pali Naka; ⊙9am-11pm) has outdoor seating and is open daily.

Brittania
PARSI $$
(Map p44; Wakefield House, Ballard Estate; mains ₹150-550; ⊙noon-4pm Mon-Sat) This Parsi institution has been around since 1923 and retains a (faded) colonial-era feel. The signature dishes are the *dhansak* (meat with curried lentils and rice) and the berry *pulao* – spiced and boneless mutton or chicken, or veg or egg, buried in basmati rice and tart barberries that are imported from Iran. It's a little tricky to find. Cash only.

Samovar Café
CAFE $$
(Map p44; Jehangir Art Gallery, MG Rd, Kala Ghoda; snacks & meals ₹90-170; ⊙11am-7pm Mon-Sat) Inside the art gallery, this cafe is perfect for a snack (try the rolls; ₹100 to ₹120) or meal (the pepper mutton chops are great). It overlooks the gardens of the Chhatrapati Shivaji Maharaj Vastu Sangrahalaya museum. Cappuccinos and beers are also on offer.

★ Koh
THAI $$$
(Map p44; ☎39879999; InterContinental, Marine Dr; mains ₹850-1850; ⊙12.30-3pm & 7.30-midnight) Destination Thai restaurant with a

real wow factor, where celeb chef Ian Kittichai works his native cuisine into an international frenzy of flavour. The massamun curry (Thai Muslim-style spiced lamb shank with cucumber relish) is his signature (and most expensive) dish, but there are lots of sublime seafood and vegetarian choices too. Well worth a splurge.

★ Mamagoto
ASIAN $$$

(Map p44; ☎022-67495660; www.mamagoto.in; 5 Surya Mahal, B Bharucha Marg; meals ₹350-550; ◷noon-11.30pm) Mamagoto means 'play with food' in Japanese and this zany little Kala Ghoda place is certainly fun, with a relaxed vibe, cool tunes and kooky decor (think pop and propaganda art). The menu really delivers, with punchy Pan-Asian flavours: combo meal deals (₹400 to ₹550) include a great juice, and the authentic Malay-style Penang curry is terrific.

There's also a branch in Bandra (☎022-26552600; www.mamagoto.in; 133 Gazebo House, Hill Rd, Bandra; ◷noon-11.30pm).

Burma Burma
ASIAN $$$

(Map p44; ☎022-40036600; www.burmaburma.in; Oak Lane, off MG Road; meals ₹330-500; ◷noon-3pm & 7-10.30pm) Sleek, stylish new restaurant that marries contemporary design with a few traditional artefacts (prayer wheels line one wall) and provides a beautiful setting for the cuisine of Myanmar. The menu is well priced, intricate and ambitious with inventive salads (try the tea leaf), curries and soups: *oh no khow suey* is a glorious coconut-enriched noodle broth. No alcohol is served.

Khyber
MUGHLAI, INDIAN $$$

(Map p44; ☎40396666; 145 MG Rd; mains ₹380-800; ◷12.30-4pm & 7.30-11.30pm) The much-acclaimed Khyber has a Northwest Frontier-themed design that incorporates murals featuring turbaned Mughal royalty, lots of exposed brickwork and oil lanterns – just the sort of place an Afghan warlord might feel at home. The meat-centric menu features gloriously tender kebabs, rich curries and lots of tandoori favourites roasted in Khyber's famous red masala sauce. Garlic or butter naan bread (₹95) is the perfect accompaniment.

Trishna
SEAFOOD $$$

(Map p44; ☎22703214; www.trishna.co.in; Ropewalk Lane, Kala Ghoda; mains ₹320-1110; ◷noon-3pm & 6.30pm-12.15am) Behind a modest entrance on a quiet Kala Ghoda lane is this often-lauded, intimate South Indian seafood restaurant. It's not a trendy place – the decor is old school, seating a little cramped and menu perhaps too long – but the cooking is superb, witness the Hyderabadi fish tikka, jumbo prawns with green pepper sauce, and outstanding crab dishes.

Mahesh Lunch Home
SEAFOOD $$$

(Map p44; ☎22023965; www.maheshlunchhome.com; Cowasji Patel St; mains ₹280-1300; ◷11.30am-4pm & 7pm-midnight) A great place to try Mangalorean or Chinese-style seafood in Mumbai. It's renowned for its ladyfish, pomfret, lobster, crab (try this with butter garlic pepper sauce) and salt-and-pepper squid (₹425). There's also a Juhu branch.

✗ Kalbadevi to Mahalaxmi

New Kulfi Centre
ICE CREAM $

(Map p50; cnr Chowpatty Seaface & Sardar V Patel Rd; kulfi per 100gm ₹40-70; ◷10am-1am) Serves the best *kulfi* (Indian firm-textured ice cream) you'll have anywhere. Killer flavours include pistachio, *malai* (cream) and mango.

Cafe Noorani
NORTH INDIAN $$

(Map p50; Tardeo Rd, Haji Ali Circle; mains ₹80-300; ◷8am-11.30pm) Inexpensive, old-school eatery that's a requisite stop before or after visiting the Haji Ali mosque. Mughlai and Punjabi staples dominate, with kebabs chargrilled to perfection and great biriyanis; try the chicken kadai (₹200).

✗ Western Suburbs

North Mumbai is home to the city's trendiest dining, centered on Bandra West and Juhu.

Hotel Ram Ashray
SOUTH INDIAN $

(Bhandarkar Rd, King's Circle, Matunga East; light meals ₹40-70; ◷5am-9.30pm) In the Tamil enclave of King's Circle, 80-year-old Ram Ashray is beloved by southern families for its spectacular dosas, *idli* (spongy, round, fermented rice cake) and *uttapa* (savoury rice pancake with toppings). Filter coffee is strong and flavoursome. The menu, written on a chalkboard, changes daily. It's just outside Matunga Rd train station's east exit.

★ Dakshinayan
SOUTH INDIAN $$

(Map p54; Anand Hotel, Gandhigram Rd, Juhu; light meals ₹90-170; ◷11am-3pm & 6-11pm, from 8am Sun) With *rangoli* on the walls, servers in lungis and sari-clad women lunching (*chappals* off under the table), Dakshinayan channels Tamil Nadu. There are delicately textured dosas (₹110 to ₹165), *idli* and *uttapam*, village-fresh chutneys and perhaps the best *rasam* (tomato soup with spices and tamarind) in Mumbai. Finish off with a South Indian filter coffee – served in a stainless-steel set.

Chilli-heads should order *molagapudi idli* (₹110), a dozen *idli* coated in 'gunpowder' (potent spices).

⭐ **Yoga House**　　　　　　CAFE **$$**
(Map p54; www.yogahouse.in; 53 Chimbai Rd, Bandra West; light meals ₹140-250; ☺8am-10pm; 🗟) This haven of pastel shades, scatter cushions and greenery in Yoga House's seaside bungalow is the perfect retreat from Mumbai's mean streets. The menu is very creative and healthy – much of it raw vegan and all of it wholesome. Signature items include its famous salads (₹195 to ₹350), soups, 10-grain bread (₹130) and hash browns (with spinach, mozzarella and peppers).

Soul Fry　　　　　　GOAN, SEAFOOD **$$**
(Map p54; ☑022-26046892; Silver Croft, Pali Mala Rd, Pali Hill; mains ₹140-390; ☺noon-3pm & 7.30pm-midnight; ✷) Rightly famous for its terrific seafood, this lively, scruffy-yet-atmospheric Goan place by Pali market is just the place to escape Bandra's Bollywood set. Crab curry, tamarind prawns and Goan meat dishes such as chicken *xacuti* are authentic and loaded with coastal flavour. There's an air-conditioned interior and bench seating on the terrace. Be warned: Monday night is karaoke night.

Raaj Bhog　　　　　　GUJARATI **$$**
(Map p54; 3rd Rd, Cosmos Commercial Center, Khar West; meals ₹180-300; ☺11am-3.30pm & 7-11pm) Modestly priced restaurants are not easy to find in this part of town so this new Gujarati place by Khar station is a welcome addition. The (unlimited) deluxe thali (₹280) is filling and varied; it's served with basmati rice and rotis.

Prithvi Cafe　　　　　　CAFE **$$**
(Map p54; Juhu Church Rd, Juhu; light meals ₹70-165; ☺9am-11pm) A bohemian cafe on a large, shady terrace attached to the Prithvi Theatre that's something of a cultural hub of intellectuals, artists and theatre types. The snacky food – croissants, sandwiches, *chaat* (savoury snacks) and Punjabi standards – is OK, but it's the setting that's special.

⭐ **Peshawri**　　　　　　NORTH INDIAN **$$$**
(Map p54; ☑28303030; ITC Maratha, Sahar Rd, Andheri East; meals ₹1100-2700; ☺12.45-2.45pm & 7-11.45pm) Make this Northwest Frontier restaurant, outside the international airport, your first or last stop in Mumbai. The buttery *dhal bukhara* (a thick black dhal cooked for a day; ₹700) is perhaps the signature dish, but its kebabs are sublime: try the *peshawri* (chargrilled lamb marinated in yoghurt and spices).

Despite the five-star surrounds (and prices) you're encouraged to eat with your hands and the seating is low.

Culture Curry　　SOUTH INDIAN, SEAFOOD **$$$**
(www.culturecurry.com; Kataria Rd, Matunga West; mains ₹260-500; ☺noon-3.45pm & 7pm-12.30am) Exquisite dishes from all over the south, from Andhra and Coorg to Kerala, are the speciality here. Best for vegie and seafood dishes; the *prawn hirva rassa* (with green mango and coconut; ₹379) is a symphony of South Indian flavour. From Matunga Rd train station, it's about 750m west along Kataria Rd.

Salt Water Café　　　　CAFE, FUSION **$$$**
(Map p54; www.saltwatercafe.in; 87 Chapel Rd, Bandra West; breakfasts ₹180-290, mains ₹410-650; ☺12.30-3.30pm & 7.30-11.50pm; 🗟) A Bandra institution where filmi producers and expats socialise in the stylish air-conditioned dining room or buzzing terrace. Stick to the classic breakfasts, omelettes and sandwiches (₹350 to ₹410) as some of the zany fusion flavour combinations are perhaps too much of a culinary clash.

Eat Around the Corner　　　　CAFE **$$$**
(Map p54; www.eataroundthecorner.in; cnr 24th & 30th Rds; light meals ₹250-400, mains ₹280-600; ☺7am-1am; 🗟) Visually it's quite a concept, its minimalist interior replete with banquette and bench seating and a long, long display counter of tempting treats (falafel, soups, salads, cakes, pastries). Prices are high, not that the young, wealthy clientele seem bothered.

🍷 **Drinking & Nightlife**

Forget the capital, Mumbai is a city that really knows how to enjoy itself. Whatever your tipple and whatever your taste, you'll find it here – from dive bar to sky bar. Colaba is rich in unpretentious publike joints (but also has some very classy places), while

Bandra and Juhu are home turf for the filmi and model set. Some of the most intriguing new places are opening in midtown areas such as Lower Parel.

Wednesday and Thursday are big nights at some clubs, as well as the traditional Friday and Saturday; there's usually a cover charge. Dress codes apply, so don't rock up in shorts and sandals. The trend in Mumbai is towards resto-lounges as opposed to full-on nightclubs. You're also technically supposed to have a license to drink in Maharashtra; some bars require you to buy a temporary one, for a nominal fee.

Colaba

★ Harbour Bar   BAR
(Map p42; Taj Mahal Palace, Mumbai, Apollo Bunder; ⊙11am-11.45pm) With unmatched views of the Gateway of India and harbour, this timeless bar inside the Taj is an essential visit. Drinks aren't uber-expensive (₹395/800 for a beer/cocktail) given the surrounds and the fact they come with very generous portions of nibbles (including jumbo cashews).

★ Colaba Social   BAR
(Map p42; www.socialoffline.in; ground fl, Glen Rose Bldg, BK Boman Behram Marg, Apollo Bunder; ⊙9am-1.30am; ☎) The Social opened with

bang in late 2014, thanks to its stellar cocktail list (most are just ₹300 or so; try the Longest Island Ice Tea) and fab Colaba location. During the day it's a social-cum-workspace for laptop-toting, brunching creative types, but by 6pm the place is crammed with a raucous young crowd. Snacks (₹120 to ₹380) and espresso coffee are available.

Also hosts DJ and live-music events, art and photography exhibits and stand-up comedy acts.

Woodside Inn   PUB
(Map p42; Wodehouse Rd, Regal Circle; ⊙10am-1am) As close as you'll get to a London pub in Mumbai, this cosy place has a gregarious vibe and serves Gateway craft beers on draught (₹300); try the wheat beer. There's comfort food (mains ₹300 to ₹450) and a great daily happy hour (4pm to 8pm).

Cafe Mondegar   PUB
(Map p42; Metro House, 5A Shahid Bhagat Singh Rd; ⊙7.30pm-12.30am) Old-school bar that draws a mix of foreigners and locals who all cosy up together in the small space, bonding over the jukebox, which is cranked up to energise the crowd.

Busaba   LOUNGE
(Map p42; www.busaba.net; 4 Mandlik Marg; ⊙6.30pm-1am; ☎) Sunken couches and contem-

---

QUEER MUMBAI

Mumbai's LGBTQ scene is still quite underground, especially for women, but it's gaining momentum. No dedicated LGBTQ bars/clubs have opened yet, but gay-friendly 'safe house' venues often host private gay parties (announced on Gay Bombay).

Humsafar Trust (Map p54; ☑022-26673800; www.humsafar.org; 3rd fl, Manthan Plaza Nehru Rd, Vakola, Santa Cruz East) Runs tons of programs and workshops; one of its support groups organises the monthly gathering 'Sunday High'. It's also closely connected to the erratically published but pioneering magazine **Bombay Dost** (www.bombaydost.co.in).

Galaxy (www.gaylaxymag.com) India's best gay e-zine; well worth consulting and has lots of Mumbai content.

Gay Bombay (www.gaybombay.org) A great place to start, with event listings including meet-ups in Bandra, GB-hosted bar and film nights, hiking trips and other info.

Kashish Mumbai International Queer Film Festival (www.mumbaiqueerfest.com) Excellent annual May event with a mix of Indian and foreign films; in 2014, 154 films from 31 countries were featured.

LABIA (Lesbian & Bisexuals in Action; labia_india@yahoo.com) Lesbian and bi support group based in Mumbai; provides a counselling service for women.

Queer Azaadi Mumbai (www.queerazaadi.wordpress.com) Organises Mumbai's Pride Parade, which is usually held in early February.

Queer Ink (www.queer-ink.com) Online publisher with excellent books, DVDs and merchandise. Also hosts a monthly arts event with speakers, workshops, poetry, comedy, music and a marketplace.

porary Buddha art give this restaurant-bar a loungey vibe. Cocktails are pricey (from ₹450) but potent and a DJ plays house on weekends. The upstairs **restaurant** (mains from ₹480) serves pan-Asian; its back room feels like a posh treehouse. Reserve ahead for dinner.

Leopold Cafe   BAR
(Map p42; www.leopoldcafe.com; cnr Colaba Causeway & Nawroji F Rd; ☺ 7.30am-12.30am) Love it or hate it, most tourists end up at this clichéd Mumbai travellers' institution at one time or another. Around since 1871, Leopold's has wobbly ceiling fans, crap service and a rambunctious atmosphere conducive to swapping tales with strangers. There's also food and a cheesy DJ upstairs on weekend nights.

Wink   NIGHTCLUB
(Vivanta by Taj, 90 Cuffe Pde; ☺ 6pm-1am) Saturday and Sunday are thumping here, but it's a classy place most nights with its sophisticated decor (low beige sofas, intricately carved screens), long whiskey list and famous Winktinis.

Fort Area & Churchgate

Dome   LOUNGE
(Map p44; Hotel InterContinental, 135 Marine Dr, Churchgate; ☺ 5.30pm-1.30am; 🐾) This white-on-white rooftop lounge has awesome views of Mumbai's crescent beach from its 8th-floor vantage. Cocktails (₹850 to ₹1200) beckon the hip young things of Mumbai each night. Indulge yourself with a Ki Garden (vodka, elderberry and cloudy apple juice) or nurse a Kingfisher (₹375).

Liv   NIGHTCLUB
(Map p44; 1st fl, 145 MG Rd, Kala Ghoda; cover per couple ₹3000; ☺ 10pm-1.30am Wed-Sat) Exclusive new Kala Ghoda club that draws an up-for-it crowd of SoBo (South Bombay) pretty young things with its out-there LED lighting and intimate feel. Musically, Wednesday is hip hop, on Friday it's Bollywood Boogie, while on Saturday EDM DJs let rip.

Kalbadevi to Mahalaxmi

Haji Ali Juice Centre   JUICE BAR
(Map p50; Lala Lajpatrai Rd, Haji Ali Circle; juices & snacks ₹30-180; ☺ 5am-1.30am) Serves fresh juices, milkshakes, mighty fine *falooda* and fruit salads. Strategically placed at the en-

trance to Haji Ali mosque, it's a great place to cool off after a visit.

Shiro   LOUNGE, NIGHTCLUB
(☑ 66511201; www.shiro.co.in; Bombay Dyeing Mills Compound, Worli; ☺ 7.30pm-1.30am) Visually this place is stunning, with water pouring from the hands of a towering Japanese goddess into lotus ponds, which reflect shimmering light on the walls. It's totally over the top, but the drinks (as well as the Asian-fusion dishes) are excellent. By 10.30pm or so it morphs into more of a club, with DJs spinning some mean salsa (Wednesday), disco (Friday) and house (Saturday). It's about 3km north of the Mahalaxmi Racecourse.

Ghetto   BAR
(Map p50; ☑ 23538418; 30 Bhulabhai Desai Marg, opp Tirupathi Apt; ☺ 7pm-1am) A grungy, graffiti-covered hang-out blaring classic and contemporary rock (Red Hot Chili Peppers, Rolling Stones) to a dedicated set of regulars. You can shoot pool here too.

Western Suburbs

★**Bonobo**   BAR
(Map p54; www.facebook.com/BonoboBandra; Kenilworth Mall, 33rd Rd, Bandra West, off Linking Rd; ☺ 6pm-1am; 🐾) The scenesters' first choice in Bandra, this bar champions indie and alternative music. DJs spin drum 'n' bass and electronica, big beats and funk tech-house, and musicians play folk and blues. There's a great rooftop terrace.

★**Aer**   LOUNGE
(Four Seasons Hotel, 34th fl, 114 Dr E Moses Rd, Worli; cover Fri & Sat after 8pm ₹2500; ☺ 5.30pm-midnight; 🐾) Boasting astounding sea, sunset and city views, Aer is Mumbai's premier sky bar. Drink prices are steep, but that's kind of the point: cocktails cost around ₹900, beers start at ₹350 and happy hour is 5.30pm to 8pm. A DJ spins house and lounge tunes nightly from 9pm.

Toto's Garage   BAR
(Map p54; ☑ 26005494; 30th Rd, Bandra West; ☺ 6pm-1am) Highly sociable, down-to-earth local dive done up in a car mechanic theme where you can go in your dirty clothes, drink draught beer (₹200 a glass) and listen to classic rock. Check out the upended VW Beetle above the bar. Always busy and has a good mix of guys and gals.

Daily BAR

(Map p54; SV Rd, Bandra; ☺6pm-1.30am; 🕾) Hip and happening new Bandra bar that take its moniker from the good news stories the owners have collated (and suspended on pages from the ceiling). Attracts a lively crowd with decadent cocktails, sangria pitchers, snappy service and a cool indoor/outdoor design. Also hosts films and live music.

Trilogy NIGHTCLUB

(Map p54; www.trilogy.in; Hotel Sea Princess, Juhu Tara Rd, Juhu; cover per couple after 11pm ₹2000; ☺10.30pm-3am Wed-Sat) This glam, glitzy Juhu club, like its clientele, is gorgeous, with two dance floors spectacularly illuminated by LED cube lights that are synced with the epic sound system. It's hip hop on Wednesday, house on Friday and EDM on Saturday.

Hoppipola BAR

(Map p54; 757 Ramee Guestline, MD Ali Quereshi Chowk, off SV Rd; ☺noon-1am; 🕾) With its wacky design (including squadrons of toy planes suspended from the roof) and abundant board games, Hoppipola doesn't take itself too seriously, with decor that's more playschool than lounge bar. Get stuck into some test-tube shots or a tower of beer and it's perfect for a session of Jenga drinking games. Bar grub (from ₹200) is tasty too.

Olive Bar & Kitchen BAR

(Map p54; ☑26058228; www.olivebarandkitch en.com; 14 Union Park, Khar West; ☺7.30pm-1am daily, plus noon-3.30pm Sat & Sun; 🕾) The watering hole of choice for Bandra's filmi elite and aspiring starlets, Olive is a Mediterranean-style bar-restaurant whose whitewashed walls, candle-lit terraces and rooms evoke Ibiza and Mykonos. It's the perfect setting for inspired Greek and Italian food (mains ₹600 to ₹1100) and vibing DJ sounds. Thursdays and weekends are packed. There's a second branch (Map p50; ☑40859595; Gate No 8, Mahalaxmi Racecourse; ☺noon-3.30pm & 7.30pm-1.30am) in Mahalaxmi.

Big Nasty BAR

(Map p54; 1st fl, 12 Union Park, Khar West, above Shatranj Napoli; ☺7pm-12.30am) The decor may be industrial, but the Nasty is fun and unpretentious. It's best known for its cheap(ish) drinks – beers from ₹220, wine from ₹350 and cocktails starting at ₹400.

Elbo Room PUB

(Map p54; St Theresa Rd, Khar West, off 33rd Rd; ☺11am-1am) This publike place has a very so-cial vibe and an Italian-Indian menu that's best enjoyed on the plant-filled terrace.

☆ Entertainment

Mumbai has an exciting live music scene, some terrific theatres, an emerging network of comedy clubs and, of course, cinemas and sporting action.

Consult **Mumbai Boss** (www.mumbai-boss.com), **Time Out Mumbai** (www.timeout mumbai.net) and www.nh7.in for live-music listings. Unfortunately, Hindi films aren't shown with English subtitles. The cinemas we've listed all show English-language movies, along with some Bollywood numbers.

Mumbai has some great arts festivals, the major ones include the excellent Mumbai Film Festival (p41) in October, May's **Kashish-Mumbai International Queer Film Festival** (www.mumbaiqueerfest.com), Prithvi Theatre's November festival for excellent drama and music, and Mumbai Sanskruti (p41), which sees two days of Hindustani classical music. The National Centre for the Performing Arts hosts numerous cultural festivals throughout the year.

★ Bluefrog LIVE MUSIC,

(☑61586158; www.bluefrog.co.in; D/2 Mathuradas Mills Compound, Senapati Bapat Marg, Lower Parel; admission ₹300-1200; ☺6.30pm-1.30am Tue-Sat, from 11.30am Sun) Mumbai cultural mecca, a world-class venue for concerts (everything from indie to Mexican), stand-up comedy and lots of DJ-driven clubby nights (hip hop, house and techno). There's also a restaurant with space-age pod seating (book ahead for dinner) in the intimate main room. Happy hour is 6.30pm to 9pm.

National Centre for the Performing Arts THEATRE, LIVE MUSIC

(NCPA; Map p44; ☑66223737, box office 22824567; www.ncpamumbai.com; Marine Dr & Sri V Saha Rd, Nariman Point; tickets ₹200-800; ☺box office 9am-7pm) This vast cultural centre is the hub of Mumbai's high-brow music, theatre and dance scene. In any given week, it might host experimental plays, poetry readings, photography exhibitions, a jazz band from Chicago or Indian classical music. Many performances are free. The box office (Map p44) is at the end of NCPA Marg.

Prithvi Theatre THEATRE

(Map p54; ☑26149546; www.prithvitheatre.org; Juhu Church Rd, Juhu; tickets ₹80-300) A Juhu institution that's a great place to see both

BOLLYWOOD DREAMS

Mumbai is the glittering epicentre of India's gargantuan Hindi-language film industry. From silent beginnings, with a cast of all-male actors (some in drag) in the 1913 epic *Raja Harishchandra*, and the first talkie, *Lama Ara* (1931), it now churns out more than 1000 films a year – more than Hollywood. Not surprising considering it has a captive audience of one-sixth of the world's population.

Every part of India has its regional film industry, but Bollywood continues to entrance the nation with its escapist formula in which all-singing, all-dancing lovers fight and conquer the forces keeping them apart. These days, Hollywood-inspired thrillers and action extravaganzas vie for moviegoers' attention alongside the more family-oriented saccharine formulas.

Bollywood stars can attain near godlike status in India and star-spotting is a favourite pastime in Mumbai's posher establishments. You can also see the stars' homes as well as a film/TV studio with **Bollywood Tours** (www.bollywoodtours.in; 8hr tour per person ₹6000), but you're not guaranteed to see a dance number and you may spend much of it in traffic.

Extra, Extra!

Studios sometimes want Westerners as extras to add a whiff of international flair (or provocative dress, which locals often won't wear) to a film.

If you're game, just hang around Colaba (especially the Salvation Army hostel) where studio scouts, recruiting for the following day's shooting, will find you. A day's work, which can be up to 16 hours, pays ₹500. You'll get lunch, snacks and (usually) transport. The day can be long and hot with loads of standing around the set; not everyone has a positive experience. Complaints range from lack of food and water to dangerous situations and intimidation when extras don't comply with the director's orders. Others describe the behind-the-scenes peek as a fascinating experience. Before agreeing to anything, always ask for the scout's identification and go with your gut.

MUMBAI (BOMBAY) ENTERTAINMENT

Hindi- and English-language theatre or an arthouse film, and there's a cafe (p67) for drinks. Its excellent international theatre festival in November showcases contemporary Indian theatre and includes international productions.

Canvas Laugh   COMEDY
(☑ 022-43485000; www.canvaslaughclub.com; 3rd fl, Palladium Mall, Phoenix Mills, Lower Parel; tickets ₹200-750) Popular comedy club that hosts around 50 shows per month, with twice-nightly programs on weekends. All comedians use English. It's 1km north of Mahalaxmi train station.

Comedy Store   COMEDY
(☑ 022-39895050; www.thecomedystore.in; D2 Mathuradas Mills Compound, Senapati Bapat Marg, Lower Parel; tickets from ₹400; ⊗ 8pm-midnight Tue & Sun) Stand-up comedy (in English) featuring established and upcoming Indian comedians that's always a good night out. It's based at the Bluefrog, but the Comedy Store also pops up at other venues across town; check the website for details.

Liberty Cinema   CINEMA, LIVE MUSIC
(Map p44; ☑ 9820027841; www.thelibertycinema.com; 41/42 New Marine Lines, near Bombay Hospital) Stunning art deco Liberty was once the queen of Hindi film – think red-carpet openings with Dev Anand. It fell on hard times in recent years, but is rebounding.

Mehboob Studios   LIVE MUSIC, GALLERY
(Map p54; ☑ 022-26421628; 100 Hill Rd, Bandra West) As well as live music, these famous film studios also host the annual Times Litfest (in December), art exhibitions and film screenings.

Wankhede Stadium   SPORTS
(Mumbai Cricket Association; Map p44; ☑ 22795500; www.mumbaicricket.com; D Rd, Churchgate; ⊗ ticket office 11.30am-7pm Mon-Sat) Test matches and one-day internationals are played a few times a year in season (October to April). Contact the Cricket Association for ticket information; for a test match you'll probably have to pay for the full five days.

D Y Patil Stadium   SPORTS
(☑ 022-27731545; Yashwantrao Chavan Marg, Nerul, Navi Mumbai) A 55,000-capacity stadium

that hosts the ISL's Mumbai City FC football team, plus occasional IPL cricket matches. It's 21km east of central Mumbai. Tickets are available at the gate.

Regal Cinema CINEMA
(Map p42; ☑22021017; Shahid Bhagat Singh Rd, Regal Circle, Colaba; tickets ₹130-180) A faded art deco masterpiece that's good for both Hollywood and Bollywood blockbusters.

Eros CINEMA
(Map p44; ☑22822335; www.eroscinema.co.in; Maharshi Karve Rd, Churchgate; tickets ₹100-170) To experience Bollywood blockbusters in situ, the Eros is the place.

Metro Big CINEMA
(☑39894040; www.bigcinemas.com; MG Rd, New Marine Lines, Fort; tickets ₹130-600) This grand dame of Bombay talkies was just renovated into a multiplex.

🛍 Shopping

Mumbai is India's great marketplace, with some of the best shopping in the country.

Be sure to spend a day at the markets north of CST for the classic Mumbai shopping experience. In Fort, booksellers, with surprisingly good wares (not all pirated), set up shop daily on the sidewalks around Flora Fountain. Snap up a bargain backpacking wardrobe at Fashion Street (MG Rd), the strip of stalls lining MG Rd between Cross and Azad Maidans. Hone your bargaining skills. Kemp's Corner has many good shops for designer threads.

Colaba

Bungalow 8 CLOTHING, ACCESSORIES
(Map p42; www.bungaloweight.com; 1st, 2nd & 3rd fls, Grants Bldg, Arthur Bunder Rd; ☺10.30am-7.30pm) Original, high-end, artisanal clothing, jewellery, home decor and other objects of beauty, spread across three loftlike floors.

Phillips ANTIQUES
(Map p42; www.phillipsantiques.com; Wodehouse Rd, Colaba; ☺10am-7pm Mon-Sat) Art deco and colonial-era furniture, wooden ceremonial masks, silver, Victorian glass and also high-quality reproductions of old photos, maps and paintings.

Cottonworld Corp CLOTHING
(Map p42; ☑22850060; www.cottonworld.net; Mandlik Marg; ☺10.30am-8pm Mon-Sat, noon-8pm Sun) Stylish Indian-Western-hybrid

goods made from cotton, linen and natural materials (including er...paper made from rhino and elephant dung). Yes, you read that right. Only in India.

Bombay Electric CLOTHING
(Map p42; www.bombayelectric.in; 1 Reay House, Best Marg; ☺11am-9pm) High fashion is the calling at this trendy, slightly overhyped unisex boutique, which it sells at top rupee alongside arty accessories and a handful of fashionable antiques.

Central Cottage Industries Emporium HANDICRAFTS, SOUVENIRS
(Map p42; ☑22027537; www.cottageempo rium.in; Chhatrapati Shivaji Marg; ☺10am-6pm) Fair-trade souvenirs including pashminas. Second branch in Colaba (Map p42; Kamal Mansion, Arthur Bunder Rd; ☺11am-7pm Mon-Sat).

🛍 Fort Area & Churchgate

⭐**Kitab Khana** BOOKS
(Map p44; www.kitabkhana.in; Somaiya Bhavan, 45/47 MG Rd, Fort; ☺10.30am-7.30pm) This bookstore has a brilliantly curated selection of books, all of which are 20% off all the time. There's a great little cafe (Map p44; www.cafefoodforthought.com; light meals ₹120-180) at the back.

⭐**Contemporary Arts & Crafts** HOMEWARES
(Map p44; www.cac.co.in; 210 Dr Dadabhai Naoroji Rd, Fort; ☺10.30am-7.30pm) Modish, high-quality takes on traditional crafts: these are not your usual handmade souvenirs.

Artisans' Centre for Art, Craft & Design CLOTHING, ACCESSORIES
(Map p44; ☑22673040; 1st fl, 52-56 Dr VB Gandhi Marg, Kala Ghoda; ☺11am-7pm) Exhibits high-end handmade goods – from couture and jewellery to handicrafts and luxury *khadi* (homespun cloth).

Khadi & Village Industries Emporium CLOTHING
(Khadi Bhavan; Map p44; 286 Dr Dadabhai Naoroji Rd, Fort; ☺10.30am-6.30pm Mon-Sat) A dusty, 1940s time warp full of traditional Indian clothing, silk and *khadi,* and shoes.

Chimanlals HANDICRAFTS
(Map p44; www.chimanlals.com; Wallace St, Fort; ☺9.30am-6pm Mon-Fri, to 5pm Sat) The beautiful traditional printed papers here will make you start writing letters.

BAZAAR DISTRICT

Mumbai's main market district is one of Asia's most fascinating, an incredibly dense combination of humanity and commerce that's a total assault on the senses. If you've just got off a plane from the West, or a taxi from Bandra – hold on tight. This working-class district stretches north of Crawford Market up as far as Chor Bazaar, a 2.5km walk away. Such are the crowds (and narrowness of the lanes), allow yourself two to three hours to explore it thoroughly.

You can buy just about anything here, but as the stores and stalls are very much geared to local tastes, most of the fun is simply taking in the street life and investigating the souklike lanes rather than buying souvenirs. The markets merge into each other in an amoeba-like mass, but there are some key landmarks so you can orientate yourself.

Crawford Market (Mahatma Phule Market; Map p50; cnr DN & Lokmanya Tilak Rds) Crawford Market is the largest in Mumbai, and contains the last whiff of British Bombay before the tumult of the central bazaars begins. Bas-reliefs by Rudyard Kipling's father, Lockwood Kipling, adorn the Norman Gothic exterior. Fruit and vegetables, meat and fish are mainly traded, but it's also an excellent place to stock up on spices. If you're lucky to be here during alphonso mango season (May to June) be sure to indulge.

Mangaldas Market (Map p50) Mangaldas Market, traditionally home to traders from Gujarat, is a minitown, complete with lanes of fabrics. Even if you're not the type to have your clothes tailored, drop by DD Dupattawala (Map p50; Shop No 217, 4th Lane, Mangaldas Market; ☺9.30am-6.30pm) for pretty scarves and dupattas at fixed prices. Zaveri Bazaar (Map p50) for jewellery and Bhuleshwar Market (Map p50; cnr Sheikh Menon St & M Devi Marg) for fruit and veg are just north of here. Just a few metres further along Sheikh Menon Rd from Bhuleshwar is a Jain pigeon-feeding station, flower market and a religious market.

Chor Bazaar (Map p50) Chor Bazaar is known for its antiques, though nowadays much of it is reproductions; the main area of activity is Mutton St, where shops specialise in 'antiques' and miscellaneous junk. Dhabu St, to the east, is lined with fine leather goods.

Royal Music Collection MUSIC STORE
(Map p44; 192 Kitab Mahal, Dr Dadabhai Naoroji Rd, Fort; ☺11am-9pm Mon-Sat) Brilliant street stall selling vintage vinyl (from ₹250).

Fabindia CLOTHING, HOMEWEARS
(Map p44; www.fabindia.com; Jeroo Bldg, 137 MG Rd, Kala Ghoda; ☺10am-8pm) Ethically sourced cotton and silk fashions and homewares in a modern-meets-traditional Indian shop.

Chetana Book Centre BOOKS
(Map p44; www.chetana.com; K Dubash Marg, Kala Ghoda; ☺10.30am-7.30pm Mon-Sat) This great spirituality bookstore has lots of books on Hinduism and a whole section on 'Afterlife/ Death/Psychic'.

Standard Supply Co PHOTOGRAPHY
(Map p44; ☎22612468; Walchand Hirachand Marg, Fort; ☺10am-7pm Mon-Sat) Everything for digital and film photography.

Oxford Bookstore BOOKS
(Map p44; www.oxfordbookstore.com; Apeejay House, 3 Dinsha Wachha Marg, Churchgate;

☺8am-10pm) Spacious store with a good selection of travel books and a **tea bar** (teas ₹35-80; ☺10am-10pm).

Kalbadevi to Mahalaxmi

Shrujan HANDICRAFTS
(Map p50; www.shrujan.org; Sagar Villa, Bhulabhai Desai Marg, Breach Candy, opp Navroze Apts; ☺10am-7.30pm Mon-Sat) Nonprofit that sells the intricately-embroidered clothing, bags, cushions covers and shawls of 3500 women in 114 villages in Kutch, Gujarat. There's also a (hard-to-find) **Juhu branch** (Map p54; Hatkesh Society, 6th North South Rd, JVPD Scheme; ☺10am-7.30pm Mon-Sat).

Mini Market/Bollywood Bazaar ANTIQUES, SOUVENIRS
(Map p50; ☎23472427; 33/31 Mutton St; ☺11am-8pm Sat-Thu) Sells vintage Bollywood posters and other movie ephemera.

BX Furtado & Sons MUSIC STORE
(Map p50; www.furtadosonline.com; Jer Mahal, Dhobi Talao; ☺10.30am-7.30pm Mon-Sat) *The*

place in town for musical instruments: si-tars, tablas, accordions and local and im-ported guitars.

Western Suburbs

Indian Hippy ART
(Map p54; ☑8080822022; www.hippy.in; 17/C Sherly Rajan Rd, Bandra West, off Carter Rd; portraits from ₹10,000; ⊙by appointment) Because you need to have your portrait hand-painted in the style of a vintage Bollywood poster. Bring (or email) a photo. Also sells LP clocks, vin-tage film posters and all manner of (frankly bizarre) Bollywood-themed products.

Play Clan SOUVENIRS, CLOTHING
(Map p54; www.theplayclan.com; Libra Towers, Hill Rd, Bandra West; ⊙11am-8.30pm) Kitschy, de-sign-y goods that are pricey but the best in town. Check out the eye masks and cartoon Hanuman cushion covers.

Kishore Silk House CLOTHING, HANDICRAFTS
(Bhandarkar Rd, Matunga East; ⊙10am-8.30pm Tue-Sun) Handwoven saris and dhotis from Tamil Nadu and Kerala.

ℹ Information

EMERGENCY
Call the **police** (☑100) for emergencies.

INTERNET ACCESS
Anita CyberCafé (Map p44; Cowasji Patel Rd, Fort; per hour ₹30; ⊙9am-10pm Mon-Sat, 2-10pm Sun) Opposite one of Mumbai's best chai stalls (open evenings).
Portasia (Map p44; Kitab Mahal, Dr Dadabhai Naoroji Rd, Fort; per hour ₹30; ⊙9am-9pm Mon-Sat) Its entrance is down a little alley.

MEDIA
To find out what's going on in Mumbai, check out the highly informative **Mumbai Boss** (www.mumbaiboss.com). The *Hindustan Times* is the best paper; its *Café* insert has a good what's-on guide. **Time Out Mumbai** (www.timeoutmumbai.net) no longer publishes a Mumbai magazine but its website is worth consulting.

MEDICAL SERVICES
Bombay Hospital (Map p44; ☑22067676, ambulance 22067309; www.bombayhospital.com; 12 New Marine Lines) A private hospi-tal with the latest medical technology and equipment.

Breach Candy Hospital (Map p50; ☑23672888, emergency 23667809; www.breachcandyhospital.org; 60 Bhulabhai Desai Marg, Breach Candy) The best in Mumbai, if not India. It's 2km northwest of Chowpatty Beach.

MONEY
ATMs are everywhere, and foreign-exchange offices changing cash are also plentiful.
Thomas Cook (Map p42; ☑66092608; Colaba Causeway; ⊙9.30am-6pm) Has a branch in the Fort area also.

POST
Main post office (Map p44; Walchand Hira-chand Marg; ⊙10am-7pm Mon-Sat, to 4pm Sun) The main post office is an imposing build-ing beside CST. Poste restante (⊙10am-3pm Mon-Sat) is at the 'Delivery Department'. Let-ters should be addressed c/o Poste Restante, Mumbai GPO, Mumbai 400 001. Bring your passport to collect mail. Opposite the post office are parcel-wallahs who will stitch up your parcel for ₹40.

TELEPHONE
Call ☑197 for directory assistance.

TOURIST INFORMATION
Indiatourism (Government of India Tourist Office; Map p44; ☑22074333; www.incredibleindia.com; Western Railways Reservation Complex, 123 Maharshi Karve Rd; ⊙8.30am-6pm Mon-Fri, to 2pm Sat) Provides information for the entire country, as well as contacts for Mumbai guides and homestays.
Maharashtra Tourism Development Cor-poration Booth (MTDC; ☑22841877; Apollo Bunder; ⊙8.30am-4pm Tue-Fri, to 9pm Sat & Sun) For city bus tours.
Maharashtra Tourism Development Corpo-ration (MTDC; Map p44; ☑22044040; www.maharashtratourism.gov.in; Madame Cama Rd, Nariman Point; ⊙10am-5pm Mon-Sat, closed 2nd & 4th Sat) The MTDC's head office has helpful staff and lots of pamphlets to give away.

TRAVEL AGENCIES
Akbar Travels (www.akbartravelsonline.com; ⊙10am-7pm Mon-Fri, to 6pm Sat); Colaba (Map p42; ☑22823434; 30 Alipur Trust Bldg, Shahid Bhagat Singh Marg); Fort (Map p44; ☑22633434; 167/169 Dr Dadabhai Naoroji Rd) Extremely helpful and can book car/drivers and buses. Also has good exchange rates.
Thomas Cook (Map p44; ☑61603333; www.thomascook.in; 324 Dr Dadabhai Naoroji Rd, Fort; ⊙9.30am-6pm Mon-Sat) Flight and hotel bookings, plus foreign exchange.

VISAS
Foreigners' Regional Registration Office (FRRO; Map p44; ☑22620446; www.immigrationindia.nic.in;

Annexe Bldg No 2, CID, Badaruddin Tyabji Marg, near Special Branch; ☺ 9.30am-1pm Mon-Fri) Tourist and transit visas can no longer be extended except in emergency situations; check the latest online.

ℹ Getting There & Away

AIR

Mumbai's **Chhatrapati Shivaji International Airport** (BOM; Map p54; ☑ 66851010; www.csia. in), about 30km from the city centre, was nearing the end of a $2 billion modernisation program at the time of research. The impressive international terminal is complete, while its new domestic terminal should be fully operational some time in 2015, creating a fully integrated airport.

At the time of writing, the airport still comprised of one international terminal and a separate domestic terminal (also known locally as Santa Cruz airport) 5km away. A free shuttle bus runs between the two terminals every half-hour (journey time 15 minutes) for ticket-holders. Both terminals have ATMs, foreign-exchange counters and tourist-information booths.

Travel agencies and airlines' websites are usually best for booking flights. The following airlines have offices in town and/or at the airport:

Air India (Map p44; ☑ 27580777, airport 28318666; www.airindia.com; Air India Bldg, cnr Marine Dr & Madame Cama Rd, Nariman Point; ☺ 9.30am-6.30pm Mon-Fri, to 5.15pm Sat & Sun) International and domestic routes.

Jet Airways (Map p44; ☑ 022-39893333; www.jetairways.com; B1, Amarchand Mansion, Madam Cama Rd, Colaba; ☺ 9am-6pm Mon-Sat) India's second-largest domestic carrier.

Major nonstop domestic flights from Mumbai include the following:

DESTINATION	FARE (₹)	DURATION (HR)
Bengaluru	3700	1½
Chennai	5800	2
Delhi	5900	2
Goa	3300	1
Hyderabad	4200	1½
Jaipur	4300	1¾
Kochi	5700	2
Kolkata	6100	2¾
Nagpur	4200	1½

BUS

Numerous private operators and state governments run long-distance buses to and from Mumbai.

Long-distance government-run buses depart from the **Mumbai Central bus terminal** (Map

ℹ **AIRPORT ARRIVAL**

Many international flights arrive after midnight. Beat the daytime traffic by heading straight to your hotel, and carry detailed landmark directions: many airport taxi drivers don't speak English and may not use official street names.

p50; ☑ enquiry 23024075; Jehangir Boman Behram Rd) right by Mumbai Central train station. They're cheaper and more frequent than private services, but standards are usually lower. The **MSRTC** (Maharashtra State Road Transport Corporation; ☑ 1800221250; www.msrtc. gov.in) website theoretically has schedules and is supposed to permit online booking, though in practice it's next to useless.

Private buses are usually more comfortable and simpler to book (if a bit more costly). Most depart from Dr Anadrao Nair Rd near Mumbai Central train station, but many buses to southern destinations depart from Paltan Rd, near Crawford Market. Check departure times and prices with **Citizen Travels** (Map p50; ☑ 23459695; www.citizenbus.com; D Block, Sitaram Bldg, Paltan Rd) or **National CTC** (Map p50; ☑ 23015652; Dr Anadrao Nair Rd). Fares to popular destinations (such as Goa) are up to 75% higher during holiday periods.

Private buses to Goa vary in price from ₹350 (bad choice) to ₹2600. Many leave from way out in the suburbs but **Chandni Travels** (Map p44; ☑ 22713901, 22676840) has six daily from in front of Azad Maidan and **Paolo Travel** (Map p44; ☑ 0832-6637777; www.paulotravels.com), with an 8pm daily departure from Fashion St, are convenient to the centre.

TRAIN

Three train systems operate out of Mumbai, but the most important services for travellers are Central Railways and Western Railways. Tickets for either system can be bought from any station that has computerised ticketing.

Central Railways (☑ 139), handling services to the east, south, plus a few trains to the north, operates from CST (also known as 'VT'). Foreign -tourist–quota tickets and Indrail passes can be bought at Counter 52.

Some Central Railways trains depart from Dadar (D), a few stations north of CST, or Lokmanya Tilak (LTT), 16km north of CST.

Western Railways (☑ 139) has services to the north from Mumbai Central train station, usually called Bombay Central (BCT). The **reservation centre** (Map p44; ☺ 8am-8pm Mon-Sat, to 2pm Sun), opposite Churchgate station, has foreign-tourist–quota tickets.

ⓘ Getting Around

TO/FROM THE AIRPORTS

International

Prepaid Taxi Taxis with set fares cost ₹700/800 (non-AC/AC) to Colaba and Fort and ₹450/550 to Bandra. The journey to Colaba takes about an hour at night (via the Sealink) and 1½ to two hours during the day.

Autorickshaws Available but they only go as far south as Bandra (daytime/night around ₹180/240).

Train If you arrive during the day (but not during 'rush hour' – 6am to 11am) and are not weighed down with luggage, consider the train: take an autorickshaw (around ₹60) to Andheri train station and then the Churchgate or CST train (₹9, 45 minutes).

Taxi From South Mumbai to the international airport should be around ₹500. Allow two hours for the trip if you travel between 4pm and 8pm.

Domestic

There's a prepaid taxi counter in the arrivals hall. A non-AC/AC taxi costs ₹600/700 to Colaba or Fort and ₹370/480 to Bandra.

Alternatively, if it's not rush hour, catch an autorickshaw (around ₹45) to Vile Parle station, where you can get a train to Churchgate (₹8, 45 minutes).

BOAT

PNP (☑ 22885220) and **Maldar Catamarans** (☑ 22829695) run regular ferries to Mandwa (one way ₹125 to ₹155), useful for access to Murud-Janjira and other parts of the Konkan Coast, avoiding the long bus trip out of Mumbai. Buy **tickets** (Map p42) near the Gateway of India.

BUS

Few travellers bother with city buses but **BEST** (www.bestundertaking.com) has a useful search facility for hardcore shoestringers and masochists – you'll also need to read the buses' Devanagiri numerals and beware of pickpockets. Fares start at ₹5.

CAR

Cars with driver can be hired for moderate rates. Air-conditioned cars start at ₹1550/1800 for half/full-day rental of around 80km.

Clear Car Rental (☑ 0888-8855220; www.clearcarrental.com)

Metro

The first section of Line 1, Mumbai's new **metro** (www.mumbaimetroone.com) opened in 2014. Initially it only connected seven stations in the far northern suburbs, well away from anywhere of interest to visitors. However Line 1 is scheduled to be extended south as far as Jacob Circle (5km north of Chhatrapati Shivaji Terminus) sometime in 2015, bringing it past Lower Parel.

Single fares cost between ₹10 and ₹20, with monthly Trip Passes (from ₹600) also available. Access to stations is by escalator, carriages are air-conditioned, and there are seats reserved for women and the disabled. Line 3 (a 33km underground line connecting Cuffe Pde south of Colaba, all the main railway terminals, Bandra and the airport) will be the next line to be constructed. It's been approved but won't open for many years.

MOTORCYCLE

Allibhai Premji Tyrewalla (Map p50; ☑ 23099313, 23099417; www.premjis.com; 205 Dr D Bhadkamkar (Lamington) Rd; ☉ 10am-7pm Mon-Sat) Sells new and used motorcycles with a guaranteed buy-back option. Long-term rental schemes (two months or more) start at around ₹25,000, with a buy-back price of around 60% after three months.

TAXI & AUTORICKSHAW

Mumbai's black-and-yellow taxis are inexpensive and the most convenient way to get around southern Mumbai; drivers *almost* always use the meter without prompting. The minimum fare is ₹21 (for up to 1.6km), a 5km trip costs about ₹50.

MAJOR LONG-DISTANCE BUS ROUTES

DESTINATION	PRIVATE NON-AC/AC SLEEPER (₹)	GOVERNMENT NON-AC (₹)	DURATION (HR)
Ahmedabad	400-650/500-2300	N/A	7-12
Aurangabad	400/550-900	472 (five daily)	9-11
Hyderabad	800-2500 (all AC)	N/A	16
Mahabaleshwar	400-2100 (all AC)	335 (three daily)	7-8
Panaji (Panjim)	600-750/700-2700	2400	14-16
Pune	250-735 (all AC)	224 (half-hourly)	3-5
Udaipur	800-1200/1500-2050	N/A	13-16

Consult www.makemytrip.com for latest schedules and prices

MAJOR TRAINS FROM MUMBAI

DESTINATION	TRAIN NO & NAME	SAMPLE FARE (₹)	DURATION (HR)	DEPARTURE
Agra	12137 Punjab Mail	580/1515/2195/3760 (A)	22	7.40pm CST
Ahmedabad	12901 Gujarat Mail	315/805/1135/1915 (A)	9	10pm BCT
	12009 Shatabdi Exp	960/1870 (C)	7	6.25am BCT
Aurangabad	11401 Nandigram Exp	235/620/885 (B)	7	4.35pm CST
	17617 Tapovan Exp	140/500 (C)	7	6.15am CST
Bengaluru	16529 Udyan Exp	505/1355/1975/3375 (A)	25	8.05am CST
Chennai	12163 Chennai Exp	570/1485/2145/3670 (A)	23½	8.30pm CST
Delhi	12951 Rajdhani Exp	2030/2810/4680 (D)	16	4.35pm BCT
Hyderabad	12701 Hussain-sagar Exp	425/1115/1590/2695 (A)	14½	9.50pm CST
Indore	12961 Avantika Exp	440/1150/1640/2780 (A)	14	7.05pm BCT
Jaipur	12955 Jaipur Exp	535/1405/2025/3455 (A)	18	6.50pm BCT
Kochi	16345 Netravati Exp	615/1635/2400 (B)	25½	11.40am LTT
Madgaon (Goa)	10103 Mandovi Exp	390/1055/1520/2575 (A)	12	7.10am CST
	12133 Mangalore Exp	420/1100/1570 (B)	9	10pm CST
Pune	11301 Udyan Exp	485/690/1150 (D)	3½	8.05am CST

Station abbreviations: CST (Chhatrapati Shivaji Terminus); BCT (Mumbai Central); LTT (Lokmanya Tilak); D (Dadar). Fares: (A) sleeper/3AC/2AC/1AC, (B) sleeper/3AC/2AC, (C) sleeper/CC, (D) 3AC/2AC/1AC

Autorickshaws are the name of the game north of Bandra. The minimum fare is ₹17, up to 1.6km, a 3km trip is about ₹30.

Both taxis and autorickshaws tack 25% onto the fare between midnight and 5am.

Tip: Mumbaikars tend to navigate by landmarks, not street names (especially new names), so have some details before heading out.

TRAIN

Mumbai's suburban train network is one of the world's busiest; forget travelling during rush hours. Trains run from 4am to 1am and there are three main lines:

Western Line The most useful; operates out of Churchgate north to Charni Rd (for Girgaum Chowpatty), Mumbai Central, Mahalaxmi (for the Dhobi Ghat), Bandra, Vile Parle (for the domestic airport), Andheri (for the international airport) and Borivali (for Sanjay Gandhi National Park), among others.

Central Line Runs from CST to Byculla (for Veermata Jijabai Bhonsle Udyan, formerly Victoria Gardens), Dadar and as far as Neral (for Matheran).

From Churchgate, 2nd-/1st-class fares are ₹5/48 to Mumbai Central, ₹8/85 to Vile Parle, and ₹9/116 to Borivali.

To avoid the queues, buy a **coupon book** (₹50), good for use on either train line, then 'validate' the coupons at the machines before boarding.

'Tourist tickets' permit unlimited travel in 2nd/1st class for one (₹75/225), three (₹115/415) or five (₹135/485) days.

Watch your valuables, and gals, stick to the ladies-only carriages except late at night, when it's more important to avoid empty cars.

Panaji & Central Goa

Best Places to Eat

➡ Viva Panjim (p87)

➡ Black Sheep Bistro (p88)

➡ Cafe Bodega (p88)

➡ Hotel Venite (p88)

➡ Upper House (p89)

Best Places to Stay

➡ Panjim Inn (p85)

➡ Backwoods Camp (p109)

➡ Goa Marriott Resort (p92)

➡ Old Quarter Hostel (p84)

➡ Casa Nova (p86)

Why Go?

Some travellers see Goa as one big beach resort, but the central region – practically beach-free – is the state's historic and cultural heart and soul. Wedged between Goa's two biggest rivers, the Mandovi and the Zuari, this region is home to the state capital, Panaji, the glorious churches of Old Goa, inland islands, bird sanctuaries and the wilds of the Western Ghats.

No visit to Goa is complete without a day or two spent cruising on the Mandovi River and exploring the old Latin Quarter in laid-back Panaji. Less than 10km away, Old Goa is the state's major cultural attraction, where the grand 17th-century churches and cathedrals are humbling in their scale and beauty. Further explorations will take you to temples and spice plantations around Ponda, to two of Goa's most beautiful wildlife sanctuaries, elephant camps and to India's second-highest waterfall. You could easily spend a week here without making it to a single beach. Don't miss it.

When to Go
Panaji

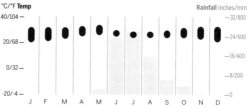

| **Nov–Mar** High season is the best time to visit Central Goa's bird sanctuaries and national parks. | **Christmas, Easter & Carnival** Goa's festivals are at their best in and around Panaji. | **Aug–Oct** Monsoon season offers a different and very green side of Central Goa. |

Panaji

POP 115,000

One of India's smallest and most relaxed state capitals, Panaji (also still widely known by its former Portuguese name, Panjim) crowds around the peninsula overlooking the broad Mandovi River, where cruise boats and floating casinos ply the waters, casting neon reflections in the night.

A glorious whitewashed church lords it over the animated city centre, a broad leafy boulevard skirts around the river, and grand colonial buildings rub shoulders with arty boutiques, old-school bookshops, state-of-the-art malls and backstreet bars.

But it's the tangle of narrow streets in the old Latin Quarter that really steal the show. Nowhere is the Portuguese influence felt more strongly than here, where the late afternoon sun lights up yellow houses with purple doors, and around each corner you'll find restored ochre-coloured mansions with terracotta-tiled roofs, wrought iron balconies and arched oyster-shell windows.

Panjim is a place for walking, enjoying the peace of an afternoon siesta, eating well, and meeting real Goans. It's also a place to catch a movie, a cultural show, or to take the kids to the planetarium.

A day or two in Panaji really is an essential part of the Goan experience.

History

The land on which Panaji stands today was once little more than a handful of fishing settlements, known to the 12th-century ruling Kadambas as Pahajani, 'the land that does not flood'.

In the late 15th century Goa came under the control of the Muslim sultan Yusuf Adil Shah, who built five hilltop forts and his own fortified summer palace here, protected by 55 cannons and conceived to guard the mouth of the Mandovi River against attackers.

When the Portuguese nobleman Afonso de Albuquerque arrived in Goa in 1510, he quickly set about conquering the palace and forts, and by the end of the year it was his. Leaving it almost untouched, however, the conquerors' efforts were instead now concentrated on aggrandising their new capital, Ela (now Old Goa), further east up the river.

For the next 300 years Panaji remained little more than a small and scruffy seafaring village, only notable for its church, where Portuguese sailors stopped off to give thanks for having survived the perilous voyage to India. However, as conditions in Old Goa became increasingly desperate, the land began to support increasing numbers of refugees from the capital, until finally, in 1759, the viceroy moved to Panjim, where he took the old Idalcao's Palace as his own residence, today the Secretariat.

By the early 19th century the city was taking shape. In 1834 Panjim became known as Nova Goa, and in 1843 it was finally recognised by the Portuguese government as Goa's state capital. A spate of building took place; among the public buildings erected were the army barracks (now the police headquarters and government offices). In essence, though, Goa was fast becoming a forgotten corner of the Portuguese empire, and lack of money and political interest meant that building work was low key in comparison to the glory days of Old Goa.

Strolling the streets of central Panaji today, you'll find that little has really changed since then. Modern building and development, for the most part, remains reasonably well planned, and the streets are as wide and leafy as they were under Portuguese dominion. Following the final exit of the Portuguese in 1961, the town's name was officially changed to the Maratha title, Panaji, though today most locals still refer to it as Panjim, as it was christened some 500 years ago on Albuquerque's arrival.

◉ Sights

★ Church of Our Lady of
the Immaculate Conception   CHURCH
(cnr Emilio Gracia & Jose Falcao Rds; ◷ 10am-12.30pm & 3-5.30pm Mon-Sat, 11am-12.30pm & 3.30-5pm Sun, English Mass 8am) Panaji's spiritual, as well as geographical, centre is this elevated, pearly white church, built in 1619 over an older, smaller 1540 chapel and stacked like a fancy white wedding cake. When Panaji was little more than a sleepy fishing village, this church was the first port of call for sailors from Lisbon, who would give thanks for a safe crossing, before continuing to Ela further east up the river. The church is beautifully illuminated at night.

By the 1850s the land in front of the church was being reclaimed and the distinctive criss-crossing staircases were added in the late 19th century. Today the entrance to its gloriously technicolour interior is along the left-hand side wall. A tangle of ropes leads up to the enormous shiny church bell in the belfry, saved from the ruins of the Augustinian monastery at Old Goa and installed here in 1871. The church is the focus for celebrations

Panaji & Central Goa Highlights

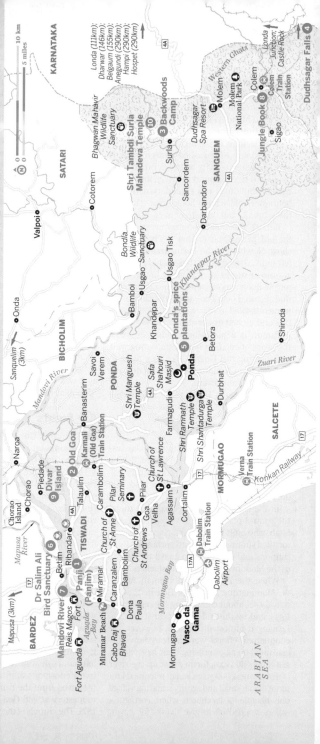

1 Explore Panaji's **Latin Quarter** (p85) on foot

2 Stand in silence in the extraordinary churches and cathedrals of **Old Goa** (p94), once larger than Lisbon

3 Enjoy birdwatching at **Backwoods Camp** (p109)

4 Trek out to **Dudhsagar Falls** (p108), India's second-highest waterfall

5 Visit an aromatic organic **spice farm** (p105) near Ponda

6 Dugout canoe it through mangroves at Choroa's **Dr Salim Ali Bird Sanctuary** (p94)

7 Take a cruise on the **Mandovi River** (p84), or try your luck at Panaji's **floating casinos** (p89)

8 Enjoy elephants at Colem's **Jungle Book** (p109) camp

9 Hop on a scooter and ferry out to **Divar Island** (p101), a little land that time forgot

10 See the last of the Kadambas at Tambdi Surla's **Shri Mahadeva Temple** (p109)

during the Feast of Our Lady of the Immaculate Conception, on 8 December.

Secretariat Building   HISTORIC BUILDING
(Dayanand Bandodkar Marg) The oldest colonial-era building in Goa is the stolid Secretariat, standing on the site of the grand summer palace of Goa's 15th-century sultan Yusuf Adil Shah, which was originally fortified and surrounded by a saltwater moat. After falling to the Portuguese in 1510, the palace was further reinforced and used as a customs post, also serving as temporary accommodation for incoming and outgoing Portuguese viceroys. It later housed Goa's State Assembly, and is today home to government offices.

Municipal Gardens   PARK
Panaji's central square is the leafy Municipal Gardens, also called Church Square (Largo da Igreja). The Ashokan Pillar at the gardens' centre was once topped by a bust of Vasco da Gama, the first Portuguese voyager to set foot in Goa in 1498, but he was replaced, upon independence in 1961, by the seal of present-day India: four lions sitting back to back, atop an abacus, with the inscription 'Truth Alone Triumphs'.

Jama Masjid   MOSQUE
(Dr Dada Vaidya Rd) Tiny Jama Masjid, barely 100m south of the Municipal Gardens and built about two centuries ago, is easy to miss. The exterior of the mosque is plain, its entrance blending in with the small shops on either side, but the interior is extremely ornate in white-marble Islamic style.

Azad Maidan   PARK
(Freedom Park) To the west of the Municipal Gardens, the grassy Azad Maidan won't win any prizes at a flower show. Its centrepiece is a small pavilion (the Corinthian pillars were reclaimed from the rubble in Old Goa), which houses a modern sculpture dedicated to freedom fighter and 'Father of Goan Nationalism' Dr Tristao de Braganza Cunha (1891–1958).

Menezes Braganza Institute   HISTORIC BUILDING
(Malaca Rd) The yellow-and-white Menezes Braganza Institute occupies part of the old buildings that were once the Portuguese army headquarters. It's worth poking your head in at the building's northeast entrance to examine the grand and dramatic *azulejos* (traditional blue-and-white painted ceramic tiles) adorning the wall, which depict scenes from *Os Lusíadas,* a famously epic Portu-

guese poem by Luís Vaz de Camões (p86) that tells the tale of Portugal's 15th- and 16th-century voyages of discovery. The bust in the centre of the foyer is the man himself.

Goa State Museum   MUSEUM
(☎ 0832-2438006; www.goamusem.gov.in; EDC Complex, Patto; ⊙ 9.30am-5.30pm Mon-Sat) **FREE** This spacious museum east of town houses an eclectic, if not extensive, collection of items tracing aspects of Goan history. As well as some beautiful Hindu and Jain sculptures and bronzes, there are nice examples of Portuguese-era furniture, coins, an intricately carved chariot and a pair of quirky antique rotary lottery machines.

The most interesting exhibit is in the furniture room: an elaborately carved table and high-backed chairs used by the notoriously brutal Portuguese Inquisition in Goa during its reign of terror. The table's legs feature carved lions and an eagle on one side and four human figures on the other.

Goa State Central Library   LIBRARY, GALLERY
(Sanskruti Bhavan, Patto; ⊙ 9am-7.30pm Mon-Fri, 9.30am-5.45pm Sat & Sun) **FREE** Panaji's ultra-modern new state library, near the state museum, has six floors of reading material, a bookshop and gallery. The 2nd floor features a children's book section and internet browsing (free, but technically only for academic research). The 4th floor has Goan history books and the 6th floor boasts a large collection of Portuguese books.

Maruti Temple   HINDU TEMPLE
(Mala) Dedicated to the monkey god Hanuman, this large orange temple built up the Altinho hillside is resplendently lit at night, and affords pleasant views over the city's Old Quarter from its verandah by day. It forms the epicentre of a roughly 10-day festival celebrated in February, when enormous and colourful statues of Hanuman are placed in the street, and festive street stalls are set up throughout the surrounding Hindu quarter of Mala.

Mahalaxmi Temple   HINDU TEMPLE
(off Dada Vaidya Rd) This modern, technicolour temple is not particularly imposing, but it's worth a look inside as it was the first Hindu shrine established in the city during Portuguese rule. It amply demonstrates that among Panaji's ubiquitous whitewashed churches there is a large and thriving Hindu community. The temple was built in 1818 and is devoted to the goddess Mahalaxmi, goddess of wealth and beauty and the Hindu deity of Panaji.

PANAJI & CENTRAL GOA PANAJI

Panaji (Panjim)

0 0
400 m
0.2 miles

Mandovi Bridge

Betim (2km); Goa Museum (4km); Torda (4km); Mapusa (13km)

Houses of Goa Museum (4km)

Mandovi River

Santa Monica Jetty

New Patto Bridge

Old Patto Bridge

Private Bus Stand (80m); Old Goa (9km); Karmali (12km); Ponda (34km)

PATTO

Dabolim (29km); Vasco da Gama (32km); Margao (34km)

Ourem Creek

Goa Tourism Development Corporation

ATMs

Dr Alvaro Costa Rd

Ourem Rd

Footbridge

Dabolim (29km); Margao (34km)

MG Rd

Avenida Dom João Castro

Statue of Abbé Faria

Steps

SÃO TOMÉ

José Falcão Rd

31st January Rd

GP Rd

CA Rd

Emilio Gracia Rd

Rua de Natal

St Sebastian Rd

Church of Our Lady of the Immaculate Conception

FONTAINHAS

31st January Rd

Fountain

Maruti Temple (250m); Baba's Wood Cafe (400m)

Panaji Jetty

Dr RS Rd

Municipal Gardens (Church Square)

Jama Masjid

Cunha-Rivara Rd

MG Rd

Ormuz Rd

Dr Pisurlekar Rd

Avenida Pe Agnelo

ALTINHO

Mahalaxmi Temple

Cafe Bodega (100m)

Ferry to Betim

Azad Maidan

Malaca Rd

Dayanand Bandodkar Marg

Menezes Braganza Rd

Dr P Shirgaonkar Rd

Dr Dada Vaidya Rd

Swami Vivekanand Rd

18th June Rd

Dr Atmaram Borkar Rd

Caculo Mall (1km); Vintage Hospitals (1.5km)

Campal Gardens (400m); Kala Academy (800m); Goa Marriott Resort (1.8km)

Municipal Market

General Bernardo Guedes Rd

Heliodoro Salgado Rd

Gen Costa Alvares Rd

Panaji (Panjim)

PANAJI & CENTRAL GOA PANAJI

Altinho Hill AREA
On the hillside above Panaji is the well-to-do residential district of Altinho. Apart from good views over the city and river, the main attraction here is the **Bishop's Palace**, an imposing building completed in 1893.

The archbishop of Goa came to reside in Panaji early in the 20th century, laying claim to the palatial residence at Cabo Raj Bhavan (p93). But when the Portuguese governor-general realised that it was the best property in Goa, the archbishop was forced to change his plans and settle instead for this palace. The pope stayed at the Bishop's Palace during his visit to Goa in 1999.

Campal Gardens PARK
The road to Miramar from Panaji runs through the Campal district. Just before you reach the Kala Academy are the strollable riverside Campal Gardens, also known as the Children's Park. The gardens offer a nice view over to Reis Magos Fort and the boats that cruise along the Mandovi River each evening.

ABBÉ FARIA

Beside Panaji's Secretariat Building, look out for the sublime, starkly black statue of a caped man, arms, hands and fingers outstretched, towering over an apparently cowering woman.

This is the **statue of Abbé Faria**, considered the 'father of modern hypnotism', a contemporary of Franz Mesmer (from where the term mesmerise derives), and a native of Goa. Born the son of a monk and a nun in a Candolim mansion in 1756, Abbé Faria is one of history's fabulously enigmatic figures. He hovered handsomely on the sidelines of the greatest events of the 18th century and flirted with its main players (the Portuguese royal family, Robespierre, Marie Antoinette and Napoleon among them), somehow ingratiating himself with every successive regime while remaining an elusive outsider, caught in a world of black magic and esoteric pursuits.

Faria was considered to be at the forefront of modern hypnotism for his explanations, and belief in, the power of suggestion – uncharted territory at the time.

Gitanjali Gallery   ART GALLERY
(📞0832-2423331; www.gallerygitanjali.com; 31st January Rd; ☉9am-7pm) FREE Worth a look while walking around Fontainhas, this bright gallery displays works by local and international artists. It also functions as an art studio and cafe, and hosts special exhibitions and workshops throughout the year.

Public Observatory   OBSERVATORY
(7th fl, Junta House, Swami Vivekanand Rd; ☉7-9pm mid-Nov–May) FREE If you're interested in checking out the clear winter night skies over Goa, the local branch of the Association of Friends of Astronomy has a public observatory on the terrace of the Junta building. The local enthusiasts are only too happy to welcome visitors and explain what you're looking at. The view over Panaji by night is lovely too, especially around dusk.

🏃 Activities

The nearest beach for swimming is at Miramar, about 4km southwest of the city, but it's really more of a people-watching place than a bathing beach. A better bet is the excellent pool at the nearby Goa Marriott Resort (p92), which nonguests can use for ₹500. In central Panaji, you can swim in the small but nice pool (₹280) at the hilltop Crown Goa (p87).

👉 Tours

Organised boat cruises are a popular way to see the Mandovi River and get a different perspective on the city. As well as the Goa Tourism cruises, there are similar privately run cruises.

Mandovi River Cruises   CRUISE
(sunset cruise ₹200, dinner cruise ₹650, backwater cruise ₹900; ☉sunset cruise 6pm, sundown cruise 7.15pm, dinner cruise 8.45pm Wed & Sat, backwater cruise 9.30am-4pm Tue & Fri) Goa Tourism operates a ran ge of entertaining hour-long cruises along the Mandovi River aboard the *Santa Monica* or *Shantadurga*. All include a live band and usually performances of Goan folk songs and dances. There are also twice-weekly, two-hour dinner cruises and a twice-weekly, all-day backwater cruise, which takes you down the Mandovi to Old Goa, stopping for lunch at a spice plantation and then heading back past Divar and Chorao Islands. All cruises depart from the Santa Monica Jetty next to the Mandovi Bridge, where you can purchase tickets.

Swastik Cruises   CRUISE
(adult/child ₹300/free; ☉6pm, 6.30pm, 7pm & 7.30pm) Private one-hour cruises depart from the main Santa Monica Jetty but you can buy tickets in advance during the day from the ticket counter next to the Betim Ferry. Cruises feature music and cultural shows. Dolphin-spotting cruises are also available.

🛏 Sleeping

Panaji has its fair share of accommodation for all budgets, but it's not saturated like the beach resorts. In the middle range are some of Goa's better boutique heritage hotels and guesthouses, mostly in the Fontainhas area, and this is reason enough to stay in Panaji.

If you're on a real budget there are a bunch of cheap guesthouses in the Old Quarter area with rooms from ₹600 but few are welcoming, let alone good value.

★ Old Quarter Hostel   HOSTEL $
(📞0832-6517606; www.thehostelcrowd.com; 31st January Rd; dm ₹450, d with AC from ₹2000; ❈🛜) Backpackers rejoice! This cool new hostel in an old Portuguese-style house in historic

Fontainhas offers slick four-bed dorms with lockers and two comfortable doubles upstairs, along with a cafe, arty murals, good wi-fi and bikes for hire. Noon checkout.

Pousada Guest House GUESTHOUSE **$**
(☑ 9850998213, 0832-2422618; sabrinateles@yahoo.com; Luis de Menezes Rd; s/d from ₹800/1050, d with AC ₹1575; ❋ 🛜) The five rooms in this bright-yellow place are simple, clean and come with comfy spring-mattress beds and TV. Owner Sabrina is friendly and no-nonsense, and it's one of Panaji's better budget guesthouses.

★ Panjim Inn HERITAGE HOTEL **$$**
(☑0832-2226523, 9823025748; www.panjiminn.com; 31st January Rd; s ₹3400-6000, d ₹3900-6500, ste ₹5950; ❋ 🛜) One of the original heritage hotels in Fontainhas, the Panjim Inn has been a long-standing favourite for its character and charm, friendly owners and helpful staff. This beautiful 19th-century mansion

has 12 charismatic rooms in the original house, along with 12 newer rooms with modern touches, but all have four-poster beds, colonial-era furniture and artworks. Buffet breakfast is included, and the Verandah restaurant serves excellent Goan food.

Panjim Pousada GUESTHOUSE **$$**
(☑0832-2226523; www.panjiminn.com; 31st January Rd; s ₹3400-4400, d ₹3900-4900; ❋ 🛜) In an old Hindu mansion, the nine divine, colonial-fantasy rooms at Panjim Pousada are set off by a stunning central courtyard, with antique furnishings and lovely art on the walls. Various doorways and spiral staircases lead to the rooms; those on the upper level are the best.

Afonso Guesthouse GUESTHOUSE **$$**
(☑9764300165, 0832-2222359; www.afonsoguesthouse.com; St Sebastian Rd; d ₹1800-3000; ❋ 🛜) Run by the friendly Jeanette, this pretty Portuguese townhouse offers

PANAJI & CENTRAL GOA PANAJI

LATIN QUARTER: FONTAINHAS & SAO TOMÉ

When the capital moved from plague-ridden Old Goa around 1843, Panjim was centred on its church square and the banks of the Mandovi River. But the settlement soon began to spread out and today the most atmospheric, Portuguese-flavoured districts of Panaji are east of the centre, squeezed between the hillside of Altinho and the banks of Ourem Creek. Fontainhas, Sao Tomé and, further south, Mala – collectively known as the Latin Quarter or Old Quarter – are unquestionably the most seductive and intriguing parts of the city, perfect for a late afternoon stroll.

Fontainhas, said to take its name from local springs, is the larger of the districts, comprising pastel-shaded houses towards Altinho Hill (p83). The land here was originally reclaimed in the late 18th century by a returning self-made Goan, known as 'the Mosmikar', so-called for the riches he had amassed during a stay in Mozambique.

Fontainhas' main thoroughfare is 31st January Rd and it's between here, Ourem Rd, Rue de Natal and further south to Altinho that you'll find many of the colourful mansions, Portuguese-era homes and bougainvillea blooms that make this district so photogenic.

Fontainhas is notable for being home to the pretty **Chapel of St Sebastian** (St Sebastian Rd; ⊘ mass 6.45am daily), built in 1818. This small whitewashed church at the end of a lovely lane contains one of only a few relics remaining as testament to the Goan Inquisition: a striking crucifix, which originally stood in the Palace of the Inquisition in Old Goa. Christ's unusual open eyes are said to have been conceived especially to strike fear into the hearts of 'heretical' suspects brought before the Inquisitors, and awaiting their usually grisly fate. In mid-November a street fair sets up outside the chapel to celebrate the Feast of Our Lady of Livrament.

To the north of Fontainhas, the tiny area around the main post office is known as Sao Tomé. The post office was once the tobacco-trading house for Panaji, and the building to the right of it was the state mint. The square that these buildings face once housed the town pillory, where justice turned into spectacle when executions took place. It was here that several conspirators involved in the Pinto Revolt (p125) were put to death for plotting to overthrow Portuguese rule in 1787.

Heritage **walking tours** (☑9823025748; per person ₹500, per person for five or more ₹250) of Fontainhas are run by the Panjim Inn if there's sufficient interest.

LUÍS VAZ DE CAMÕES

Luís Vaz de Camões (1524–80), regarded as Portugal's greatest poet, was banished to Goa in 1553 at the age of 29, after being accused of fighting with, and wounding, a magistrate in Lisbon. He was obviously no soft touch, for he enlisted in the army and fought with some distinction before attracting further official disapproval for publicly criticising Goa's Portuguese administration.

His reward this time was to be exiled to the Moluccas, and he returned to Goa only in 1562 to write his most famous work, *Os Lusíadas*, an epic poem glorifying the adventures of Vasco da Gama, which, classical in style and imperialist in sentiment, has since become an icon of Portuguese nationalism.

A statue of Camões, erected in 1960, stood at the centre of Old Goa until 1983, when many Goans decided that it was an unacceptable relic of colonialism. An attempt by radicals to blow it up met with failure, but the authorities took the hint and removed the statue. It now stands, along with Afonso de Albuquerque and various other disgraced Portuguese colonials, in the Archaeological Museum (p98) in Old Goa.

spacious, well-kept rooms with timber ceilings. The little rooftop terrace makes for sunny breakfasting (extra) with Fontainhas views. Add ₹200 for air-con. It's a simple, serene stay in the heart of the most atmospheric part of town. Checkout is 9am and bookings are accepted online but not by phone.

★**Casa Nova**　　　　　GUESTHOUSE $$
(☑ 9423889181; www.goaholidayaccommodation. com; Gomes Pereira Rd; ste ₹4300; ❇ ☎) In a gorgeous Portuguese-style house (c 1831) in Fontainhas, Casa Nova comprises just one stylish, exceptionally comfy double-bed apartment, accessed via a little alley and complete with arched windows, wood-beam ceilings, and mod-cons like a kitchenette and wi-fi.

Mayfair Hotel　　　　　HOTEL $$
(☑ 0832-2223317; manishafernz@yahoo.com; Dr Dada Vaidya Rd; s/d from ₹1105/1330, d with AC ₹1690; ❇ ☎) The oyster-shell windows and mosaic tiling in the lobby of this popular corner hotel are promising but the rooms are not quite as bright. Ask to see a few as there are new and old wings with rooms of varying quality, some overlooking a potentially nice back garden. Friendly family owners have been sheltering travellers for many years.

Casa Paradiso　　　　　HOTEL $$
(☑ 0832-3290180; www.casaparadisogoa.com; Jose Falcao Rd; d/tr with AC ₹1911/2200; ❇) A neat and welcoming little stay in the heart of the city. Up a small flight of stairs, the simple but clean rooms come with TV, hot water and noon checkout.

Abrigo de Botelho　　　　BOUTIQUE HOTEL $$
(☑ 9527778884; www.hadbgoa.com; Rue de Natal; r incl breakfast ₹3000-5000; ❇ ☎) At the end of a quiet lane in the Old Quarter, the six rooms in this lovely baby-blue heritage house are spacious, neatly furnished and enhanced with antiques, but still offer cable TV, air-con and wi-fi.

Hotel Sona　　　　　HOTEL $$
(☑ 0832-2222226; www.hotelsonagoa.com; Ourem Rd; d ₹1900-2200; ❇ ☎) With a nice location opposite Ourem Creek, Sona is a sound but slightly boring choice in a good area. Not all of the 30 clinical-but-clean air-con rooms of this four-storey building face the river, so check out a few.

Hotel Ria Residency　　　　HOTEL $$
(☑ 0832-2220002; www.riahotels.com; Ourem Rd; d ₹1500-1800; ❇) Contrasting starkly with its heritage neighbours, this characterless place doesn't look very appealing but at this price it's not bad value for the location and reasonably comfortable air-con rooms.

Panjim Peoples　　　　　HOTEL $$$
(☑ 0832-2226523, 0832-2435628; www.panjiminn. com; 31st January Rd; d ₹9000; ❇ ☎) The Panjim Peoples is an atmospheric heritage hotel with just four enormous upstairs rooms. There are mosaic-covered bathrooms, deep bath-tubs, antique furnishings and nautical ship lights. Downstairs is the Gitanjali Gallery & Cafe.

★**La Maison**　　　　　BOUTIQUE HOTEL $$$
(☑ 0832-2235555; www.lamaisongoa.com; 31st January Rd; r ₹4400-6600; ❇ ☎) The newest of the upcoming boutique heritage hotels in Fontainhas, La Maison is historic on the outside

but thoroughly modern and swanky within. The eight rooms are deceptively simple and homely five-star comfortable with soft beds, cloud-like pillows, writing desks and flat-screen TVs. Breakfast is included and attached is the contemporary Fogo Restaurant.

Crown Goa HOTEL $$$
(☑ 0832-2400000; www.thecrowngoa.com; Bairo Alto Dos Pilotos, Jose Falcao Rd; d incl breakfast ₹9000-10,650, ste from ₹11,200; ❄ @ ☒) Perched on a small hill above the Sao Tomé district, with fine views over the Mandovi, this spa-hotel-casino is a good option for a little bit of luxury in the heart of the city. A lift takes you up to a lovely terrace with swimming pool (nonguests ₹280) and bar. Spacious rooms are airy and tastefully done in mustards and whites, some with balconies. Along with the casino (no live gaming), there's a day spa and well-equipped gym.

Hotel Fidalgo HOTEL $$$
(☑ 0832-2226291-99; www.hotelfidalgo-goa. com; 18th June Rd; d/ste ₹7000/14,000; ❄ @ ☒) The city centre's smartest hotel is the business-style, slightly stuffy and old-fashioned Fidalgo, with snappy service and a good range of cuisines courtesy of its 'food enclave,' including a good vegetarian Indian restaurant, Legacy of Bombay. Cheaper deals online.

Hotel Mandovi HOTEL $$$
(☑ 0832-2426270; www.hotelmandovigoa.com; Dayanand Bandodkar Marg; s/d standard ₹4500/5060, executive ₹5625/6200, ste ₹12,400; ❄ ☏) A Panaji institution for more than 50 years, the Mandovi offers comfortable, though dated, rooms, many looking out onto the wide Mandovi River. For ambience, style and facilities, it's outdone by other top-end hotels in town. There are a couple of good restaurants.

🍴 Eating

There's not a beach shack in sight, but you'll never go hungry in Panaji, where food is enjoyed fully and frequently and new boutiquey restaurants are popping up each year. A stroll down 18th June or 31st January Rds will turn up a number of cheap but tasty canteen-style options, as will a quick circuit of the Municipal Gardens. Lots of these are pure veg, and offer up good thalis, *bhaji-pau* (bread roll dipped in curry) breakfasts and South Indian snacks.

The Latin Quarter has a developing foodie scene, where you can dine on traditional Goan specialities or Western comfort food.

★**Viva Panjim** GOAN $
(☑ 0832-2422405; 31st Jan Rd; mains ₹100-170; ☺ 11.30am-3.30pm & 7-11pm Mon-Sat, 7-11pm Sun) Well known to tourists, this little sidestreet eatery, in an old Portuguese-style house and with a few tables on the laneway, still delivers tasty Goan classics at reasonable prices. There's a whole page devoted to pork dishes, along with tasty *xacuti* and

PANAJI & CENTRAL GOA PANAJI

PANAJI'S CRAZY CARNIVAL

Panaji's annual carnival has been hitting the city centre for three chaotic days, sometime in late February or early March, since the 18th century, when it was introduced by the Catholic Portuguese as one last opportunity for excess before the strictures of Lent.

However, the origins of Carnival are far older, dating back as far as the Bacchanalias of ancient Rome, and later enlivened by African slaves in the Portuguese colonies. Once introduced to Goa, of course, an entirely local twist was added to the fun-filled goings on, with the inclusion of *tiatrs*, the satirical folk plays that are still performed throughout Carnival today.

Carnival begins with the arrival in Panaji of a character called King Momo on *Sabato Gordo* (Fat Saturday), and his instruction to the people of the city to, in essence, 'don't worry, be happy'. Dancing, drinking, processions of floats through the streets, cross-dressing and *assaltos* (amiable battles) – with sticky mixtures of flour, coloured tikka powder and water – ensue.

Though various criticisms of Carnival have emerged over the years – ranging from its post-Independence shunning due to its 'colonialism', to its recent commercialisation and excuse for the over-consumption of alcohol – Panaji's three days of mayhem are still celebrated by many thousands each year, seeing hotels booked solid, streets filled with revellers, and bars doing a brisk trade. Don't come dressed in your best, and prepare to be soaked to the skin.

cafreal-style dishes, seafood such as kingfish vindaloo and crab *xec xec,* and desserts such as *bebinca* (richly layered Goan cake made from egg yolk and coconut). Fair drink prices and good service too.

Vihar Restaurant   INDIAN $
(MG Rd; mains ₹40-130, veg thali from ₹90; ☺11am-11pm) A vast menu of 'pure veg' food, great big thalis, South Indian dosas and a plethora of fresh juices make this clean, simple canteen a popular place for locals and visitors. One of the few places in this area that's still busy late into the evening.

Cafe Bhonsle   CAFE $
(Ormuz Rd; veg thali ₹80, mains ₹100-170; ☺9am-10pm) Well known for its delicious lunchtime thalis and *puri bhaji,* Cafe Bhonsle has expanded with an upstairs section into a multicuisine place serving fish thalis and other seafood dishes. Thalis are served between around noon and 2.30pm.

Anandashram   INDIAN, GOAN $
(31st January Rd; thalis ₹80-130, seafood ₹200-350; ☺noon-3.30pm & 7.30-10.30pm Mon-Sat) This little place is renowned locally for seafood, serving up simple but tasty fish curries, as well as veg and nonveg thalis for lunch and dinner.

Gujarat Sweet Mart   SWEETS $
(Gujarat Lodge, 18th June Rd; drinks ₹20-50) If you have a sweet tooth, this hole-in-the-wall sweets counter is the place to indulge it, with a panoply of Indian confectioneries. There's also a range of cheap snacks and some of the best sweet lassis and milkshakes in town.

George Bar & Restaurant   GOAN $
(Municipal Gardens; mains ₹90-200; ☺9.30am-10.30pm) There's something very rustic and local about this cramped restaurant in the shadow of Panaji's main church. Seafood and Goan classics are done well at prices that attract a healthy mix of families and drinkers. The upstairs section has air-con.

★Cafe Bodega   CAFE $$
(☑0832-2421315; Altinho; mains ₹120-320; ☺10am-7pm Mon-Sat, to 4pm Sun; 📶) It's well worth a trip up to Altinho Hill for this serene cafe-gallery in a lavender-and-white Portuguese-style mansion in the grounds of Sunaparanta Centre for the Arts. Enjoy good coffee, juices and fresh-baked cakes around the inner courtyard or lunch on super pizzas and sandwiches.

★Hotel Venite   GOAN $$
(31st January Rd; mains ₹210-260; ☺9am-10.30pm) With its cute rickety balconies overhanging the cobbled street, Venite has long been among the most atmospheric of Panaji's old-school Goan restaurants. The menu is traditional, with spicy sausages, fish curry rice, pepper steak and *bebinca* featuring, but Venite is popular with tourists and prices are consequently rather inflated. It's not to be missed though.

Drop in for a cold beer or shot of *feni* (Goan liquour) before deciding on lunch or dinner.

Verandah   GOAN $$
(☑0832-2226523; 31st January Rd; mains ₹180-360; ☺11am-11pm) The breezy 1st-floor restaurant at Panjim Inn is indeed on the balcony, with just a handful of finely carved tables and Fontainhas street views. Goan cuisine is the speciality, but there's also a range of Indian and continental dishes and local wines.

Route 66   DINER, STEAK $$
(☑9623922796; Ourem Rd; mains ₹160-500; ☺noon-11.30pm) Styled on an American diner, this new 1st-floor place opposite Old Patto Bridge has hot dogs, burgers, cheese chilli fries, hickory barbecue ribs and New York–style pizzas. The steaks might blow your budget, but for comfort fast food it's hard to beat. On-site bakery and full bar.

Sher-E-Punjab   NORTH INDIAN $$
(☑0832-227204; www.sher-e-punjab.com; 18th June Rd; mains ₹110-300; ☺10.30am-11.30pm) Sheer-E-Punjab is widely regarded as one of the best North Indian places in Panaji, catering to well-dressed locals and business visitors with its generous, carefully spiced Punjabi dishes, including tandoori classics and rich butter chicken. The pleasant garden terrace out back is refreshing. There's another branch at Hotel Aroma.

★Black Sheep Bistro   EUROPEAN, TAPAS $$$
(☑0832-2222901; www.blacksheepbistro.in; Swami Vivekanand Rd; tapas ₹180-225, mains ₹320-450) One of the new breed of Panaji boutique restaurants, Black Sheep's impressive pale-yellow facade gives way to a sexy dark-wood bar and loungy dining room. The tapas dishes are light, fresh and expertly prepared in keeping with their farm-to-table philosophy. Salads, pasta, local seafood and dishes like lamb osso bucco also grace the menu, while an internationally trained

PANAJI'S FLOATING CASINOS

Live gaming is illegal in India, but back in 2001 the powers that be in Goa decided that if the gambling was offshore, it could circumvent this law. The result is floating casinos moored on the Mandovi River! The casinos remain controversial though, and the Goan government has indicated that the mini cruise ships must relocate out to sea by 2015 or have their licenses revoked.

The casinos vary a little in size and shape, but are quite luxurious and all offer gaming tables with croupiers, including blackjack, poker, roulette, baccarat, Indian flush and slot machines. Buffet meals, free drinks and entertainment are part of the deal in the evenings. Dress codes apply.

Deltin Royale (☑ 8698599999; www.deltingroup.com/deltin-royale; Noah's Ark, RND Jetty, Dayanand Bandodkar Marg; weekday/weekend ₹2500/3000, premium weekend ₹4000-4500; ⊙ 24hr, entertainment 9pm-1am) Goa's biggest luxury floating casino, Deltin Royale has 123 tables, the Vegas Restaurant, a whisky bar and a creche. Entry includes gaming chips worth ₹1500/2000 weekday/weekend and to the full value of your ticket with the premium package. Unlimited food and drinks included.

Deltin JAQK (☑ 7798740004; www.deltingroup.com/deltin-jaqk; Fisheries Jetty, Dayanand Bandodkar Marg; weekday/weekend ₹2000/2500, premium ₹3500; ⊙ 24hr, entertainment 9pm-1am) Deltin JAQK has three floors with 50 tables, including a learners' table. Admission includes gaming chips to the value of ₹1500/2000 weekday/weekend or ₹5000 in chips with the premium ticket. There's a lavish buffet on the dining floor and floorshow entertainment from 9pm. All tickets include free drinks until midnight (then free drinks only at gaming tables).

Casino Pride (☑ 0832-6516666; www.bestgoacasino.com; Dayanand Bandodkar Marg; weekday/weekend ₹1500/2000; ⊙ 24hr, entertainment 9-11pm) These two casino boats are loosely modelled on Mississippi-style paddle boats. *Pride I* has 40 gaming tables, a kids' play room and an outdoor party deck. Admission includes ₹1000 coupon for gaming. Unlimited dinner buffet is included, as well as free drinks if you're playing a table. *Pride II* is the same deal but smaller.

sommelier matches wine to food. The Black Sheep is serious about food and it shows.

Baba's Wood Cafe   ITALIAN $$$
(☑ 0832-3256213; 49 Mala; pizza & pasta ₹300-500; ⊙ noon-3pm & 7-11.30pm) Sharing an interesting premises with a wood-craft gallery, this upmarket Italian restaurant in a quiet street near the Maruti Temple has a lovely little alfresco dining area and a menu featuring more than 20 different pasta dishes from ravioli to carbonara. Pizzas are wood-fired and pasta homemade, while desserts include tiramisu and chocolate fondue. Good for a splurge.

Upper House   GOAN $$$
(☑ 0832-2426475; www.theupperhousegoa.com; Cunha-Rivara Rd; mains ₹220-440; ⊙ 11am-10pm; ❀) Climbing the stairs to the Upper House is like stepping into a cool European restaurant, with a modern but elegant dining space overlooking the Municipal Gardens, a chic neon-lit cocktail bar and a more formal restaurant at the back. The food is very

much Goan though, with regional specialities such as crab *xec xec,* fish curry rice and pork vindaloo prepared to a high standard at relatively high prices.

🍷 Drinking & Nightlife

Panaji's local drinking scene is in the town's tiny, tucked-away bars, mostly equipped with rudimentary plastic tables, a fridge, a few stools and an almost-exclusively male clientele. They're good places to mingle with the locals, and generally open up towards lunchtime, closing for a siesta mid-afternoon, and cranking up again come sundown. More upscale bars can be found in high-end hotels.

Cafe Mojo   BAR
(www.cafemojo.in; Menezes Braganza Rd; ⊙ 10am-4am Mon-Thu, to 6am Fri-Sun) The decor is cosy English pub, the clientele young and up for a party, and the hook is the e-beer system. Each table has it's own beer tap and LCD

screen: you buy a card (₹1000), swipe it at your table and start pouring – it automatically deducts what you drink (you can also use the card for spirits, cocktails or food). Wednesday night is ladies night, Thursday karaoke, and the weekends go till late.

Riverfront & Down the Road BAR
(cnr MG & Ourem Rds; ⊙11am-1am) This restaurant's balcony overlooking the creek and Old Patto Bridge makes for a cosy beer or cocktail spot with carved barrels for furniture. The ground-floor bar (from 6pm) is the only real nightspot on the Old Quarter side of town, with occasional live music.

Top Gear Pub BAR
(Dayanand Bandodkar Marg; ⊙11am-3pm & 6.30pm-midnight) One of Panaji's hole-in-the-wall bars, this tiny, retro place is hidden behind unassuming doors. There's no food – just cold beer and *feni* by the shot.

Quarterdeck BAR
(Dayanand Bandodkar Marg; ⊙11am-11pm) The riverside location on the banks of the Mandovi is the main redeeming feature of this open-air garden restaurant and bar near the Betim Ferry dock. Drinks are overpriced, as is the food (mains ₹150 to ₹350), but it's a nice place to enjoy a sundowner and watch the casino boats light up.

☆ Entertainment

Panaji's most visible form of entertainment is aboard the casino boats anchored out in the Mandovi River, but the city is also home to India's biggest international film festival and the cultural offerings of the excellent Kala Academy.

Kala Academy CULTURAL CENTRE
(✉0832-2420452; www.kalaacademygoa.org; Dayanand Bandodkar Marg) On the west side of the city, in Campal, is Goa's premier cultural centre, which features a program of dance, theatre, music and art exhibitions throughout the year. Many shows are in Konkani, but there are occasional English-language productions. The website has an up-to-date calendar of events.

INOX Cinema ´ CINEMA
(✉0832-2420900; www.inoxmovies.com; Old GMC Heritage Precinct; tickets ₹180-200) This comfortable, plush multiplex cinema shows Hollywood and Bollywood blockbusters. Book online to choose your seats in advance.

Cine Nacional CINEMA
(Ormuz Rd; tickets ₹60) Dismal, dark and dank, but an interesting experience if you're looking for an unforgettable dose of Bollywood with local flavour. The only filmic quality the toilets possess is their likeness to a certain scene in *Trainspotting*. Films are shown about four times daily; check the posters outside the box office for current screenings.

🛍 Shopping

Panaji is a decent place for a boutique-style shopping stop, with international brand-name stores dotting Mahatma Gandhi (MG) Rd (at around a third of European prices), Goa's largest shopping mall, and a slew of 'lifestyle stores' selling high-end faux antiques, well-made textiles and richly illustrated coffee-table tomes. For local grit and grime head to the municipal markets.

Municipal Market MARKET
(Heljogordo Salgado Rd; ⊙from 7.30am) This atmospheric place, where narrow streets have been converted into covered markets, makes for a nice wander, offering fresh produce, clothing stalls and some tiny, enticing eateries. The fish market is a particularly interesting strip of activity.

New Municipal Market MARKET
(⊙from 7.30am) This light-filled building comprises mostly stacks of fresh fruit and vegetables downstairs and a few drab electronics shops and tailors upstairs. Less atmosphere than the nearby old Municipal Market.

Caculo Mall MALL
(✉0832-2222068; 16 Shanta, St Inez Rd; ⊙8am-11pm) Goa's biggest mall is four levels of air-conditioned family shopping heaven, with brand-name stores, food court, kids' toys, Time Zone arcade games and a movie theatre.

Marcou Artifacts CRAFTS
(✉0832-2220204; www.marcouartifacts.com; 31st Jan Rd; ⊙9am-8pm) This small shop displays one-off painted tiles, fish figurines and hand-crafted Portuguese and Goan ceramics at reasonable prices. Also showrooms at the Hotel Delmon and Margao's market.

Sosa's CLOTHING
(✉0832-2228063; E245 Ourem Rd; ⊙10am-7pm Mon-Sat) A boutique carrying local labels such as Horn Ok Please, Hidden Harmony and Free Falling, Sosa's is among the best places in Panaji to source upscale Indian fashion.

Book Fair
BOOKS

(Hotel Mandovi, Dayanand Bandodkar Marg; ⊙9am-9pm) A small, well-stocked bookshop in the Hotel Mandovi lobby, with plenty of illustrated books on Goa.

Singbal's Book House
BOOKS

(Church Sq; ⊙9.30am-1pm & 3.30-7.30pm Mon-Sat) On the corner opposite Panaji's main church, Singbal's has an excellent selection of international magazines and newspapers, and lots of books on Goa and travel.

Velha Goa Galeria
HANDICRAFTS

(Ourem Rd; ⊙10am-1pm & 3-7pm Mon-Sat) One of several places in town specialising in *azulejos* (tin-glazed ceramic tiles), this nice place offers tiles, vases and other ceramic objects reproduced in the old style by Portuguese artist, Anabela Cardosa. Pricey, but great gifts or souvenirs.

Barefoot
HANDICRAFTS

(31st January Rd; ⊙10am-8pm Mon-Sat) Part of Panaji's new wave of high-end shops, specialising in design. Though pricey, it has some nice gifts ranging from traditional Christmas paintings on wood to jewellery and beaded coasters.

Khadi Gramodyog Bhavan
HANDICRAFTS

(Dr Atmaram Borkar Rd; ⊙9am-noon & 3-7pm Mon-Sat) Goa's only outpost of the government's Khadi & Village Industries Commission has an excellent range of hand-woven cottons, oils, soaps, spices and other hand-made products that come straight from (and directly benefit) regional villages.

ℹ Information

INTERNET ACCESS

Cozy Nook (18th June Rd; per hour ₹40; ⊙9am-8.30pm) Fast and friendly internet, and a good travel agency.

MEDICAL SERVICES

Goa Medical College Hospital (☑0832-2458700; www.gmc.goa.gov.in; Bambolin) This 1000-bed hospital is 9km south of Panaji on NH17 in Bambolim.

Vintage Hospitals (☑0832-6644401, ambulance 9764442220; www.vintagehospitals.com; Caculo Enclave, St Inez; ⊙24hr) Central Panaji's best hospital in an emergency; it's just west of the centre near Caculo Mall.

MONEY

International 24-hour ATMs are widespread in Panaji; look out for HDFC, State Bank of India, ICICI and Axis.

Thomas Cook (☑0832-2221312; 8 Alcon Chambers, Dayanand Bandodkar Marg; ⊙9.30am-6pm Mon-Sat) Changes travellers cheques commission-free and gives cash advances on Visa and MasterCard.

POST

Hidden in the lanes around the main post office, there are privately run parcel-wrapping outfits that charge reasonable prices for their essential services.

Main Post Office (MG Rd; ⊙9.30am-5.30pm Mon-Sat) Offers swift parcel services and Western Union money transfers.

TOURIST INFORMATION

Goa Tourism Development Corporation (Goa Tourism, GTDC; ☑0832-2437132; www.goa-tourism.com; Paryatan Bhavan, Dr Alvaro Costa Rd; ⊙9.30am-5.45pm Mon-Sat) Better known as Goa Tourism, the GTDC office is in the slick new Paryatan Bhavan building across the Ourem Creek and near the bus stand. However, it's more corporate office than tourist office and is of little use to casual visitors, unless you want to book one of GTDC's host of tours.

Government of India Tourist Office (☑0832-2223412; www.incredibleindia.com; Communidade Bldg, Church Sq; ⊙9.30am-1.30pm & 2.30-6pm Mon-Fri, 10am-1pm Sat) The staff at this central tourist office can be helpful, especially for information outside Goa. This office is expected to move to the same building as Goa Tourism by the time you read this.

TRAVEL AGENCIES

There are several travel agencies where you can book and confirm flights; many are along 18th June Rd.

E-zy Travels (☑0832-2435300; www.ezytravels.in; shop 8-9, Durga Chambers, 18th June Rd) A professionally run travel agent that can book international flights.

ℹ Getting There & Away

AIR

Dabolim Airport is around 30km south of Panaji. There are no direct bus services between the airport and Panaji, though some higher-end hotels offer a minibus service, often included in the room tariff.

A taxi from Panaji to the airport costs ₹800 and takes about 45 minutes, but allow an hour for traffic. From Dabolim, the prepaid taxi fare is ₹670 (₹770 for AC). Alternatively, if you don't have much luggage, you can catch a bus from the main road to Vasco da Gama, then a bus direct from Vasco to Panaji (₹30, 45 minutes).

BOAT

Taking the rusty but free passenger/vehicle ferry across the Mandovi River to the fishing village of Betim makes a fun shortcut en route to the northern beaches. It departs the jetty on Dayanand Bandodkar Marg roughly every 15 minutes between 6am and 10pm. From Betim there are regular buses onwards to Calangute and Candolim.

BUS

All local buses depart from Panaji's **Kadamba bus stand** (☑ interstate enquiries 0832-2438035, local enquiries 0832-2438034; www. goakadamba.com; ⊙ reservations 8am-8pm), with frequent local services (running to no apparent timetable) heading out every few minutes; major destinations are Mapusa in the north, Margao to the south and Ponda to the east. Most bus services run from 6am to 10pm. Ask at the bus stand to be directed to the right bus for you, or check the signs on the bus windscreens. Fares range from ₹10 to Old Goa to ₹30 to Margao. To get to the beaches in South Goa, take an express bus to Margao (45 minutes) and change there; to get to beaches north of Baga, it's best to head to Mapusa (20 minutes) and change there. There are direct buses to Candolim, Calangute and Baga.

State-run long distance services also depart from the Kadamba bus stand, but prices offered by private operators are similar and they offer greater choice in type of bus and departure times. Many private operators have booths outside the entrance to the Kadamba bus stand (go there to compare prices and times), but most private interstate services depart from the interstate bus stand across the highway next to the New Patto Bridge.

The main thing to note about private bus services is that fares are seasonal and can change dramatically depending on the type of bus, time of year and even day of the week. December to February, festivals/holidays and weekends are the peak times to travel.

The Kadamba bus stand has an internet cafe, an ATM and lots of cheap snack joints.

Paulo Travels (☑ 0832-2438531; www.phm goa.com; G1, Kardozo Bldg) is a reliable private operator with offices just north of the Kadamba bus stand. It operates a number of services with varying levels of comfort to Mumbai (₹350 to ₹700, 11 to 15 hours), Pune (₹450 to ₹600, 10 to 12 hours), Hampi (₹450 to ₹650, 10 hours), Bengaluru (Bangalore, ₹450 to ₹750, 14 to 15 hours) and various other long-distance destinations.

TRAIN

The closest train station to Panaji is Karmali (Old Goa), 12km to the east near Old Goa. A number of long-distance services stop here, including services to and from Mumbai, and many trains coming from Margao also stop here – but check in advance. Panaji's **Konkan Railway Reservation Office** (☑ 0832-2712940; www.konkan-railway.com; ⊙ 8am-8pm Mon-Sat) is on the 1st floor of the Kadamba bus stand – not at the train station. You can also check times, prices and routes online at www.konkanrailway.com and www.indianrail.gov.in.

🛈 Getting Around

It's easy enough to get around central Panaji and Fontainhas on foot, which is just as well because taxis and autorickshaws charge extortionate prices for short trips. A taxi to Old Goa costs around ₹350, and an autorickshaw should agree to take you there for ₹250. Lots of taxi drivers hang around at the Municipal Gardens, making it a good place to haggle for the best price. Autorickshaws and motorcycle taxis can also be found in front of the post office, on 18th June Rd, and just south of the church.

Local buses run to Miramar, Dona Paula and to Old Goa.

West of Panaji

Miramar

Miramar, 3km southwest of the city, is Panaji's nearest beach. The couple of kilometres of exposed sand facing Aguada Bay are hardly inspiring compared to other Goan beaches but are a popular local place to watch the sun sink into the Arabian Sea. It's not a great place for swimming and bikinis are likely to attract unwanted attention.

Along the seafront road, at the start of Miramar Beach, is Gaspar Dias. Originally a fort stood here, designed for defence, directly opposite the fort at Reis Magos on the other side of the Mandovi. There's no fort now, but the most prominent position on the beachfront is taken up by a statue representing Hindu and Christian unity.

Kids and families will enjoy the Goa Science Centre & Planetarium (www.goascience centre.in; Marine Hwy, Miramar; admission ₹10, planetarium ₹15; ⊙ 10am-6pm) with an outdoor park, hands-on interactive displays, 3D movies and a planetarium.

Miramar's plush Goa Marriott Resort (☑ 0832-2463333; www.marriott.com; Miramar Beach; d ₹7000-15,000; ❀ 🗧 ☒) is the best in the Panaji area, with the 5-star treatment beginning in the lobby and extending right up to the rooms-with-a-view. The 24-hour Waterfront Terrace & Bar is a great place for a sundowner overlooking the pool (nonguests ₹500), while its Simply Grills restaurant (bookings advised) is a dinner favourite with well-heeled Panjimites.

Frequent local buses run along the Panaji riverfront to Miramar.

Dona Paula

Situated on the headland that divides the Zuari and Mandovi Rivers, 9km southwest of Panaji, Dona Paula allegedly takes its name from Dona Paula de Menenez, a Portuguese viceroy's daughter who threw herself into the sea from the clifftop after being prevented from marrying a local fisherman. Her tombstone still stands in the chapel at nearby Cabo Raj Bhavan. Though the views over Mormugao Bay are nice enough, and down on the promenade boat operators offer trips, the village is drab, the small beaches raggedy and the hawkers persistent.

For the last 40 years, Baroness Yrsa von Leistner's (1917–2008) whitewashed *Images of India* statue has graced a mock acropolis on an outcrop of rock at the end of the Dona Paula road. It portrays a couple looking off in different directions, the man towards the past and the woman towards India's future.

◉ Sights

Cabo Raj Bhavan   FORT
(Cabo Raj Niwas; www.rajbhavangoa.org; ☺ chapel Sun Mass 9.30-10.30am, Christmas, Easter & feast days) On the westernmost point of the peninsula stands an old fortress, Cabo Raj Bhavan, nowadays the official residence of the Governor of Goa. Plans to build a fortress here, to guard the entrance to the Mandovi and Zuari Rivers, were first proposed in 1540, and although the 16th century had become the 17th before work on the fortress began, a chapel was raised on the spot almost immediately. The fortress was subsequently completed and the chapel extended to include a Franciscan friary. The fort itself, though equipped with several cannons, was never used in defence of Goa, and from the 1650s was instead requisitioned as a grand and temporary residence for Goa's lucky archbishop.

From 1799 to 1813 the site (along with Fort Aguada and Reis Magos Fort, to the north) was occupied by the British who, during the Napoleonic Wars, deemed it necessary in order to deter the French from invading Goa. Now all that remains of the British presence is a forlorn little British cemetery, with gravestones spanning just over a century. It's tucked away behind the Institute of Oceanography – look for the hand-painted sign to the cemetery and the clam-shaped Oceanography Institute roof off the main roundabout. Cabo Raj Bhavan's 500-year-old chapel also draws thousands of locals to its Feast of the Chapel for prayers and festivities each 15 August.

After the departure of the British, the buildings were once again inhabited by the archbishop of Goa, but it didn't remain long in his possession: in 1866 the Portuguese viceroy took a shine to the buildings, and had them refurbished and converted into the governor's palace, packing the poor old archbishop off to the hilltop Bishop's Palace (p83) in Altinho.

🛏 Sleeping & Eating

Dona Paula offers several guesthouses and higher-end hotels, but it's hardly an appealing beach destination. There's a cluster of simple cafes along the seafront.

O Pescador   HOTEL $$
(☎0832-2453863; www.opescador.com; d without/ with AC ₹3900/6000, ste ₹7100; ❋🅿🛜🏊) Also known as the Dona Paula Beach Resort, O Pescador's site has been utilised to create well-decorated mock-Portuguese villas with a view of the 'private' beach. It's a firm favourite among the UK package-holiday crowd and is the base for Dive Goa (☎93250 30110; www.divegoa.com; Jetty Rd, Dona Paula).

Cidade de Goa   HOTEL $$$
(☎0832-2454545; www.cidadedegoa.com; d from ₹15,000; ❋@🛜🏊) Indulgence is the order of the day at this swanky village-style place, designed by renowned local architect Charles Correa, located 1km down the coast from Dona Paula at Vanguinim Beach. All the usual opulence is on offer, including pool, spa and casino, and eight restaurants.

ℹ Getting There & Away

Frequent buses to Dona Paula depart the Kadamba bus stand in Panaji (₹6, 20 minutes), running along riverfront Dayanand Bandodkar Marg, and passing through Miramar.

Panaji to Old Goa

Ribandar

The old riverside road joining Panaji to Old Goa, via the quaint village of Ribandar, seems to have changed little since it was first built on land reclaimed from marshes some 400 years ago. Considering it's so close to the capital, driving this route towards Old Goa gives you the distinct impression that time has stood still. Ribandar makes a nice place to pause, and is one of several free ferry access points to Chorao and Divar Islands.

Chorao Island

Lazy Chorao Island, accessible by the free ferry from Ribandar or Divar Island, is mainly known for its beautiful bird sanctuary. If you arrive here with your own transport it's worth a ride through the countryside to little Chorao village, with its handful of whitewashed village churches and picturesque Portuguese homes. You can also ride or drive to the Divar ferry crossing, explore that island and ferry back to the mainland at Old Goa.

◎ Sights

Dr Salim Ali Bird Sanctuary   BIRD SANCTUARY
(Chorao Island; admission ₹75, forest department boat ₹900; ⊙6am-6pm) Named after the late Dr Salim Moizzudin Abdul Ali, India's best-known ornithologist, this serene sanctuary on Chorao Island was created by Goa's Forestry Department in 1988 to protect the birdlife that thrives here and the mangroves that have grown up in and around the reclaimed marshland. Apart from the ubiquitous white egrets and purple herons, you can expect to see colourful kingfishers, eagles, cormorants, kites, woodpeckers, sandpipers, curlews, drongos and mynahs, to name just a few.

Marsh crocodiles, foxes, jackals and otters have also been spotted by some visitors, along with the bulbous-headed mudskipper fish that skim across the water's surface at low tide. There's a birdwatching tower in the sanctuary that can be reached by boat when the river level, dependent on the tide, is not too low.

Even for those not especially interested in the birds themselves, a leisurely drift in dug-out canoe through the sanctuary's mangrove swamps offers a fascinating insight into life on this fragile terrain.

The best time to visit is either in the early morning (around 8am) or in the evening (a couple of hours before sunset), but since the Mandovi is a tidal river, boat trips depend somewhat on tide times. You'll find boatmen, in possession of dugout canoes to take you paddling about the sanctuary, waiting around at the ferry landing on Chorao Island; the going rate is around ₹700 for a 1½-hour trip. The forest department also operates a boat, which can hold up to 12 people. Don't forget to bring binoculars and a field guide to all things feathered if you're a keen birdwatcher.

To get to Chorao Island by bus, board a bus from Panaji bound for Old Goa and ask to be let off at the Ribandar ferry crossing.

Old Goa

Life in Old Goa, the principal city of the Portuguese eastern empire from 1510 until its abandonment in 1835, was anything but dull. Its rise was meteoric. Over the course of the century following the arrival of the Portuguese in Goa, the city became famous throughout the world. One Dutch visitor compared it with Amsterdam for the volume of its trade and wealth; at its 17th-century zenith, Old Goa (then known as Ela) was bigger than Lisbon and known as the 'Rome of the East'.

Its fall, however, was just as swift, and eventually, plagued by epidemic after deadly epidemic – cholera, malaria and typhoid among them – the city was completely abandoned. Today in Old Goa, 9km east of Panaji on the course of the broad Mandovi River, only a handful of imposing churches and convents remain from the original city, but they are beautifully preserved, impressive in scale and a must-visit while in central Goa.

The site makes an excellent day trip but it can get crowded; try to visit early on a weekday morning or late afternoon.

History

The first records of a settlement on the site of Old Goa date back to the 12th century and a Brahmin colony known as Ela. Though continuously occupied, it wasn't until the 15th century that Ela rose to prominence, with the Muslim Bahmani rulers choosing it as the site for a new Goan capital, in place of the ransacked and silted-up port capital of Govepuri (today Goa Velha).

Within a short time the new capital was a thriving place. Contemporary accounts tell of the magnificence of the city, enlarged and strengthened with ramparts and a moat, and of the grandeur of its royal palace. It became a major trading centre and departure

Old Goa

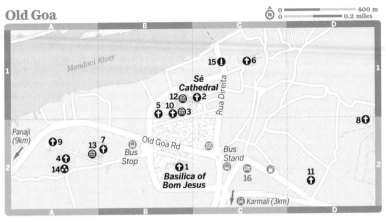

0   400 m
0   0.2 miles

Old Goa

◎ Top Sights

1	Basilica of Bom Jesus	B2
2	Sé Cathedral	C1

◎ Sights

3	Archaeological Museum	B1
4	Chapel of St Anthony	A2
5	Chapel of St Catherine	B1
6	Church & Convent of St Cajetan	C1
7	Church & Convent of St Monica	B2
8	Church of Our Lady of the Mount	D2
9	Church of Our Lady of the Rosary	A2
10	Church of St Francis of Assisi	B1
11	Church of St Francis Xavier	D2
12	Kristu Kala Mandir Art Gallery	B1
13	Museum of Christian Art	A2
14	Ruins of the Church of St Augustine	A2
15	Viceroy's Arch	C1

◎ Sleeping

16	Old Goa Residency	C2

point for pilgrims to Mecca, and also gained prominence for its shipbuilding.

With the arrival of the Portuguese in the 16th century, Ela became the new Portuguese capital and a base for the shipment of spices back to the Old World. Soon came missionaries (including the young Francis Xavier), intent on converting the natives, and in 1560 the Inquisition, to put paid to the legendary licentious behaviour of both locals and colonials. Though their methods were gruesome, the behaviour they were targeting was widespread: despite the proliferation of churches and cathedrals, Old Goa was a city of drunkenness and debauchery; even the clerics themselves sometimes kept harems of slave girls, and death from syphilis was rife.

Syphilis, however, wasn't to be Old Goa's most widespread disease. The city had been built on swamps, a breeding ground for mosquitos and malaria, while water sources tainted with sewage caused cholera to sweep its streets. Moreover, by the end of the 16th century the Mandovi River was silting up and Portuguese supremacy on the seas had

been usurped by the British, Dutch and French. The city's decline was accelerated by another devastating cholera epidemic in 1635. Finally, by 1759, the Portuguese had had enough, and the Viceroy moved his official residence to Panjim.

In 1843 Panjim was officially declared the new capital, and by 1846 only Old Goa's convent of Santa Monica was in regular use, though that was also eventually abandoned, leaving the shadow of a grand and desolate city behind.

From the late 19th century until the mid-20th century, Old Goa remained a city of ghosts, empty but for one or two buildings used as military barracks. When archaeological interest started to increase, work was done to clear the area, and some buildings were returned to their former uses. But for many of the once-glorious buildings, plundered for building materials or simply falling victim to the elements, the reprieve came too late; the starkest reminder of this is the skeletal tower of the Church of St Augustine, which can be seen for miles around.

ⓘ VISITING OLD GOA

As Goa's top historical attraction and a focal point for pilgrims and domestic bus tours, Old Goa can get very crowded on weekends and feast days. The best time to visit is on a weekday morning, when you can take in Mass at Sé Cathedral or the Basilica of Bom Jesus and explore the rest of the site before the afternoon heat sets in. Remember to cover your shoulders and legs when entering the churches and cathedral, and observe the various signs – for instance, still photography is allowed in the churches, but not photos of people posing in the church. So no selfies.

⊙ Sights

★ Basilica of Bom Jesus   CHURCH

(⊙ 7.30am-6.30pm) Famous throughout the Roman Catholic world, the imposing Basilica of Bom Jesus contains the tomb and mortal remains of St Francis Xavier, the so-called Apostle of the Indies. St Francis Xavier's missionary voyages throughout the East became legendary. His 'incorrupt' body is in the mausoleum to the right, in a glass-sided coffin amid a shower of gilt stars.

Construction on the basilica began in 1594 and was completed in 1605 to create an elaborate late-Renaissance structure, fronted by a facade combining elements of Doric, Ionic and Corinthian design.

Prominent in the design of the facade is the intricately carved central rectangular pediment, embellished with the Jesuit emblem 'IHS', an abbreviation of the Latin '*Iesus Hominum Salvator*' (Jesus, Saviour of Men).

This is the only church in Old Goa not plastered on the outside, the lime plaster having been stripped off by a zealous Portuguese conservationist in 1950. Apparently his notion was that exposed to the elements, the laterite stone of which the basilica is built would become more durable and thus the building would be strengthened. Despite proof to the contrary, no one has got around to putting the plaster back yet; hence, some of the intricate carving is eroding with the dousing of each successive monsoon.

Inside, the basilica's layout is simple but grand, contained beneath a simple wooden ceiling. The huge and ornate gilded reredos (ornamental screen), stretching from floor to ceiling behind the altar, takes pride of place, its baroque ornament contrasting strongly with the classical, plain layout of the cathedral itself. It shows a rather portly St Ignatius Loyola protecting a tiny figure of the infant Jesus. His eyes are raised to a huge gilded sun above his head, on which 'IHS' is again emblazoned, above which is a representation of the Trinity.

To the right of the altar is the slightly grisly highlight for the vast majority of visitors: the body of St Francis Xavier himself. The body was moved into the church in 1622, and installed in its current mausoleum in 1698 courtesy of the last of the Medicis, Cosimo III, Grand Duke of Tuscany, in exchange for the pillow on which St Francis' head had been resting. Cosimo engaged the Florentine sculptor Giovanni Batista Foggini to work on the three-tiered structure, constructed of jasper and marble, flanked with stars, and adorned with bronze plaques that depict scenes from the saint's life. Topping it all off, and holding the shrivelled saint himself, is the casket, designed by Italian Jesuit Marcelo Mastrili and constructed by local silversmiths in 1659. The sides were originally encrusted with precious stones which, over the centuries, have been picked off.

Crowds are heaviest at the basilica during the **Feast of St Francis Xavier**, held annually on 3 December and preceded by a nine-day devotional novena, with lots of lighthearted festivity alongside the more solemn open-air Masses. Once every 10 years, the saint is given an exposition, and his body hauled around Old Goa before scores of pilgrims. The last one was in 2014, so you'll have to wait until 2024.

Passing from the chapel towards the sacristy there are a couple of items relating to St Francis' remains and, slightly further on, the stairs to a gallery of modern art.

Next to the basilica is the **Professed House of the Jesuits**, a two-storey laterite building covered with lime plaster. It actually pre-dates the basilica, having been completed in 1585. It was from here that Jesuit missions to the east were organised. Part of the building burned down in 1633 and was partially rebuilt in 1783.

Mass is held in the basilica in Konkani at 7am and 8am Monday to Saturday, at 8am and 9.15am on Sunday, and at 10.15am in English on Sunday. Confession is held daily in the sacristy from 5pm to 6pm.

★ **Sé Cathedral**   CATHEDRAL

(🕐9am-6pm; Mass 7am & 6pm Mon-Sat, 7.15am, 10am & 4pm Sun) At over 76m long and 55m wide, the cavernous Sé Cathedral is the largest church in Asia. Building work commenced in 1562, on the orders of King Dom Sebastiao of Portugal, and the finishing touches where finally made some 90 years later. The exterior of the cathedral is notable for its plain style, in the Tuscan tradition. Also of note is its rather lopsided look resulting from the loss of one of its bell towers, which collapsed in 1776 after being struck by lightning. The remaining tower houses the famous **Sino de Ouro** (Golden Bell), the largest in Asia and renowned for its rich tone, which once tolled to accompany the Inquisition's notoriously cruel *autos-da-fé* (trials of faith), held out the front of the cathedral on what was then the market square.

The huge interior of the cathedral is surprisingly plain. To the right as you enter is a small, locked area that contains a font made in 1532, said to have been used by St Francis Xavier. Two small statuettes, inset into the main pillars, depict St Francis Xavier and St Ignatius Loyola. There are four chapels on either side of the nave, two of which have screens across the entrance. Of these, the **Chapel of the Blessed Sacrament** is outstanding, with every inch of wall and ceiling gorgeously gilded and decorated – a complete contrast to the austerity of the cathedral interior.

Opposite, to the right of the nave, is the other screened chapel, the **Chapel of the Cross of Miracles**. The story goes that in 1619 a simple cross (known as the Cruz dos Milagres) made by local shepherds was erected on a hillside near Old Goa. The cross grew bigger and several witnesses saw an apparition of Christ hanging on it. A church was planned on the spot where the vision had appeared and while this was being built the cross was stored nearby. When it came time to move the cross into the new church it was found that it had grown again and that the doors of the church had to be widened to accommodate it. The cross was moved to the cathedral in 1845, where it soon became, and remains, a popular place of petition for the sick.

Towering above the main altar is the huge gilded reredos, its six main panels carved with scenes from the life of St Catherine, to whom the cathedral is dedicated. She was beheaded in Alexandria, and among the images here are those showing her awaiting execution and being carried to Mt Sinai by angels.

Kristu Kala Mandir Art Gallery   GALLERY

(admission ₹10; 🕐9.30am-5.30pm Tue-Sun) This gallery, sandwiched between the Church of St Francis of Assisi and Sé Cathedral, is located in what used to be the archbishop's house, and contains a hodgepodge collection

PANAJI & CENTRAL GOA OLD GOA

OLD GOA'S ARCHITECTURE

In order to make the most of what you encounter in Old Goa, it's worth a brief brush-up on its architectural heritage.

Most churches are made of laterite, a local red and highly porous stone, which was traditionally coated in white lime wash mixed with crushed clam shells in an effort to prevent erosion. Some were embellished with harder-wearing basalt, much of it quarried from Bassein, near Mumbai, though some is thought to have been brought as ballast by ships from Portugal.

Built in an era of glorious colonialism, much of what's on display today is staunchly European, inspired by the building fashions of late-Renaissance Rome. The pinnacle of building here (in the early 17th century) collided with the rise, in Europe, of the baroque movement, characterised by its love of dripping gilt, scrollwork and ornamentation. This pomp and splendour served an important purpose for its priests and missionaries, as it kept the locals awed into submission, feeling dwarfed and vulnerable when confronted with an immense gold altarpiece.

The second style evident at Old Goa is more wholly Portuguese, known as Manueline, after its main patron King Manuel I. This vernacular approach saw the embellishment of buildings with symbols reflecting Portuguese might; anchors, ropes and other maritime motifs represent Portugal's ascendency on the high seas. Though not too much Manueline architecture has survived the test of time, the Church of Our Lady of the Rosary (p100) remains a well-preserved example.

WORTH A TRIP

CHURCH OF OUR LADY OF THE MOUNT

This church is often overlooked due to its location on a wooded hilltop, some 2km east of the central area. A sealed road leads to an overgrown flight of steps (don't walk it solo) and the hill on which the church stands commands an excellent view of Old Goa, with the church spires seemingly rising out of a sea of palms.

The church was built by Afonso de Albuquerque, completed in 1519, and has been rebuilt twice since; it now makes the perfect, suitably sorrowful place to watch the sunset over the ruins of once-mighty Old Goa. Usually locked, you can gain entry during the Feast of St Francis Xavier in December, and the Monte Music Festival in February, when concerts are held here.

of contemporary Christian art and religious objects.

Church of St Francis of Assisi   CHURCH

West of the Sé Cathedral, the Church of St Francis of Assisi is no longer in use for worship, and consequently exudes a more mournful air than its neighbours.

The church started life as a small chapel, built on this site by eight Franciscan friars on their arrival in 1517. In 1521 it was replaced by a church consecrated to the Holy Ghost, which was then subsequently rebuilt in 1661, with only the doorway of the old building incorporated into the new structure. This original doorway, in ornate Manueline style, contrasts strongly with the rest of the facade, the plainness of which had become the fashion by the 17th century.

Maritime themes – unsurprising given Old Goa's important port status – can be seen here and there, including navigators' globes and coats of arms, which once adorned ships' sails.

The interior of the church, though now rather ragged and faded, is nevertheless beautiful, in a particularly 'folk art' type style. The walls and ceiling are heavily gilded and decorated with carved wood panels, with large paintings depicting the works of St Francis adorning the walls of the chancel. Look out for the huge arch that supports the choir, painted vividly with floral designs, and

the intricately carved pulpit. The reredos dominates the gilded show, although this one is different to others in Old Goa, with a deep recess for the tabernacle. The four statues in its lower portion represent apostles, and above the reredos hangs Christ on the cross. The symbolism of this scene is unmistakable: Jesus has his right arm free to embrace St Francis, who is standing atop the three vows of the Franciscan order – Poverty, Humility and Obedience.

Archaeological Museum   MUSEUM

(adult/child ₹10/free; ⊘9am-5pm) Part of the Franciscan monastery at the back of the Church of St Francis of Assisi is now an archaeological museum, housing some lovely fragments of sculpture from Hindu temple sites in Goa, and some Sati stones, which once marked the spot where a Hindu widow committed suicide by flinging herself onto her husband's funeral pyre.

You'll also find two large bronze statues here: one of the Portuguese poet Luís Vaz de Camões (p86), which once stood more prominently in the central grassy area of Old Goa, and one of Afonso de Albuquerque, the Portuguese conqueror and first governor of Goa, which stood in the Azad Maidan in Panaji, before being moved here after Independence.

Upstairs, a gallery contains portraits of some 60 of Goa's Portuguese viceroys, spanning more than 400 years of Portuguese rule. Not particularly exciting in terms of portraiture, they're an interesting insight into Portugal's changing fashions, each as unsuitable for the tropical heat as the last.

Chapel of St Catherine   CHURCH

About 100m to the west of the Church of St Francis of Assisi stands the small Chapel of St Catherine. An earlier chapel was erected on this site by Portuguese conqueror Afonso de Albuquerque in 1510 to commemorate his triumphant entry into the city on St Catherine's Day. In 1534 the chapel was granted cathedral status by Pope Paul III and was subsequently rebuilt; the inscribed stone added during rebuilding states that Afonso de Albuquerque actually entered the city at this spot, and thus it's believed that the chapel stands on what used to be the main gate of the Muslim city, then known as Ela.

Church & Convent of St Cajetan   CHURCH

Modelled on the original design of St Peter's in Rome, this impressive church was built by Italian friars of the Order of Theatines, sent here by Pope Urban VIII to preach Christianity in the kingdom of Golconda (near Hyderabad). The friars, however, were refused entry to Golconda, so settled instead at Old Goa in 1640. The construction of the church began in 1655, and although it's perhaps less interesting Old Goa's other churches, it's still a beautiful building and the only domed church remaining in Goa.

Though the altar is dedicated to Our Lady of Divine Providence, the church is named after the founder of the Theatine order, St Cajetan (1480–1547), a contemporary of St Francis Xavier. Born in Vicenza, St Cajetan spent his whole life in Italy, establishing the Order of Theatines in Rome in 1524. He was known for his work in hospitals and with 'incurables', and for his high moral stance in an increasingly corrupt Roman Catholic church. He was canonised in 1671.

The facade of the church is classical in design and the four niches on the front contain statues of apostles. Inside, clever use of internal buttresses and four huge pillars have given the interior a cruciform construction, above the centre of which is the towering dome. The inscription around the inside of the base of the dome is a verse from the Gospel of St Matthew. The largest of the altars on the right-hand side of the church is dedicated to St Cajetan himself. On the left side are paintings illustrating episodes in the life of St Cajetan; in one it appears, quite peculiarly, that he is being breastfed at some distance by an angel whose aim is remarkably accurate. Traditionally, the last mortal remains of deceased Portuguese governors were kept in the church's crypt, beneath the reredos, in lead coffins until their shipment home to their final resting place. The last few, forgotten for more than three decades, were finally sent back to Lisbon in 1992.

Adjoining the church, the Convent of St Cajetan is nowadays a college for recently ordained priests; next door, immediately to the west, you'll see a freestanding basalt doorway, atop five steps, which is the only remains of the grand palace of Goa's 16th-century Muslim ruler Adil Shah. This was later converted into the notorious Palace of the Inquisition, in whose dungeons countless 'heretics' languished, awaiting their dreadful fate. The palace was torn down in the 18th century and its materials repurposed for building in Panaji.

Ruins of the Church of St Augustine   RUIN
Standing on Holy Hill (Monte Santo) is perhaps the most mournful memorial to Old Goa's fallen might. All that's left today of the Church of St Augustine is the 46m-high tower, which served as a belfry and formed part of the church's facade. The few other remnants are choked with creepers and weeds, making picking your way among them rather difficult. The church was constructed in 1602 by Augustinian friars who had arrived in Old Goa in 1587 and was abandoned in 1835.

As Old Goa emptied due to a continual series of deadly epidemics, the church fell into neglect and the vault collapsed in 1842. In 1931 the facade and half the tower fell down, followed by more sections in 1938. The tower's huge bell was moved in 1871 to the Church of Our Lady of the Immaculate Conception (p79) in Panaji, where it can be seen (and heard) today.

Church & Convent of St Monica   CHURCH
Work on this three-storey laterite church and convent commenced in 1606 and was completed in 1627, only to burn down nine years later. Reconstruction began the following year and it's from this time that

THE TALE OF CATERINA & GARCIA

Old Goa at one time was full of sex and scandal, and the graves of Garcia de Sá and Caterina a Piró, in Old Goa's demure Church of Our Lady of the Rosary (p100), have their own lascivious tale to tell.

Caterina a Piró, a 'commoner' by birth, was the first Portuguese woman to arrive in the new colony of Old Goa, apparently departing Portugal in an attempt to flee the scandal surrounding her affair with a Portuguese nobleman named Garcia de Sá. The star-crossed pair, however, were destined to meet again, when de Sá was made one of Goa's earliest governors.

Under pressure from the newly arrived St Francis Xavier, de Sá was finally persuaded to do the honourable deed and marry Caterina, who, unfortunately, was already on her deathbed at the time. Her finely carved tomb, at a 'respectful' distance from Garcia's, might suggest to some that the relationship was never *exactly* true love.

the current buildings date. Once known as the 'Royal Monastery' because of the royal patronage that it enjoyed, the building comprised the first nunnery in the East but, like the other religious institutions, it was crippled by the banning of the religious orders and, though it didn't immediately close, it was finally abandoned when the last sister died in 1885.

During the 1950s and '60s the buildings housed first Portuguese and then Indian troops, before being returned to the church in 1968. The building is now used by nuns of the Mater Dei Institute and was closed for renovations at the time of writing, but might open to visitors in the future. The high point of a visit is a peek at the 'miraculous' cross behind the high altar, said to have opened its eyes in 1636, when blood began to drip from its crown of thorns.

Museum of Christian Art   MUSEUM
(www.museumofchristianart.com; admission ₹50, camera ₹100; ⊘9am-6pm) This excellent museum, in a stunningly restored space within the 1627 Convent of St Monica, contains a collection of statues, paintings and sculptures, though the setting warrants a visit in its own right. Interestingly, many of the works of Goan Christian art made during the Portuguese era, including some of those on display here, were produced by local Hindu artists.

Church of Our Lady of the Rosary   CHURCH
Passing beneath the buttresses of the Convent of St Monica, about 250m further along the road is the Church of Our Lady of the Rosary, which stands on the top of a high bluff. It's one of the earliest churches in Goa; legend has it that Afonso de Albuquerque surveyed the action during his troops' attack on the Muslim city from this bluff and vowed to build a church there in thanks for his victory. It's also thought to be here that St Francis Xavier gave his first sermon upon his arrival in Old Goa.

The church, which has been beautifully restored, is Manueline in style and refreshingly simple in design. There are excellent views of the Mandovi River and Divar Island from the church's dramatic position, but unfortunately the building is frequently locked.

The only ornaments on the outside of the church are simple rope-twist devices, which bear testimony to Portugal's reliance on the sea. Inside the same is true; the reredos is wonderfully plain after all the gold decoration in the churches down in the centre of Old Goa, and the roof consists simply of a layer of tiles. Set into the floor in front of the altar is the tombstone of one of Goa's early governors, Garcia de Sá, and set into the northern wall of the chancel is that of his wife, Caterina a Piró.

Chapel of St Anthony   CHURCH
The Chapel of St Anthony, dedicated to the saint of the Portuguese army and navy, was one of the earliest to be built in Goa, again on the directions of Afonso de Albuquerque in order to celebrate the assault on the city. Like the other institutions around it, St Anthony's was abandoned in 1835 but was brought back into use at the end of the 19th century and is now partly in use as a convent.

Viceroy's Arch   MONUMENT
Perhaps the best way to arrive in Old Goa is the same way that visitors did in the city's heyday. Approaching along the wide Mandovi River, new arrivals would have first glimpsed the city's busy wharf just in front of the symbolic arched entrance to the city.

This archway, known as the Viceroy's Arch, was erected by Vasco da Gama's grandson, Francisco da Gama, who became viceroy in 1597. On the side facing the river the arch (which was restored in 1954 following a collapse) is ornamented with the deer emblem on Vasco da Gama's coat of arms. Above it in the centre of the archway is a statue of da Gama himself.

On the side facing the city is a sculpture of a European woman wielding a sword over an Indian, who is lying under her feet. No prizes for guessing the message here, as the Inquisition made its way liberally across the city. The arch originally had a third storey with a statue of St Catherine.

🛏 Sleeping & Eating

The only real reason to stay in Old Goa's solitary hotel is to be here early in the morning before the day-trippers arrive, and at night after they've left. A string of little tourist restaurants near the bus stop offer snacks, chai and thalis.

Old Goa Residency   HOTEL $
(✔0832-2285013, 0832-2285327; d without/with AC ₹980/1250; ❋) The GTDC's hotel isn't flash, but it's reasonably good value and a comfortable distance from everything you're here to see in Old Goa.

❶ Information

Old Goa has no tourist office, but willing tour guides linger outside the main churches. Ask at the Museum of Christian Art about walking tours of the whole site. You can also enquire at the Archaeological Museum (p98), which stocks books on Old Goa, including S Rajagopalan's excellent booklet *Old Goa*, published by the Archaeological Survey of India. One of the most comprehensive is *Old Goa: the Complete Guide* by Oscar de Noronha (2004).

❶ Getting There & Away

There are frequent buses to Old Goa (₹10, 25 minutes) from the Kadamba bus stand in Panaji. Buses to Panaji or Ponda leave when full (around every 10 minutes) from either the main roundabout or the bus stop/ATM just beside the Tourist Inn restaurant.

DIVAR'S FESTA DAS BANDEIRAS

Many of the visible inhabitants of Divar Island are women, since a large number of Divar's male population have left home to seek their fortunes on the construction sites of the Middle East and elsewhere in Asia. Each year, in January, they return home to celebrate the Festa das Bandeiras (Flag Festival), during which they parade around Piedade, waving flags from their adoptive homes. The tradition is thought to stem from an ancient pagan Harvest Festival, during which the villagers marked the boundaries of their land by marching about it, wielding weapons. Today the most dangerous part of the proceedings is the brandishing of pea-shooters.

Divar Island

Stepping off the ferry from Old Goa onto beautiful little riverine Divar Island, you have the distinct feeling of entering the land that time forgot. Surrounded by marshy waters and criss-crossed with sleepy single-lane roads, the island makes for lovely, languid exploration, and though there's not much particularly to see, it's a serene and seldom-visited place to take in the atmosphere of old-time rural Goa.

The largest settlement on the island is sleepy but picturesque Piedade. But Divar, whose name stems from the Konkani *dev* and *vaddi* (translated as 'place of the Gods'), has an important Hindu history that belies its modern day tranquillity.

Before the coming of the Portuguese, Divar was the site of two particularly important temples – the Saptakoteshwara Temple (moved across the river to Bicholim when the Portuguese began to persecute the Hindus), as well as a Ganesh temple that stood on the solitary hill in Piedade. The former contained a powerful Shivalingam (phallic symbol representing the god Shiva), which was smuggled during the Inquisition to Naroa on the opposite side of the river, just before more than 1500 Divar residents were forcibly converted to Christianity. It's likely that the Ganesh temple, meanwhile, was destroyed by Muslim troops near the end of the 15th century, since the first church on this site was built in around 1515.

The church that occupies the hill today, the Church of Our Lady of Compassion, combines an impressive facade with an engagingly simple interior. The ceiling is picked out in plain white stucco designs, and the windows are set well back into the walls, allowing only a dim light to penetrate into the church; the views alone, however, make Piedade and its church worth the trip.

Beside the church, a small cemetery offers one of only a few fragments of the once grand Kadamba dynasty. The small chapel in its grounds was converted from an older Hindu shrine, and the carving, painted plaster ceiling and faint stone tracery at the window all date from before the death of the Kadamba dynasty in 1352. Look around for the priest, who'll unlock the chapel for you to take a look.

Divar Island Retreat (☎0832-2280605, 9823993155; www.divarretreatgoa.com; r incl breakfast ₹3500; 🖥🗶), a divine family-run homestay in a beautiful old Portuguese-style mansion, is reason enough to stay on Divar. The 12 individually decorated rooms come with bathroom and flat-screen TV and are arranged around a pretty garden and pool. It's in the main village but there's no sign – call ahead.

Divar Island can only be reached by one of three free vehicle ferry services. A boat from Old Goa (near the Viceroy's Arch) runs to the south side of the island, while the east end of the island is connected by ferry

CHURCH OF ST LAWRENCE, AGASSIM

About 3km south of Goa Velha, at the south end of the small village of Agassim, is the Church of St Lawrence, a plain and battered-looking building that houses one of the most flamboyantly decorated reredos (ornamental screen) in Goa. The heavily gilded construction behind the altar is unique not only for its wealth of detail but also for its peculiar design, which has multitudes of candlesticks projecting from the reredos itself. The panelled blue-and-white ceiling of the chancel sets the scene.

to Naroa in the Bicholim taluk (district). Another ferry operates to Ribandar from the southwest of the island. Ferries run frequently from around 7am to 8pm.

Goa Velha

Though it's hard to believe it today, the little village of Goa Velha – nowadays just a blur of roadside buildings on a trip south towards Margao along the national highway NH17 – was once home to Govepuri, a grand international port and capital city, attracting Arab traders who settled the surrounding area, rich from the spoils of the spice trade.

Before the establishment of Old Goa (then known as Ela) as Goa's Muslim capital around 1472, Govepuri, clinging to the banks of the Zuari River, flourished under the Hindu Kadamba dynasty. It was only centuries later, long after grand Govepuri had fallen, that the place was renamed Goa Velha by the Portuguese, to distinguish it from their new capital, Old Goa, known to them simply as Goa.

The city, which in its heyday was southwest India's wealthiest, was established by the Kadambas around 1054, but in 1312 was almost totally destroyed by Muslim invaders from the north, and over the following years was repeatedly plagued by Muslim invasions. It wasn't until Goa came under the control of the Hampi-based Vijayanagar Empire in 1378 that trade revived, but by this time the fortunes of the old capital had declined beyond repair, due to both its crushing destruction and the gradual silting-up of its once lucrative port. In 1472

the Muslim Bahmani sultanate took Goa, destroyed what remained of Govepuri, and moved the capital to Old Goa.

Just off the main road at the northern extent of Goa Velha is the Church of St Andrew, which hosts an annual festival. On the Monday a fortnight before Easter, 30 statues of saints are taken from their storage place in Old Goa and paraded around the roads of the village. The festivities include a small fair, and the crowds that attend this festival are so vast that police have to restrict movement on the NH17 highway that runs through the village.

The procession has its origins in the 17th century when, at the prompting of the Franciscans, a number of lavishly decked-out life-sized statues were paraded through the area as a reminder to locals of the lives of the saints and as an attempt to curb the licentiousness of the day. Originally the processions started and ended at Pilar, but in 1834 the religious orders were forced to leave Goa and the statues were transferred to the Church of St Andrew. Processions lapsed and many of the original sculptures were lost or broken, but in 1895 subscriptions were raised to obtain a new set, which is still used today, and the procession was reinstated with gusto.

Pilar

A few kilometres north of Goa Velha, and 12km southeast of Panaji, set on a hill high above the surrounding countryside, is Pilar Seminary, one of four theological colleges built by the Portuguese. Only two of these seminaries still survive, the other being Rachol Seminary near Margao. The hill upon which the seminary stands was once the site of a large and ancient Hindu temple, dedicated to Shiva; it's thought that this was the Goveshwar Mandir, from which the name Goa is thought to have derived. The college was established here in 1613 by Capuchin monks, naming it Our Lady of Pilar, after the statue they brought with them from Spain.

Abandoned in 1835 when the Portuguese expelled the religious orders, the seminary was rescued by the Carmelites in 1858 and became the headquarters of the Missionary Society of St Francis Xavier in 1890. The movement gradually petered out and in 1936 the buildings were handed over to the Xaverian League. Today the seminary is still in use, as a training centre for missionaries, and is also the site of local pilgrimages by those who come to give thanks for the life of Father Agnelo de Souza, a director of the seminary in the early 20th century who was beatified after his death.

Aside from the beautiful views afforded from its roof terrace, the seminary is home to a small **museum** (⊙ 8am-1pm & 3-6pm Mon-Sat) FREE, which holds some of the Hindu relics discovered on-site, as well as some lovely religious paintings, carvings and artefacts. The 1st floor of the building houses a small, but brilliantly lit, chapel.

At the bottom of the hill is the old **Church of Our Lady of Pilar**, which still contains the original statue brought from Spain, along with lots of tombstones of Portuguese nobility, the grave of the locally famed Father Agnelo, and some attractive paintings in an alcove at the rear of the chapel.

Ponda

Workaday Ponda city has few attractions in its own right, but it's the urban gateway to Goa's interesting Hindu temple heartland, as well as to the fragrant spice plantations that pepper the countryside to the north and east.

◎ Sights

Safa Shahouri Masjid
MOSQUE

(Safa Masjid) The Safa Shahouri Masjid, Goa's oldest remaining mosque, is 2km from the town centre, on Ponda's northern outskirts. Built by Bijapuri ruler Ali Adil Shah in 1560, it was originally surrounded by gardens, fountains and a palace, and is said to have matched the mosques at Bijapur in size and quality. Today little remains of the former grandeur, despite attempts at restoration by the Archaeological Survey of India..

🛏 Sleeping & Eating

There's little reason to stay overnight in Ponda, but it has a scattering of unremarkable hotels ranged along the main road, with budget rooms priced from ₹600.

Hotel Sungrace
HOTEL $

(☑ 0832-2311241; www.hotelsungrace.in; 9 Sadar; s/d without AC ₹700/800, s/d/ste with AC ₹800/900/1700; ❄) Clean, bright but not terribly exciting rooms are stacked atop a busy restaurant, which serves up the usual range of Indian and Chinese dishes. Book ahead during festival and holiday periods, as its 28 rooms are frequently filled with Indian tourists.

Ponda & Around

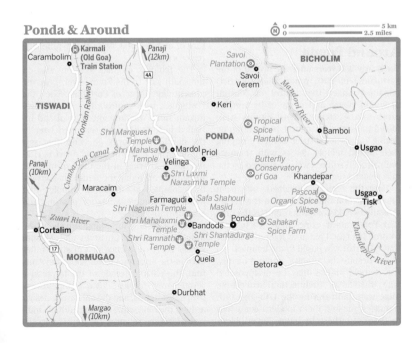

Hotel Sun Inn HOTEL $$

(☑0832-2318180; www.hotelsuninn.com; s/d incl breakfast from ₹1900/2500; ✲) Sun Inn is a comfortable multistorey business hotel a few kilometres from central Ponda on the highway to Panaji. Expect clean, orderly rooms with TV and air-con. The upper-floor rooms have good views over the countryside.

Sandeep Cold Drinks FAST FOOD $

(snacks ₹20) This little cart on the main highway specialises in just one thing: *vada pau* (deep-fried spicy fried potato served with a fluffy fresh bun). Filling and cheap.

Cafe Bhonsle INDIAN $

(☑0832-2318725; thalis from ₹80; ◷7am-10pm Mon-Sat, to 3pm Sun) This all-vegetarian restaurant, on the right-hand side of the main road when entering town from the south, makes a good lunch stop, whipping out high-speed thalis, an extensive menu of Indian and Chinese food, and a mean *bhaji-pau*.

ⓘ Getting There & Away

There are regular buses from Ponda to Panaji (₹20, 1½ hours) and Margao (₹18, one hour). To explore the region's surrounding temples and spice farms, you'll need your own transport or a taxi; alternatively, take one of the GTDC's lightning day trips.

Around Ponda

For nearly 250 years after the arrival of the Portuguese in 1510, Ponda taluk (district) remained under the control of Muslim or Hindu rulers, and many of its temples came into existence when Hindus were forced to escape Portuguese persecution by fleeing across its district border, bringing their sacred temple deities with them as centuries-old edifices were destroyed by the new colonial regime.

Here the temples remained, safe from the destruction that occurred in the Velhas Conquistas (Old Conquests), and by the time that Ponda itself came under Portuguese control, increased religious tolerance meant that no threat was posed to the temples.

But despite the temples' intrepid history, true temple junkies may be disappointed with the area's architectural collection. Most were built during the 17th and 18th centuries, making them modern compared to those elsewhere in India. Nevertheless,

what they lack in ancient architecture they make up for with their highly holy ancient deities, salvaged on devout Hindus' flights from probable death at the hands of the Inquisition.

The temples are clustered in two main areas: the first in the countryside 5km west of town, and the second north along the route of the NH4A highway. If you're not a true temple-traipser, the two with most appeal are the Shri Mahalsa and Shri Manguesh temples, both near the villages of Priol and Mardol. Close to the busy highway, they are easy to reach by bus; take any bus between Panaji and Margao that runs via Ponda and ask your driver to drop you off near the temples. To get to other temples of the region, it's easiest to hire a scooter or motorbike, or negotiate a day rate with a taxi from Panaji, Ponda or Margao.

The other reason to visit the Ponda region is to visit one of the touristy but aromatic spice plantations offering lavish lunches, elephants and informative tours.

◉ Sights

Shri Manguesh Temple HINDU TEMPLE

Around 9km north of Ponda, this temple is one of the most visited of Goa's Hindu temples, admirably combining two key features of Goan Hinduism: first, it's dedicated to a solely Goan deity (in this case the local god Manguesh), and second, it exhibits the mixture of architectural styles that typifies the region's temples.

The temple's original location was on the south side of the Zuari River, near the present-day village of Cortalim. When the Portuguese took control, its ancient Shivalingam stone was brought to Priol and installed in a new temple (enlarged later in the mid-18th century), an effort that saw Hindus from Portuguese-held districts risking death, arriving in the dead of night to worship here. Today the temple has grown to encompass a substantial complex that includes accommodation for pilgrims and administrative offices.

Architecturally, Shri Manguesh shows the influences of both Christian and Muslim styles. There's evidence of Christian influence in the octagonal tower above the sanctum, the pillared facade of the impressive seven-storey *deepastambha* (lamp tower), the largest in Goa, and the balustrade design around the roof, while the domed roofs indicate a Muslim influence. The tank (reservoir)

PONDA'S SPICE PLANTATIONS

The Ponda region is the centre of commercial spice farms in Goa and several have opened their doors as tourist operations, offering a guided tour of the plantation, buffet thali-style lunch, and in some cases, elephant rides and cultural shows.

These farms typically produce spices such as vanilla, pepper, cardamom, nutmeg, chilli and turmeric, along with crops such as cashew, betel nut, coconut, pineapple and papaya.

Savoi Plantation (✆0832-2340272, 9822133309; adult/child ₹600/300; ◔9am-4.30pm) This 200-year-old plantation, 12km north of Ponda, is the least touristy, elephant-free and the cream of the crop in the region. You'll be welcomed with fresh pomegranate juice, cardamom bananas and other organic treats, and find knowledgeable guides keen to walk you through the 40-hectare plantation at your own pace. Local crafts are also for sale and there are a couple of cottages for overnight stays.

Sahakari Spice Farm (✆0832-2312394; www.sahakarifarms.com; admission incl lunch ₹400; ◔8am-4.30pm) This well-touristed farm just 2km from Ponda, near the village of Curti, is also a good place for elephant rides (₹700) and elephant bathing (₹700) in the small river.

Pascoal Organic Spice Village (✆0832-2344268; www.pascoalfarm.com; farm tour & lunch adult/child ₹400/200; ◔9am-4pm) About 7km east of Ponda, Pascoal offers bamboo river-rafting, elephant rides and cultural shows, along with farm tours and lunch. You can stay here overnight in innovative mud cottages.

Tropical Spice Plantation (✆0832-2340329; www.tropicalspiceplantation.com; Keri; admission incl lunch ₹400; ◔9am-4pm) Accessed via a bamboo bridge, around 5km north of Ponda, this is one of the most popular farms with tour groups and visitors. An entertaining 45-minute tour of the spice plantation is followed by a banana-leaf buffet lunch. Elephant rides/bathings are available for an extra ₹700.

PANAJI & CENTRAL GOA AROUND PONDA

in front of the temple is the oldest part of the complex. If you walk down to the right-hand side of the temple you can also see the giant *raths* (chariots) that are used to parade the deities during the temple's festival, which takes place in the last week of January or the first week of February.

Manguesh, the temple's god, is said in Goan Hindu mythology to be an incarnation of Shiva. The story goes that Shiva, having lost everything to his wife Parvati in a game of dice, came to Goa in a self-imposed exile. When Parvati eventually came looking for him, he decided to frighten her and disguised himself as a tiger. In horror, Parvati cried out 'Trahi mam girisha!' (Oh lord of mountains, save me!), whereupon Shiva resumed his normal form. The words *mam girisha* became associated with the tale and Shiva's tiger incarnation, with time, became known as Manguesh. The Shivalingam left to mark the spot where all this happened was eventually discovered by a shepherd, and a temple was built to house it at the temple's original location near Cortalim.

Shri Mahalsa Temple   HINDU TEMPLE

The Mahalsa Temple, 1km down the road from the Shri Manguesh Temple, is in the tiny village of Mardol. This temple's deity originally resided in an ancient shrine in the village of Verna in Salcete *taluka* in the south. The buildings were reputedly so beautiful that even the Portuguese priest whose job it was to oversee their destruction requested that they should be preserved and converted into a church. Permission was refused, but before the work began in 1543 the deity was smuggled to safety.

Mahalsa is a uniquely Goan deity, this time an incarnation of Vishnu in female form. Various legends suggest how Mahalsa came into being. In one, Vishnu, who was in a particularly tight corner during a struggle with the forces of evil, disguised himself as Mohini, the most beautiful woman ever seen, in order to distract his enemies. The trick worked and Mohini, with her name corrupted to Mahalsa, was born. To complicate matters, Mahalsa also fits into the pantheon as an incarnation of Shiva, the destroyer. In general, however, she is regarded

THE CAVES OF KHANDEPAR

In the village of Khandepar, 5km northeast of Ponda, and set back in the dense forest behind the Mandovi River, are four small (well-hidden) rock-cut **caves** believed to have been carved into the laterite stone around the 12th century, though some archaeologists date their origin back as early as the 9th century. These are among Goa's oldest remaining historical treasures, but were only rediscovered in 1970. Ask around locally for the exact whereabouts of the caves – someone will eventually point you in the right direction.

Thought to have been used by a community of Buddhist monks, each of the four caves consists of two simple cells, with tiered roofs added in the 10th or 11th centuries by the Kadamba dynasty who, it's thought, appropriated the caves and turned them into Hindu temples. The fourth cave supports the Buddhist theory, containing a pedestal used for prayer and meditation. There are also niches in the walls for oil lamps, and pegs carved for hanging clothes. The first cave, meanwhile, has a lotus medallion carved into its ceiling, typical of the later Kadambas.

by her devotees as a representative of peace; for this, and for her multifaceted identity, she has many devotees.

Once you pass through the entrance gate, off the busy side street, the temple is pleasantly peaceful. The inner area is impressive, with huge wooden pillars and slatted windows and, like most of the other temples in this area, an ornamented silver frame surrounds the doorway to the sanctum. Walk around to the back of the main building and peer through the archway to the water tank; the combination of the ancient stonework, palm trees and paddy fields beyond is quite a sight.

In front of the temple stands a large *deepastambha* and a 12.5m-high brass oil lamp that is lit during festivals; it's thought to be the largest such lamp in the world.

In addition to the annual chariot procession held in February for the **Zatra festival**, the temple is also famous for two other festivals. Jasmine flowers are offered in tribute to the god Mahalsa during the **Zaiyanchi Puja festival**, which falls in August or September. The full-moon festival of **Kojagiri Purnima** is also celebrated here; on this particular night (usually in September) the goddess Lakshmi (Laxmi) descends to earth to bestow wealth and prosperity on those who stay awake to observe the night-time vigil.

Shri Laxmi Narasimha Temple   HINDU TEMPLE
Almost immediately after leaving the village of Mardol on the main road, a side road to the right takes you up a hill towards the little village of Velinga and the Laxmi Narasimha Temple, one of the most attractive and secluded temples around Ponda. It's dedicated to Narasimha, or Narayan, a half-lion

half-human incarnation of Vishnu, which he created to defeat a formidable adversary. The deity was moved here from the district of Salcete in 1567, and the most picturesque part of the temple is the old water tank, to the left of the compound as you enter, spring-fed and entered via a ceremonial gateway.

Although the temple has a sign by the door announcing that entry is for the 'devoted and believers only,' respectful nonbelievers will probably be allowed to have a look.

Shri Naguesh Temple   HINDU TEMPLE
South of Shri Laxmi Narasimha, in the village of Bandode, is the small and peaceful Naguesh Temple. The most striking part of the temple is the ancient water tank, with its overhanging palms, fishy depths and weathered stones. Also of note are colourful images in relief around the base of the *deepastambha,* and the frieze of Ramayana scenes running inside along the tops of the pillars. Unlike its neighbours, this temple was in existence well before Albuquerque ever set foot in Goa, but the buildings you see today are newish and rather uninteresting. The temple is dedicated to Shiva, known in this incarnation as Naguesh, and is particularly rich in animal representation.

Shri Mahalaxmi Temple   HINDU TEMPLE
Only 4km outside Ponda, and a stone's throw from Naguesh Temple, is the relatively uninspiring Mahalaxmi Temple. The goddess Mahalaxmi, looked upon as the mother of the world, was particularly worshipped by the Shilahara rulers and by the Kadambas, and thus has featured prominently in the Hindu pantheon in southern India. Here

she wears a lingam (phallic symbol of Shiva) on her head, symbolising her connection with Shiva.

Shri Ramnath Temple   HINDU TEMPLE
Though undoubtedly one of Ponda's all-round uglier temples, Shri Ramnath is notable for the impressive and extravagant silver screen on the door to the sanctum. Other temples have similar finery but the work here is exceptional, in particular the two unusual scenes depicted at the top of the lintel. The lower of the two depicts kneeling figures worshipping a lingam, while the upper one shows Vishnu lying with Lakshmi, his consort, on a couch made up of the coils of a snake. The lingam installed in the sanctum was brought from Loutolim in Salcete taluk in the 16th century.

Shri Shantadurga Temple   HINDU TEMPLE
Surrounded by forest and paddy fields, the Shri Shantadurga Temple is one of the most famous shrines in Goa and is consequently packed with those who come to worship, as well as day-trippers brought in by the bus load. Hustle past the rows of roadside hawkers to get a look at this heavily European-inspired creation, built in 1738, 200 years after its deity had been smuggled in from Quelossim, not far from present-day southern Colva.

The goddess Shantadurga is another form taken by Parvati, Shiva's consort. As the most powerful of the goddesses, Parvati could either adopt a violent form, Durga, or she could help to bring peace, as Shanta. The legend goes that during a particularly savage quarrel between Shiva and Vishnu she appeared in her Durga form and helped to make peace between the two gods – thus embodying the contradiction that the name Shantadurga implies. In Goa she has come to be worshipped as the goddess of peace and has traditionally had a large following.

Butterfly Conservatory of Goa   BUTTERFLY PARK
(☑0832-2985174; www.bcogoa.org; Priol; admission ₹100; ⊙9am-4.30pm) Also called Mystic Meadows, this small butterfly sanctuary, 5km north of Ponda, houses more than 100 species of free-flying butterflies (eg it's not enclosed). It's a labour of love for the owners and worth a look if you're visiting nearby spice plantations

Bondla Wildlife Sanctuary

At only 8 sq km, Bondla Wildlife Sanctuary (adult/child ₹20/10, camera/video camera ₹30/150; ⊙9am-5.30pm Fri-Wed) is Goa's smallest protected wildlife sanctuary. Though not particularly remote, it's really only accessible if you have your own transport or a car and driver. You're unlikely to see animals just by wandering around the sanctuary, though the park's jungly reaches are home to wild boar, gaurs (Indian bison), monkeys, jackals, leopard and deer. If you're committed, however, it's a butterfly-spotter and birdwatcher's paradise. The sanctuary is about 10km from Usgao village. A one-way taxi here from Panaji should cost around ₹1000, or ₹500 from Ponda.

Bondla has Goa's only zoo, a very small moated offering, which is a bit sad considering it's within a wildlife sanctuary; still, it gives you a look at tigers, elephants, porcupines and snakes. There's also a nature interpretation centre and botanical gardens (neither of which are worth the trip out here in themselves).

There are some Forest Department cottages here if you want to spend the night.

Molem & Around

If you're keen to visit Goa's largest protected wildlife area, the state's oldest temple, or the second-largest waterfalls in India, then make tracks for Molem, a dusty village on the main road east into Karnataka state.

Molem's sole and upscale accommodation option, Dudhsagar Spa Resort (☑0832-2612319; www.dudhsagarsparesort.com; d/tent incl breakfast ₹4500/6600; ✳@☀) is a relatively slick series of bungalows and luxury tents, set up around a garden. The tents are a delight, with huge beds, sleek modern furnishings and gorgeous deep baths, set on the quiet side of the site amid tall trees filled with monkeys. Frogs, geckos and assorted wildlife are likely to make an appearance, possibly in your tent. It's situated near the Molem forest checkpoint. Staff can organise excursions into the park. There is also a spa with steam baths and sauna, three restaurants and a nice garden pool, and a range of ayurvedic and detox treatment programs.

PANAJI & CENTRAL GOA BONDLA WILDLIFE SANCTUARY

GOA'S TEMPLE ARCHITECTURE

Though Goa's temples often exhibit a strange and colourful blend of traditional Hindu, Christian and Muslim architectural elements, several of their key components remain constant.

On entering a temple, you'll first reach the *prakara* (courtyard), which surrounds the whole complex, often encompassing a *tirtha* (water tank), in which worshippers bathe before continuing into the temple. Next you'll pass one or two pillared *mandapas* (pillared pavilion), used for music, dancing and congregational prayer.

Through these, you'll arrive at the *antarala* (main shrine), surrounded by a *pradakshina* (passage) for circumambulation, and flanked by two shrines of the temple's lesser deities. Within the main shrine is the *garbhagriha* (inner sanctum), which houses the *devta* (sacred deity) – in elaborate statue or simple stone form – and forms the most sacred part of the temple. Only high-caste Brahmin priests are admitted to the shrine room, where they perform regular ritual purifications. Topping off the shrine room is the *sikhara* (sanctuary tower), which symbolises the Divine Mountain, the source of the sacred River Ganges.

Sanctuary towers tend to have been influenced by Portuguese church trends, often resulting in octagonal towers topped by a copper dome. *Mandapa* roofs are often terracotta-tiled, decorated with oriental images imported from Macau, another Portuguese colony, and embellished with Muslim motifs. The most distinct of all, however, are the Maratha-conceived *deepastambhas* or *deepmals* (lamp towers) – multistoreyed pagodas usually standing beside the temple's main entrance, in which multiple cubby holes hold dozens of oil lamps stunningly illuminated on special occasions and during the weekly ceremonial airing of the *devta*.

Bhagwan Mahavir Wildlife Sanctuary

The entrance to Bhagwan Mahavir Wildlife Sanctuary (adult/child ₹20/10, camera/video camera ₹30/150; ◎8.30am-5.30pm) lies a stone's throw from Molem and, with an area of 240 sq km, this is the largest of Goa's four protected wildlife areas; it also encompasses the 107-sq-km Molem National Park. Unless you're on a tour, however, you might have problems actually gaining access to the park's quiet, unmarked trails. Tickets are available at the Forest Interpretation Centre, 2km before the park entrance, close to Molem town.

The best way to explore the park is to organise a tour through a travel agent or hire a jeep for the day in Molem or Colem. Most tours will also visit Dudhsagar Falls and the Devil's Canyon. At Dudhsagar Spa Resort staff can arrange trips into the park's interior.

Shy and hard-to-spot wildlife includes jungle cats, Malayan giant squirrels, gaurs, sambars, leopards, chitals (spotted deer), slender loris, Malayan pythons and cobras. There's an observation platform a few kilometres into the park; as with most parks, the best time to see wildlife is in the early morning or late evening.

Dudhsagar Falls

Situated in the far southeastern corner of the Bhagwan Mahavir Wildlife Sanctuary, Goa's most impressive waterfall splashes down just west of the border with Karnataka state, and at 603m this is the second highest in India after Jog Falls. The falls are best visited as soon after monsoon as possible (October is perfect), when the water levels are highest and the cascades earn their misty nomenclature, Dudhsagar, meaning, in Konkani, 'Sea of Milk'.

Getting to the falls starts with a trip to the village of Colem, around 7km south of Molem, either by car or by the scenic 8.15am local train from Margao – the South Central Railway line actually crosses over the falls offering excellent views. Check return train times in advance, as they vary seasonally. From Colem, pick up a shared jeep (₹400 per person for six people) for the bumpy 45-minute journey, then it's a quick clamber up over the rocks to reach the falls.

The jeep takes you into the sanctuary, through a number of extremely scenic jungle and forest areas (there are three streams to be forded, which would make this trip tricky – though not impossible – by Enfield or other motorbike). En route, you'll pass

Devil's Canyon, a beautiful gorge with a river running between the steep-sided rocks.

At the falls themselves swimming is possible (life jackets are provided for ₹50), but don't picture yourself taking a romantic swim on your own – there will be plenty of other bathers joining in. You can also walk the distance to the head of the falls (though it's unwise without a local to guide you), a real uphill slog, but affording beautiful views.

Goa Tourism runs one of its trademark whirlwind day trips, the 'Dudhsagar Special' (₹1200) to the waterfall, with stops at Old Goa and Ponda, lunch at Molem, then the Shri Mahadeva Temple at Tambdi Surla. Tours depart at 9am from Calangute, Mapusa, Panaji or Miramar on Wednesday and Sunday, departing 9am and returning 6pm. Private travel agents also offer tours.

It's possible to trek the 11km from Colem to the falls in around four hours, but organise a local guide in advance and start early.

Colem

The small village of Colem (Kulem) is a train stop on the South Central Railway and the jumping off point for Dudhasaghar Falls and other Western Ghats hotspots.

Jungle Book   ELEPHANT PARK
(☑ 9822121431; www.goaecotourism.com; Bazar Wada, Colem; elephant rides/wash from ₹700) If you're looking to interact with elephants, Jungle Book, in the village of Colem, is the place. As well as elephant rides and bathing, a host of other activities are on offer, including jungle trekking, ziplining, village visits, spice plantation tours and trips to Dudhsagar Falls. Organised half-/full-day trips cost from ₹4200/5400, while an overnight trip with basic mud-hut accommodation and meals costs ₹9200. Travel agents at the beach resorts can also book these tours.

Dudhsagar Plantation   SPICE PLANTATION
(☑ 9769048726; www.dudhsagarplantation.com; guided tour per person incl lunch ₹900) A less-touristy alternative to the Ponda region spice plantations, this relatively remote farm is about 30km from Margao on the road to Colem. As well as a spice tour and lunch, you can take a dip in the river or arrange transport to the Dudhsagar Falls. Tours require a minimum five people. There's also farmstay accommodation.

Tambdi Surla

Shri Mahadeva Temple   HINDU TEMPLE
If you're a history or temple buff, don't miss the atmospheric remains of the unusual little Hindu Shri Mahadeva Temple at Tambdi Surla, 12km north of Molem. Built around the 12th century by the Kadamba dynasty, it's the only temple of dozens of its type to have survived both the years and the various conquerings and demolishings by Muslim and Portuguese forces, and probably only made it thus far due to its remote jungle setting.

No one quite knows why this spot was chosen, since historically there was no trade route passing here and no evidence of there having been any major settlement nearby.

The temple itself is very small, facing eastward so that the rays of dawn light up its deity. At the eastern end, the open-sided *mandapa* (assembly hall) is reached through doorways on three sides. The entrance to the east faces a set of steps down to the river, where ritual cleansing was carried out before worship. Inside the *mandapa* the plain slab ceiling is supported by four huge carved pillars. The clarity of the designs on the stone is testimony not only to the skill of the artisans, but also to the quality of the rock that was imported for the construction; look out for the image on one of the bases

PANAJI & CENTRAL GOA MOLEM & AROUND

BACKWOODS CAMP

For birdwatching enthusiasts, quiet, rustic **Backwoods Camp** (☑ 9822139859; www.backwoodsgoa.com; Matkan, Tambdi Surla; 1-/2-/3-day per person ₹4500/7500/11,000) ✿, in the village of Matkan near Tambdi Surla, offers one of Goa's richest experiences; you'll spot everything from Ceylon frogmouths and Asian fairy bluebirds, to puff-throated babblers and Indian pittas. Accommodation is in tents on raised forest platforms, bungalows or farmhouse rooms, and the camp makes a valiant attempt to protect this fragile bit of the Goan ecosystem, through measures including waste recycling, replanting indigenous tree species, and employing local villagers. Rates include three guided birdwatching walks daily.

THE DHANGARS

Goa's green eastern reaches are home to the Dhangars, one of the state's nomadic tribes who have lived, for centuries, on buffalo-herding. Their lifestyle, like that of many other nomadic tribes, is today threatened (in their case by deforestation and high levels of alcoholism), and many have been forced to move to cities in search of work, or attempt settled forms of agriculture. You might, however, still see them in far-flung stretches of the park, tending their lowing, leathery livestock.

of an elephant crushing a horse, thought to symbolise Kadambas' own military power at the time of the temple's inauguration.

The best examples of the carvers' skills, however, are the superb lotus-flower relief panel set in the centre of the ceiling and the finely carved pierced-stone screen that separates the outer hall from the *antarala* (main shrine), flanked by an image of Ganesh and several other deities. Finally, beyond the inner hall is the *garbhagriha* (inner sanctum), where the lingam resides.

The exterior of the temple is plain, with a squat appearance caused by the partial collapse of its *sikhara* tower. On the remains of the tower are three relief carvings depicting the three most important deities in the Hindu pantheon; on the north side is Vishnu, to the west is Shiva and to the south is Brahma.

BEYOND GOA

Hampi

📳 08394

Unreal and bewitching, the forlorn ruins of Hampi, in Karnataka state, dot an unearthly landscape that will leave you spellbound the moment you cast your eyes on it. Heaps of giant boulders perch precariously over miles of undulating terrain, their rusty hues offset by jade-green palm groves, banana plantations and paddy fields. While it's possible to see the ancient ruins and temples of this World Heritage Site in a day or two, this goes against Hampi's relaxed grain.

The main travellers' ghetto has traditionally been Hampi Bazaar, a village crammed with budget lodges, shops and restaurants, and towered over by the majestic Virupak-

sha Temple. However, recent demolitions have seen tranquil Virupapur Gaddi across the river become the new hang-out. Both offer different experiences, and it's recommendable to spend a few nights at each.

Hampi is generally a safe, peaceful place, but don't wander around the ruins after dark or alone, as it can be dangerous terrain to get lost in, especially at night.

History

Hampi and its neighbouring areas find mention in the Hindu epic Ramayana as Kishkinda, the realm of the monkey gods. In 1336 Telugu prince Harihararaya chose Hampi as the site for his new capital Vijayanagar, which – over the next couple of centuries – grew into one of the largest Hindu empires in Indian history. By the 16th century it was a thriving metropolis of about 500,000 people, its busy bazaars dabbling in international commerce, brimming with precious stones and thronging with merchants from faraway lands. All this, however, ended in a stroke in 1565, when a confederacy of Deccan sultanates razed Vijayanagar to the ground, striking a grievous blow from which it never recovered.

◉ Sights

Set over 36 sq km, there are some 3700 monuments to explore in Hampi, and it would take months if you were to do it full justice. The ruins are divided into two main areas: the Sacred Centre, around Hampi Bazaar with its temples, and the Royal Centre, towards Kamalapuram, where the Vijayanagara royalty lived and governed.

Sacred Centre

★ Virupaksha Temple   HINDU TEMPLE

(admission ₹2, camera ₹50; ☉ dawn-dusk) The focal point of Hampi Bazaar is the Virupaksha Temple, one of the city's oldest structures, and Hampi's only remaining working temple. The main *gopuram* (gateway tower), almost 50m high, was built in 1442, with a smaller one added in 1510. The main shrine is dedicated to Virupaksha, an incarnation of Shiva.

If Lakshmi, the temple elephant, and her attendant are around, she'll smooch (bless) you for a coin; she gets her morning bath at 8am down by the river ghats.

To the south, overlooking Virupaksha Temple, Hemakuta Hill has a few early ruins, including monolithic sculptures of Narasimha (Vishnu in his man-lion incarnation) and

Ganesha. At the east end of the recently abandonded Hampi Bazaar is a monolithic **Nandi statue**, around which stand colonnaded blocks of the ancient marketplace. Overlooking the site is Matanga Hill, whose summit affords dramatic views of the terrain at sunrise.

Within the now-derelict bazaar is the **Hampi Heritage Gallery** (⊙10am-1pm & 3-6pm Tue-Sun) **FREE**, exhibiting interesting historical photos of the ruins.

★**Vittala Temple**   HINDU TEMPLE
(Indian/foreigner ₹10/250, child under 15 free; ⊙8.30am-5.30pm) The undisputed highlight of the Hampi ruins, the 16th-century Vittala Temple stands amid the boulders 2km from Hampi Bazaar. Work possibly started on the temple during the reign of Krishnadevaraya (r 1509–29). It was never finished or consecrated, yet the temple's incredible sculptural work remains the pinnacle of Vijayanagar art.

The ornate **stone chariot** that stands in the courtyard is the temple's showpiece and represents Vishnu's vehicle with an image of Garuda within. Its wheels were once capable of turning. The outer 'musical' pillars reverberate when tapped. They were supposedly designed to replicate 81 different Indian instruments, but authorities have placed them out of tourists' bounds for fear of further damage, so no more do-re-mi.

As well as the main temple, whose sanctum was illuminated using a design of reflective waters, you'll find the marriage hall and prayer hall, the structures to the left and right upon entry, respectively.

Lakshimi Narasmiha   HINDU TEMPLE
An interesting stop-off along the road to the Virupaksha Temple is the 6.7m monolithic statue of the bulging-eyed Lakshimi Narasmiha in a cross-legged lotus position and topped by a hood of seven snakes.

Krishna Temple   HINDU TEMPLE
Built in 1513, the Krishna Temple is fronted by a D-cupped *apsara* and 10 incarnations of Vishnu. It's on the road to the Virupaksha Temple near Lakshimi Narasmiha.

Sule Bazaar   HISTORIC SITE
Halfway along the path from Hampi Bazaar to Vittala Temple, a track to the right leads over the rocks to deserted Sule Bazaar, one of ancient Hampi's principle centres of commerce and reputedly its red-light district. At the southern end of this area is the beautiful 16th-century **Achyutaraya Temple**.

Royal Centre & Around

While it can be accessed by a 2km foot trail from the Achyutaraya Temple, the **Royal Centre** is best reached via the Hampi–Kamalapuram road. A number of Hampi's major sites stand here.

Mahanavami-diiba   RUIN
The Mahanavami-diiba is a 12m-high three-tiered platform with intricate carvings and panoramic vistas of the walled complex of ruined temples, stepped tanks and the king's audience hall. The platform was used as a royal viewing area for the Dasara festivities, religious ceremonies and processions.

Hazarama Temple   HINDU TEMPLE
Hazarama Temple features exquisite carvings that depict scenes from the Ramayana, and polished black granite pillars.

PANAJI & CENTRAL GOA HAMPI

DEMOLISHMENT OF HAMPI BAZAAR

While in 1865 it was the Deccan sultanates who leveled Vijayanagar, today a different battle rages in Hampi, between conservationists bent on protecting Hampi's architectural heritage and the locals who have settled there.

In mid-2012 the government's master plan, which had been in the works since the mid-2000s, and which aims to classify all of Hampi's ruins as protected monuments, was dramatically and forcefully put into action. Overnight, shops, hotels and homes in Hampi Bazaar were bulldozed, reducing the atmospheric main strip to rubble, as villagers who'd made the site a living monument were evicted.

While residents were compensated with a small plot of land in Kaddirampur, 4km from the bazaar (where there is talk of new guesthouses eventually opening up), many locals remain displaced years later as they await their pay out.

While at the time of writing, rubble from the demolished buildings remained, iconic hang-outs had been destroyed and the main temple road resembled a bombed-out town, guesthouses and restaurants on the fringes of the bazaar remained intact.

Hampi & Anegundi

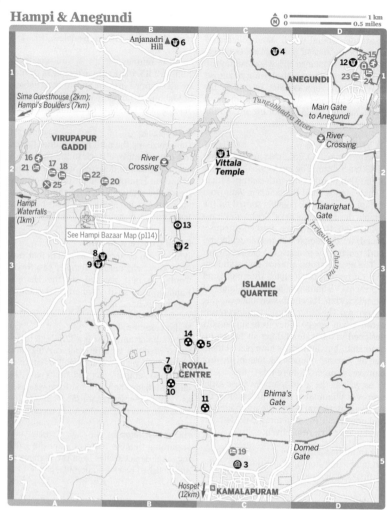

Anjanadri Hill

ANEGUNDI

Tungabhadra River

Sima Guesthouse (2km);
Hampi's Boulders (7km)

VIRUPAPUR
GADDI

River
Crossing

Main Gate
to Anegundi

River
Crossing

Vittala
Temple

Hampi
Waterfalls
(1km)

Talarighat
Gate

See Hampi Bazaar Map (p114)

Irrigation Channel

ISLAMIC
QUARTER

ROYAL
CENTRE

Bhima's
Gate

Domed
Gate

Hospet
(12km)

KAMALAPURAM

Zenana Enclosure RUIN

(Indian/foreigner ₹10/250; ⊙8.30am-5.30pm)
Northeast of the Royal Centre within the walled ladies' quarters is the Zenana Enclosure. Its peaceful grounds and manicured lawns feel like an oasis amid the arid surrounds. Here is the **Lotus Mahal**, a delicately designed pavilion that was supposedly the queen's recreational mansion. It overlooks the 11 grand **Elephant Stables** with arched entrances and domed chambers. There's also a small museum and army barracks within the high-walled enclosure.

Queen's Bath RUIN

(⊙8.30am-5.30pm) South of the Royal Centre you'll find various temples and elaborate waterworks, including the Queen's Bath, deceptively plain on the outside but amazing within, with its Indo-Islamic architecture.

Archaeological Museum MUSEUM

(Kamalapuram; ⊙10am-5pm Sat-Thu) Worth popping in for its quality collection of sculptures from local ruins, plus neolithic tools, fascinating coins, 16th-century weaponry and a large floor model of the Vijayanagar ruins.

Hampi & Anegundi

Activities

Hampi Waterfalls   WATERFALL

About a 2km walk west of Hampi Bazaar, past shady banana plantations, you can scramble over the boulders to reach the attractive Hampi 'waterfalls', a series of small whirlpools among the rocks amid superb scenery.

Bouldering & Rock Climbing

Hampi is the undisputed bouldering capital of India. The entire landscape is a climber's adventure playground made of granite crags and boulders, some bearing the marks of ancient stonemasons. *Golden Boulders* (2013) by Gerald Krug and Christiane Hupe has a ton of info on bouldering in Hampi.

Tom & Jerry   BOULDERING

(☑8277792588, 9482746697; luckykoushik1@gmail.com; Virupapur Gaddi; 2½hr class ₹500) Two local lads who are doing great work in catering to climbers' needs, providing quality mats, shoes and local knowledge. They also organise climbing trips upcountry to Badami.

Thimmaclimb   BOULDERING

(☑8762776498; www.thimmaclimb.wix.com/hampi-bouldering; Shiva Guesthouse, Virupapur Gaddi; class from ₹350-500) A small operation run by local pro Thimma, who guides, runs lessons and stocks professional equipment for hire and sale.

Birdwatching

Kishkinda Trust (TKT; ☑08533-267777; www.thekishkindatrust.org) in Anegundi has info on birdwatching in the area, which has over 230 species, including the greater flamingo. *The Birds of Hampi* (2014) by Samad Kottur is the definitive guide.

✿ Festivals & Events

Vijaya Utsav   RELIGIOUS

(Hampi Festival; ◔ Jan) Hampi's three-day extravaganza of culture, heritage and the arts in January.

Virupaksha Car Festival   FESTIVAL

(◔Mar/Apr) The Virupaksha Car Festival in March/April is a big event, with a colourful procession characterised by a giant wooden chariot (the temple car from Virupaksha Temple) being pulled along the main strip of Hampi bazaar.

🛏 Sleeping

Most guesthouses are cosy family-run digs, perfect for the budget traveller. A handful of places also have larger, more comfortable rooms with air-con and TV.

Hampi Bazaar

★ Padma Guest House   GUESTHOUSE $

(☑08394-241331; padmaguesthouse@gmail.com; d from ₹800; ❄ 🖥) In a quiet corner of Hampi

Hampi Bazaar

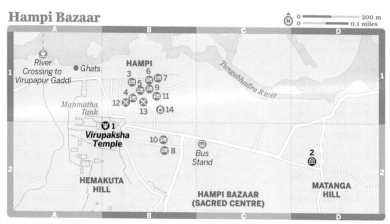

Hampi Bazaar

Bazaar, this amiable guesthouse feels more like a homestay, with basic, squeaky-clean rooms, many of which have views of Virupaksha Temple.

Archana Guest House
GUESTHOUSE $
(☎ 08394-241547; addihampi@yahoo.com; d from ₹600; ☎) On the riverfront, quiet and cheerful Archana is one of the few places in the bazaar with a view. It's set over two houses opposite each other, with rooms painted in vivid purple and green, and has an open-air restaurant overlooking the river.

Pushpa Guest House
GUESTHOUSE $
(☎ 9448795120; pushpaguesthouse99@yahoo.in; d from ₹850, with AC from ₹1200; ❄ ☎) The highly recommended Pushpa is a top all-rounder that gets you a comfortable, attractive and spotless room. It has a lovely sit-out on the 1st floor, and a reliable travel agency.

Vicky's
GUESTHOUSE $
(☎ 9480561010; vikkyhampi@yahoo.co.in; r ₹600; ☎) An old faithful done up in pop purple and green, with decent rooms and friendly owner.

Netra Guesthouse
GUESTHOUSE $
(☎ 9480569326; r without/with bathroom from ₹250/400) Basic but relaxed rooms for shoe-stringers, with ambient open-air restaurant.

Ganesh Guesthouse
GUESTHOUSE $
(vishnuhampi@gmail.com; r ₹400-800, with AC ₹1200-2000; ❄ ☎) The small family-run Ganesh has been around for 20 years, yet only has downstairs rooms, giving it an appealing intimacy. Also has a nice rooftop restaurant.

Kiran Guest House
GUESTHOUSE $
(☎ 9448143906; kiranhampi2012@gmail.com; r ₹400-600; ☎) Chilled-out guesthouse overlooking the riverfront and banana groves.

Ranjana Guest House   GUESTHOUSE $$
(☑ 08394-241696; ranjanaguesthouse@gmail.com;
r from ₹1000; ✳) Run by a tight-knit family,
Ranjana prides itself on well-appointed
rooms and killer temple-views from its
sunny rooftop terrace.

Gopi Guest House   GUESTHOUSE $$
(☑ 08394-241695; www.gopiguesthouse.com; r
₹1200; ✳ @ ☏) Split over two properties on
the same street, long-standing Gopi offers
quality rooms that are almost upscale by
Hampi standards. Its rooftop cafe is a nice
place to hang out.

🛏 Virupapur Gaddi

Many travellers prefer the tranquility of Virupapur Gaddi, across the river from Hampi
Bazaar.

Hema Guest House   GUESTHOUSE $
(☑ 8762395470; rockyhampi@gmail.com; d ₹350;
☏) Rows of cute and comfy colourful cottages in a shady grove, all with hammocks,
and a restaurant perpetually full with lazing
tourists.

Sunny Guesthouse   GUESTHOUSE $
(☑ 9448566368; www.sunnyguesthouse.com; r
₹200-750; @ ☏) Sunny both in name and
disposition, this popular guesthouse is a
hit among backpackers for its cheap rooms,
tropical garden, hammocks and chilled-out
restaurant.

Gopi Guesthouse   GUESTHOUSE $
(☑ 9481871816; www.hampiisland.com; r ₹300-
1200; ☏) A classic Hampi setup with basic
huts and hammocks in its garden as well
as a chilled-out restaurant. Also has plush
rooms with tiled floors and hot water.

Shanthi   GUESTHOUSE $
(☑ 9449260162; shanthi.hampi@gmail.com; cottage
₹800-1500; @) A more upmarket choice,
Shanthi's earth-themed, thatched cottages
have rice-field, river and sunset views, with
couch swings dangling in the front porches.

Manju's Place   GUESTHOUSE $
(☑ 9449247712; r ₹300, without bathroom from
₹100) The place for those who like things
quiet, with attractive mudbrick huts in a
bucolic setting among rice fields.

Sima Guesthouse   GUESTHOUSE $
(☑ 9481664504; r with shared bathroom ₹200-
300) A quirky guesthouse away from the
crowds, low-key Sima has *very* basic but

ℹ HAMPI RUINS TICKET

The ₹250 entrance fee for Vittala Temple entitles you to same-day admission
into most of the paid sites across the
ruins (including around the Royal Centre
and the Archaeological Museum), so
don't lose your ticket.

---

memorable rooms incorporated into boul-
der faces. Unexpectedly has a tiny skate
ramp, along with a couple of boards.

Hampi's Boulders   LODGE $$$
(☑ 9448034202; www.hampisboulders.com; Naray-
anpet; r incl full board from ₹7000; ✳ ☏ 🏊) The
only luxury option in these parts, this 'eco-wil-
derness' resort sits amid leafy gardens 7km
west of Virupapur Gaddi. There's a choice of
themed rooms, but by far the best are the chic
cottages with elegant furnishing, river views
and outdoor showers. Rates include guided
walks and transfer from Hampi.

🛏 Kamalapuram

Hotel Mayura Bhuvaneshwari   HOTEL $$
(☑ 08394-241574,   8970650025;   s/d from
₹1620/1800; ✳ ☏) This tidy government
operation, about 3km south of the Royal
Centre, has well-appointed but dated rooms,
a lovely big garden, much-appreciated bar,
and a good multicuisine restaurant.

✗ Eating

Due to Hampi's religious significance, meat
is strictly off the menu in all restaurants,
and alcohol is banned (though some restaurants can order it for you).

★ **Laughing Buddha**   MULTICUISINE $
(Virupapur Gaddi; mains from ₹80; ⊙ 8am-10pm;
☏) Now that Hampi's famous riverside
restaurants have closed on the other side,
Laughing Buddha has taken over as the most
atmospheric place to eat, with serene river
views that span beyond to the temples and
ruins. Its menu is curries, burgers, pizzas,
you know the drill...

Ravi's Rose   MULTICUISINE $
(mains from ₹100; ⊙ 8am-10pm) This slightly
sketchy rooftop-restaurant is the bazaar's
most social hang-out, with a good selection
of dosas, but most are here for the, erm,
tasty lassis (cough, cough). It also has a nearby guesthouse built into the rock face.

Mango Tree   MULTICUISINE $$
(mains ₹90-310; ◷ 7.30am-9.30pm) Hampi's most famous restaurant may no longer sit beneath its iconic mango tree or boast river views, but its spirit lives on since relocating to the bazaar, inside an ambient tented restaurant.

Prince Restaurant   MULTICUISINE $$
(mains from ₹80; ◷ 7.30am-9.30pm) Food here takes ages to arrive, so thankfully this atmospheric shady hut is a good place to chill out with cushioned seating on the floor. Does *momos* (Tibetan dumplings), pizzas etc.

Shopping

Akash Art Gallery & Bookstore   BOOKS
(Hampi Bazaar; ◷ 6am-9pm) Excellent selection of books on Hampi and India, plus secondhand fiction. It has a free Hampi map.

Information

There's no ATM in Hampi; the closest is 3km away in Kamalapuram – an autorickshaw costs ₹100 for a return trip.

Internet (per hour ₹40) is ubiquitous in Hampi Bazaar, though most guesthouses have free wi-fi these days. A good tourist resource for Hampi is www.hampi.in.

Tourist Office (☑ 08394-241339; ◷ 10am-5.30pm Sat-Thu) This dingy office inside Virupaksha Temple has brochures but is more useful for arranging cycling tours (per person ₹400 including bike and guide), walking guides (half-/full day ₹600/1000) and bus tours (₹350, seven hours), all of which head to the ruins.

Getting There & Away

A semideluxe bus connects Hampi Bazaar to Bengaluru (₹550, eight hours) leaving at 8pm, but otherwise you'll have to head to Hospet for onward travel. Travel agents in Hampi Bazaar can book tickets.

The first bus from Hospet (₹22, 30 minutes, half-hourly) is at 5.45am; the last one back leaves Hampi Bazaar at 7.30pm. An autorickshaw costs ₹150 to ₹200.

Hospet is Hampi's nearest train station.

Getting Around

Bicycles cost ₹30 per day in Hampi Bazaar, while mopeds can be hired for around ₹150. Petrol is ₹100 a litre.

A small **boat** (person/bicycle/motorbike ₹10/10/20; ◷ 7am-6pm) shuttles frequently across the river to Virupapur Gaddi. A large backpack will cost ₹10 extra, while a special trip after 6pm is ₹50 to ₹100 per person depending on how late you cross.

Walking the ruins is possible, but expect to cover at least 7km just to see the major sites. Autorickshaws and taxis are available for sightseeing. Hiring an autorickshaw for the day costs ₹750.

Organised tours depart from Hospet and Hampi.

Around Hampi

Anegundi

Across the Tungabhadra River, about 5km northeast of Hampi Bazaar, sits Anegundi, an ancient fortified village that's part of the Hampi World Heritage Site but predates Hampi by way of human habitation. Gifted with a landscape similar to Hampi, Anegundi has been spared the blight of commercialisation, and thus continues to preserve the local atmosphere minus the touristy vibe.

Sights & Activities

Mythically referred to as Kishkinda, the kingdom of the monkey gods, Anegundi retains many of its historic monuments, such as sections of its defensive wall and gates, and the Ranganatha Temple (◷ dawn-dusk) devoted to Rama. Also worth visiting is the Durga Temple (◷ dawn-dusk), an ancient shrine closer to the village.

Hanuman Temple   HINDU TEMPLE
(◷ dawn-dusk) The whitewashed Hanuman Temple, accessible by a 570-step climb up the Anjanadri Hill, has fine views of the rugged terrain around. Many believe this is the birthplace of Hanuman, the Hindu monkey god who was Rama's devotee and helped him in his mission against Ravana. The hike up is pleasant, though you'll be courted by impish monkeys, and within the temple you'll find a large group of chillum-puffing sadhus.

Kishkinda Trust   CULTURAL, OUTDOORS
(TKT; ☑ 08533-267777; www.tktkishkinda.org; Main Rd, Anegundi) ✎ For cultural events, activities and volunteering opportunities, get in touch with Kishkinda Trust, an NGO based in Anegundi that works with local people.

Sleeping & Eating

A great place to escape the hippies in Hampi, Anegundi has fantastic homestays in restored heritage buildings. Most guesthouses in Anegundi are managed by Uramma Heritage Homes (☑ 9449972230; www.urammaheritagehomes.com).

Peshagar Guest House   GUESTHOUSE **$**
(☑09449972230; www.urammaheritagehomes.
com; s/d ₹450/850) Six simple rooms done
up in rural motifs open around a pleasant
common area in this heritage house with
courtyard garden and basic rooftop.

★**Uramma Cottage**   COTTAGE **$$**
(☑08533-267792; www.urammaheritagehomes.
com; s/d from ₹2000/2500; ❋🛜) Delightful
thatched-roof cottages with rustic farm-
house charm that are both comfortable and
attractive and set in a relaxed landscaped
garden setting.

Uramma House   GUESTHOUSE **$$**
(☑09449972230; www.urammaheritagehomes.
com; s/d ₹2000/3500, house for 4 people ₹7000;
🛜) This 4th-century heritage house is a
gem, with traditional-style rooms featuring
boutique touches.

Hoova Craft Shop & Café   CAFE **$**
(mains ₹60-100; ⊙8.30am-9.30pm) A lovely place
for an unhurried flavoursome local meal.

🛍 Shopping

Banana Fibre Craft Workshop   HANDICRAFTS
(⊙10am-1pm & 2-5pm Mon-Sat) Watch on at
this small workshop as craftspeople ply their
trade making a range of handicrafts and
accessories using the bark of a banana tree,
and recycled materials. They sell it all too.

ℹ Getting There & Away

Anegundi is 7km from Hampi, and reached by
crossing the river on a coracle (₹10) from the
pier east of the Vittala Temple. By far the most
convenient way is to hire a moped or bicycle (if
you're feeling energetic) from Virupapur Gaddi.
An autorickshaw costs ₹200.

Hospet (Hosapete)

☑08394 / POP 164,200
A hectic, dusty regional centre, Hospet (renamed as Hosapete in 2014) is certainly
nothing to write home about, and notable
only as a transport hub for Hampi.

🛏 Sleeping & Eating

Hotel Malligi   HOTEL **$$**
(☑08394-228101; www.malligihotels.com; Jabu-
natha Rd; r ₹990-5000; ❋@🛜🏊) Hotel Malli-
gi has built a reputation around clean and
well-serviced rooms, aquamarine swimming
pool and a good multicuisine restaurant.

DAROJI SLOTH BEAR SANCTUARY

Daroji Sloth Bear Sanctuary (admis-
sion ₹25; ⊙9.30am-6pm) About 30km
south of Hampi, amid scrubby undu-
lating terrain, lies the Daroji Sloth Bear
Sanctuary, which nurses a population
of around 150 free-ranging sloth bears
in an area of 83 sq km. You have a very
good chance of spotting them, as honey
is slathered on the rocks to coincide
with the arrival of visitors. However,
you can only see them from afar at the
viewing platform. Bring binoculars, or
basically there's no point turning up.
Generally 4pm to 6pm is the best time
to visit.

The sanctuary is also home to leop-
ards, wild boars, hyenas, jackals and
other animals, but you're unlikely to see
anything other than peacocks. You'll
need to arrange transport to get here,
which should costs around ₹600 for an
autorickshaw and ₹1000 for a car.

Udupi Sri Krishna Bhavan   SOUTH INDIAN **$**
(Bus Stand; thali ₹45, mains ₹50-70; ⊙6.30am-
10.30pm) Opposite the bus stand, this clean spot
dishes out Indian veggie fare, including thalis.

ℹ Information

You'll find ATMs along the main drag and Shan-
bagh Circle. Internet cafes (₹40 per hour) are
common.

ℹ Getting There & Away

BUS
Hospet's bus stand has services to Hampi
from Bay 10 every half-hour (₹22, 30 minutes).
Overnight private sleeper buses ply to/from Goa
(10 hours) and Gokarna (eight hours) for ₹850
to ₹1150, and to Bengaluru (₹340 to ₹700, 6½
hours) and Mysore (₹380 to ₹605, 8½ hours).

TRAIN
Hospet's train station is a ₹20 autorickshaw ride
from town. The Amaravathi Express and KCG
YPR Express head to Magdaon, Goa (sleeper/2AC
₹225/855, 7½ hours) at 6.30am on Monday,
Wednesday, Thursday and Saturday. The Hampi
Express departs nightly at 9pm for Bengaluru
(3AC/2AC/1AC ₹680/970/1635, nine hours) and
Mysore (₹860/1240/2075, 12½ hours).

North Goa

Best Places to Eat

➡ Go With the Flow (p132)

➡ Thalassa (p147)

➡ La Plage (p151)

➡ Villa Blanche Bistro (p141)

➡ Café Chocolatti (p124)

Best Places to Stay

➡ Siolim House (p149)

➡ Wanderers Hostel (p150)

➡ Jungle Hostel (p145)

➡ Mandala (p152)

➡ Marbella Guest House (p124)

Why Go?

North Goa is the Goa you might have heard all about: the crazy nightlife, Goan trance, hippie markets and yoga retreats. If you like a fast pace and plenty to do, this is the place.

The region is framed by two great rivers – the Mandovi in the south and the Terekhol in the north – and in between is some 35km of golden beaches, interrupted only by the occasional rocky headland and the mouth of the broad Chapora River. Calangute and Baga are the epicentre of the region, with one of the few beaches still humming in the low season. Anjuna, with its famous Wednesday market, and Vagator still exude some hippy cool and party vibe, while the laid-back beaches of Morjim, Aswem and Mandrem are low-key but burgeoning family-friendly resorts with some flashy beachfront huts. In the far north, Arambol is a popular budget traveller enclave with cheap clifftop accommodation and paragliding.

It's not for everyone, but if you like to dance, practice yoga or meditation, shop and eat well, it's hard to beat.

When to Go

Anjuna

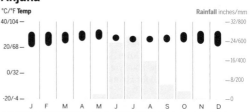

Nov–Mar High season; fine weather, beach shacks and yoga classes

mid-Dec–early Jan Crowds and prices peak but Christmas and NYE parties are legendary.

Oct & Apr Shoulder season; good weather, fewer crowds and cheaper rooms.

Panaji to Fort Aguada

Heading north from Panaji you can either take the expansive four-lane Mandovi River bridge and main highway through Porvorim to Mapusa (or detour west to the beaches via Saligao), or try the more scenic 'back road' along the north bank of the Mandovi to Fort Aguada. The latter option allows you to shortcut across the river on the free vehicle ferry to Betim.

Reis Magos

Travelling west from Betim, turn left at the crossroads in the small village of Verem and continue about 1.5km to tiny Reis Magos (Three Wise Men) village, notable for its 16th-century church and Goa's oldest and best preserved fort.

Opened to the public in 2012 as a cultural centre, **Reis Magos Fort** (☑0832-2904649; www.reismagosfort.com; adult/student/child ₹50/25/free, Sun & holidays ₹10; ⊘11am-sunset) overlooks the narrowest point of the Mandovi River estuary, making it easy to appreciate the strategic importance of the site. It was originally built in 1551, after the north bank of the river came under Portuguese control, and was rebuilt in 1703, in time to assist the desperate Portuguese defence against the Hindu Marathas (1737–39). It was then occupied by the British army in 1799 when they requisitioned Reis Magos, Cabo Raj Bhavan and Fort Aguada in anticipation of a possible attack by the French.

After the British withdrawal in 1813 the Reis Magos fort gradually lost importance, and was eventually abandoned. Like Fort Aguada nearby, the fort was turned into a prison in 1900 until it was abandoned again in 1993.

In 2011 the fort underwent extensive restoration and is now a cultural and heritage centre with exhibition spaces, including a gallery of works by cartoonist Mario Miranda and a room devoted to the history of the fort and its restoration. You can wander the ramparts for great views and inspect the original cannons pointing out over the Mandovi.

Reis Magos Church (⊘9am-noon & 4-5.30pm Mon-Sat, service 8am Sun) was built below the fortress walls in 1555, shortly after the construction of the fort itself. A Franciscan seminary was later added, and over the years it became a significant seat of learning.

The seminary is gone but the church is well worth a look, with its steep steps up from the road and fine views of the Mandovi River from the main doors. Outside the church, the lions portrayed in relief at the foot of the steps show signs of Hindu influence, and a crown tops off the facade. The colourful interior contains the tombs of three viceroys, including Dom Luis de Ataide, famous for holding 100,000 Muslim attackers – along with their 2000 elephants – at bay for 10 months in 1570, with his own force of just 7000 men.

Reis Magos is famous for the colourful **Three Kings Festival** on 6 January, when the story of the three wise men is recreated, with young local boys acting the parts of the Magi, complete with gifts for the infant Jesus.

Nerul (Coco) Beach

Nerul Beach (also known as Coco Beach), where the Nerul River meets the Mandovi, affords a great view across to Miramar and Panaji in Central Goa and is popular with day-trippers. The beach itself and the murky tidal waters are not much to look at, but it has a slight air of isolation as it can only be reached by a narrow one-way road through paddy fields.

Boat operators hang out at the beach, ready to take you on dolphin-spotting trips along the estuary, and there are a couple of restaurants on the beachfront.

There's not much reason to stay here, unless you're checking in to the swanky **Coco Shambhala** (www.cocoshambhala.com; villa per week ₹200,000; ❄🛜🏊), a luxurious collection of four villas, each of which come with their own private jetpool, and car and driver.

Candolim, Sinquerim & Fort Aguada

Candolim's long and languid beach, which curves to join smaller Sinquerim Beach to the south, is largely the preserve of slow-basting package tourists from the UK, Russia and, increasingly, elsewhere in India. It's fringed with an unabating line of beach shacks, all offering sunbeds and shade in exchange for your custom.

Back from the beach and running parallel to it, bustling Fort Aguada Rd is among the best resort strips in Goa for shops and services, and is home to dozens of restaurants and bars that awaken each evening to

North Goa Highlights

1 Sleep in style and stretch out with a good book at peaceful **Mandrem** (p151)

2 Haggle for a bargain at the touristy but still charming **Anjuna flea market** (p138)

3 Drop in to a yoga class at Anjuna, Arambol, **Assagao** (p142) or Mandrem

4 Stroll the lanes of pretty little **Assagao village** (p141)

5 Paraglide from the hill

above Sweetwater Lake near **Arambol** (p153)

6 Dine at one of the clifftop restaurants then party into the night at **Vagator** (p143)

7 Enjoy Goan village life in

style with a stay at a heritage hotel in **Siolim** (p148)

8 Experience the neon lights, buskers and food stalls at one of the Saturday night markets in **Baga** (p134)

9 Take a boat trip down the **Nerul River** (p119) to spot dolphins and crocodiles

10 Learn to surf, kitesurf or paddleboard in **Aswem** (p150)

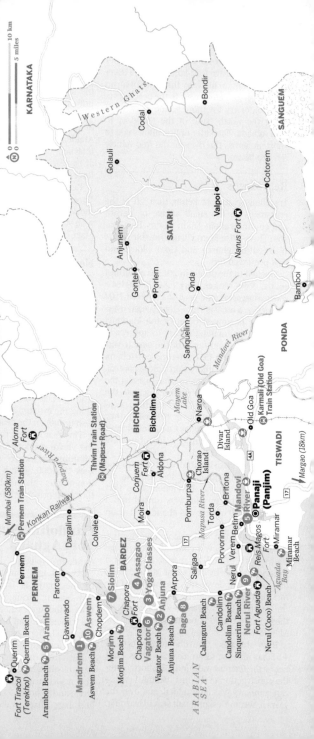

provide cocktails, international cuisine and occasional live music. In all it's an upmarket, happy holiday strip, but independent travellers may find it a little soulless.

◉ Sights

Fort Aguada   FORT
(◷ 8.30am-5.30pm) **FREE** Standing on the headland overlooking the mouth of the Mandovi River, Fort Aguada occupies a magnificent and successful position, confirmed by the fact it was never taken by force. A highly popular spot to watch the sunset, with uninterrupted views both north and south, the fort was built in 1612, following the increasing threat to Goa's Portuguese overlords by the Dutch, among others.

One of the great advantages of the site was the abundance of water from natural springs on the hillside, making the fort an important first watering point for ships just arrived from Portugal; the spring also gave the fort its name, *agua* being Portuguese for 'water'. Like Reis Magos and Cabo Raj Bhavan, the British occupied the fort in 1799 to protect Goa from possible French invasion.

Today visitors flock to the bastion that stands on the hilltop – though when compared with the overall area surrounded by defences, this is only a fraction of the original fort. To get to the hilltop fort, take the 4km winding road that heads east from Sinquerim Beach and loops up around the headland. Otherwise there's a steep 2km walking trail to the fort that starts just past Marbella Guest House. You can also walk out to the sea-level fort walls at Sinquerim along the road past the Taj Hotel.

Fort Aguada Lighthouse   LIGHTHOUSE
The old Portuguese lighthouse, which stands in the middle of Fort Aguada, was built in 1864 and once housed the great bell from the Church of St Augustine in Old Goa before it was moved to the Church of Our Lady of the Immaculate Conception in Panaji. It's the oldest of its sort in Asia, but is usually not open to the public. Outside the fort bastions, the new lighthouse (Indian/foreigner ₹10/50, camera ₹25; ◷ 3-5.30pm), built in 1976, can usually be visited; climb to the top for a good view along the coast.

Church of St Lawrence   CHURCH
A short way to the east of the bastion is the pretty Church of St Lawrence, which also occupies a magnificent viewpoint. The church was built in 1643 to honour St Lawrence, the patron saint of sailors, whose image stands on the gilded *reredos* (ornamental screen), holding a model ship.

Fort Aguada Jail   LANDMARK
Below Fort Aguada is the local jail, Goa's largest prison, whose cells stand on the site that once formed the square-shaped citadel of the hilltop fort. Today the prison houses inmates mostly serving sentences for drug possession or smuggling, including a dozen or so long-staying foreigners.

The road down to the jail's entrance passes a weird and wonderful compound known as **Jimmy's Palace**, home to reclusive tycoon Jimmy Gazdar. Designed by Goan architect Gerard da Cunha, it's a closely guarded froth of fountains, foliage and follies, of which you'll catch glimpses as you whiz past. Obviously neither place is open to the public.

☞ Tours

Sinquerim Dolphin Trips   BOAT TOUR
(per person ₹300; ◷ 8.30am-5pm) The boatmen on the Nerul River below Fort Aguada have banded together, so trips are now fixed price. A one-hour dolphin-spotting and sightseeing trip costs ₹300 per person with a minimum of 10 passengers. Trips pass Nerul (Coco) Beach, Fort Aguada Jail, the fort, and 'Jimmy's Palace'.

John's Boat Tours   TOUR
(☏ 0832-6520190, 9822182814; www.johnboattours.com; Fort Aguada Rd, Candolim; ◷ 9am-9pm) A respected and well-organised Candolim-based operator offering a wide variety of boat and jeep excursions, as well as overnight houseboat cruises (₹5500 per person including meals). Choose from dolphin-watching cruises (₹1000), a return boat trip to the Wednesday Anjuna flea market (₹800), or the renowned 'Crocodile Dundee' river trip, to catch a glimpse of the Mandovi's mugger crocodile.

🛏 Sleeping

Though Candolim is largely frequented by package tourists and 5-star luxury guests bussed straight in from Dabolim Airport, there's a surprising range of accommodation for the independent traveller. Most of the best value budget choices are situated either in the northern part of Candolim or in the Sinquerim area further south. Laneways spread like tendrils from the main Fort Aguada Rd to the beach and are lined with midrange hotels and restaurants.

Candolim, Sinquerim & Fort Aguada

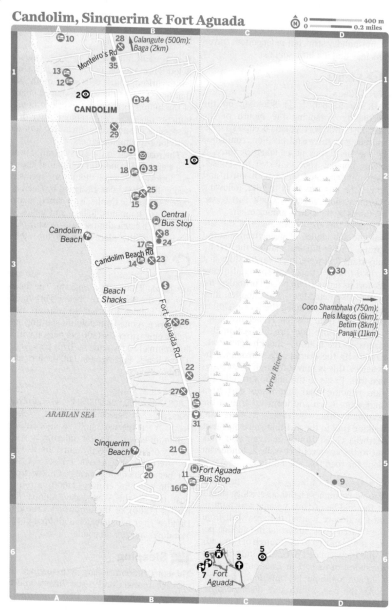

Zostel   HOSTEL **$**

(☏ 917726864942; www.zostel.com; Candolim; dm
₹450-550, d ₹1800; ❉ ☎) The first Goan addition
to this funky Indian hostel chain has popped
up on the Candolim–Calangute border, bringing budget dorm beds to package-tour central.

There are six- and eight-bed dorms with air-
con, a 10-bed dorm and a female-only dorm,
all in a whitewashed two-storey house set
back from Fort Aguada Rd. Facilities include
a kitchen, free wi-fi, a common room and lockers. There's just one double room.

Candolim, Sinquerim & Fort Aguada

NORTH GOA CANDOLIM, SINQUERIM & FORT AGUADA

Villa Ludovici Tourist Home GUESTHOUSE **$**
(☑0832-2479684; Fort Aguada Rd, Candolim; d incl breakfast ₹945) For over 30 years Ludovici has been welcoming travellers into its well-worn, creaky rooms in a grand old Portuguese-style villa, which is slowly being swallowed by its five-star neighbours. Four-poster beds on a budget; rooms are large, if definitely faded, and the hosts (and ghosts) are kind and amiable.

Dona Florina HOTEL **$**
(☑9923049076, 0832-2489051; www.donaflorina. co.in; Monteiro's Rd, Escrivao Vaddo; r ₹1000-2000; ❈🛇) Friendly Dona Florina is a good value, spotless place in a pleasant tangle of laneways and family-run hotels just back from the beach. Front-facing upper-floor rooms have sea views, there's daily yoga on the roof terrace, and the lack of vehicle access ensures a peaceful experience.

D'Mello's Sea View Home HOTEL **$$**
(☑0832-2489650; www.dmellos.com; Monteiro's Rd, Escrivao Vaddo; d ₹1200-1700; ❈@🛇) D'Mello's has grown up from small beginnings but is still family run and occupies four buildings around a lovely garden. The front building has the sea-view rooms so check out a few, but all are clean and

well-maintained. Add ₹500 if you want aircon. Wi-fi is available in the central area.

★ Bougainvillea Guest House GUESTHOUSE **$$**
(☑0832-2479842, 9822151969; www.bougainvillea goa.com; Sinquerim; r/penthouse ₹2500/6000; ❈🛇) A lush, plant-filled garden leads the way to this gorgeous family-run guesthouse, located off Fort Aguada Rd. The eight light-filled suite rooms are spacious and spotless, with fridge, flat-screen TV and either balcony or private sit-out; the top-floor penthouse has its own rooftop terrace. This is the kind of place guests come back to year after year. Book ahead.

Tina's Inn GUESTHOUSE **$$**
(☑7720003889; Fort Aguada Rd, Candolim; d incl breakfast ₹3500; ❈🛇) This attractive whitewashed Portuguese-style mansion has eight rather plain but comfortable air-con rooms at the back, with TV, fridge and spring mattresses.

Ruffles Beach Resort HOTEL **$$**
(☑9850752662; www.rufflesgoa.com; Fort Aguada Rd, Candolim; d ₹2800-3500; ❈🛇▣) A pleasant courtyard pool and well-equipped rooms make this a reliably good midrange choice. There's a good little restaurant and bar facing the road.

Horizon View GUESTHOUSE **$$**
(📞 0832-2479727; www.horizonview.co.in; Candolim Beach Rd; d ₹2000-2500; ❋ 🛜 🖵) One of the few midrange places in town catering solely to independent tourists, this small, family-run hotel is a good-value option, with simple rooms set around a small swimming pool. Don't expect luxury, but for the price it's nice. The grill restaurant serves up highly popular English breakfasts.

★**Marbella Guest House** BOUTIQUE HOTEL **$$**
(📞 0832-2479551, 9822100811; www.marbella-goa.com; Sinquerim; r ₹3400-4200, ste ₹4900-6400; ❋ 🛜) This stunning Portuguese-era villa, filled with antiques and enveloped in a peaceful courtyard garden, is a romantic and sophisticated old-world remnant. Rooms are individually themed, including Moghul, Rajasthani and Bouganvillea. The penthouse suite is a dream of polished tiles, four-poster bed with separate living room, dining room and terrace. Its kitchen serves up some imaginative dishes. Located off Fort Aguada Rd. No kids under 12.

Lemon Tree Amarante Beach Resort HOTEL **$$$**
(📞 0832-3988188; www.lemontreehotels.com; Fort Aguada Rd; r from ₹7000; ❋ @ 🛜 🖵) This boutiquey, luxe place on the main strip conjures up a strange mixture of Thai-spa style and medieval motifs. It works, though, with swish rooms equipped with wi-fi and DVD players, a luxurious spa, and a roomy courtyard pool with swim-up bar.

Aashyana Lakhanpal VILLA, COTTAGES **$$$**
(📞 0832-2489225; www.aashyanalakhanpal.com; Fort Aguada Rd; villa per week ₹117,000-607,000; ❋ @ 🛜 🖵) A five-bedroom villa filled with art, a three-bedroom villa, three two-bedroom *casinhas* (little houses) and other cottages, set amid 1.6 hectares of lush, landscaped grounds spilling down to the beach, make Aashyana one of Candolim's – if not Goa's – most exclusive retreats. This is high-society luxe at its best and it puts the nearby Taj hotels in the shade for both style and price.

Vivanta by Taj Holiday Village HOTEL **$$$**
(📞 1800 111825, 0832-6645858; www.vivantabytaj.com; Fort Aguada Rd; cottage ₹12,000-18,000; ❋ @ 🛜 🖵) The Taj's garden complex comprises 142 cottages and villas in a smart variation on a five-star theme, with all the luxuries you'd expect from this top-end chain.

The palm-filled garden spills down to the beach, and its Banyan Tree Thai restaurant is well known for good food in beautiful alfresco surroundings.

Vivanta by Taj Fort Aguada HOTEL **$$$**
(📞 0832-6645858, 1800-111825; www.vivantabytaj.com; d incl breakfast ₹10,000-20,000, villa from ₹35,000; ❋ @ 🛜 🖵) Dominating the headland above Sinquerim Beach, the Taj Group's sprawling beach resort looks a little dated, but its service is still top-notch and the location impressive. Its Jiva Spa offers soothing balms and palms, and the resort has a gym, a pool, and three quailty restaurants.

✕ Eating

Candolim has some excellent upmarket restaurants – many attached to resort hotels. Then there's the long string of seafront beach shacks serving world cuisine and fresh seafood. Much of the best on offer is ranged along Fort Aguada Rd, though if you take the side streets towards the beach you'll find a few gems, along with local joints serving a cheap and tasty breakfast *bhaji-pau* or lunchtime thali.

Viva Goa! GOAN, SEAFOOD **$**
(Fort Aguada Rd; mains ₹90-180; ⏰ 11am-midnight) This inexpensive, locals-oriented little place, also popular with in-the-know tourists, serves fresh fish and Goan seafood specialities such as a spicy mussel fry. Check market price of seafood before ordering.

Zappa's CAFE **$**
(📞 9767019410; Candolim; mains ₹40-120; ⏰ 8am-2pm) A tiny cafe sandwiched between the beach and busy Fort Aguada Rd, Zappa's serves up tasty breakfast and brunch dishes and some of the freshest pasta dishes in town. The owner has spent many years living and cooking in Europe. Zappa's beach shack is directly west.

★**Café Chocolatti** CAFE, BAKERY **$$**
(409A Fort Aguada Rd; sweets ₹50-200, mains ₹270-420; ⏰ 9am-5.30pm) The lovely garden tearoom at Café Chocolatti may be on the main Fort Aguada Rd but it's a divine and peaceful retreat where chocolate brownies, waffles and banoffee pie with a strong cup of coffee or organic green tea seem like heaven. It also offers a great range of salads, paninis, crepes and quiches for lunch. Take away a bag of chocolate truffles, homemade by the in-house chocolatier.

THE PINTO REVOLT

In 1787 Candolim was the scene of the first serious local attempt to overthrow the Portuguese. The founders of the conspiracy were mostly churchmen, angry at the ingrained racial discrimination that meant they were not allowed to occupy the highest clerical positions. Two of them, Father Caetano Francisco Couto and Jose Antonio Gonsalves, travelled to Portugal to plead their case in the court at Lisbon. Unsuccessful in their attempts, they returned to Goa and began plotting at the home of the Pinto family in Candolim. Gradually the number of conspirators grew, as army officers and others disaffected with their Portuguese overlords joined the cause.

The plans were so close to completion that a date had been fixed for the proposed coup, when the plot was discovered by the Portuguese authorities. A total of 47 conspirators, including 17 priests and seven army officers, were arrested. The lucky ones were sentenced to the galleys or deported to Portugal for a 20-year prison stint, while 15 of the lowlier and less fortunate were hanged, drawn and quartered in Panaji and their heads mounted on stakes as a deterrent to other would-be revolutionaries.

L'Orange   MULTICUISINE $$

(www.lorangegoa.com; Fort Aguada Rd; mains ₹130-250; ⊗ noon-3pm & 6pm-midnight) A fusion of European and Indian cuisines specialising in tasty barbecued meats and seafood, L'Orange works hard at standing out from Candolim's crowded restaurant scene. Regular live music and a happy vibe certainly give it an edge.

Stone House   STEAK, SEAFOOD $$

(Fort Aguada Rd; mains ₹150-500; ⊗ 11am-3pm & 7pm-midnight) Surf 'n' turf's the thing at this venerable old Candolim venue, inhabiting a stone house and its leafy front courtyard, with the improbable-sounding 'Swedish Lobster' topping the list. It's also a popular blues bar, with live music most nights of the week in season.

⭐**Bomra's**   BURMESE $$$

(⊡ 9767591056; www.bomras.com; 247 Fort Aguada Rd; mains from ₹300; ⊗ noon-2pm & 7-11pm) Wonderfully unusual food is on offer at this sleek little place serving interesting modern Burmese cuisine with a fusion twist. Aromatic curries include straw mushroom, lychee, water-chestnut, spinach and coconut curry and duck curry with sweet tamarind and groundnut shoot. Decor is palm-thatch style huts in a lovely courtyard garden.

Banyan Tree   THAI $$$

(⊡ 0832-6645858; Vivanta by Taj Holiday Village; mains from ₹600; ⊗ 12.30-2.30pm & 7.30-10.30pm) Refined Thai food is the trademark of the Taj's romantic Banyan Tree, its swish courtyard set beneath the branches of a vast old banyan tree. If you're a fan of green

curry, don't miss the succulent, signature version on offer here. Ambience, and dress, is formal.

Tuscany Gardens   ITALIAN $$$

(⊡ 0832-6454026; www.tuscanygardens.in; Fort Aguada Rd; mains ₹240-410; ⊗ 1-11pm) You can easily be transported to Tuscany at Candolim's cosy, romantic Italian restaurant, where perfect antipasti, pasta, pizza and risotto are the order of the day. Try the chicken breast stuffed with gorgonzola and ham, the seafood pizza or the buffalo-mozzarella salad.

Republic of Noodles   ASIAN FUSION $$$

(Lemon Tree Amarante Beach Resort; mains ₹375-450; ⊗ 11.30am-3pm & 7-11pm) For a sophisticated dining experience, the RoN at the Lemon Tree Amarante delivers with its dark bamboo interior, Buddha heads and floating candles. Seeking to recreate Southeast Asian street food, you'll get delicious, huge and award-winning noodle plates, including a fabulous pad thai and some exciting options for vegetarians.

🍷 Drinking & Nightlife

Candolim's drinking scene is largely hotel-based, but its plentiful beach shacks are a popular place for a relaxed beer or sunset cocktail. A couple of big-name nightclubs are in the area; solo males (or groups of men) might have trouble gaining entry.

Bob's Inn   BAR

(Fort Aguada Rd, Candolim; ⊗ noon-4pm & 7pm-midnight) The African wall hangings, palm-thatch, communal tables and terracotta sculptures are a nice backdrop to the *rava* (semolina) fried mussels or the prawns 'chilly fry' with potatoes, but this Candolim institution is really just a great place to drop in for a drink.

LPK Waterfront
CLUB

(www.lpkwaterfront.com; couples ₹1500; ⊙9.30pm-4am) The initials stand for Love, Peace and Karma: welcome to North Goa's biggest new club, the whimsical, sculpted waterfront LPK. It's actually across the Nerul River from Candolim (so technically in Nerul) but its club nights attract party-goers from all over with huge indoor and outdoor dance areas.

SinQ
CLUB

(☑8308000080; www.sinq.co.in; Fort Aguada Rd; couples ₹1500, women ₹500; ⊙10pm-3am) Candolim's latest party place, SinQ is almost directly opposite Taj Holiday Village so the clientele is upmarket – only the cool people get in. Inside are some interesting dance spaces and an outdoor party area with curtained cabanas beside the pool. Events vary but Wednesday is ladies night, with free drinks and DIY cocktails for the girls, Thursday is retro night, and Friday and Saturday are 'open bar' nights with free drinks.

🛍 Shopping

Newton's
SUPERMARKET

(Fort Aguada Rd; ⊙9am-midnight) If you're desperately missing Edam cheese or Pot Noodles, or just want to do some self-catering, Newton's is Goa's biggest supermarket.

There's a good line in toiletries, wines, children's toys and luxury food items. The downside is that it's usually packed and security guards won't allow bags inside.

Fabindia
SOUVENIRS, HOMEWARES

(www.fabindia.com; Fort Aguada Rd; ⊙10.30am-9pm) Popular nationwide chain selling fair-trade bed and table linens, home furnishings, clothes, jewellery and toiletries. Fabindia makes for a great, colourful browse, and is perfect for picking up high-end gifts or treating yourself to a traditional kurta or *salwar kameez* (traditional dresslike tunic and trouser combination for women).

Sotohaus
HOMEWARES

(☑0832-2489983; www.sotodecor.com; Fort Aguada Rd; ⊙10am-6pm Mon-Sat) Offering cool, functional items dreamed up by a Swiss expat team, this is the place to invest in a natural-form-inspired lamp, mirror or dining table, to add a twist of streamlined India to your pad back home.

Broadway Book Centre
BOOKS

(☑0832-6519777; www.booksingoa.com; Fort Aguada Rd, Candolim; ⊙10am-8pm) With five stores in Goa, Broadway is the state's biggest bookstore chain, so you should be able to find what you're looking for here. Staff are friendly and helpful.

ℹ Information

The post office, supermarkets, travel agents, pharmacies and plenty of banks with ATMs are all located on the main Fort Aguada Rd, running parallel to the beach.

CANDOLIM'S MANSIONS

Despite the wholesale development of this once-sleepy seaside village, some intriguing architectural remnants of a rather different past remain hidden in Candolim's quiet back lanes.

In the 17th and 18th centuries, Candolim saw the arrival of a number of wealthy Goan families, fleeing from the capital at Old Goa due to the ravages of typhoid, cholera and malaria epidemics. The homes they built were lavish and ornate, filled with oyster-shell windows, fine materials from Macau and China, and scrolling carved stonework.

Casa dos Costa-Frias Though it's not open to the public, seek out the beautiful Casa dos Costa-Frias, down a side road just opposite Candolim's football field, which belonged to relatives of the influential Pinto family. It was built in the early 18th century, and stands behind a white, cross-topped gateway, with a family chapel tucked behind it.

Casa dos Monteiros Near the beach, the Casa dos Monteiros is an example of the peak of Candolim's architectural splendour. Built by Goa's most powerful family, the Monteiros, it has the pretty 1780 Nossa Senhora dos Remedios (Our Lady of Miracles) chapel standing opposite the entrance to the house. Still occupied by descendants of the Monteiros, the house is not open to visitors but is worth a look from the outside.

Davidair (☑ 0832-2489303/4; www.com2goa. com; Fort Aguada Rd; ⊘ 9am-6pm) Reputable travel agency specialising in flights out of Goa and organised tours throughout India.

ℹ Getting There & Around

Buses run about every 10 minutes to and from Panaji (₹15, 35 minutes), and stop at the central bus stop near John's Boat Tours. Some continue south to the Fort Aguada bus stop at the bottom of Fort Aguada Rd, then head back to Panaji along the Mandovi River road, via the villages of Verem and Betim.

Frequent buses also run from Candolim to Calangute (₹8, 15 minutes) and can be flagged down on Fort Aguada Rd.

Calangute & Baga

POP 16,000

Calangute and Baga move to the beat of their own drum – and a pretty noisy one it is.

For many visitors, particularly cashed-up young Indian tourists from Bangalore and Mumbai, plus Russians on package holidays, this is Goa's party town, where the raves and hippies have made way for modern thumping nightclubs and wall-to-wall drinking.

At times the Calangute market area and the main Baga road are a traffic-clogged nightmare where buses, taxis and scooters fight for space and frequently end up at a stand still. But there's a good reason why this relentless stretch of beach is among Goa's most popular. Everything you could ask for – from a Thai massage to a tattoo – is in close proximity and the beach is lined with an excellent selection of restaurant shacks with sunbeds, wi-fi and attentive service.

Stretching between the blurred lines of Candolim and Baga, Calangute is centred on the busy market road leading to the beachfront. To the south of the market the beach is more relaxed and upscale with some fancy restaurants and quiet lanes winding down to the beach. To the north things get a little more cramped and slightly downmarket, eventually morphing into the packed party strip known as Baga.

Baga beach consists of jostling shacks, peppered with water-sports and boat-trip touts, and row upon row of sunbeds. The crowd here is young and excitable and the music plays loud and late, especially around infamous Tito's Lane. Things are noticeably more sedate across the Baga River where you'll find some excellent restaurants.

Once little more than a couple of fishing villages, Calangute and Baga were among the first beaches in Goa to attract the long-staying hippies in the '60s, before they moved north to Anjuna. How times have changed.

🏃 Activities

Local fishermen congregate around the northern end of Baga Beach, offering dolphin-spotting trips (₹500 per person), boat trips to Anjuna flea market (₹400) and whole-day coastal excursions up to Arambol, Mandrem and back.

Yoga classes pop up around Calangute and Baga each season, though it's not as organised as in the resorts and retreats further north. Look out for up-to-date flyers and noticeboards for the latest.

You don't have to go far to find beach water sports along the Calangute–Baga strip.

Goa Aquatics DIVING
(☑ 9822685025; www.goaaquatics.com; 136/1 Gaura Vaddo, Calangute; dive trip from ₹5000, dive course ₹14,000-25,000) This professional dive resort based at Little Italy restaurant offers a range of PADI courses and boat dives to Grande and Netrani islands. An introductory dive for beginners is ₹5000 and a four-day PADI Open Water course is ₹20,000.

Ayurvedic Natural Health Centre AYURVEDA, YOGA
(☑ 0832-2409275; www.healthandayurveda.com; Chogm Rd, Saligao; ⊘ 7.30am-7.30pm) This Saligao-based centre, about 2.5km east of central Calangute, offers a range of courses in reflexology, aromatherapy, acupressure, short- and long-term yoga courses and various other regimes. We've received unhappy reports from travellers though, and complaints of inexperienced staff; check in for a day treatment before committing.

Atlantis Watersports WATER SPORTS
(www.atlantiswatersports.com; Baga Bazar) A long-running water-sports operator on Baga Beach (near Tito's) offering parasailing (₹800), banana boat rides (₹250), speedboat rides (₹250), tubing (₹350) and two-hour dolphin trips (₹600 per person), along with fishing, windsurfing and rafting trips.

Calangute & Baga

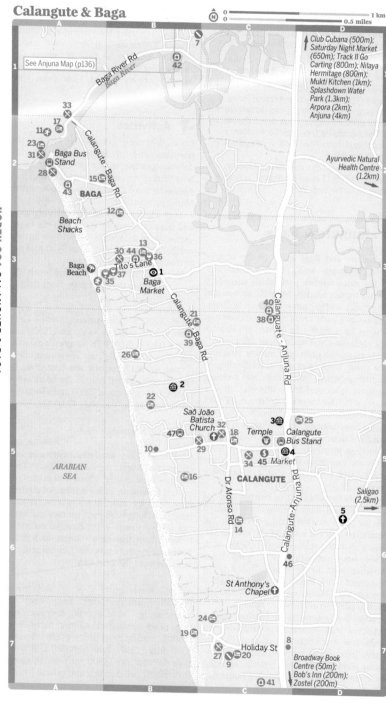

0   1 km
0   0.5 miles

See Anjuna Map (p136)

Baga River Rd
Baga River

Calangute - Baga Rd

Club Cubana (500m);
Saturday Night Market
(650m); Track II Go
Carting (800m); Nilaya
Hermitage (800m);
Mukti Kitchen (1km);
Splashdown Water
Park (1.3km);
Arpora (2km);
Anjuna (4km)

Ayurvedic Natural
Health Centre
(1.2km)

BAGA

Beach
Shacks

Baga
Beach

Tito's Lane

Baga
Market

Calangute - Baga Rd

Calangute - Anjuna Rd

ARABIAN
SEA

Saõ João
Batista
Church

Temple

Calangute
Bus Stand

Market

CALANGUTE

Saligao
(2.5km)

Dr Afonso Rd

Calangute - Anjuna Rd

St Anthony's
Chapel

Holiday St

Broadway Book
Centre (50m);
Bob's Inn (200m);
Zostel (200m)

Calangute & Baga

Sights

Activities, Courses & Tours

Sleeping

Eating

Drinking & Nightlife

Shopping

Information

Transport

Barracuda Diving   DIVING
(📞9822182402, 0832-2279409; www.barracuda diving.com; Sun Village Resort, Baga; dive trip/course from ₹4500/6000) This long-standing dive school offers a vast range of PADI and SSI classes, dives and courses, including a 1½-hour 'Bubblemakers' introduction to scuba class for children eight years and older (₹1000), Discover Scuba for ₹6000 and PADI Open Water for ₹23,000. For qualified divers a two-tank dive to Grande Island is ₹4500. Barracuda Diving is also notable for its 'Project Aware,' which undertakes marine-conservation initiatives and annual underwater and beach clean-ups.

Jungle Guitars   MUSIC
(📞9823565117; www.jungleguitars.com; Baga; course US$1500) A unique experience for committed guitarists, Jungle Guitars offers 15- to 20-day courses teaching you how to build your very own steel string or classical guitar from scratch, overseen by resident master guitar-builder Chris. The course cost includes all materials, expert instruction and a case for the finished product.

 Tours

Day Tripper   TOUR
(📞0832-2276726; www.daytrippergoa.com; Gaura Vaddo, Calangute; ⊙9am-5.30pm Mon-Sat Nov-Apr) Calangute-based Day Tripper is one of Goa's biggest and most reliable tour agencies. It runs a wide variety of minibus and boat trips around Goa, including two-hour dolphin trips (₹500 per person), trips to Dudhsagar Falls (₹1530), a houseboat stay (₹5300 per person) and also interstate tours to Hampi and the Kali River (for rafting and birdwatching trips) in Karnataka.

GTDC Tours   TOUR
(Goa Tourism Development Corporation; 📞0832-2276024; ⊙www.goa-tourism.com) Goa Tourism's tours can be booked online or at the refurbished GTDC Calangute Residency hotel beside the beach. The full-day North Goa tour (₹225, 9.30am to 6pm daily) departs from Calangute or Mapusa and takes in the Mandovi estuary, Candolim, Calangute, Anjuna and inland to Mayem Lake.

📖 Sleeping

Calangute and Baga's sleeping options are broad and varied, though it's not a particularly budget-friendly destination except in low season – quite a few places here remain open year-round. Both beach strips are built up with concrete-block hotels catering to charter planes full of British, Russian and European tourists, but with a few worthwhile offerings for the independent traveller.

📍 Calangute

⭐ Ospy's Shelter   GUESTHOUSE $
(☎7798100981, 0832-2279505; ospys.shelter@gmail.com; d ₹800-900) Tucked away between the beach and St Anthony's Chapel, in a quiet, lush little area full of palms and sandy paths, Ospy's is a traveller favourite and only a two-minute walk from the beach. Spotless upstairs rooms have fridges and balconies, and the whole place has a cosy family feel. Take the road directly west of the chapel – but it's tough to find, so call ahead.

Johnny's Hotel   HOTEL $
(☎0832-2277458; www.johnnyshotel.com; s ₹400-600, d ₹700-900, with AC ₹1000-1200; ❄🛜) The 15 simple rooms at this backpacker-popular place make for a sociable stay, with a downstairs restaurant-bar and regular yoga and reiki classes. A range of apartments and houses are available for longer stays. It's down a lane lined with unremarkable midrange hotels and is just a short walk to the beach.

Coco Banana   GUESTHOUSE $
(☎0832-2279068; www.cocobananagoa.com; d ₹950, with AC ₹1500; ❄🛜) Among the palms south of the main entrance to Calangute Beach, colourful Coco Banana has been providing a soothing retreat for travellers for many years. Run by the friendly Walter, rooms are spacious and spotless and the vibe is mellow. For families or groups, ask about the self-contained apartments at nearby Casa Leyla.

Garden Court Resort   GUESTHOUSE $
(☎0832-2276054; luarba@dataone.in; r ₹600-900, with AC ₹1200-1800; ❄🛜) Rooms here are fronted by a Portuguese-style family home, set among pretty gardens and remarkably quiet, despite being on the busy market road. They're not flashy but are reasonable value and come with balconies.

Hotel Seagull   HOTEL $$
(☎0832-2179969; Holiday St; d with AC ₹2500; ❄🛜🏊) Bright, friendly and welcoming, the Seagull's rooms, set in a cheerful blue-and-white house in south Calangute, are light and airy with air-con and a small pool out back. Downstairs is the fine **Blue Mariposa** bar-restaurant, serving Goan, Indian and continental dishes.

Hotel Golden Eye   HOTEL $$
(☎9822132850, 0832-2277308; www.hotelgoldeneye.com; Holiday St; d without/with AC ₹2000/2500, sea-facing rooms from ₹4500, apt ₹5000-8000; ❄🛜) This popular beach-front hotel at the end of 'Holiday St' has a fine range of rooms and apartments, from cheaper but tidy ones at the back to the boutique sea-facing rooms with modern decor, AC and cable TV. Unlike some midrangers it's welcoming to independent walk-in travellers, though you'll need to book ahead in season. The Flying Dolphin beach shack is out front.

Vila Goesa   HOTEL $$
(☎0832-2277535; www.vilagoesa.com; d without/with AC from ₹3300/4500, ste ₹5000-8000; ❄🛜🏊) Nicely situated between south Baga and north Calangute, and hidden in the palm thickets 200m back from the beach, this is a great place for lingering with a good book by the pool. Rooms are simple but pleasantly furnished; the higher the tariff, the closer you get to the beach.

⭐ Pousada Tauma   BOUTIQUE HOTEL $$$
(☎0832-2279061; www.pousada-tauma.com; ste incl meals €280-385; ❄🛜🏊) If you're looking for luxury with your ayurvedic regime, check right into this gorgeous little boutique hotel in busy Calangute but appropriately shielded from the outside world. Spacious, nicely furnished suites are set around a super fountain-fed pool. Rates include all meals at the romantic open-air **Copper Bowl** restaurant, though ayurvedic treatments in the private centre are extra. There's also a shuttle to its beach restaurant.

Casa de Goa   HOTEL $$$
(☎0832-6717777; www.casadegoa.com; Dr Afonso Rd, Tivai Vaddo; r/ste/villa incl breakfast from ₹7000/11,000/12,500; ❄@🛜🏊) The beautiful Casa de Goa is popular with Indian families and books up months in advance for weekends and high season – it's really only a good deal from April to October when rates are less than half. Portuguese-style

COLONIAL CALANGUTE

It's hard to find traces of the old, gentile or 'authentic' Calangute among the holiday mayhem, but it's still there. On the road to Saligao, don't miss **St Alex's Church**, with its magnificently golden and ornamented *reredos* (ornamental screen) and pulpit. Next, look out for the stately 18th-century **Casa Braganza** *palácio* (palace), and **Casa dos Proença**, a grand mansion built in the early 18th century by Calangute's then-wealthiest family. You'll notice the grand, tower-shaped verandah, screened off with oyster-shell windows, while the mansion's pitched roof was designed to create a natural air-conditioning system, channelling in cool air from the building's doors and windows.

Another relic of Calangute's past can be found at the **old customs post**, at the market crossroads. Several of these posts were built during Portuguese rule to monitor the coming and going of goods, and to deter smuggling. Nearby, the **covered market** makes for good local wandering, among a crush of Goans all here to buy fresh produce, spices, coffee, meat and fish – still a very local Calangute experience.

yellow ochre buildings orbit a pretty pool courtyard, decor is bright and fresh, and the big, clean rooms have safes, flat-screen TVs and new fridges, with other high-end and thoughtful touches.

Baga

★ **Indian Kitchen** GUESTHOUSE $
(✆9822149615, 0832-2277555; www.indiankitchen-goa.com; s/d/chalet ₹770/990/1500; ❄@✆☎) If a colourful budget stay is what you're after, look no further than this family-run guesthouse, which offers a range of accommodation from basic to more spacious, comfy apartments, but all with lots of effort at individual charm. There's a neat central courtyard and, surprisingly for a budget place, a sparklingly clean pool out the back. Each room has its own terrace or sit-out. Air-con is charged at an extra ₹600; wi-fi costs ₹100 per day.

Melissa Guest House GUESTHOUSE $
(✆9822180095, 0832-2279583; Baga River Rd; d ₹800) Across the Baga River, Melissa Guest House has just four neat little rooms, all with attached bathrooms and hot-water showers, in a tatty garden. Good value for the location.

Alidia Beach Cottages GUESTHOUSE $$
(✆0832-2279014; Calungute–Baga Rd, Saunta Waddo; d ₹2000, with AC from ₹3300; ❄☎☎) Set back behind a whitewashed church off busy Baga Rd, this convivial but quiet place has beautifully kept Mediterranean-style rooms orbiting a gorgeous pool. The cheaper, non-AC rooms at the back are not as good, but all are in reasonably good condi-

tion, staff are eager to please, and there's a path leading directly to Baga Beach.

Divine Guest House GUESTHOUSE $$
(✆0832-2279546, 9370273464; www.indivinehome.com; Baga River Rd; s ₹600, d ₹1200-1300, with AC ₹1650-3000; ❄@☎) Not the bargain it once was, Divine still sits pretty on the relatively quiet headland north of the Baga River. The 'Praise the Lord' gatepost offers a little gentle proselytising from the friendly family, while the rooms are homey and bright with the odd individual touches. Wi-fi is prepaid.

Cavala Seaside Resort HOTEL $$
(✆0832-2276090; www.cavala.com; Calungute–Baga Rd; s/d incl breakfast from ₹1500/3000, d & ste with AC ₹3500-5500; ❄☎☎) Idiosyncratic, ivy-clad Cavala has been harbouring Baga-bound travellers for over 25 years and is often full. Perhaps as a result, service is indifferent, but there's a big range of rooms, pool and a bar-restaurant with frequent live music.

Casa Baga BOUTIQUE HOTEL $$$
(✆0832-6517779, 0832-2253204; www.casaboutiquehotels.com; d ₹6600-10,000; ❄@☎☎) The 24 luxury Balinese-style rooms, some with huge four-poster beds, make for a classy and tranquil stay in the midst of Baga's action, with all the little stylish touches the Casa boutique team is so adept at providing.

★ **Nilaya Hermitage** HOTEL $$$
(✆0832-2269793; www.nilaya.com; Arpora; ❄@☎) The ultimate in Goan luxury, set 3km inland from the beach at Arpora, a stay here will see you signing the guestbook with Bollywood stars and the likes of Giorgio

NORTH GOA CALANGUTE & BAGA

Armani, Sean Connery and Kate Moss. Eleven beautiful red-stone rooms undulate around a swimming pool. The food is as dreamy as the surroundings, and the spa will see you spoiled rotten.

✖ Eating

Calangute and Baga boast probably the greatest concentration of dining options anywhere in Goa, with everything from the simplest street food to the finest fillet steak.

The beach shacks are an obvious go-to, but there are some interesting gems along the 'Strip' and excellent upmarket offerings on the north side of the Baga River.

✖ Calangute

Plantain Leaf INDIAN $
(☑0832-2279860; veg thali ₹100, mains ₹90-270; ⊗8am-11pm) In the heart of Calangute's busy market area, 1st-floor Plantain Leaf has consistently been the area's best veg restaurant for many years. It's gone through a change though, dumping the classic South Indian banana leaf thalis, adding nonveg (meat) to the menu and expanding its repertoire to more North Indian flavours. It's still a good place for a thali, along with seafood (fish thali ₹150), kebabs and biryani, and it just sneaks in to the budget category.

Infantaria BAKERY, ITALIAN $$
(Calangute-Baga Rd; pastries ₹50-200, mains ₹160-440; ⊗7.30am-midnight) Infanteria began life as Calangute's best bakery but has developed into an extremely popular Italian-cum-Indian restaurant. The bakery roots are still there, though, with homemade cakes, croissants, little flaky pastries and real coffee. Get in early for breakfast before the good stuff runs out. For lunch and dinner it's Goan and Italian specialities and a full bar. Regular live music in season.

Cafe Sussegado Souza GOAN $$
(☑8652839651; Calangute-Anjuna Rd; mains ₹160-280; ⊗noon-midnight) In a little yellow Portuguese-era house just south of the Calangute market area, Cafe Sussegado is the place to come for Goan food such as fish curry rice, chicken *xacuti* (a spicy coconut dish) and pork *sorpotel* (a vinegary stew made from liver, heart and kidneys), with a shot of *feni* (Goan liquour) to be going on with. Authentic, busy and good atmosphere.

Casandré GOAN, MULTICUISINE $$
(mains ₹130-300; ⊗noon-3pm & 6pm-midnight) Housed in an old Portuguese-style bungalow, this dim and tranquil taverna seems a little out of place amid the tourist tat of Calangute's main beach drag. With a long and old-fashioned menu encompassing everything from 'sizzlers' to Goan specialities, and a cocktail list featuring the good old gimlet, this is a loveable time-warp.

★A Reverie INTERNATIONAL $$$
(☑9823505550; www.areverie.com; Holiday St; mains ₹475-700; ⊗7pm-late) A gorgeous award-winning lounge bar, all armchairs, cool jazz and whimsical outdoor space, this is the place to spoil yourself, with the likes of Serrano ham, grilled asparagus, French wines and Italian cheeses. Although fine dining, A Reverie likes to style itself as 'fun dining' and doesn't take itself too seriously. On the snack list, check out the Indian taco truck (₹275), wasabi prawns or barbecue pulled-pork rolls.

✖ Baga

Britto's MULTICUISINE $$
(☑0832-2277331; Baga Beach; mains ₹180-460; ⊗8.30am-midnight) Long-running Britto's is an arena-sized Baga institution at the north end of the beachfront, with a sandy floor if you've forgotten you're on the beach. It's a good spot for breakfast and gets busy for lunch and dinner. The drinks list is longer than the food menu and young Indian tourists are fond of ordering the iced Kingfisher mini-kegs. All good fun and there's live music most nights in season.

★Go With the Flow BRAZILIAN, INTERNATIONAL $$$
(☑7507771556; www.gowiththeflowgoa.com; Baga River Rd; dishes ₹200-650; ⊗6pm-late Mon-Sat) Stepping into the fantasy neon-lit garden of illuminated white-wicker furniture is wow factor enough, but the food is equally out of this world. With a global menu leaning towards European and South American flavours, Brazilian chef Guto brings a wealth of experience and culinary imagination to the table. Try some of the small bites (ask about a tasting plate) or go straight for the pork belly or duck ravioli. If you don't suffer vertigo, check out the 30ft-high dining tower with superb views back over Baga Beach.

★ **Fiesta** CONTINENTAL **$$$**

(✆ 0832-2279894; www.fiestagoa.in; Tito's Lane; mains ₹250-600; ⊙ 7pm-late) Follow the lamplights off happening Tito's Lane; there's something magical about stepping into Fiesta's candlelit split-level tropical garden. Soft music and exotic furnishings add to an upmarket Mediterranean-style dining experience that starts with homemade pizza and pasta and extends to French-influenced seafood dishes and some of the finest desserts around. Worth a splurge.

Le Poisson Rouge FRENCH **$$$**

(✆ 0832-3245800; www.gregorybazire.com; Baga River Rd; mains ₹390-480; ⊙ 7pm-midnight) The Baga River area manages to do fine dining with aplomb, and this Indo-French restaurant is one of the best. Simple local ingredients are combined into winning dishes such as king prawns ravioli with lemongrass, vegetable ratatouille, river crab with tender coconut tempura vegetables, and crème brûlée, all served up in romantic surroundings beneath the stars.

🍷 Drinking & Nightlife

Baga's boisterous club scene, centred on Tito's Lane, has long been well known among the tourist crowd looking for a good time. It certainly amped up after the late-night music bans cancelled all-night parties around Anjuna and Vagator. Some find the scene here a little sleazy and the bar staff indifferent. Solo women are welcomed into clubs (usually free) but should exercise care and take taxis to and from venues.

Baga is still a go-to place for many, but nightlife has spread out to places like Arpora's long-running Club Cubana and some new nightclubs down south in Candolim.

Tito's CLUB

(✆ 9822765002; www.titosgroup.com; Tito's Lane, Baga; cover charge couples/women from ₹500/ free; ⊙ 8pm-3am) The long-running titan on Goa's clubbing scene, Tito's has done its best to clean up the locals-leering-at-Western-women image of yesteryear. It's couples or ladies only – solo men can forget it, though partying lads are known to bribe solo ladies to accompany them in.

Café Mambo CLUB

(✆ 7507333003; www.cafemambogoa.com; Tito's Lane, Baga; cover charge couples ₹500; ⊙ 10.30pm-3am) Part of the Tito's empire, Mambo is one of Baga's most happening

CHURCH OF NOSSA SENHORA, MAE DE DEUS

Church of Nossa Senhora, Mae de Deus (Church of Our Lady, Mother of God) As you explore the countryside, don't miss a peek into the Church of Nossa Senhora, Mae de Deus, with its unusual neo-Gothic Christmas-cake style topped with a row of fanciful turrets. Built in 1873, it houses a rather technicolour, and allegedly 'miraculous', statue of the Mother of God herself, rescued from the ruins of an old convent at Old Goa. It's situated 2km from Calangute, on the road towards the village of Saligao.

The church is brightly lit every evening – making it a useful landmark for navigating the surrounding country lanes.

clubs with an indoor/outdoor beachfront location and nightly DJs pumping out house, hip hop and Latino tunes. Couples or females only.

Club Cubana CLUB

(✆ 9823539000; www.clubcubanagoa.com; Arpora; ⊙ 9.30pm-4am) Billing itself as the 'nightclub in the sky,' this hilltop place in Arpora (a few kilometres north of Baga) has been providing a late-night pool party scene for more than a decade. As with most clubs it's couples or ladies only (though solo males can usually pay a premium to get in) and, depending on the night, it's open bar with a cover charge of ₹1000 to ₹2000. Wednesday is ladies night.

Cape Town Cafe BAR

(www.capetowncafe.com; Tito's Lane, Baga; ⊙ 11am-1am; 🛜) The most laid-back of the Tito's venues, Cape Town has a street-front lounge bar with wi-fi and live sports on big screens, while inside international DJs play until late. Goan food and bar snacks available.

🛍 Shopping

In line with its status as the tourist capital of Goa, Calangute has likewise grown to become the shopping capital. Flashy neon-lit international brand shops line the main Calangute–Candolim road. Upmarket gold and jewellery shops, boutique fashion stores and dozens of arts-and-craft emporia are also here.

The attractions here are as much about food stalls and entertainment as shopping, but there's a big range of colourful stalls, flashing jewellery, laser pointers and other novelties that would be difficult to sell during daylight hours.

Both start up in late November and are occasionally known to be cancelled at short notice, so check locally or with taxi drivers.

Saturday Night Market (www.snmgoa.com; Arpora; ☉6pm-late Sat Nov-Mar) The original Saturday Night Market (formerly Ingo's) is up the hill in Arpora, about 2km northest of Baga.

Mackie's Saturday Nite Bazaar (www.mackiesnitebazaar.com; ☉6pm-late Sat Nov-Apr) Colourful Saturday night market on the Baga River with music, entertainment, shopping and food stalls.

However, it's probably the small-time stalls that will catch the eye of most foreign visitors. Calangute and Baga have been swamped by Kashmiri traders eager to cash in on the tourist boom. There is a fantastic range of things to buy: Kashmiri carpets, embroideries and papier mâché boxes, as well as genuine and reproduction Tibetan and Rajasthani crafts, bronzes, carvings and miniature paintings. Check out the market on Baga Rd near Tito's Lane to compare prices. This is the same sort of stuff you'll see in abundance at the Anjuna flea market.

Karma Collection
SOUVENIRS
(www.karmacollectiongoa.com; Calangute-Arpora Rd, Calangute; ☉9.30am-10.30pm) Beautiful home furnishings, textiles, ornaments, bags and other enticing stuff – some of it antique – has been sourced from across India, Pakistan and Afghanistan and gathered at Karma Collection, which makes for a mouth-watering browse. Fixed prices mean there's no need to bargain, though it's not cheap.

All About Eve
CLOTHING, ACCESSORIES
(☑0832-2275687; Calangute-Arpora Rd; ☉10am-8pm) Attached to Karma Collection, All About Eve stocks unusual clothes, bags and accessories, many designed by the owners themselves, and which are unlike any of the usual array you'll find on a beach-road stall.

Casa Goa
HOMEWARES
(☑0832-2281048; Calangute-Baga Rd; ☉10am-8pm) A lovely collection of furniture, textiles and home accessories housed in an old Portuguese-era mansion. Browse Casa Goa for a nice vase, a cute picture frame or even a four-poster bed.

Star Magic Shop
MAGIC
(Baga Beach Rd; ☉9am-late, closed Wed Nov-Apr) Learn magic tricks in just two minutes (that's the claim!) at this little Baga shop. Star also has a stall at the Anjuna flea market and the Saturday night markets in season.

Tara Bookshop
BOOKS
(☑9822116925; Tito's Lane; ☉9am-midnight Mon-Sat) A good selection of new and second-hand books in Baga central; it's also a book exchange and travel agency.

Literati Bookshop & Cafe
BOOKS
(☑0832-2277740; www.literati-goa.com; Calangute; ☉10am-6.30pm Mon-Sat) A refreshingly different bookstore, in the owners' South Calangute home, and a very pleasant Italian-style garden cafe. Come for a fine espresso and browse the range of books by Goan and Indian authors as well as antiquarium literature. Check the website for readings and other events.

❶ Information
Currency-exchange offices, ATMs, supermarkets and pharmacies cluster around Calangute's main market and bus stand, and south on the road to Candolim.

There are still a few internet cafes around charging ₹40 per hour, but wi-fi is widespread in hotels and beach shacks.

❶ Getting There & Away
Frequent buses go to Panaji (₹15, 45 minutes) and Mapusa (₹12, 30 minutes) from both the Calangute and Baga bus stands.

A taxi from Calangute or Baga to Panaji costs around ₹400 and takes about half an hour.

Paulo Tours & Travels (☑ 08322281274; www.phmgoa.com; ☻ 9am-9pm) One of the most dependable operators for private buses to Hampi and Mumbai; pick-up is available in Calangute. Has an office near the beach.

❶ Getting Around

Motorcycle and scooter hire is easy to arrange in Calangute and Baga. Prices are fairly steady at around ₹250 for a gearless Honda Kinetic and ₹350 to ₹400 for an Enfield, but high demand means you might have to pay much more in peak season. Definitely try bargaining in quieter times or for rentals of more than a week.

A local bus runs between the Calangute and Baga stands every few minutes; catch it anywhere along the way, though when traffic is bad it might be quicker to walk.

Taxis between Calangute and northern Baga Beach charge an extortionate ₹100.

Anjuna

Dear old Anjuna has been a stalwart of the hippie scene since the 1960s and still drags out the sarongs and sandalwood each Wednesday (in season) for its famous – and once infamous – flea market. Though it continues to pull in droves of backpackers, midrange tourists are increasingly making their way here for a dose of hippie-chic, and Anjuna continues to evolve with its beach party scene and a small flowering of new restaurants and bars.

The village itself is certainly a bit ragged around the edges these days and is spread out over a wide area – if you arrive at the bus stand around the northern cliff-edge you're likely to be a bit nonplussed by the place. But do as most do: hire a scooter or motorbike and explore the back lanes and southern beach area and you'll find a place that suits, along with a bit of the old-style Anjuna vibe and some party action. Anjuna will grow on you.

🏃 Activities

Anjuna's charismatic, narrow beach runs for almost 2km from the rocky, low-slung cliffs at the northern village area right down beyond the flea market in the south. There's reasonable paddling at the southern and middle sections (beware of strong currents), but even here the beach shrinks to almost nothing when the high tide washes in. When the tide goes out, it becomes a lovely – and often surprisingly quiet – stretch of sand.

On market days in season there's often **paragliding** from the headland at the southern end of the beach.

Lots of yoga, ayurveda and other alternative therapies and regimes are on offer in season; look out for noticeboards at popular cafes.

Tito's White House　　　YOGA, MARTIAL ARTS
(☑ 9960589987; www.karatetaichi.com; Anjuna–Calangute Rd; ☻ 7-8.30pm Mon, Wed & Fri, 7-8.30am Tue, Thu & Sat) Tito's White House, on the Anjuna–Calangute Rd, is a base for yoga as well as karate, tai-chi and Zumba classes.

Brahmani Yoga　　　YOGA
(☑ 9545620578; www.brahmaniyoga.com; Tito's White House, Aguada-Siolim Rd; classes ₹600, 10-class pass ₹4500) This friendly drop-in centre offers daily classes from November to April in ashtanga, vinyasa, hatha and dynamic yoga, as well as pranayama meditation. No need to book: just turn up 15 minutes before the beginning of class to secure space enough to spread your yoga mat.

Splashdown Water Park　　　SWIMMING
(☑ 0832-2273008; www.splashdowngoa.com; Anjuna-Baga Rd, Arpora; weekdays/weekends ₹380/420, spectators ₹260/300; ☻ 10.30am-6pm) This fabulous collection of pools, fountains and waterslides will keep kids (and adults) happy all day long. A nice cafe and bar overlook the action. It's in Arpora, roughly halfway between Anjuna and Baga.

Mukti Kitchen　　　COOKING
(☑ 08007359170; Anjuna-Baga Rd, Arpora; veg/nonveg ₹1500/1800; ☻ 11am-2pm & 5-8pm) Mukti shares her cooking skills twice daily at these recommended classes on the Anjuna Rd in Arpora. Courses include five dishes that can be tailored – veg or nonveg, Goan, Indian or ayurvedic. Minimum four people, maximum six; book one day ahead.

🛏 Sleeping

Anjuna has a good range of budget and midrange accommodation spread over a wide area. Dozens of basic rooms are strung along Anjuna's northern clifftop and beach stretch, charging ₹600 to ₹1000 outside of peak periods. Plenty of small, family-run guesthouses are also tucked back from the main beach strip, offering nicer double rooms for a similar price; look out for signs announcing 'rooms to let' or 'house to let.'

Anjuna

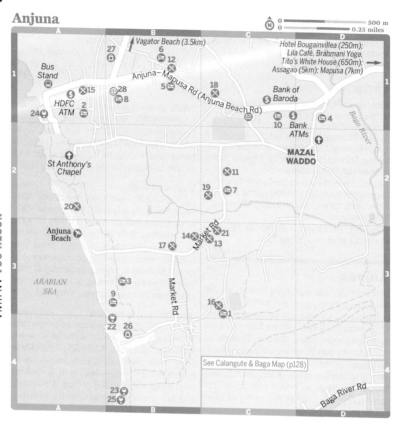

ARABIAN
SEA

See Calangute & Baga Map (p128)

Prison Hostel
HOSTEL **$**

(☑0832-2273745; www.thehostelcrowd.com; 940 Market Rd; dm ₹350-400, with AC ₹450, d ₹1400; ❉🛜) Cell-like rooms are not uncommon in India, but this quirky new backpacker hostel on Anjuna's Market Rd goes a step further and is themed like a jail. Apart from the bars on the windows and black-and-white decor, there's no sense of incarceration here, however. Clean four-to 10-bed dorms have individual lockers and bed-lights, there's a good kitchen, and breakfast and wi-fi are included. Expect loud music and partying guests.

Florinda's
GUESTHOUSE **$**

(☑9890216520; s/d ₹500/700, with AC ₹1500; ❉🛜) One of the better budget places near the beach, Florinda's has clean rooms, with 24-hour hot water, window screens and mosquito nets, set around a pretty garden. The few air-con rooms fill up fast.

Vilanova
GUESTHOUSE **$**

(☑0832-6450389, 9225904244; mendonca90@rediffmail.com; Anjuna Beach Rd; d ₹600-700, with AC ₹1200; ❉) Big, clean rooms have a fridge, TV, 24-hour hot water and window screens, and are set in three Portuguese-style bungalows in a cute little compound. Good vibes and a comfortable family atmosphere, with friendly staff and a good restaurant.

Red Door Hostel
HOSTEL **$**

(☑0832-2274423; reddoorhostels@gmail.com; dm without/with AC ₹500/600, d without/with AC ₹1600/2000; ❉🛜) A recent addition to North Goa's hostel scene, Red Door is a welcoming place close to Anjuna's central crossroads. It offers clean four- and six-bed dorms plus a few private rooms. Facilities include lockers, free wi-fi, a garden and good communal areas, including a well-equipped kitchen. Laid-back vibe and resident pet dogs.

Anjuna

Paradise   GUESTHOUSE $
(☑ 9922541714; janet_965@hotmail.com; Anjuna-Mapusa Rd; d ₹800-1000, with AC ₹2000; ✳ @ 📶) This friendly place is fronted by an old Portuguese home and offers neat, clean rooms with well-decorated options in the newer annexe. The better rooms have TV, fridge and hammocks on the balcony. Friendly owner Janet and her family also run the pharmacy, general store, restaurant, internet cafe, Connexions travel agency and money exchange!

Peace Land   GUESTHOUSE $
(San Miguel's; ☑ 9822685255, 0832-2273700; s/d from ₹600/800, with AC ₹1200-1500; ✳ 📶) A good budget deal with small but tidy rooms arranged around a tranquil courtyard garden back from the main Anjuna road. It's run by a friendly family, and there's a pool table, chill-out area, hammocks and a decent restaurant.

Sea Horse   HUT $$
(☑ 9764465078; www.vistapraiaanjuna.com; ☺ hut without/with AC ₹1500/1800; ✳ 📶) A line-up of timber cabins behind the beach restaurant of the same name, Sea Horse is decent value for the location. The huts are small and have modern bathrooms, but get a little hot – go for the air-con rooms if it's humid. Staff are friendly and accommodating. The same owners have a pricier beachfront set-up called Praia Anjuna.

Palacete Rodrigues   HERITAGE HOTEL $$
(☑ 0832-2273358; www.palacetegoa.com; Mazal Vaddo; d & ste ₹3000-6000; ✳ 📶 ♨) This lovely family-run mansion, filled with antiques and ornate furniture, is absolutely as quirky as you could hope for in Anjuna – perhaps too over-the-top for some. Some of the 14 rooms and suites are themed and decorated along ethnic cultural lines: French, Chinese, Japanese and Goan. Outside is a neat garden and pool area.

Banyan Soul   BOUTIQUE HOTEL $$
(☑ 9820707283; www.thebanyansoul.com; d ₹2200; ✳ 📶) A slinky 12-room option, tucked down the lane off Market Rd, and lovingly conceived and run by Sumit, a young Mumbai escapee. Rooms are chic and well equipped with TV, and there's a pleasant library and a shady seating area beneath a banyan tree.

Hotel Bougainvillea   HERITAGE HOTEL $$
(Granpa's Inn; ☑ 0832-273270; www.granpasinn.com; Anjuna-Mapusa Rd; d/ste incl breakfast from ₹4400/5000; ✳ 📶 ♨) An old-fashioned hotel housed in a pretty, yellow 200-year-old ancestral mansion, 'Granpa's Inn' offers charm and a touch of luxury with a lovely pool and well-decorated cottages. The grounds are lush, shady and make a cool retreat, though some find it a little far from the beach for this price.

Casa Anjuna   HERITAGE HOTEL $$$
(☑ 0832-2274123-5; www.casaboutiquehotels.com; D'Mello Vaddo 66; r from ₹7700; ✳ 📶 ♨) This heritage hotel is enclosed in lovely plant-filled gardens around an inviting pool, managing to shield itself from the hype of central Anjuna. All rooms have antique furnishings and period touches; like many upmarket places it's better value out of season when rates halve.

NORTH GOA ANJUNA

ANJUNA FLEA MARKET

Anjuna Flea Market (⊙8am-late Wed, Nov-late Mar) Anjuna's weekly Wednesday flea market is as much part of the Goan experience as a day on the beach. More than three decades ago, it was conceived and created by hippies smoking jumbo joints, convening to compare experiences on the heady Indian circuit and selling pairs of Levi jeans or handmade jewellery to help fund the rest of their stay.

Nowadays things are far more mainstream and the merchandise comes from all over India: sculptures and jewellery courtesy of the Tibetan and Kashmiri traders; bejewelled Gujarati tribal women selling T-shirts; richly coloured saris, mirror bags and bedspreads from Rajasthan; and sacks of spices from Kerala. It's hard to miss the tribal girls from Karnataka pleading passers-by to 'come look in my shop.' Weaving in among this syrupy blend of stalls are the remaining hippies, the backpackers, weekenders from Mumbai, and bus- and taxi-loads of package tourists from Russia and Europe.

Such purchasing power has inevitably pushed market prices up, but with plenty of competition you can still find some good bargains if you know the right price. These days the market sprawls back from the beach to the entrance road in the paddy fields; the endless stalls can become repetitive after a while. For a rest from the shopping there are chai stalls and a couple of restaurant-bars with live music. **Cafe Looda** has a fabulous sunset beachfront location and live music from 5pm.

You might still find Westerners trading goods and services (tattoos, piercings and the like) but it's much more a souvenir market these days. Despite changes over the years, the market shows no sign of waning in popularity, so dive in and enjoy the ride. The best time to visit is early (from 8am) or late afternoon (around 4pm till close just after sunset). The first market of the season is around mid-November, continuing till the end of April.

🍴 Eating

Anjuna has always had a reasonably good range of eating options, from clifftop restaurant-bars and cafes hidden in the back lanes to the big beachfront places near the market site. New places are popping up, keeping things fresh. Self-caterers will love Oxford Stores (p140), Anjuna's excellent expat-oriented supermarket.

★ Artjuna Cafe
CAFE $

(☑0832-2274794; www.artjuna.com; Market Rd; mains ₹80-290; ⊙8am-10.30pm) Artjuna is right up there with our favourite cafes in Anjuna. Along with all-day breakfast, outstanding espresso coffee, salads, sandwiches and Middle Eastern surprises like baba ganoush, tahini and falafel, this sweet garden cafe has an excellent craft and lifestyle shop, yoga classes and one of Anjuna's best noticeboards. Great meeting place.

Café Diogo
CAFE $

(Market Rd; snacks ₹60-140; ⊙8.30am-3pm) Excellent fruit salads are sliced and diced at Café Diogo, a small locally run cafe on the way down to the market. The generous avocado, cheese and mushroom toasted sandwiches and the unusual gooseberry lassi are also worth a try.

Cafe Orange Boom
CAFE $

(Market Rd; mains from ₹80; ⊙8.30am-3pm) Orange Boom, a popular cafe on the road to the market, specialises in breakfast and lunch and has friendly service and a useful noticeboard.

Whole Bean Tofu
CAFE $

(Market Rd; mains ₹70-180; ⊙8am-5pm) This simple, tasty, tofu-filled health-food cafe focuses on all things created from the most versatile of beans.

Dhum Biryani & Kebabs
INDIAN $$

(Anjuna-Mapusa Rd; mains ₹180-350; ⊙9am-1am) Loved by visitors and locals alike, Dhum Biryani serves up consistently good kebabs as well as plates of biryani and other usual suspects.

German Bakery
MULTICUISINE $$

(www.german-bakery.in; bread & pastries ₹50-90, mains ₹100-450; ⊙8.30am-11pm; 🖘) Leafy and filled with prayer flags, occasional live music and garden lights, German Bakery is a long-standing favourite for hearty and healthy breakfast, fresh-baked bread and organic food, but these days the menu runs to pasta, burgers and seafood. Prices are up and service is down though. Healthy juices (think wheatgrass) and espresso coffee.

Om Made Cafe
MEDITERRANEAN **$$**

(D'Mello Vaddo; dishes ₹120-250; ◷9am-sunset) A highlight on Anjuna's same-same clifftop strip, this cheery little place offers striped deckchairs from which to enjoy the views and the super breakfasts, sandwiches and salads. The food is fresh and organic, the preparation thoughtful.

Lila Café
CAFE **$$**

(www.lilacafegoa.com; Tito's White House, Aguada-Siolim Rd; mains ₹80-280; ◷8.30am-6pm) This German-expat–run cafe was a traveller favourite down at Baga for many years before moving up to its new location at Tito's White House. It still serves great home-baked breads and specialises in buffalo cheese and smoked ham.

Heidi's Beer Garden
GERMAN **$$**

(☑9886376922; Market Rd; mains ₹100-400; ◷11am-11pm) It may well be Goa's first German-style beer garden and restaurant, which is reason enough to call into Heidi's. Another is the range of some 40 international beers from Germany, Belgium, Mexico, Japan, Portugal and more. The imported beers are relatively expensive, but you can still order local beers, including a Goan draught. The food is mostly German and European, including bratwurst sausages and the acclaimed German thali (₹400).

Martha's Breakfast Home
CAFE **$$**

(meals ₹60-300; ◷7.30am-1.30pm) As the name suggests, welcoming Martha's speciality is breakfast, served up in a quiet garden on the way down to the flea-market site. Omelettes, fresh juice and cereal are de rigueur, but the stars of the show are the waffles with maple syrup and strawberries (in season). There are some nice rooms (₹700) here and a two-bedroom house to rent (₹10,000 per week). Located off Market Rd.

★Burger Factory
BURGERS **$$$**

(Anjuna-Mapusa Rd; burgers ₹250-450; ◷noon-11pm) There's no mistaking what's on offer at this little alfresco diner. The straightforward menu is chalked up on a blackboard at the side, and though the burgers aren't cheap, they are interesting and expertly crafted. Choose between beef or chicken burgers and toppings such as cheddar, wasabi and mayo or beetroot and aioli.

La Tomatina
SPANISH **$$$**

(☑8007966409; www.latomatina-goa.com; Anjuna-Mapusa Rd; tapas plates ₹150-270; mains ₹350-450; ◷noon-11pm) Anjuna's Spanish cantina is very true to its name – the tapas and main dishes, including paella (₹350), are authentic and tasty. Sample *patatas bravas,* Andalucian calamari or fish croquettes, or share a two-person tasting plate (₹750). The Serrano ham is imported, of course. Live flamenco music and dancing some nights.

Drinking & Nightlife

Though Anjuna is no longer trance-party central, at the southern end of the beach several nightclubs are some of the most happening places in North Goa when the night is right. Market day is always fun, with live music at one or both of the two bars there.

Party nights also crank up at one or more of the clifftop bars, at the northern end of the beach. All places double as restaurants and usually have some form of accommodation.

Purple Martini
COCKTAIL BAR

(www.mypurplemartini.com; ◷6pm-midnight) The clifftop sunset views, blue-and-white colour scheme and swanky bar at this beautifully situated restaurant-bar could easily transport you to Santorini. Come for a sundowner cocktail (from ₹300) and check out the menu of Greek kebabs and Mediterranean salads.

Curlies
BAR

(www.curliesgoa.com; ◷9am-3am) At the southern end of Anjuna Beach, Curlies mixes laid-back beach-bar vibe with sophisticated night spot – the party nights here are notorious. There's a parachute-silk-covered rooftop lounge bar and an enclosed late-night dance club. Thursdays and Saturdays are big nights, as are full moon nights.

NORTH GOA ANJUNA

ⓘ DANGERS & ANNOYANCES

Despite regular crackdowns and party restrictions, Anjuna and Vagator are still well-known places for procuring illicit substances, though they're not quite so freely available (or as cheap) as in Goa's trance-party heyday. Participate at your peril – the police Anti-Narcotics Cell has been known to carry out checks on foreigners and the Fort Aguada Jail currently accommodates a number of international 'guests' on 10-year drug-related stretches. Even bribes might not get you out of trouble.

Take great care of your wallet, camera and the like on market day, when pickpocketing can be a problem.

Cafe Lilliput
BAR, CLUB

(☎ 0832-2274648; www.cafelilliput.com; ⊗ 8am-
1am, to 4am party nights; ☎) Hovering over the
beach near the flea-market site, Lilliput has
built itself a reputation as one of the go-to
nightspots, but it also has a good all-day
restaurant and some interesting accommodation at the back.

Shiva Valley
CLUB

(⊗ 8am-3am) At the very southern end of
Anjuna Beach, Shiva Valley has grown from
small beach shack to fully fledged club, with
Tuesday the main party night.

🛍 Shopping

Oxford Stores
SUPERMARKET

(Anjuna-Vagator Rd; ⊗ 8.30am-9pm) The huge
Oxford Stores, 100m from the Starco crossroads on the road to Vagator, is a fully
fledged supermarket, complete with shopping trolleys and checkout scanners. It's
an awesome place to stock up on toiletries,
cheap booze and all those little international
luxuries.

ℹ Information

Anjuna has a group of ATMs clustered together
on Anjuna Beach Rd, and one close to the bus
stand.

Internet joints come and go but with free wi-fi
so widespread they're becoming harder to find.

There are plenty of reliable travel agents in
town that can book train tickets, flights and local
tours.

Bank of Baroda (Anjuna-Mapusa Rd;
⊗ 9.30am-2.30pm) Gives cash advances on
Visa and MasterCard.

Manali Guest House (per hour ₹40;
⊗ 9.30am-8.30pm) Has an internet cafe and is
also notable for its good bookshop and travel
agency.

ℹ Getting There & Away

Buses to Mapusa (₹15) depart every half-hour
or so from the main bus stand at the end of the
Anjuna–Mapusa Rd near the beach; some buses
coming from Mapusa continue on to Vagator and
Chapora.

A couple of direct daily buses head south to
Calangute; otherwise, take a bus to Mapusa and
another from there.

Plenty of motorcycle taxis and autorickshaws
gather at the main crossroads and you can also
easily hire scooters and motorcycles here from
₹250 to ₹400 – most Anjuna-based travellers
get around on two wheels.

Mapusa

POP 40,500

Mapusa (pronounced 'Mapsa') is the largest
town in northern Goa, and is most often
visited for its busy Friday market, which
attracts scores of buyers and sellers from
neighbouring towns and villages, as well as
a healthy intake of tourists from the northern beaches. It's a good place to pick up the
usual range of embroidered bed sheets and
the like, at prices far lower than in the beach
resorts.

Many travellers pass through Mapusa
anyway as it's the major transport hub for
northern Goa buses. Most amenities are arranged around the Municipal Gardens, just
north of the Kadamba bus station and main
market site.

Environmental action group **Goa Foundation** (☎ 0832-2256479; www.goafoundation.
org; St Britto's Apts, G-8 Feira Alta, Mapusa) has its
headquarters in Mapusa, while numerous
charity organisations, including International Animal Rescue and El Shaddai are
nearby in Assagao.

◉ Sights

Church of Our Lady of Miracles
CHURCH

Founded in 1594 and rebuilt several times
since, the Church of Our Lady of Miracles
(also known as St Jerome's), around 600m
east of the Municipal Gardens, is famous
more for its annual festival than for its architecture. It was built by the Portuguese on
the site of an old Hindu temple, and thus
the Hindu community still holds the site as
sacred.

On the 16th day after Easter, the church's
annual feast day is celebrated here by both
Hindus and Christians – one of the best examples of the way in which Hinduism and
Christianity often coexist merrily in Goa.

Maruti Temple
HINDU TEMPLE

In the centre of town, the small,
pastel-coloured Maruti temple was built in
the 1840s at a site where the monkey god
Hanuman was covertly worshipped during
more oppressive periods of Portuguese rule.
After temples had been destroyed by the
Portuguese, devotees placed a picture of
Hanuman at the fireworks shop that stood
here, and arrived cloaked in secrecy to perform their *pujas* (prayers).

In April 1843 the picture was replaced by
a silver idol and an increasing number of

WORTH A TRIP

ASSAGAO

On the road between Mapusa and Anjuna or Vagator, Assagao is one of North Goa's prettiest villages, with almost traffic-free country roads passing old Portuguese-era mansions and whitewashed churches. The area is inspiring enough to be home to several of North Goa's best yoga retreats (p142).

Local organisation **El Shaddai** (☑0832-2461068, 0832-6513286; www.childrescue.net; El Shaddai House, Socol Vaddo, Assagao), a child protection charity, has several schools based here.

Spicy Mama's (☑9623348958; www.spicymamasgoa.com; 138/3 Bairo Alto, Assagao; veg/nonveg 1-day course ₹2000/3000, 3-day ₹5000/7000, 5-day ₹10,000/12,000) For cooking enthusiasts, Spicy Mama's specialises in spicy North Indian cuisine, from butter chicken to *aloo gobi* and *palak paneer*, prepared at the country home of Suchi. The standard one-day course is four hours; book ahead for in-depth multiday masterclasses.

Sunbeam (www.justjivi.com/goa.html; Anjuna-Mapusa Rd, Assagao; ste from ₹10,000; ❄ 🛜 🏊) This collection of three incredible suites is one of North Goa's most idiosyncratic properties. Owned and overseen by Jivi Sethi, a well-known and flamboyant Indian stylist, Sunbeam is all heirlooms, high theatrics, and lots and lots of luxury – as well as fabulous food.

Villa Blanche Bistro (www.villablanche-goa.com; 283 Badem Church Rd, Assagao; mains ₹180-350; ⊙9am-5.30pm Mon-Sat, 10.30am-3pm Sun) This lovely, chilled garden cafe in the back lanes of Assagao is run by a German-Swiss couple. Salads, sandwiches, filled bagels, desserts and cakes are the speciality. For an indulgent breakfast or brunch try the waffles and pancakes.

---

worshippers began to gather here. Eventually the business community of Mapusa gathered enough funds to acquire the shop, and the temple was built in its place.

The intricate carvings at the doorway of the temple are the work of local artisans.

🛏 Sleeping

With the northern beaches so close and most long-distance buses departing in the late afternoon or early evening, it's hard to think of a good reason to stay in Mapusa, but there are a few options if you do.

Hotel Vilena HOTEL $
(☑0832-2263115; Feira Baixa Rd; d without/with bathroom ₹630/840, with AC ₹1575; ❄) Mapusa's best budget choice, with 14 plain double rooms, is not much to look at, but staff are welcoming.

Mapusa Residency HOTEL $
(☑0832-2262694; d without/with AC ₹1100/1430, ste ₹1790; ❄) Rooms are in the bland-but-functional mould you'd expect from GTDC accommodation, but the borderline budget–midrange price tag is reasonable value for the location across from the bus stand.

Hotel Satyaheera HOTEL $$
(☑0832-2262949; www.hotelsatyaheeragoa.com; d without/with AC from ₹2500/2800; ❄) Next to the little Maruti temple in the town centre, this is widely considered Mapusa's best hotel, which isn't saying much. Rooms are comfortable enough but overpriced. Ruchira (p141), the roof garden restaurant, is a decent place to eat.

🍴 Eating & Drinking

Several cafes within the market area serve simple Indian snacks, dishes and cold drinks to a local clientele.

Hotel Vrundavan INDIAN $
(thalis from ₹75; ⊙7am-10pm Wed-Mon) This all-veg place bordering the Municipal Gardens is a great place for a hot chai, *pav bhaji* or quick breakfast.

Ruchira Restaurant INDIAN, MULTICUISINE $
(Hotel Satyaheera; mains ₹90-180; ⊙11am-11pm) On the top floor of Hotel Satyaheera, this rooftop garden restaurant and bar is popular with tourists and widely deemed one of Mapusa's better family restaurants, serving tasty Goan, Indian and continental dishes (including seafood) at lower prices than the beach shacks.

INLAND YOGA RETREATS

North Goa is well known and rightly popular for its beachy yoga shalas. But back in the countryside, mostly around Assagao, are some top-notch yoga retreats where the Zen-like silence of the forest more than makes up for the lack of ocean views.

Purple Valley Yoga Retreat (☑ 0832-2268363; www.yogagoa.com; 142 Bairo Alto, Assagao; dm/s 1 week from £600/750, 2 weeks £980/1200; ☎) This popular yoga resort in Assagao offers one- or two-week residential courses in ashtanga yoga; weekly rates include accommodation, daily classes, vegetarian meals and full use of resort facilities. Nonresidential two-week courses cost £700. A range of beauty therapies and ayurvedic treatments is also available on-site for course participants.

Sushumna Yoga (☑ 9923219254; www.sushumna.in; 290 Socal Vaddo, Assagao; drop-in class from ₹500, 3-/5-day workshops ₹12,500/20,000) Reputable yoga school with drop-in classes, weekly workshops and teacher-training courses. Specialises in vinyasa flow but also offers beginners' hatha, iyengar, pranayama and restorative yoga.

Swan Yoga Retreat (☑ 0832-2268024, 8007360677; www.swan-yoga-goa.com; Assagao; per person 1 week from ₹17,500) Enveloped in the jungle in a peaceful corner of Assagao, Swan Retreat is a very Zen yoga experience in the Satyananda tradition. Minimum week-long yoga retreats start every Saturday and include eco-accommodation, ayurvedic veg meals, meditation, daily classes and an optional afternoon 'masterclass'. Several levels of cottage and teepee accommodation are spread around the property.

Yoga Magic (☑ 0832-6523796; www.yogamagic.net; Anjuna; s/d lodge ₹6750/9000, ste ₹9000/12,000; ☎) Solar lighting, compost toilets and local building materials (including cow dung and rammed earth) are some of the worthy initiatives practised in this ultraluxurious village of Rajasthani tented lodges and bamboo-villa suites. Organic gourmet vegetarian food and serious yoga and meditation are the order of the day here.

Prices include breakfast and afternoon tea; daily yoga classes cost extra, or you can opt for one of the all-inclusive week-long yoga holidays from ₹38,000. It's located on the Mapusa-Chapora Rd, about 2km from Vagator Beach.

Golden Oven BAKERY $
(Market Rd; pastries from ₹10, mains from ₹50; ⊙ 9am-6.30pm Mon-Sat) For some clean and shiny comfort, duck into this bakery opposite the market, a cool respite from the shopping chaos across the street. As well as cakes and pastries, they serve mini pizzas and sandwiches.

Ruta's World Cafe INTERNATIONAL $$
(☑ 0832-2250757; www.caferuta.com; St Xavier's College Rd, opp Ashirwad Bldg; mains ₹110-270; ⊙ 10am-8pm Mon-Sat) The second branch of Ruta's excellent brand of fresh and tasty American-inspired cuisine has given travellers a good culinary reason to visit Mapusa. The sandwiches, salads and comfort foods such as jambalaya are all delicious. It's north of the centre, in the same Portuguese house as Fabindia.

Pub PUB
(⊙ 10am-4pm & 7-11pm Mon-Sat) Don't be put off by the dingy entrance or stairwell: once you're upstairs, this breezy place opposite the market is great for watching the milling crowds over a cold beer or *feni*. Eclectic daily specials make it a good spot for lunch (mains from ₹100).

🛍 Shopping

Mapusa Market MARKET
(⊙ 8am-6.30pm Mon-Sat) The Mapusa market goes about its business all days except Sunday, but it really gets going on Friday morning. It's a raucous affair that attracts vendors and shoppers from all over Goa, with an entirely different vibe to the Anjuna flea market. Here you'll find locals haggling for clothing and produce, and you can also hunt out antiques, souvenirs and textiles. So significant is the market locally that the town's name is derived from the Konkani words *map* (meaning 'measure') and *sa* (meaning 'fill up'), in reference to the trade in spices, vegetables and fruit that's plied here daily.

Other India Bookstore BOOKS
(☑0832-2263306; www.otherindiabookstore.com; Mapusa Clinic Rd; ☺9am-5pm Mon-Fri, to 1pm Sat) This friendly and rewarding little bookshop, at the end of an improbable, dingy corridor, specialises in books about Goa and India, with a focus on spirituality, environment, politics and travel. It's sign-posted near the Mapusa Clinic, a few hundred metres up the hill from the Municipal Gardens.

ℹ️ Information

There are plenty of ATMs scattered about town, including around the Municipal Gardens and market area.

Mapusa Clinic (☑ 0832-2263343; Mapusa Clinic Rd; ☺ consultations 9.30am-1pm & 4-8pm Mon-Sat) A well-run private medical clinic with 24-hour emergency services. Look for signs to the 'new' Mapusa Clinic, behind the 'old' one.

Pink Panther Travel Agency (☑0832-2263180; panther_goa@sancharnet.in; Coscar Corner; ☺10am-6pm Mon-Fri, to 1.30pm Sat) A useful travel agent that can book bus, train and air tickets (both international and domestic) as well as perform currency exchange. It's just east of the Municipal Gardens.

ℹ️ Getting There & Away

If you're coming to Goa by bus from Mumbai, Mapusa's Kadamba bus stand is the jumping-off point for the northern beaches. Local bus services run every few minutes; look for the correct destination on the sign in the bus windshield – and try to get an express. For buses to the southern beaches, take a bus to Panaji, then Margao, and change there.

Local services include:

Anjuna ₹15, 20 minutes
Arambol ₹30, one hour
Calangute/Candolim ₹12/15, 20/35 minutes
Panaji ₹27, 30 minutes
Thivim ₹15, 20 minutes

Long-distance services are run by both government and private bus companies. Private operators' services are more frequent and have more choice of bus type. Fares are variable based on the season and even day of the week. Private operators have booking offices outside the bus stand (opposite the Municipal Gardens). There's generally little difference in price, comfort or duration between them, but shop around for the best fare. You can check fares and timings for government buses at www.goakadamba.com.

Most long-distance buses depart in the late afternoon or evening. Sample fares include:

Bengaluru ₹900, with AC ₹1200; 13 to 14 hours
Mumbai ₹700, with AC ₹900; 12 to 15 hours
Pune ₹700, with AC ₹900, 11 to 13 hours
Hampi sleeper ₹1000; 9½ hours

There's a prepaid taxi stand outside the bus terminal; it has a handy signboard of prices. Cabs to Anjuna or Calangute cost ₹280; Candolim ₹350; Panaji ₹300; Arambol ₹600; and Margao ₹1100. An autorickshaw to Anjuna or Calangute should cost ₹200.

Thivim, about 12km northeast of town, is the nearest train station on the Konkan Railway. Local buses to Mapusa meet trains (₹15); an autorickshaw to or from Thivim station costs around ₹200.

Vagator & Chapora

Dramatic red stone cliffs, dense green jungle and a crumbling 17th-century Portuguese fort provide Vagator and its diminutive village neighbour Chapora with one of the prettiest settings on the North Goan coast. Once known for wild trance parties and heady, hippie lifestyles, things have slowed down considerably these days, but Chapora – reminiscent of the Mos Eisley Cantina in *Star Wars* – remains a favourite for hippies and long-staying smokers, with the smell of charas (resin of the marijuana plant) clinging heavy to the light sea breeze.

Chapora is a working fishing harbour nestled at the broad mouth of the Chapora River, so it doesn't have much in the way of beach, whereas Vagator has three small, charismatic coves to choose from. The most northerly and largest is **Vagator Beach**, a beautiful stretch of sand, which fills up for a few hours each afternoon when domestic coach tours unload their swift-clicking tourist hordes making the most of its good swimming. Avoid this time of day and you'll have plenty of room for lounging on its pretty, boulder-studded sands.

Vagator's two southerly coves are known as **Little Vagator Beach** and **Ozran Beach**; they're accessible by steep footpaths running down from near the Nine Bar and Thalassa respectively. With shacks occupying the sands, Goa trance heavy on the sound systems, and cows thronging among the people, there's a distinctly laid-back vibe, overseen at Ozran by the huge, happy carved Shiva face that gazes out serenely from the rocks.

Vagator & Chapora

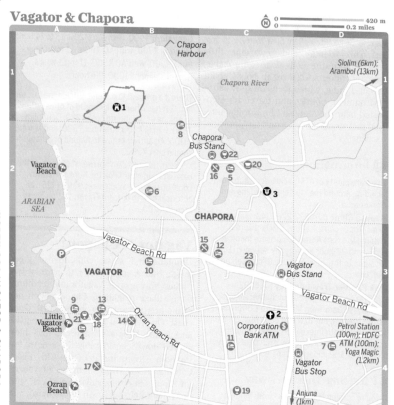

☉ Sights & Activities

There's plenty of yoga and ayurveda on offer seasonally in both Vagator and Chapora; check the noticeboards at local cafes or look for flyers.

Chapora Fort   FORT

Chapora's old laterite fort, standing guard over the mouth of the Chapora River, was built by the Portuguese in 1617, to protect Bardez taluk (district), in Portuguese hands from 1543 onwards, from the threat of invaders. It was built over the remnants of an older Muslim structure, hence the name of the village itself, from 'Shahpura', meaning 'town of the Shah.'

Today it is a crumble of picturesque ruins with only the outer walls remaining, though you can still pick out the mouths of two escape tunnels and a scattering of pre-Portuguese Muslim tombstones. The main reason to make the climb up the hill is

for the sensational views out along the coast from atop the fort walls – north to Morjim beach and the Chapora River, and south to Vagator and Ozran beaches. The best time to climb up is about an hour before sunset.

Though heavily fortified, Chapora Fort was nevertheless captured several times by invaders: first by several groups of Hindu raiders, and next, in 1684, when it was reportedly conquered without a shot being fired. On this occasion the Portuguese captain of the fort decided to surrender to the Maratha forces of the chieftain Sambhaji, his decision perhaps stemming, if legend is to be believed, from the manner in which Sambhaji's forces managed to breach the fort's defences: it's said that they clung tight to tenacious 1.5m-long monitor lizards, who were able to scale the rocky walls with ease.

The Portuguese rebuilt the fort in 1717, adding features such as tunnels that led

Vagator & Chapora

from the bastion down to the seashore and the river bank to enable resupply or escape in times of trouble, but Chapora fell again to the Marathas in 1739. Soon the northerly taluk of Pernem came into Portuguese hands, forming part of the Novas Conquistas (the 'New Conquests', the second wave of Portuguese conquests in Goa), and the significance of Chapora faded. The fort was finally abandoned to the ravages of the elements in 1892.

Chapora Harbour   HARBOUR
The narrow road northwest of the village leads you past lots of village homes with rooms for rent, up to a small harbour where the day's catch is hauled in from colourful, bobbing fishing boats. Self-caterers with the desire for fresh fish can haggle directly with fishermen or go mussel fishing at low tide. In any case, it makes for a scenic photo opportunity and provides an interesting window into traditional village life.

🛏 Sleeping
Vagator has the greater choice of accommodation, spread over a wide area back from the beach.

🛏 Vagator
Budget accommodation, much of it in private rooms, ranges along Ozran Beach Rd and Vagator Beach Rd; you'll see lots of signs for 'rooms to let' on the side roads, too, in simple private homes and guesthouses, from ₹400 to ₹600 per double.

⭐ **Jungle Hostel**   HOSTEL $
(☑0832-2273006; www.thehostelcrowd.com; Vagator Beach Rd; dm without/with AC ₹450/500, s/d ₹900/1400; ❄@🛜) True backpacker hostels are on the rise in Goa, but this place (formerly Asterix) was one of the originals, bringing the dorm experience and an international vibe to Vagator. The six-bed dorms are clean and bright and things like lockers, wi-fi, breakfast, communal kitchen and travel advice are free.

Bean Me Up   GUESTHOUSE $
(Enterprise Guest House; ☑7769095356; www.beanmeup.in; 1639/2 Deulvaddo; d without/with bathroom ₹900/1200; 🛜) Set around a leafy, parachute-silk courtyard that's home to Vagator's best vegan restaurant, rooms at the Enterprise Guest House look simple but are themed with individual exotic decor, earthy shades, mosquito nets and shared verandahs. The mellow yoga-friendly vibe matches the clientele.

Garden Villa   GUESTHOUSE $
(☑9822104780, 0832-6529454; Vagator Beach Rd; s/d from ₹600/700; 🛜) Just four clean rooms and two spacious bungalows in the garden behind an old Portuguese-style house.

Shalom   GUESTHOUSE $
(☑919881578459, 0832-2273166; www.shalomguesthousegoa.com; d ₹800-1400, with AC ₹1800; ❄🛜) Arranged around a placid garden not far from the path down to Little Vagator Beach, this established place run by a friendly family (whose home is on-site) offers a variety of extremely well-kept rooms and a two-bedroom apartment for long-stayers.

Julie Jolly   HOTEL $$
(☑0832-2273620, 2274897; www.hoteljollygoa.com; d from ₹1900, with AC ₹2300-2700, tr/q from ₹3000/4000; ❄@💺) Rooms are neat and

TRANCE PARTIES

Goa has a far longer and more vibrant history of hosting parties than most people realise. As far back as the 16th century, the Portuguese colony was notorious as an immoral outpost where drinking, debauching and dancing lasted till dawn, and, despite a more strait-laced interlude at the hands of the notorious Goan Inquisition, the tradition was finally resurrected full-force when the 'Goa Freaks' arrived on the state's northern beaches in the 1960s.

But the beach parties and full-moon raves of the 1970s and '80s came to seem like innocent affairs compared with the trance parties that replaced them in the '90s. At the peak of Goa's trance period, each high season saw thousands of revellers choosing synthetic substances (such as ecstasy) over marijuana and dancing to techno beats in Day-glo stupors, sometimes for days at a time.

In 2000 a central government 'noise pollution' ban on loud music in open spaces between 10pm and 6am was handed down. This, combined with increasing crackdowns on drug possession, seriously put the brakes on the trance-party scene, with police teams swooping in to close down parties before they even began. This was largely greeted with relief from locals, who were becoming increasingly worried at the peak of the trance-party phenomenon about the effects of drug dealing, alcohol and attendant promiscuity on Goa's own youth population.

With a tourist industry to nurture and the potential for baksheesh, the police still tend to turn a blind eye to a handful of parties during the peak Christmas and New Year period or on full-moon nights. Indoor venues, including clubs in Baga and Candolim, are able to keep pumping till 4am or later, but entry rules are restrictive, particularly for men. In Vagator and Anjuna, several clubs still carry on by partying indoors after 10pm. Down south in Palolem, 'silent discos' are the new thing. Other parties, like the **Sunburn Festival** (www.sunburn.in), simply take place during the day.

If you're determined to experience the remnants of Goa's true trance scene, hang around long enough in Anjuna or Vagator and you'll likely be handed a flyer for a party (many with international DJs). Taxi drivers are one of the best sources of information as it's in their interests to ferry party-goers around. Other locals get involved setting up chai and omelette stands, and selling cigarettes and laser pointers.

Keep an ear close to the ground – if you're lucky, you might get a taste of the Goa of old.

---

spacious, like little Spanish villas around a small pool. It's back from the beach action but has its own resort-style atmosphere. The owners also run two cheaper guesthouses in Vagator – Jolly Jolly Lester and Jolly Jolly Roma.

Alcove Resort HOTEL $$
(☏ 0832-2274491; www.alcovegoa.com; Little Vagator Beach; d without/with AC from ₹3300/3850, cottage ₹4400/4950; ❀@☎☒) The location overlooking Little Vagator Beach is hard to beat at this price. Attractively furnished rooms, slightly larger cottages and four suites surrounding a decent central pool, restaurant and bar, make this a good place for those who want a touch of affordable luxury.

Casa Vagator HOTEL $$$
(☏ 0832-2416738; www.casaboutiquehotels.com; d incl breakfast from ₹7000; ❀@☎☒) A successfully rendered outfit in the de-luxe Casa boutique mould, this is Vagator's most stylish accommodation option, with gorgeous rooms offering equally gorgeous views out to the wide blue horizon. The only downside is its proximity to techno-heavy Nine Bar, which pumps out Goa trance every night from 6pm until the 10pm shutdown.

🛏 Chapora

Head down the road to the harbour and you'll find lots of rooms – and whole homes – for rent, which is precisely what most long-stayers do.

Casa de Olga GUESTHOUSE $
(☏ 0832-2274355, 9822157145; eadsouza@yahoo.co.in; r ₹600-1200, without bathroom from ₹300) This welcoming family-run homestay, set around a nice garden on the way to Chapora harbour, offers spotless rooms of var-

ying sizes in a three-storey building. The best are the brand-new top-floor rooms with swanky bathrooms, TV and balcony. Budget travellers will be happy with the compact ground-floor rooms with shared bathroom.

Baba
GUESTHOUSE $

(☑0832-2273339;babavilla11@yahoo.in;d without/ with bathroom ₹250/500) At this price, and with its laid-back Chapora location, Baba is often full with long-stayers but you might be lucky as a walk-in. The 14 rooms are clean and simple but serviceable. Located behind the Baba Restaurant on the main street.

Baba Place
GUESTHOUSE $

(☑9822156511; babaplace11@yahoo.com; Chapora Fort Rd; d without/with AC ₹800/1200; ✳🖭) Brand new at the time of writing, Baba Place features a rooftop terrace with views of Chapora Fort, immaculate, decent-sized rooms with verandah, and a nice, quiet Chapora location.

Eating

Vagator

Vagator has a handful of outstanding dining spots, along with the usual range of much-of-a-muchness shacks down on the beach.

Yangkhor Moonlight
TIBETAN, MULTICUISINE $

(mains ₹80-200; ⊙9am-10pm) Well known locally for its fresh Tibetan food like *momos* (Tibetan dumpling) and soups, as well as pasta dishes. The chairs and tablecloths are plastic and the decor downmarket compared with some of its beachfront neighbours, but most travellers enjoy the food.

Bluebird
GOAN $$

(www.bluebirdgoa.com; Ozran Beach Rd; mains ₹250-370; ⊙8.30am-11pm) Bluebird specialises in Goan cuisine, with genuine vindaloos, chicken *cafreal* (marinated in a sauce of chillies, garlic and ginger), fish curry rice and Goan sausages among the temptations, as well as some delicately spiced seafood dishes. Dine in the lovely open garden cafe. The attached guesthouse has some nice rooms.

★ Bean Me Up Soya Station
VEGAN $$

(www.beanmeup.in; 1639/2 Deulvaddo; mains ₹180-350; ⊙8am-11pm; 🖭) Bean Me Up has gone all vegan, but even nonveg travellers will be blown away by the taste, variety and filling plates on offer in this relaxed garden restaurant. The extensive menu includes vegan pizzas, ice creams and innovative salads. Ingredients are as diverse as coconut, cashew milk and cashew cheese, quinoa, tofu and lentil dhal.

Mango Tree Bar & Cafe
MULTICUISINE $$

(Vagator Beach Rd; mains ₹120-550; ⊙24hr) With loud reggae, crappy service, dark-wood furniture, a sometimes rambunctious bar scene, ancient expats leaning over the bar, draught beer and an overall great vibe, the Mango Tree is a classic Vagator meeting place. It's open late (24 hours if it's busy enough), the food is pretty good – from Goan to European, pizza, Thai and Mexican – and films or sports are sometimes shown on the big screen.

★ Thalassa
GREEK $$$

(☑9850033537; www.thalassagoa.com; mains ₹300-750; ⊙4pm-midnight) Authentic and ridiculously good Greek food is served alfresco on a breezy terrace to the sound of the sea just below. Kebabs, souvlaki and thoughtful seafood dishes are the speciality, but vegie dishes are also excellent; the *spanakorizo* (spinach and rice cooked with Greek olive oil and herbs and topped with feta) is outstanding. Wash it all down with a jug of sangria. It's very popular around sunset – book ahead for a beachside table.

Greek dancing – complete with plate-smashing – livens up the night on some weekends. Thalassa also has huts (double per night ₹3000 to ₹4000), which are almost as classy as the restaurant.

Chapora

Little Chapora doesn't have the breadth of eating choices of Vagator, but that's what the people who hang out here like about it. With a couple of popular juice joints and a handful of nondescript restaurants, Chapora stays cool while the fine dining is elsewhere.

Sunrise Restaurant
CAFE $

(mains ₹90-200; ⊙7am-10.30pm) Sunrise doesn't pretend to be anything special but it does open early for breakfast and has perfectly edible food and a decent little garden on the main road out of Chapora.

🍷 Drinking & Nightlife

Vagator, along with Anjuna, was once the epicentre of Goa's infamous all-night trance party scene. To its credit, Vagator still has two or three of the most happening late-night places along this coast, and over the Christmas and New Year period parties can crank up at surprisingly short notice.

Jai Ganesh Fruit Juice Centre   CAFE
(Chapora; juices ₹40-80; ⊘8.30am-midnight) Thanks to its corner location, with views up and down Chapora's main street, this may be the most popular juice bar in Goa. It's a prime meeting spot and, once parked, most people are reluctant to give up their seat. Enjoy the juices, shakes and lassis, including an avocado variation.

Scarlet Cold Drinks   CAFE
(juices & snacks ₹30-80; ⊘8.30am-midnight) Selling juice, lassis, fruit salads and muesli to travellers, Scarlet is the second-most popular of Chapora's juice bars. There's a useful noticeboard with news of the latest local yoga classes, reiki courses and the like.

Hilltop   CLUB
(⊡0832-2273665; ⊘sunset-late) Hilltop is a long-serving Vagator trance and party venue that's deserted by day but comes alive from sunset. Its edge-of-town neon-lit coconut grove location allows it, on occasion, to bypass the 10pm noise regulations to host concerts, parties and the occasional international DJ. Sunday sessions (5pm to 10pm) are legendary here, and in season there's usually an evening market and techno party on Friday night.

Paulo's Antique Bar   BAR
(Chapora; ⊘11.30am-11pm) In season this hole-in-the-wall bar on Chapora's main street overflows with good music and cold beer at night. Even during the afternoon the few tables on the verandah are a good spot to watch the world go by.

Nine Bar   BAR
(⊘6pm-4am) Once the regular go-to place in Goa's trance scene, the open-air Nine Bar, on the clifftop overlooking Little Vagator Beach, has now moved into an indoor space so the parties can still go all night. Look out for flyers and local advice to see when the big party nights are on.

🛍 Shopping

Rainbow Bookshop   BOOKS
(Vagator Beach Rd; ⊘10am-2pm & 3-7pm) Long-running shop stocking a good range of secondhand and new books.

ℹ Information

There's a HDFC ATM at the petrol station on the back road to Anjuna.

ℹ Getting There & Away

Fairly frequent buses run to both Chapora and Vagator from Mapusa (₹15, 30 minutes) throughout the day, many via Anjuna. The bus stand is near the road junction in Chapora village. Practically anyone with legs will rent you a scooter/motorcycle from ₹250/400 per day.

Siolim

POP 12,000

The busy village of Siolim straddles the Chapora River and is a major road junction between Anjuna, Chapora, Mapusa and the road north to Arambol. Though all travellers heading north will pass through Siolim, it's often overlooked due to its riverside location some way from the nearest beach, but if you're looking for a change from sea and sand, it makes an interesting place to stay with quite a few budget and midrange guesthouses for rent, and some fine top-end heritage hotels.

◉ Sights & Activities

Siolim is home to an atmospheric daily **market** near the ferry landing stage on the banks of the Chapora River, where you can watch women open mussel shells at high speed. On Wednesday mornings another small **market** (from 7.30am to 10am), full of homegrown produce, sets up near the central **St Anthony Church**, a building that dates back to the 16th century.

Siolim Cooking School   COOKING
(⊡0832-2272138, 9604887740; www.cooking-classesgoa.com; Little Siolim House; 4hr class ₹2500) This upmarket and very reputable cooking school run by Siolim House specialises in traditional Goan cuisine. Visit the market to select produce then learn to cook (and eat) four dishes.

SIOLIM'S ZAGOR FESTIVAL

Held annually on the first Sunday and Monday after Christmas, Siolim's Zagor Festival offers a glimpse into the peaceful coexistence of Goa's diverse religious communities. Taking place on the Christian feast day of Nossa Senhora de Guia, the night-time festival blends both Hindu and Christian traditions, centring on a small Hindu shrine near the ferry dock, which is believed to house Zagoryo, the village deity.

The guardian of the village *bunds* (the dams that keep the river from the rice fields), Zagoryo is offered thanks during the festival by every Siolim family. Hindu families offer the deity oil, Christians bring candles, and everyone also offers up *pohe* (small cakes of pressed rice). Beginning with a midnight candlelit procession, villagers file through the streets of Siolim bearing an effigy of Zagoryo, stopping at both roadside Hindu and Christian shrines for blessings along the way. Next comes a traditional dance drama, during which legends are re-enacted by members of two important Siolim families – the Catholic D'Souzas and Hindu Shirodkars – who've inherited the roles from their forebears.

At first light the next morning, Hindu and Christian blessings are chanted by village priests, and the deity is carried back to his shrine, amid a shower of further offerings. Huge crowds attend but if you're in the area at the right time it's an event not to be missed.

🛏 Sleeping

★ **Siolim House**　　　HERITAGE HOTEL **$$$**
(☎ 9822584560, 0832-2272138; www.siolimhouse.com; annexe ₹4300-5000, ste ₹5600-7600; ❋ 🛜 🌊) Comprising the seven-room Siolim House hotel and the smaller, three-bedroom Little Siolim, Siolim House is without doubt one of North Goa's boutique treats. Situated in an old *palácio* (palace) that was once home to the Governor of Macau, the hotel is elegant and carefully restored and, though it has a lovely pool, is devoid of many 'luxury' trappings such as TV and only three rooms have air-con.

The rooms are all unique, some with grand four-poster beds and enormous stepped, throne-like bathrooms.

Noi Varo　　　VILLA **$$$**
(☎ 9011071911; www.shunyachi.com; villa from US$700, min 2 nights; ❋ 🛜 🌊) This wonderful villa, strictly for families or groups looking to book the whole place, is as exclusive as it gets. It's a spacious, stunning refurbished Portuguese mansion with three double bedrooms and a variety of extra sleeping spaces if your party requires it. You can kick back amid antiques, hang out in its river-view tree house, consult with its gourmet chef and float in a cool swimming pool. Artists, writers, musicians and the like should ask about special creative rates.

Teso Waterfront　　　RESORT **$$$**
(☎ 0832-2270096; www.tesogoa.com; Vaddy Siolim; luxury tent ₹9000-12,000; ❋ 🛜 🌊) This loungy upmarket party place has a cool location looking out on the lake-like mouth of the Chapora River. The safari Rajasthani tents are pricey but deluxe with air-con, fluffy beds, fridge, flat-screen TV, wardrobe and dresser. Muslin-wrapped cabanas make a great place to sip a cocktail overlooking the waterfront, and the dancefloor kicks off after sunset.

Morjim

The broad mouth of the Chapora River splits the North Goa coast, and Morjim Beach is the first village and beach resort heading north – it's reached by back roads heading west from the main highway after you cross the Siolim Bridge.

Morjim was once a very low-key – almost deserted – beach and the southern end is still protected due to the presence of rare olive ridley turtles, which come to lay their annual clutches of eggs between November and February. A Goa Forest Department hut is set up here to monitor the turtles and to provide environmental information in season. As with many pockets of Goan beaches, Morjim has become extremely popular with long (and shorter) staying Russian tourists, so many little guesthouses

THE TURTLE WIND

Each November, a strong breeze known as the 'turtle wind' heralds the arrival of olive ridley turtles to lay eggs on a clutch of Goan beaches. It's believed that these females – who live for over a century – return to the beach of their birth to lay eggs, courtesy of an incredible in-built 'homing device', often travelling thousands of kilometres to do so.

One such beach is Morjim, but turtle numbers over the last century have slowly dwindled to dangerous levels due to poaching. On investigation, it was found that locals were digging up the eggs and selling them as delicacies at the market, and any turtle found out of the water was generally killed for its meat and shell. Increased tourism to Goa has also taken its toll; eggs were, for years, trampled unwittingly at rave parties, while sea and light pollution continue to threaten the survival of those turtles that manage, against the odds, to hatch. Since nesting is influenced by lunar cycles, some environmentalists believe increasing unnatural lighting contributes to the turtles' confusion.

In 1996 the Goa Foundation, on the urging of several concerned local residents, finally stepped in and enlisted the help of the Goa Forest Department to patrol the beach and instigate a turtle conservation program. Locals who once profited from selling the eggs are now paid to guard them at the several turtle protection sites (at Morjim, Agonda and Galgibag beaches) established for this very purpose. Drop into one of its information huts, or go to www.goaenvis.nic.in/marineturtle.htm, to learn more.

and beach shacks have set up here with Cyrillic signs and menus, while domestic tourists and travellers from other beaches are also drifting here.

Still, it's not as developed as Mandrem or Arambol, and though there are lovely views down the headland to Chapora Fort, the beach is more black sand than golden.

🛏 Sleeping

★**Wanderers Hostel**　　　　　HOSTEL $
(☎9619235302; www.wandererhostel.com; Morjim; dm incl breakfast ₹500, luxury tent d ₹2000; ❄️🛜🏊) This relatively new hostel about five minutes' walk back from Morjim Beach is a real find. The main building, decorated with original travellers murals, has 40 beds in spotless air-con dorms with lockers, bed lights and free wi-fi, full kitchen, clean bathrooms, cosy communal areas and a pool table. In the garden next door is a tent village with swimming pool and yoga retreat centre (classes free to guests).

It's an interesting mix of yoga-meets-party atmosphere, and with an enthusiastic young owner, it's hard to think of a downside. Morjim's only ATM is across the road.

Rainbow Bar & Restaurant　　　HUTS $
(hut ₹1000) Rainbow has some colourful huts behind its beachfront restaurant and bar. It's at the end of Morjim Beach Rd, on the beach.

Goan Café & Resort　　　　RESORT $$
(☎0832-2244394; www.goancafe.com; apt & cottage from ₹1800, with AC ₹2200, treehouse without/with bathroom from ₹1200/1700; ❄️🛜) Fronting Morjim Beach, this excellent family-run resort has a fine array of beachfront stilted 'treehouse' huts and more solid rooms (some with air-con) at the back. The **Friends Corner** restaurant is good; it's not licensed but you're welcome to BYO.

Aswem

Aswen is a wide stretch of beach growing busier each year, but is still a little overshadowed by Mandrem to the north (though it's increasingly hard to tell where Aswem ends and Morjim or Mandrem begins). Beach-hut accommodation and beach-shack restaurants spring up each season on a very broad stretch of clean, white-sand beach with few hawkers and the main Morjim–Mandrem road set some way back from the sands.

Yoga, ayurvedic massage and water sports are on offer here in season, including Goa's best new surf outfit.

🏃 Activities

Vaayu Waterman's Village　　　SURFING
(☎9850050403; www.vaayuvision.org; Aswem; surfboard hire per hr ₹500, lessons ₹2700) Goa's only surf shop is also an activity and art

centre where you can arrange lessons and hire equipment for surfing, kiteboarding, stand-up paddleboarding, kayaking and wakeboarding. Enthusiastic young owners also run an art gallery, cafe and funky accommodation across the road from Asvem beach.

🛏 Sleeping

Aswem boasts a stylish and growing range of beach huts. Most places are steadily moving upmarket but you can still find basic beach huts and rooms back from the beach for ₹1000 (less out of high season), depending on the view, facilities and proximity to the beach.

Meems' Beach Resort   RESORT $$
(☎ 0832-2247015; www.meemsbeachresort.com; r ₹2000, with AC ₹2500, f ₹4000; ❄ 🛜) A solid guesthouse with 11 very clean rooms, Meems' is just across the road from the beach. A feature here is the atmospheric garden restaurant with low tables and floor cushions, specialising in Kashmiri cuisine and Vietnamese barbecue.

Yab Yum   HUT $$$
(☎ 0832-6510392; www.yabyumresorts.com; hut from ₹5800; 🛜) 🌿 This top-notch choice has unusual, stylish, dome-shaped huts – some look like giant hairy coconuts – made of a combination of all-natural local materials, including mud, stone and mango wood. A whole host of yoga and massage options are available, and it's all set in one of the most secluded beachfront jungle gardens you'll find in Goa.

Marbela Beach Resort   LUXURY TENTS $$$
(☎ 9158881180, 0832-6450599; www.marbela beach.com; tent ₹12,000-20,000; 🛜) The luxury tents and 'Spanish-style' rooms at this slick resort are pricey but fitted out like five-star hotel rooms. Even if you don't stay here, the beachfront cabanas are a divine spot for a drink and the resort's thumping Club M parties late from Thursday to Sunday.

Amarya Shamiyana   TENTS $$$
(☎ 7350711882; www.amaryagroup.com/amarya-shamiyana; tent from ₹7900; ❄ 🛜) Four huge, luxurious tents with all the modern trimmings (including wi-fi, room service and rain showers), located just off the beach, makes this a highly tranquil spot to splurge.

Leela Cottages   BEACH HUTS $$$
(☎ 0832-22822874; www.leelacottage.com; cottage ₹6500-7500; ❄ @ 🛜) The 15 cute luxury beach cottages (deluxe and grand) are situated in a nice leafy garden, just steps from the beach. Stand-out touches include antiquey pieces in each cottage, ornate furniture, individually named rooms and lots of cute throw pillows, plus air-con and minibar. There's a quality spa and yoga classes.

🍴 Eating

There are plenty of beach shacks along this bit of coast and the restaurants at Marbela and Leela are top-notch.

La Plage   MEDITERRANEAN $$
(mains ₹210-400; ⏱ 9am-10pm) Renowned in these parts, La Plage takes beach shack to the next level with its inspired gourmet French-Mediterranean food. Along with excellent salads, seafood and fabulous desserts (try the chocolate thali), La Plage stocks great wines. It's usually open from late November to April.

Mandrem

Mellow Mandrem has developed in recent years from an in-the-know bolt-hole for those seeking respite from the relentless traveller scene of Arambol and Anjuna to a fairly mainstream but still incredibly lovely beach hang-out.

An unusual feature of Mandrem is the narrow river inlet separating the white-sand beach from most of the accommodation strip and the road – rickety bamboo bridges connect you to the beach, where seasonal beach shacks set up. Some pretty sophisticated hut villages are springing up each year, too. Development is still low-key compared to most resorts in Goa, and the beaches are largely free of hawkers, sunbeds and tourist crowds. There's plenty of yoga, meditation and ayurveda on offer, though, plus good dining and space to lay down with a good book. Many believe there's no better place in North Goa.

🏃 Activities

Mandrem is something of a 'spiritual central', and there's plenty of yoga on offer. Many classes and courses change with the season, but there are a few places that reappear year after year.

Amalia Camp SPIRITUAL COURSES

(www.neeru.org) Learn the spiritual art of 'Open Clarity' at Amalia Camp, where local guru Neeru hosts *satsangs* (devotional speech and chanting sessions) to help ease you towards ever-elusive enlightenment. Check the website for a schedule of events or to book accommodation.

Ashiyana Retreat Centre YOGA

(☑ 9850401714; www.ashiyana-yoga-goa.com; Junas Waddo, Mandrem) This 'tropical retreat centre' situated right on Mandrem Beach has a long list of classes and courses available from November to April, from retreats and yoga holidays to spa, massage and 'massage camp'. Accommodation is in one of its gorgeous, heritage-styled rooms or huts.

Ayurvedic Massage Centre AYURVEDA, MASSAGE

(☑ 9420896843; 1/1½hr massage from ₹1000/ 1500; ⊘9am-8pm) Ayurvedic massage is provided here by the delightful Shanti. Try the rejuvenating 75-minute massage and facial package, or go for an unusual 'Poulti' massage, using a poultice-like cloth bundle containing 12 herbal powders, which is dipped in warm oil and comes especially recommended for treating back pain. You'll find her place on the right-hand side as you head down the beach road.

There's another branch at Sea Paradise Resort on the beach.

Himalaya Yoga Valley YOGA

(☑ 9960657852; www.yogagoaindia.com; Mandrem Beach) The winter home of a popular Dharamsala outfit, HYV specialises in hatha and ashtanga residential teacher-training courses, but also has daily drop-in classes (₹400; 1½ hours; 8am, 10am and 3pm daily) and 10-day yoga refresher courses.

Oceanic Yoga YOGA

(☑ 9049247422; www.oceanicyoga.com; Junas Waddo, Mandrem; drop-in class ₹300-400) Oceanic offers drop-in classes, seven-day yoga and meditation retreats, reiki and yoga teacher-training courses.

🛏 Sleeping & Eating

Mandrem has a growing number of beach huts fronting the beach or river inlet for around ₹1000, though many of the operations are moving more upmarket. As with most destinations in Goa, the huts change appearance, owner and prices seasonally. You'll also find plenty of houses and rooms

for rent throughout the village; just look for signs. Dining options are largely of the standard beach-shack variety, with most places dishing up a decent range of Indian and international cuisine.

⭐**Dunes Holiday Village** HUT $

(☑ 0832-2247219; www.dunesgoa.com; r & hut ₹900-1100; @☎) The pretty huts here are peppered around a palm-filled lane leading to the beach; at night, globe lamps light up the place like a palm-tree dreamland. Huts range from basic to more sturdy 'treehouses' (huts on stilts). It's a friendly, good-value place with a decent beach restaurant, massage, yoga classes and a marked absence of trance.

⭐**Mandala** RESORT $$

(☑ 9158266093; www.themandalagoa.com; r & hut ₹1600-5500; ❄☎) Mandala is a shanti and beautifully designed eco-village with a range of huts and a couple of quirky air-con rooms in the 'Art House'. Pride of place goes to the barn-sized two-storey villas inspired by the design of a Keralan houseboat. There are no beach views or even direct beach access but the location, overlooking the tidal lagoon, is serene with a large garden, daily yoga sessions and an organic restaurant.

The Brit owner also runs adventure trips, kayaking and cruises.

Beach Street RESORT $$

(Lazy Dog; ☑ 0832-3223911; Mandrem Beach; r & hut ₹3300-4400; ☎❄) This large and relatively new beachfront villa has neat and tidy rooms, while the seasonal beachfront huts are spacious and well designed. The pool is a nice touch, but it's only a short walk over the bamboo bridge to the beach.

Villa River Cat GUESTHOUSE $$

(☑ 9823610001, 0832-2247928; www.villarivercat. com; 438/1 Junasawaddo; d ₹3015, with bathroom ₹3770-4800; ❄) This fabulously quirky circular guesthouse – filled with art, light, antiques, and an owner with a decidedly creative inclination – is popular with arty types, potential screenwriters and return guests. Animal lovers will enjoy the resident cats and dogs.

Riva Beach Resort RESORT $$$

(☑ 0832-2247612; www.rivaresorts.com; d ₹6000-7000; ❄☎) This sprawling set of hotel-style rooms and seasonal cottages tumbles down from the main road to the inlet where bamboo bridges provide access to the beach. Spring mattresses, ocean-view balconies and a good restaurant.

Elsewhere   COTTAGE, TENT **$$$**

(www.aseascape.com; tent/r/house per week from US$811/1314/2435; @) The exact location of this heavenly set of historic beachfront houses and Otter Creek Tents, on some 500m of beachfront, is a closely guarded secret – though Google Earth will give you a clue. Choose from four beautiful beachfront houses, intriguingly named the Piggery, Bakery, Priest's House and Captain's House, or from three luxury tents (each sleeping two) and revel in the solitude that comes with a hefty price tag and a 60m walk across a bamboo bridge. Minimum one-week stay. Book ahead.

ⓘ Information

There are motorbike and scooter hire places, travel agents and shops along the beach road to Mandrem. There's an international ATM on the main road in Mandrem village.

ⓘ Getting There & Around

Although local buses run between Siolim and Mandrem village, it's a nightmare trying to get anywhere in a hurry on public transport. Most travellers taxi to their chosen accommodation, then either hire a scooter/motorbike or use taxis from there.

Arambol (Harmal)

Arambol (also known as Harmal) is the most northerly of Goa's developed beach resorts and is still the beach of choice for many long-staying budget-minded travellers in the north.

Arambol first emerged in the 1960s as a mellow paradise for long-haired long-stayers. Today things are still decidedly cheap and cheerful, with much of the village's budget accommodation arranged in simple little huts along the cliffsides, though the main beach is now an uninterrupted string of beach shacks, many with beach-hut operations stacked behind.

The covelike beach is gently curved and safe for swimming, making it popular among families with children, along with the usual array of travellers. A short walk around the northern headland, past shops and cheap guesthouses, brings you to little Kalacha Beach, another popular place

thanks to the 'Sweetwater Lake' back from the beach. The headland above here is the best place in Goa for paragliding.

🏃 Activities

Aside from yoga and beach lounging, popular pursuits in Arambol are **paragliding** from the headland above Kalacha Beach (Sweetwater Lake) and **kite surfing** and **surfing** down at the southern end. Several operators give lessons and rent equipment; look out for flyers and noticeboards.

Arambol Paragliding   PARAGLIDING

(10min flight ₹1500; ⊙ noon-6pm) The headland above Kalacha Beach (Sweetwater Lake) is an ideal launching point for paragliding. There are a number of independent operators: ask around at the shack restaurants on the beach, arrange a pilot, then make the short hike to the top of the headland. Most flights are around 10 minutes, but if conditions are right you can stay up much longer.

Surf Wala   SURFING

(www.surfwala.com; Surf Club; 1½hr lesson from ₹2000, 3-/5-day course ₹5000/8000) If you're a beginner looking to get up on a board, join the international team of surfers based at Arambol's Surf Club. Prices include board hire, wax and rashie. Check the website for instructor contact details – between them they speak English, Russian, Hindi, Konkani and Japanese! Board-only rental is ₹500.

Himalayan Iyengar Yoga Centre   YOGA

(www.hiyogacentre.com; Madhlo Vaddo; 5-day course ₹4000; ⊙ 9am-6pm Tue-Sun Nov-Mar) Arambol's reputable Himalayan Iyengar Yoga Centre, which runs five-day courses in hatha yoga from mid-November to mid-March, is the winter centre of the iyengar yoga school in Dharamkot, near Dharamsala in North India. First-time students must take the introductory five-day course, then can continue with more advanced five-day courses at a reduced rate.

Booking and registration must be done in person at the centre. Accommodation is available for students in simple huts or tents (single/double ₹650/800).

🛏 Sleeping

Accommodation in Arambol has mushroomed from the basic huts and rooms along the clifftop walk and the guesthouses back

WORTH A TRIP

QUERIM & FORT TIRACOL (TEREKHOL)

Just a few kilometres north of Arambol, quiet Querim's beach (also called and signposted as Keri Beach) is a little-visited patch of sand where you can while away the hours in peace, with just a few beach shacks in residence from mid-November. Backed by a shady cover of fir and casuarina trees, there's not much to do here but have a leisurely swim, settle back with a book, and enjoy the tranquillity that's missing from Arambol these days. You can reach Querim the long way by scooter or taxi, or tackle the headland walk (about one hour) from Kalacha Beach.

If you're keen to stay here, wander around the village set back from the beach where there are numerous 'rooms for rent' signs, and some entire village houses up for grabs.

To get to Terekhol (the most northerly point in Goa) and its fort, it's fun to hop on board Querim's free **ferry** (every 30min; ⊙ 7am-10pm) that chugs passengers and vehicles across the Terekhol River from the ferry landing at the very end of the village road. If the ferry isn't operating, a huge new bridge (completed in 2012) crosses the river along the main highway.

Not far from the ferry landing, you'll find Fort Tiracol (Terekhol), perched high above the banks of the river of the same name. Originally built by the Marathas in the early 17th century, the fort was captured by viceroy Dom Pedro de Almeida in 1746 and was rebuilt; the little **Chapel of St Anthony**, which takes up almost all of the available space within it, was added at that time.

The fact that the fort falls on the 'wrong' side of Goa's natural northern border, the Terekhol River, led it to be involved in considerable controversy. In the late 18th century the British demanded that it be handed over to the Empire, and in 1825, when the first Goan-born governor, Dr Bernardo Peres da Silva, was ousted, his supporters took over the fort. His own forces mutinied at the last moment, and met their deaths at the hands of the Portuguese. Finally, in 1954, Goa's entire northern border came to be at the centre of anti-Portuguese demonstrations. Several pro-India supporters hoisted an Indian flag over the fort's ramparts, and two were killed as a result; a plaque here memorialises the event.

The fort has operated as a private hotel in past years but was closed and waiting for a buyer at the time of writing. The gates are guarded but you can still enter and look at the chapel and the views down the coast from the ramparts.

in the village to a mini-Palolem collection of beach huts spawning behind the shacks along the main beach. Enter at the 'Glastonbury St' beach entrance and walk north to find plenty of places clinging to the headland between here and Kalacha Beach, or enter at the south end and ask at any of the beach shacks.

Arambol has a budget reputation and you can get basic huts – especially around the clifftops – for ₹400 or less, but prices are creeping up and anything seafacing is likely to be around ₹1000, more in peak season.

Most of the budget cliffside places don't bother with advance booking – simply turn up early in the day to see who's checking out – except, of course, in peak Christmas season when you might even have to book a minimum of a week.

Chilli's HOTEL $
(☑ 9921882424; d ₹600, apt with AC ₹1000; ﹡) Near the beach entrance on Glastonbury St,

this clean and friendly canary-yellow place is one of Arambol's better non-beachfront bargains. Chilli's offers 10 decent, no-frills rooms, all with attached bathroom, fan and a hot-water shower. The top-floor apartment with air-con and TV is great value. Owner Derek hires out motorbikes and scooters and offers free advice. It's open year-round.

Shree Sai Cottages HUT $
(☑ 0832-3262823, 9420767358; shreesai_cottages @yahoo.com; hut without bathroom ₹400-600) A good example of what's on offer along the cliffs, Shree Sai has simple, cute, sea-facing huts on the cliffs overlooking Kalacha Beach.

Om Ganesh HUT $
(☑ 9404436447; r & hut ₹400-800) Popular seasonal huts along the cliff path and a good restaurant, Om Ganesh has been around for a while and also has solid rooms in a building on the hillside.

Ludu Guest House HUT **$**
(☑9404434332, 0832-2242734; r ₹500-1000)
A cut above many other Arambol options, Ludu offers simply decorated, clean and bright cliffside rooms with attached cold-water showers. Hot water can be ordered by the bucketful.

Pitruchaya HUT **$**
(☑9881811098, 9404454596; r & hut from ₹500)
This relatively spaciously situated little place, with a slightly Mediterranean feel, has very neat sea-facing huts. There are also eight good-value rooms on the back side of the path.

Surf Club GUESTHOUSE **$$**
(www.surfclubgoa.com; d ₹1200-1600; ☎) In its own space at the end of a lane, on the very southern end of Arambol Beach, the Surf Club is one of those cool little hang-outs that offer a bit of everything: simple but clean rooms, a funky bar with live music, surf lessons (p153) and a seasonal kindergarten.

Arambol Plaza Beach Resort HOTEL **$$**
(☑9545550731, 0832-2242052; Arambol Beach Rd; r & cottage ₹1800-2500; ✻☎✈) On the road between the upper village and the beach, Arambol Plaza is a reasonable mid-range choice with cute timber cottages around a decent pool. All rooms are air-con but avoid the poorly maintained rooms in the building at the side.

✗ Eating & Drinking

Despite Arambol's backpacker-hippie vibe it certainly hasn't escaped the beach shack invasion, so you'll find about two dozen of them wall to wall along the main beach in season, complete with sunbeds and beach umbrellas out front. Most are pretty good (and many have accommodation behind). They change seasonally but a few are consistent.

The northern cliff walk has a string of budget restaurants with good views, and the road leading down to the beach is punctuated by some interesting dining options. In the upper village, chai shops and small local joints will whip up a chai for ₹5 and a thali for ₹70. The Surf Club is well known for good burgers and for hosting live music concerts in season.

Shimon MIDDLE EASTERN **$**
(meals ₹100-160; ⊙9am-11pm) Just back from the beach, and understandably popular with Israeli backpackers, Shimon is the place to fill up on exceptional falafel. For something more unusual go for *sabich,* crisp slices of eggplant stuffed into pita bread along with boiled egg, boiled potato and salad. The East-meets-Middle-East thali (₹360) comprises a little bit of almost everything on the menu.

Follow up with a strong Turkish coffee or its signature iced coffee.

Outback Bar MULTICUISINE **$**
(mains from ₹90; ⊙8am-late) Among the many little clifftop restaurants, Outback is consistently good for seafood and is always a great place for a sundowner, preferably right after you've hit the thermals over nearby Kalacha Beach.

German Bakery BAKERY **$**
(Welcome Inn; pastries ₹30-90) This popular little cafe bakes a good line in cakes and pastries, including lemon cheese pie and chocolate biscuit cake. It's a cool meeting spot close to the beach but away from the beach shacks.

Dylan's Toasted & Roasted CAFE **$**
(☑9604780316; www.dylanscoffee.com; coffee & desserts from ₹60; ⊙9am-11pm late Nov-Apr) The Goa (winter) incarnation of a Manali institution, Dylan's is a fine place for an espresso, a chocolate chip cookie and old-school dessert. A nice hang-out just back from the southern beach entrance.

Fellini ITALIAN **$$**
(mains ₹180-350; ⊙6.30pm-late) On the left-hand side just before the beach, this unsignposted but long-standing Italian joint is perfect if you're craving a carbonara or calzone. More than 20 wood-fired, thin-crust pizza varieties are on the menu, but save space for a very decent rendition of tiramisu.

Double Dutch MULTICUISINE **$$**
(mains ₹110-390, steaks ₹420-470; ⊙7am-10pm) In a peaceful garden set back from the main road to the Glastonbury St beach entrance, Double Dutch has long been popular for its steaks, salads, Thai and Indonesian dishes, and famous apple pies. It's a very relaxed meeting place with secondhand books, newspapers and a useful noticeboard for current Arambolic affairs.

Rice Bowl ASIAN **$$**
(mains ₹110-280; ⊙8am-11pm) Rice Bowl specialises in Chinese and Japanese cuisine

WORTH A TRIP

HOUSES OF GOA MUSEUM

Turning right to take the main highway north just after Britona, it's worth a quick detour away from the Mandovi riverbanks to reach the little village of Torda, where you'll find the interesting **Houses of Goa Museum** (☑ 0832-2410711; www.archgoa.org; near Nisha's Play School, Torda; adult/child ₹100/25; ◷ 10am-7.30pm Tue-Sun), created by well-known local architect Gerard de Cunha to illuminate the history of Goan homes, apparent statewide in various states of picturesque decrepitude. The multilevel, triangular building is an architectural oddity in itself, and the museum traces Goan architectural traditions, building materials and styles in an in-depth but accessible style.

Next door is the **Mario Gallery** (☑ 0832-2410711; ◷ 10am-5.30pm Mon-Fri, to 1pm Sat) FREE with works by one of India's favourite cartoonists, Loutolim local Mario de Miranda, who died in December 2011 at the age of 85.

Marooned shiplike in the middle of a traffic island, the museum is hard to miss. Turn right at the O'Coqueiro junction and then left at the fork, and you'll find it just there. If you don't have your own transport, a taxi here from Panaji should cost around ₹300 one-way.

and does it well. With a good view down to Arambol Beach, this is a great place to settle in with a plate of gyoza and a beer.

🛍 Shopping

Arambol Hammocks　　　　　HAMMOCKS
(☑ 9822389005; www.arambol.com; ◷ 9am-6pm) At the north end of the main beach, Arambol Hammocks designs and sells hammocks, including their 'flying carpets' and 'flying chairs'. You can also organise paragliding from here.

ℹ Information

The closest ATM is on the main highway in Arambol's village, about 1.5km back from the beach. If it's not working there's another about 3km north in Paliyem or about the same distance south in Mandrem.

Everything else you'll need in the way of services – internet, travel agents, moneychangers and the like – you'll find in abundance on what's commonly known as 'Glastonbury St', the road leading down to Arambol's beach. Wi-fi is widespread, and mostly free, in beach huts and restaurants.

ℹ Getting There & Away

Frequent buses to and from Mapusa (₹30, one hour) stop on the main road at the 'backside' (as locals are fond of saying) of Arambol village, where there's a church, a school and a few local shops. From here, it's a 1.5km trek down through the village to the main beach drag (head straight for the southern beach entrance or bear right for the northern 'Glastonbury St' entrance another 500m further on). An autorickshaw or taxi will charge at least ₹50 for the ride.

Plenty of places in the village advertise scooters and motorbikes for hire for ₹250 and ₹350 respectively, per day.

A taxi to Mapusa or Anjuna should cost around ₹600. If you're heading north to Mumbai, travel agents can book bus tickets and you can board at a stop on the highway in the main village.

Inland Bardez & Bicholim

There's not as much to explore in North Goa's interior as there is in the central and southern parts of the state, but with your own wheels you can leave the beach behind for a day or two and head east into the districts of Bardez and Bicholim. There are some fine old churches, sleepy villages, forts and a part of the Goan countryside that relatively few tourists see.

Britona & Pomburpa

On the Mandovi River east of the national highway is the pretty riverside village of Britona. Its parish church, **Nossa Senhora de Penha de Franca** (Our Lady of the Rock of France), is a grand old dame, occupying a fine location at the confluence of the Mandovi and Mapusa Rivers, looking across to Chorao Island on one side and to the Ribandar Causeway on the other.

Nossa Senhora de Penha de Franca was a Spanish saint who, after one hair-raising voyage in which the sailors saved themselves from certain death by appealing to Nossa Senhora, became associated with seafarers, and thus was favoured by many of those who had survived the voyage to India.

The interior of the church is beautifully decorated, with a high-vaulted ceiling and a simple *reredos* embellished with painted scenes. This church is best visited in the morning and holds one service (in Konkani) on most days.

Britona has plenty of old-fashioned village character, and makes a nice place to stay for the night. **Casa Britona** (☎0832-2416737; www.casaboutiquehotels.com; d from ₹7200; ✴@☀) is a 300-year-old converted customs warehouse, with luxurious antique-filled rooms, fine outdoor dining beneath the stars and a lovely riverside swimming pool.

Continue 5km to the village of Pomburpa, peek in at the equally beautiful **Church of Nossa Senhora Mae de Deus** (Our Lady Mother of God), noteworthy for its stunning interior and elaborate gold-leaf *reredos*.

Aldona

Around 5km north of Pomburpa, the large and picturesque village of Aldona is home to the **Church of St Thomas** on the banks of the Mapusa River, which makes a grand sight, particularly when viewed from the village's now-defunct ferry crossing. The church, built in 1596, is attached to a strange, saintly legend. The story goes that one day, as a group of thieves crossed the river to Aldona, to strip the church of its riches, they were met by a young boy who warned them to reconsider carrying out their crime. While they were nonetheless attempting to remove valuables, the church bells began to peal; fleeing in a panic, some of the thieves drowned, while the others were captured. As the leader was led sorrowfully away, he recognised the church's statue of St Thomas as the boy who had cautioned him against his misdeeds.

Corjuem Island

On this inland island around 2km northeast of Aldona and now accessible by modern road bridges, you'll find the only still-intact inland fort, the abandoned and atmospheric **Corjuem Fort**. Around 1705 Corjuem came to mark the easternmost boundary of Portugal's colonial conquest, and the small fort was quickly built to protect the territory from raids by the Rajputs and Marathas.

Squat and thick walled, standing alone on a small hillock, the fort has a lonely feel about it, and although there's not a whole lot to see here, it's easy to imagine this place as a solitary outpost in the jungle nearly

Inland Bardez & Bicholim

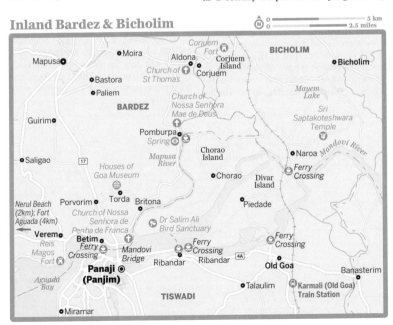

DEFENDER OF HEARTH & HOME

Corjuem Fort's most famous Portuguese defender was Ursula e Lancastre, a Portuguese noblewoman who travelled the world disguised as a man, eventually finding herself stationed here as a soldier. It was not until she was suspected and stripped that her secret was discovered; however, this did not put an end to her military career. She promptly went on to marry the captain of the guard, following what was, in retrospect, probably one of the most interesting strip searches in the history of warfare.

three centuries ago, filled with homesick Portuguese soldiers just waiting to be overrun by bloodthirsty attackers.

Naroa & Shri Saptakoteshwara Temple

For the most scenic entry to the little village of Naroa, clinging to the banks of the Mandovi, venture here by **ferry** (free; ⊙ every 20-30 min) from picturesque Divar Island (p101). Just 2km from the ferry point, the **Shri Saptakoteshwara Temple** is tiny, tucked away in a narrow emerald-green valley and undisturbed by anything apart from a few mopeds and the occasional tour bus.

The deity worshipped at the temple is a lingam (a phallic symbol of Shiva, the destroyer), which underwent considerable adventures before arriving here. Having been buried to avoid early Muslim raids, it was recovered and placed in a great Kadamba temple on Divar Island, but when the Portuguese desecrated the spot in 1560 it was smuggled away and subsequently lost. Miraculously rediscovered in the 17th century by Hindus, who found it being used as part of a well shaft, it was smuggled across the Mandovi River to safety in the temple. It's said that the great Maratha rebel leader Shivaji used to come here to worship, and personally saw to it that the temple was reconstructed in 1668, creating the small, solid structure that stands here today.

To find the temple, follow the road from the ferry point at Naroa (from Divar Island) for approximately 2km, before forking right down a small tarmac lane. You'll find the temple about 1.5km along, to your left; follow the red and green archaeology arrows until you arrive. You'll know it from its shallow, Mughal-style dome, tall lamp tower, and vaulted arches. Look out for the equestrian mural of Shivaji, above the entrance.

Mayem Lake

East of Naroa and about 35km from Panaji, glistening Mayem Lake is a pleasant sort of place that's popular among local picnickers, while the GTDC's North Goa bus tour also sets down daily for lunch here.

If you're keen to stay for longer than lunchtime, Goa Tourism's **Mayem Lake View** (☑0832-2362144; www.goa-tourism.com; d ₹1049, with AC ₹1380-1710, ste ₹2200; ❋) is almost certainly the nicest of all the GTDC's hotels. Its rooms are cheerful, clean and good value, particularly those perched at the lake's edge.

South Goa

Why Go?

South Goa is the more serene half of the state, and for many travellers that's the attraction. There are fewer activities and not as many bars, clubs or restaurants as in the north, but overall the beaches of the south are cleaner, whiter and not as crowded as those in North Goa.

Bounded to the north by the wide Zuari River and to the south by the neighbouring state of Karnataka, south Goa's coast is a series of resorts that range from the five-star hotel strips of Cavelossim and the village feel of Benaulim, to the backpacker-friendly beach-hut bliss of Palolem, Patnem and Agonda.

Take the time to explore inland, where you'll find some fabulous historic sights, Goa's finest Portuguese mansions, winding country lanes and wildlife reserves. If you want to take it easy, the south is a redolent, rewarding and re-energising place to base yourself.

Best Places to Eat

➜ Ruta's World Cafe (p163)
➜ Ourem 88 (p187)
➜ Space Goa (p186)
➜ Home (p189)
➜ Zeebop by the Sea (p173)

Best Places to Stay

➜ Ciaran's (p185)
➜ Blue Lagoon (p181)
➜ Bamboo House Goa (p179)
➜ H2O Agonda (p182)
➜ Art Resort (p185)

When to Go
Palolem

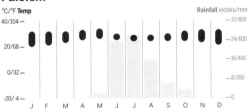

Dec–Mar High season; brilliant cloudless days, beach huts, yoga and festivals in full swing.

Oct–Nov & Apr–May Pre- and post-season – prices much lower, fewer crowds, humid weather.

Mid-Dec–early Jan Peak season; prices sky-high, crowds, lots of parties, Christmas festivities.

South Goa Highlights

1 Check into a beach hut in beautiful **Palolem** (p159), where you can kayak, learn to cook or just relax

2 Marvel at colonial mansions and *palácio* in the villages of **Chandor** (p166) and **Quepem** (p168)

3 Learn about Goa's traditional past at **Goa Chitra Museum** (p176) in Benaulim

4 Trek down to secluded **Cola Beach** (p180), one of the prettiest in Goa

5 Hire a bike and take the beautiful drive from Patnem to Galgibag's **Turtle Beach** (p190)

6 Cruise out to remote **Tanshikar Spice Farm** (p188) and stop in at the bizarre 'bubble lake' along the way

7 Book into a luxurious beachfront hut on serene **Agonda Beach** (p181)

8 Take a break from the beach in busy **Margao** (p162), visiting the market, Municipal Library and church

9 Go scuba diving at Grande Island from **Bogmalo** (p170)

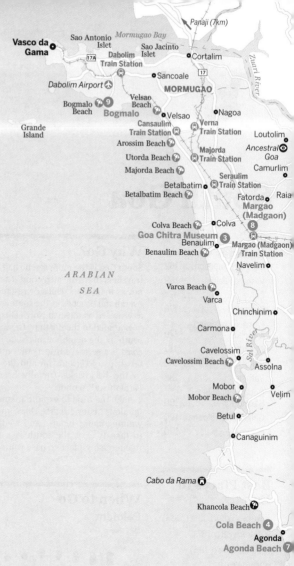

Londa (111km);
Dharwar (146km);
Belgaum (155km)

Ponda

PONDA

4A

Rachol Seminary &
Church

South Central Railway

Bhagwan Mahavir
Wildlife Sanctuary

SALCETE

Curtorim

Chandorgoa
Train Station

Sanvordem
Train Station

Sanvordem

2 **Chandor**

Curchorem

Sanguem River

Darguina

Paroda

Shri Chandreshwar
(Bhutnath) Temple

Sanguem

2 **Quepem**

Seraulim
Train Station

Shri Damodar
Temple

Zambaulim

SANGUEM

Cuncolim

Rivona
Buddhist
Caves

Rivona

Bali
Train Station

Usgalimal
Rock
Carvings

Fatorpa

Netravali
Protected
Area

Konkan Railway

QUEPEM

Paroda River

Netorli

Savare
Waterfall

Barcem
Train Station

Quisconda

6 **Tanshikar
Spice Farm**

Netravali
Bubble Lake

17

Shri Malikarjun
Temple

Animal
Rescue
Centre

Savare

Honeymoon
Beach

Butterfly
Beach

Palolem

CANACONA

Cotigao
Wildlife
Sanctuary

Salginim

1

Char Rasta

Patnem **Chaudi**

anacona
Island

Canacona Train Station

Talpona River

Colomb Bay

Rajbag

Rajbag Beach

Talpona Beach

Poinguinim

Entrance to
Cotigao Wildlife
Sanctuary

Turtle Beach **5** Galgibag

KARNATAKA

Masher

Matem

Karwar (21km);
Gokarna (68km)

0 _____ 10 km
N 0 _____ 5 miles

Polem

Polem Beach

Margao (Madgaon)

POP 94,400

Margao (also known as Madgaon) is the capital of South Goa, a busy – at times traffic-clogged – market town of a manageable size for getting things done. As the major transport hub of the south, lots of travellers pass through Margao's train station or Kadamba bus stand; fewer choose to stay here, but it's a useful place for shopping, catching a local sporting event or simply enjoying the busy energy of big-city India in small-town form.

Though the modern town favours commerce over culture – it certainly lacks Panaji's charms – this wasn't always the case. Before the Portuguese conquests of the 16th century onward, Margao was a centre for both pilgrimage and learning, with dozens of Hindu temples and a library of thousands upon thousands of volumes. However, all traces were destroyed by the Portuguese, as Margao became absorbed into their 17th-century Novas Conquistas (New Conquests). The small Shiva temple, just south of the covered market, still attracts Hindus each evening, to light candles and incense, and to leave offerings of garlanded marigolds and coconuts to the ever-popular god.

Margao's compact town centre ranges around the oblong Municipal Gardens, with shops, restaurants, ATMs and the covered market all within easy reach. To the north of town, is the old Portuguese-flavoured Largo de Igreja district; about 1km north further is the main (Kadamba) bus station, and 1.5km southeast of the Municipal Garden is Margao's train station.

◉ Sights & Activities

Church of the Holy Spirit CHURCH

Margao's whitewashed main church was first built in 1565, on the site of an important Hindu temple. Before demolition started on the temple, local Hindus managed to rescue the statue of the god Damodara, to whom the building was dedicated. It was secretly moved to a new site in the village of Zambaulim, around 30km southeast, where there is still a large temple today.

However, the new church didn't last long and was burned to the ground by Muslim raiders the same year it was built. It was soon replaced and a seminary was established, but both were subsequently destroyed, again by Muslim forces, after which the seminary was moved to Rachol, to the northeast.

The present church, built in 1675, remains in use as a parish church and is finely decorated inside. The impressive *reredos* (ornamental screen) is dedicated to the Virgin Mary, rising from ground level to the high ceiling, made more distinguished by the gilded and carved archway that stands in front of it. The church doors are usually unlocked throughout the day, and access is via the side entrance on the northern side.

Largo de Igreja AREA

Largo de Igreja, the area around the Church of the Holy Spirit, features a number of traditional old Portuguese-style mansions, in various states of decay or repair. The most famous is the grand 1790 Sat Burnzam Ghor (Seven Gabled House). Originally, as its name suggests, there were seven of the distinctive high-peaked gables, of which only three remain, though it is still an impressive edifice. Built by Sebastiao da Silva, private secretary to the viceroy, it sports an especially beautiful private chapel, dedicated to St Anna, and noteworthy for being the first private chapel in which a Goan family was permitted to privately perform Mass It's currently not open to the public.

Mount Church CHURCH

Located about 500m southeast of Sat Burnzam Ghor and a fair climb up Monte Hill, Margao's only hill, Mount Church is a simple whitewashed building, faced by a similarly diminutive piazza cross. A detour up here is worth it for the view, all the way out to Colva.

Municipal Library LIBRARY

(Abade Faria Rd; ⊙8am-8pm Mon-Fri, 9am-noon & 4-7pm Sat & Sun) On the west side of the canary-yellow Secretariat Building, you'll find respite from the sun in the prim Municipal Library, which houses some good books about Goa. Don't miss the library's newspaper reading room, in which you're required to collect your newspaper at the counter and then sit in the seat designated only for readers of that particular paper – it's popular enough that it's often full.

Fatorda Stadium SPORT

(☑0832-2743050) With a capacity of almost 28,000, Margao's modern Fatorda Stadium (officially known as Jawarharlal Nehru Stadium) is Goa's premier sports venue. State and international football (soccer) and cricket matches are staged here. It's 2km northeast of Municipal Gardens.

Tours

Canopy Ecotours   TOURS
(☑0832-2710650, 9764261711; www.canopygoa. com; 8 Sapna Arcade, Malbhatt) This eco-friendly outfit based in Margao offers birdwatching, butterfly-spotting and wildlife photography trips into the Western Ghats. Canopy also runs Nature's Nest, a set of rustic cottages on the outskirts of Bhagwan Mahavir Wildlife Sanctuary, with packages including meals and treks.

🛏 Sleeping

Unlike Panaji, Margao doesn't have the range of accommodation that you'd expect in a town of this size. But with the beaches of the south so close, there's really no pressing reason to stay here.

Hotel Tanish   HOTEL $
(☑0832-2735858; www.hoteltanishgoa.com; Reliance Trade Centre, Valaulikar Rd; s/d ₹900/1200, s/d/ste with AC ₹1100/1500/2000; ❄) Oddly situated inside a modern mall, this top-floor hotel offers good views of the surrounding countryside, with stylish, well-equipped rooms. Suites come with a bathtub, a big TV and a view all the way to Colva; just make sure you get an outside-facing room, as some overlook the mall interior.

Nanutel Margao   HOTEL $$
(☑0832-6722222; Padre Miranda Rd; s/d incl breakfast ₹3780/4100, ste ₹4750-5300; ❄🛜🏊) Margao's best business-class hotel by some margin, Nanutel is modern and slick with a lovely pool, good restaurant, bar and coffee shop, and clean air-con rooms. The location, between the Municipal Gardens and Largo de Igreja district, is convenient for everything.

Om Shiv Hotel   HOTEL $$
(☑0832-2710294; www.omshivhotel.com; Cine Lata Rd; d ₹2750-3850, ste ₹5000; ❄@🛜) In a bright-yellow building tucked away behind the Bank of India, Om Shiv does a decent line in fading 'executive' rooms, all of which have air-con and balcony. The suites have good views, there's a gym and the 7th-floor Rockon Pub.

Margao Residency   HOTEL $$
(☑0832-2715528; Luis Miranda Rd; d ₹1270, with AC ₹1570; ❄) The omnipresent GTDC's outfit in town is an acceptable choice for the price, with clean rooms and a good location opposite the Municipal Library.

🍴 Eating & Drinking

Café Tato   INDIAN $
(Valaulikar Rd; thalis ₹90; ⏱7am-10pm Mon-Sat) A favourite local lunch spot: tasty vegetarian fare in a bustling backstreet canteen, and delicious all-you-can-eat thalis.

Gaylin   CHINESE $
(Valaulikar Rd; mains ₹80-130; ⏱noon-3pm & 6.30-11pm) Hidden behind opaque glass doors decorated with dragon motifs, you'll find generous, garlicky renditions of Chinese favourites dispensed by friendly Darjeeling-derived owners. Recipes are suitably spiced up to cater to resilient Indian palates.

Casa Penguim de Gelados   SNACKS, INDIAN $
(opposite Municipal Gardens; veg thali ₹70; ⏱8.30am-8pm Mon-Sat) Tea and ice creams are the speciality here, but they also do a good vegetarian thali and an array of South Indian snacks.

★Ruta's
World Cafe   AMERICAN, INTERNATIONAL $$
(☑0832-2710757; www.caferuta.com; Fr Miranda Rd; mains ₹150-350; ⏱10am-7pm Mon-Sat) Ruta's is a quality addition to Margao's otherwise average dining scene and an excellent reason to get off the beach. After years working as an award-winning cook, teacher and recipe-book author on the San Francisco scene, chef Ruta Kahate has brought some of her culinary magic to Goa (there's another restaurant in Mapusa; see p142).

Simple things like soups, salads and toasties sit alongside 'comfort food' such as pulled pork burgers and New Orleans jambalaya.

★Longhuino's   GOAN, MULTICUISINE $$
(Luis Miranda Rd; mains ₹95-205; ⏱8.30am-10pm) A local institution since 1950, quaint old Longhuino's has been serving up tasty Indian, Goan and Chinese dishes, popular with locals and tourists alike. Go for a Goan dish like *ambot tik*, and leave room for the retro desserts such as rum balls and tiramasu. Service is as languid as the slowly whirring ceiling fans, but it's a great place to watch the world go by over a coffee or beer.

SOUTH GOA MARGAO (MADGAON)

Margao (Madgaon)

N
0 _____ 200 m
0 _____ 0.1 miles

Panaji (33km)

Bus Stand

Market

Fatorda Stadium (200m)

Chandor (15km);
Ponda (17km)

Kadamba Bus Stand

Colva (6km)

1

4

LARGO DE IGREJA

2
MONTE HILL

Damodar Temple

Apollo Victor Hospital

14
19
8

Abade Faria Rd

Padre Miranda Rd

16

15

Old Bus Stand

Thomas Cook

10 **12**

Valaulikar Rd

6

Municipal Gardens

Central Bus Stand

Isidoro Baptista Rd

Cyberlink

11
13
3 **5**
7 **18**
9

Luis Miranda Rd

Miguel LF Rd

Erasmo Carvalho Rd

Rue F de Loiola

17

Station Rd

(2km);
Palolem (37km)

Canopy Ecotours (450m)

Margao (Madgaon)

Underground Pub BAR
(☑ 9975791123; Abade Faria Rd; ☺5pm-late)
Margao isn't much of a party town but you can enjoy a drink, listen to music or watch sports at this cute underground bar north of the post office.

🔒 Shopping

Golden Heart Emporium BOOKS
(Confidant House, Abade Faria Rd; ☺10am-1.30pm & 4-7pm Mon-Sat) One of Goa's best bookshops, Golden Heart is crammed from floor to ceiling with fiction, nonfiction, children's books, and illustrated volumes on the state's food, architecture and history. It also stocks hard-to-get titles by local Goan authors. It's down a little lane off Abade Faria Rd, on the right-hand side as you're heading north.

MMC New Market MARKET
(☺8.30am-9pm Mon-Sat) Margao's crowded, covered canopy of colourful stalls is a fun place to wander around, sniffing spices, sampling soaps and browsing the household merchandise.

🛈 Information

There are plenty of banks offering currency exchange and 24-hour ATMs ranged around the Municipal Gardens. GTDC trips can be booked at the front desk of the Margao Residency (p163).

Apollo Victor Hospital (☑ 0832-672888; www.apollovictorhospital.com; Station Rd, Malbhat) Has a casualty department, reliable medical services and a 24-hour pharmacy.

Cyberlink (Caro Centre, Abade Faria Rd; per hr ₹40; ☺8.30am-7.30pm Mon-Sat; 🛜) Reasonably swift internet access.

Maharaja Travels (☑ 0832-2732744; Luis Miranda Rd; ☺9am-1pm & 3-6pm Mon-Sat) A reliable hole-in-the-wall place for long-distance bus tickets.

Main Post Office (☺9am-1.30pm & 2.30-5pm Mon-Sat) North side of the Municipal Gardens.

Thomas Cook (☑ 0832-2714768; Mabai Hotel Bldg; ☺9.30am-6pm Mon-Sat) A reliable place to change money and perform money transfers.

🛈 Getting There & Around

BUS
Local and long-distance buses use the Kadamba bus stand, about 2km north of the Municipal Gardens. Buses to Palolem (₹40, one hour), Colva (₹15, 20 minutes), Benaulim (₹15, 20 minutes) and Betul (₹20, 40 minutes) stop both at the Kadamba bus stand and at the central bus stand on the east side of the Municipal Gardens. Services run to no particular timetable but are frequent.

Regular express local buses also run to Panaji (₹30) from where you can change for buses to Mapusa and the northern beaches.

Daily air-con state-run buses go to Mumbai (₹900, 16 hours), Pune (₹900, 13 hours) and Bangalore (₹800, 13 hours), which can be booked online at www.goakadamba.com. Non-AC buses are about one-third cheaper. For greater choice and flexibility but similar prices, private long-distance buses depart from the stand opposite Kadamba. You'll find booking offices all over town; **Paulo Travels** (☑ 0832-2702405; ww.phmgoa.com; Hotel Nanutel, Padre Miranda Rd) is among the best, and also has the only buses to Hampi (sleeper ₹800 to ₹1000, 10 hours).

TAXI
Taxis are plentiful around the Municipal Gardens and Kadamba bus stand, and are a quick and comfortable way to reach any of Goa's beaches, including Palolem (₹900), Calangute (₹1000), Anjuna (₹1200) and Arambol (₹1700). Be sure to wear your best bargaining cap when negotiating your fare. Prepaid taxi stands are at the train station and main bus stand. For Colva and Benaulim, autorickshaws will do the trip for around ₹120.

TRAIN

Margao's well-organised train station (known as Madgaon on train timetables), about 2km south of town, serves both the Konkan Railway and local South Central Railways routes, and is the main hub for trains from Mumbai to Goa and south to Kochi and beyond. Its **reservation hall** (☑ PNR enquiry 0832-2700730, information 0832-2712790; ⊙ 8am-2pm & 2.15-8pm Mon-Sat, 8am-2pm Sun) is on the 1st floor.

Outside the station you'll find a useful prepaid taxi stand; use this to get to your beachside destination and you'll be assured a fair price. Alternatively, a taxi or autorickshaw to or from the town centre to the station should cost around ₹80.

Around Margao

As tempting as it is to head directly west to the beach from Margao, the area to the east and northeast of town is a rich patchwork of rice paddy fields, lush countryside, somnolent rural villages, superb colonial houses, and a smattering of historical and religious sites. With a day or two to spare and a hired motorcycle, car or taxi, you can cover most of the sights of interest and experience a rewarding side of Goa that has nothing to do with beaches.

Rachol Seminary & Church

Rachol Seminary & Church   CHURCH

Built in 1580 atop an old Muslim fort, the Rachol Seminary and Church stands near the village of Raia, 7km from Margao. Although it's not officially open to visitors, you'll likely be able to find a trainee priest to show you around its beautiful church and cloistered theological college.

The seminary, built by the Jesuits, soon became a noted centre of learning, graced with one of India's first printing presses. Among the seminary's most famous members were Father Thomas Stevens, who by 1616 had busily translated the Bible into Konkani and Marathi, to help with the conversion of the locals, and Father Ribeiro, who produced the first Portuguese-Konkani dictionary in 1626.

Work on the church (dedicated to Jesuit founder St Ignatius Loyola) began in 1576, four years before the founding of the seminary, and it has been maintained in excellent condition. Its splendid gilded *reredos* fills the wall above the altar, featuring an image of St Constantine, the first Roman emperor to convert to Christianity; fragments of St Constantine's bones are on display near the main doorway. One of the side altars also displays the original Menino Jesus, which was first installed in the Colva church, before being taken up to Rachol amid much controversy.

Loutolim

Architectural relics of Goa's grand Portuguese heritage can be seen around the unhurried village of Loutolim, some 10km northeast of Margao.

The centre of the village is the brooding whitewashed Church of Salvador do Mundo. Walk downhill from there to reach **Ancestral Goa** (☑ 0832-2777034; www.ancestralgoa.com; adult/child ₹50/25, camera ₹20; ⊙ 9am-6pm), a high kitsch park with a series of sculptures depicting traditional Goan lifestyle. Follow the numbered trail to the mysterious 'Big Foot', a footprint in the rock that you can touch and make a wish on, and Sant Mirabai, the largest laterite sculpture in India.

The village hosts a number of impressive Portuguese-style mansions but just one, **Casa Araujo Alvares** (☑ 0832-2750430; adult/child ₹100/50, camera ₹20; ⊙ 9am-5.30pm), opposite Ancestral Goa, is officially open to the public. You can tour the interior of the 250-year-old house on an automated half-hour 'sound-and-light show', which illuminates rooms and furnishings to accompanying commentary.

Though Loutolim's other mansions (Miranda House, Roque Caetan House and Salvador Costs House among them) aren't officially open to the public, you can always peer through the great wrought-iron gates.

About 1km from the church, British-run **Casa Susegad** (☑ 0832-6483368; www.casasusegad.com; s/d ₹6200/7300; ❉ ⬆ ❉) has just five lovely, antique-filled rooms, and makes a wonderful upmarket retreat. An organic vegetable garden supplies the ingredients for delicious dinners, and a menagerie of parakeets, monkeys, cats and dogs inhabit the extensive gardens, complete with terrace swimming pool.

Without your own wheels, Loutolim is best accessed by taxi from Margao; a one-way fare should be about ₹180.

Chandor

The small village of Chandor, about 15km east of Margao, is an important stop for its collection of once-grand Portuguese-era

BRAGANZA HOUSE

Braganza House, built in the 17th century and stretching along one whole side of Chandor's village square, is the biggest Portuguese-era mansion of its kind in Goa and the best example of what Goa's scores of once grand and glorious mansions have today become. Granted the land by the King of Portugal, the Braganza family built this oversized house and later divided it into the east and west wings when it was inherited by two sisters from the family.

Both sides are open to the public daily. There are no set tour times but if you enter either side a family member or representative should give you a guided tour and regale you with a few stories of the lifestyles of the landed gentry during Goa's years of Portuguese rule. The entry fee at each side is a suggested donation and goes towards the considerable upkeep of the homes, which receive no official funding.

The **West Wing** (☑ 0832-2784201; donation ₹150; ⊘ 9am-5pm) belongs to one set of the family's descendants, the Menezes-Braganças. It's beautifully maintained and more like a museum than a home, filled with gorgeous Belgian glass chandeliers, Italian marble floors and antique treasures from Macau, Portugal, China and Europe. Also here is the extensive library of Dr Luis de Menezes Braganca, a noted journalist and leading light in the Goan Independence movement. Despite the passing of the elderly Mrs Aida Menezes-Braganca in 2012, the grand old home remains open to the public. Photography is not allowed.

Next door, the **East Wing** (☑ 0832-2784227; donation ₹100; ⊘ 10am-6pm) is owned by the Pereira-Braganza family, descendants of the other half of the family. It's not as grand and well-maintained as its counterpart but is beautiful in its own lived-in way and is also crammed with antiques and collectibles from around the world. It features a large ballroom with marble floor, but the high point is the small family chapel, which contains a carefully hidden fingernail of St Francis Xavier.

mansions, exemplified by the wonderful Braganza House. It's a photogenic place with fading but still grand facades and gables – many topped with typically Portuguese carved wooden roosters – and the looming white Nossa Senhora de Belem church.

Between the late 6th and mid-11th centuries it was better known as Chandrapur, the most spectacular city on the Konkan coast. This was the grand seat of the ill-fated Kadamba dynasty until 1054 when the rulers moved to a new, broad-harboured site at Govepuri, at modern-day Goa Velha. When Govepuri was levelled by the Muslims in 1312, the Kadambas briefly moved their seat of power back to Chandrapur, though it was not long before Chandrapur itself was sacked in 1327, and then its glory days were finally, definitively, over. Few signs remain of once-glorious Chandrapur, though the village has an archaeological site, where the foundations of an 11th-century Hindu temple and a headless stone Nandi bull (the vehicle of Shiva) still mark the spot.

A kilometre east past the church, and open to the public, is the **Fernandes** House (☑ 0832-2784245; donation ₹200; ⊘ 9am-6pm), whose original building dates back more than 500 years, while the Portuguese section was tacked on by the Fernandes family in 1821. The secret basement hideaway, full of gun holes and with an escape tunnel to the river, was used by the family to flee attackers. Admission includes a guided tour.

Heading north across the railway line you'll find another Portuguese-era mansion, an impressive canary-yellow building that now houses **Achies Art Gallery** (☑ 9822139680; www.achiesgrandeza.com; ⊘ 9am-6pm Mon-Sat) **FREE**. Call in to see the regular changing exhibitions of contemporary Goan and Indian art. The 'Grandeza' is also used for weddings, parties and film shoots.

The best way to reach Chandor is with your own transport, or by taxi from Margao (₹400 round-trip, including waiting time). On 6 January, Chandor hosts the colourful **Feast of the Three Kings**, during which local boys re-enact the arrival of the three kings from the Christmas story.

SOUTH GOA CRUISING

Take your moped, Enfield Bullet or hired taxi and hit the open road – avoiding cows, pedestrians, careening trucks, chickens, dogs, bicycles, pigs, water buffalo and the other assorted obstacles that make Goan roads something of a thrilling ride.

Palolem to the Sal River This beautiful stretch of coastal road winds from Palolem via Agonda Beach then through thick forested hills before dropping down to the Sal River. Along the way, detour to pretty Cola Beach and Cabo da Rama fort.

Chandor–Quepem–Loutolim circuit Delve deep into the world of Goan colonial-era mansions with this back-road circuit from Margao; detour to the petro-glyphs of Usgalimal and the Buddhist caves at Rivona.

Colva to Velsao Head north from busy beachfront Colva, up the scenic coast road past dozens of crumbling Portuguese-era palaces. Stop off here and there to discover desert-ed stretches of beach, and climb up to Velsao's Our Lady of Remedios chapel for the view back down.

Palolem to Netravali Head inland through farmland and protected forest to a spice farm, waterfalls and the mysterious bubble lake around Netravali. A superb day trip.

Curtorim

About 5km north of Chandor is the small village of Curtorim, another of Goa's many peaceful pastoral places. If you're passing through, stop to have a look at the **Church of St Alex**, a large whitewashed affair with a rusty tin-roofed porch and a lovely, lavish interior, which looks out serenely onto a vast lily-studded lake. It's one of Goa's oldest churches and makes a grand spot to break a countryside journey.

Quepem

About 8km southeast of Chandor is the busy small town of Quepem. Here the **Palácio do Deão** (☎0832-2664029, 9823175639; www.palaciododeao.com; ☉10am-5pm Sat-Thu), the renovated 18th-century palace built by the town's founder, Portuguese nobleman Jose Paulo de Almeida, sits across from the Holy Cross Church on the banks of the Kushavati River.

Today the restored house and its beautiful, serene gardens are open to the public. Call ahead to book a tour or arrange a delicious Portuguese-inspired lunch or afternoon tea on its lovely terrace. All donations are used to continue restoration work and eventually create a cultural centre here.

A taxi from Margao, 14km away, will cost ₹650 round-trip, including waiting time; the bus (₹10, every few minutes) stops just a few minutes' walk down the road.

Shri Damodar Temple

Shri Damodar Temple   TEMPLE
Approximately 12km southeast of Chandor and 22km from Margao, on the border of Quepem and Sanguem *talukas*, is the small village of **Zambaulim**, home to the Shri Damodar Temple. Though the temple itself is uncompromisingly modern, the deity in its sanctum is anything but, having been rescued in 1565 from the main temple in Margao, which was destroyed by the Portuguese to make way for their Church of the Holy Spirit.

The ablutions area, built 200m back from the main buildings on the banks of the Kushavati River, is an ancient Hindu site, and its water – if you're feeling simultaneously brave and under the weather – is said to have medicinal properties.

Rivona Buddhist Caves

Continuing south from Zambaulim for about 3km, the road passes through **Rivona**, which consists of little more than a few houses spread out along the roadside. As the road leaves the village, curling first to the left and then right, there is a small sign on the left, pointing to Shri Santhsa Gokarn. A short way up the dirt track, which comes to an end at a tiny temple, the **Rivona Buddhist caves** (also called Pandava caves) are on the left. Look out for strips of red cloth, hung auspiciously from an old tamarind tree nearby. The main cave's entrance is just beside an ablutions tank and small well.

It's thought that the caves were occupied by Buddhist monks, who settled here some time in the 6th or 7th century AD. There's little to see, but the tiny compartments are an interesting reminder that religions other than Hinduism, Islam and Christianity also made it to Goa. There's a small staircase cut through the rock between the upper and lower levels of the caves. If you plan to have a poke about inside, you'll need a torch and be mindful to keep a very sharp eye out for snakes – the caves are teeming with these modern-day tenants.

Usgalimal Rock Carvings

One of Goa's least visited but most fascinating sights is tucked far into the depths of the countryside at Usgalimal. The destination is a series of prehistoric petroglyphs (rock art), carved into the laterite-stone ground on the banks of the Kushavati River, and depicting various scenes including bulls, deer and antelope, a dancing woman, a peacock and 'triskelions' – a series of concentric circles thought by some archaeologists to have been a primitive means of measuring time.

These underfoot carvings are thought to be the work of one of Goa's earliest tribes, the Kush, and were only discovered by archaeologists in 1993, after being alerted to their existence by locals. The images are thought to have been created some 20,000 to 30,000 years ago, making them an important, if entirely unexploited, prehistoric site. In order for you to make out the carvings better, you'll likely have a helping hand from a local, who sits patiently at the site waiting to drizzle water from a plastic bottle into the grooves; he appreciates a tip for his efforts.

To get here, continue past Rivona for about 6km and keep an eye out for the circular green-and-red Archaeological Survey of India signs. An unsealed road off to the right of the main road leads 1.5km down to the river bank and carvings.

Shri Chandreshwar (Bhutnath) Temple

Approximately 14km southeast of Margao near the village of Paroda, a number of hills rise out of the plain, the highest of which is Chandranath Hill (350m). At the top, in a small clearing stands the Shri Chandreshwar (Bhutnath) Temple, a small but attractive 17th-century building in a lovely, solitary setting.

Although the present buildings date from the 17th century, legend has it that there has been a temple here for almost 2500 years, since the moment a meteor hit the spot. The site is dedicated to Chandreshwar, an incarnation of Shiva who is worshipped here as 'Lord of the Moon'. Consequently it's laid out so that the light of the full moon shines into the sanctum and illuminates the glittering gold deity. At the rear of the shrine, two accessory stone deities keep Chandreshwar company: Parvati (Shiva's consort) to the west, and Ganesh (his son) to the east. It's said that when the moonlight falls on it, the shrine's lingam (phallic symbol of Shiva) oozes water.

Leaving through the side entrance there is another small shrine standing separately that is dedicated to the god Bhutnath, who is worshipped in the form of a simple stone pinnacle that sticks out of the ground.

To get here, you'll need your own transport, since buses don't service this road. Head to Paroda, and ask there for the turn-off that takes you up the narrow, winding hillside road. There's a small parking area near the top, from which the approach to the temple is via a steep flight of steps.

Vasco da Gama

POP 150,000

Industrial Vasco da Gama is a busy port town, and was once a major transport hub for travellers until its train station was eclipsed by Margao's. Situated at the base of the isthmus leading to Mormugao Harbour, Vasco sports both an oil refinery and Goa's biggest red-light district, at Baina, where there's a steady influx of sailors and truck drivers. The city also has a reputation for being the crime centre of Goa, largely because of its outlying shanty towns, inhabited by migrant workers looking for employment in its port, iron-ore and barge-building industries.

It's really not an unpleasant place, though, and the city centre, along Swatantra Path and FL Gomes Rd, is quite nice by workaday Indian town standards. But with no sights of interest there's really no compelling reason for travellers to come here.

🛏 Sleeping & Eating

Vasco Residency   HOTEL **$$**
(☑ 0832-2513119; Swatantra Path; d without/with AC ₹1300/1920; ☀) Secure, central and as

bland as they come, the GTDC's Vasco offering is serviceable if you get lost in Vasco.

Hotel La Paz Gardens HOTEL **$$**
(☏0832-2512121; www.hotellapazgardens.com; Swatantra Path; s/d standard ₹2700/3400, premium ₹4900/5700, deluxe ste ₹4600/5200; ❀🛜❄) Vasco's best hotel, La Paz is a comfortable but unexceptional business hotel. All rooms have air-con and satellite TV, and facilities are good, with a gym, sauna, swimming pool and three restaurants, including the locally popular Chinese restaurant, **Sweet-n-Sour**. Free airport transfers are included in the room rates.

Welcome Restaurant SOUTH INDIAN **$**
(Swatantra Path; thalis ₹70; ⊙7am-10pm) Considered by many locals to be the best veg restaurant in Vasco, this *udupi,* just a couple of doors down from La Paz Gardens, churns out dosas and *idlis* in the morning, thalis and *puri-bhajis* at lunch, and a full Indian menu come dinnertime.

❶ Getting There & Away

Express minibuses run nonstop from the minibus stand off FL Gomes Rd to Margao (₹25, 45 minutes) and Panaji (₹30, 45 minutes). There are also regular buses from here to the airport (₹10) and Bogmalo (₹12). For long-distance state buses or trains, head to Margao.

A taxi from the airport costs around ₹180 and an autorickshaw ₹100.

Around Vasco da Gama

Sao Antonio Islet

If you have the taste for truly local flavour on a Sunday afternoon, venture about 6km east from Vasco da Gama, on the riverside road that takes you to the main highway, where you'll find the tiny Sao Antonio Islet in the middle of the Zuari estuary, joined by a thin isthmus to the main land. Here, at low tide, hundreds of locals converge to pick clams, wading waist-deep into the muddy tidal waters, accompanied by copious quantities of *feni* (Goan liquor) and general merrymaking.

Sao Jacinto

A kilometre along from Sao Antonio Islet, you'll reach Sao Jacinto, a second little river island connected to the mainland by a causeway, where you'll find an old lighthouse and two small whitewashed chapels. It's home to a small village of mostly fishermen and toddy (palm beer) tappers, and makes a pleasant place to pause for a few minutes, to have a quick look around.

Sancoale

A mournful monument to Portugal's past glories is on display at Sancoale, a kilometre past Sao Jacinto, where you'll find all that's left of **Nossa Senhora de Saude** (Our Lady of Health), a once-impressive 1566 church, built to commemorate the spot where the first Jesuits touched down in Goa in 1560. A fire ravaged the church in 1834, and all that's left now is a highly decorative part of the facade, worth stopping off to see by following the Archaeological Survey of India sign that leads the way off the main road.

Bogmalo to Betalbatim

The northern section of South Goa's coastline extends from Bogmalo, just a few kilometres south of Dabolim Airport, down to Mobor, perched on the headland above the mouth of the Sal River. Between the two is some 35km of virtually uninterrupted beach – golden sands in an almost dead-straight line lapped by the Arabian Sea. The main village-based resorts here are Colva and Benaulim, but there are numerous other beach villages with a mixture of five-star resorts, midrange package-holiday hotels, family-run guesthouses and, of course, beach shacks. What you won't find much of here, is the beach-hut accommodation so popular further south in Agonda and Palolem or north in Aswem and Mandrem.

Bogmalo

Only 4km from the Dabolim Airport, Bogmalo is a thin crescent of sand with a scruffy village and a slightly isolated air, given there are no other beaches around it. One end of the bay is marred by the monstrous '70s-style Bogmalo Beach Resort, which somehow evaded the restriction requiring all high-rise hotels to be built at least 500m from the high-tide line.

It makes a decent stop if you've got a day to kill before a flight, or if you're into scuba diving – India's most experienced dive operator is based here and the popular Grande Island dive site is only 10 minutes away by boat. Otherwise, while it never feels overcrowded, it's not one of South Goa's better beaches.

There's a reliable international ATM at the entrance to the Naval Aviation Museum above the village.

◉ Sights & Activities

A couple of jet skis are usually available for hire on the beach in season, along with a kayak or windsurfer or two. Ask around, or wander along the beach to find a vendor and negotiate a price.

Naval Aviation Museum   MUSEUM
(☑0832-5995525; adult/child ₹20/5, camera/video ₹20/50; ⊙10am-5pm Tue-Sat) The Naval Aviation Museum, at the naval base on the road above Bogmalo Beach, makes an interesting diversion if you're interested in ships and planes. Full of men idling about, especially around its Cockpit Cafe, the museum offers a neat and interesting presentation of India's naval history, and its connection to machines of the air.

Full Moon Cruises   BOAT TOUR
(☑9764625198; rahul54293@gmail.com; Full Moon Cafe; boat trip per couple ₹5500) Rahul, at the Full Moon Cafe, operates these daily half-day boat trips, tailored to customers' requirements, but usually involving a spot of dolphin-watching, a bit of fishing and a visit to Bat Island just off the Bogmalo coast. Boats can carry up to six – add ₹1500 per person after the first two.

★ Goa Diving   DIVING
(☑9049442647; www.goadiving.com; courses from ₹11,000, one-/two-tank dive ₹3000/5000) Mainland India's original dive operator, with 25 years experience, Goa Diving is an internationally respected outfit and a good place to earn your PADI certificate. It has an office on the road into Bogmalo but usually maintains a booth at the southern entrance to the beach in season.

It offers all the PADI courses, from Open Water to Divemaster, and runs dive trips to nearby Grande Island (where you can explore the remains of the British-built SS *Mary*), and Pigeon (Netrani) Island, 85km to the south. Local dives start at ₹3000 for a one-tank dive; four dives plus transfers and one night's accommodation near Pigeon Island is ₹17,000. An introductory dive costs ₹5000, an Open Water course costs ₹20,000. Courses include theory and instruction in a swimming pool.

🛏 Sleeping & Eating

Bogmalo has a handful of decent but over-priced places to stay, including a few village guesthouses on the back road running parallel to the beach. Not surprisingly, most hotels offer free airport transfers. In season there are just a few beach shacks offering a standard Indian menu and decent seafood.

Sarita's Guest House   GUESTHOUSE $$
(☑0832-2538965; www.saritasguesthouse.com; d ₹1725; ❈ 🛜) Beachfront Sarita's has clean but unremarkable and rather overpriced rooms with air-con and TV, and a common balcony offering an unimpeded view of the beach. Also offers a bar and restaurant.

Joets Guest House   GUESTHOUSE $$
(☑0832-2538036; d ₹5000; 🛜) At the northern end of the beachfront, this clean and simple guesthouse, run by the same operators as Coconut Creek, offers spacious rooms and a popular, rowdy bar and restaurant. Rates include free use of the swimming pool at Coconut Creek.

Coconut Creek   COTTAGES $$$
(☑0832-2358100, 2538090; www.coconutcreek goa.com; cottage without/with AC ₹7200/9000; ❈ 🛜 🏊) Stylish cottages are set around an inviting pool in a coconut grove just back from the northern end of the beach. Coconut Creek is easily the nicest place to stay in Bogmalo, but it's aimed squarely at package tourists and is a little overpriced for independent walk-ins.

❶ Getting There & Away

An irregular bus service runs between Bogmalo and Vasco da Gama (₹10, 25 minutes). Buses depart from the car park in front of the entrance to the Bogmalo Beach Resort. Taxis and auto-rickshaws wait around in the same area; a taxi to the airport should cost ₹250 and an autorick-shaw around ₹150.

Velsao & Arossim

About 10km east of Bogmalo, the coast road leaves the main highway and heads south to Velsao, the northerly starting point of South Goa's beaches. Despite the gloomy presence of the vast and looming Zuari Agro chemical plant to the north, Velsao's beach makes a quiet place to get away from it all, in the company of just a lifeguard, a scattering of tourists and a flock or two of milling seabirds. Further south, Arossim and neighbouring Cansaulim beaches are quiet and clean with some five-star action.

The coast road travels some way back from the beach, through thick coconut groves past dozens of old bungalows and paddy fields, while occasional laneways lead you down to the beach.

If you're travelling the coast under your own steam, it's the view, rather than the plain little chapel itself, that should entice you to take the steep road east off the coastal road up to **Our Lady of Remedios**, at the top of the hill. On clear days, you'll have a gorgeous view south – just ignore the uglier northerly and easterly views up towards the monstrous fertiliser factory and surrounding industrial sprawl.

Sleeping & Eating

Park Hyatt Resort & Spa　　　HOTEL **$$$**
(☑ 0832-2721234; www.goa.park.hyatt.com; Arossim; d from ₹12,000; ❋ @ ☲) The top sleeping option in Arossim is the 18-hectare Park Hyatt. Rooms are lavish and large, and the resort has plenty of features that would entice even the most adventurous to stay put. Its Sereno Spa is spread over a series of stunning outdoor pavilions and offers a magical Abhyanga massage, performed simultaneously by two therapists. Nonguests can take in some of the glitz at one of the restaurants.

Starfish Beach Shack　　　MULTICUISINE **$$**
(mains from ₹130) This simple beach shack is, unusually, the only one on Arossim Beach so it's naturally popular with British and Russian package holidayers staying nearby. Sun beds and beach umbrellas occupy a very quiet patch.

Casa Sarita　　　GOAN **$$$**
(☑ 0832-2721234; Park Hyatt Hotel; mains from ₹650; ☉ noon-3pm & 6-11pm) Gorgeous upmarket Goan cuisine is crafted at this fabulous Park Hyatt restaurant, which offers the piquant flavours of the region's specialities in all their glory. Try the vindaloo or the kingfish curry and you won't be disappointed.

Utorda

A clean, if slightly characterless, stretch of beach, approached on sandbag stepping-stones and rickety bridges over a series of creeks, Utorda makes for a pleasant afternoon on its sands. Take your pick from a ragtag bunch of beach shacks, though it's mostly popular with holidaymakers from the surrounding swish resorts.

🏃 Activities

Banana Surf School　　　SURFING
(☑ 7057998120; www.goasurf.com; Utorda Beach; lessons €45-250; ☉ 7.30am-12.30pm Oct-Mar) South Goa's very gentle surf is a good place for beginners and Banana Surf School,

---

FADING FISHERIES

Somewhere in the region of 50,000 Goans are dependent on fishing for their family income, but Goa's once-abundant waters are today facing a serious threat from overfishing, and locals now reminisce about their younger days when *ramponkars* (fishermen), in their simple wooden outriggers, would give away 60cm-long kingfish because they had so many to spare. These days it's difficult to buy fish direct from boats, and even local markets offer slim pickings because much of the best fish is sold directly to upmarket hotels, exported, or shipped to interstate markets where the best prices are fetched. Naturally this has driven up the price of seafood, not only for tourists, but for Goans who rely on their staple fish-curry-rice.

Overfishing has become a phenomenon since modern motorised trawlers, owned and operated by wealthy businesspeople, started to eclipse the simple traditional fishing methods of the *ramponkars* in the 1970s. Despite a law limiting trawlers to beyond a 5km shoreline 'exclusion zone', trawlers stay relatively close to the shore, adversely affecting the catch of the *ramponkars*, while their use of tightly knit nets, which don't allow juvenile fish to escape (these are either thrown away or used for fertiliser) has further dwindled fish stocks. Although the *ramponkars* continue to press for change, Goan state legislature seems helpless in the face of powerful trawler owners, while the seas slowly empty and irreversible damage is done to maintaining this precious resource. Meanwhile, many fishing boats now spend as much time ferrying tourists around for dolphin-spotting trips as they do catching fish.

based at Zeebop by the Sea, can get you up and surfing with a one-hour trial (€45), two-hour lesson (€70), three-day course (€180) or five-day course (€250). Instructors speak English and Russian.

🛏 Sleeping & Eating

Dom Pedro's Haven GUESTHOUSE $$
(☑ 9922909432; r without/with AC ₹1500/1800; ❄ 🌐) A down-to-earth option (unusual on this strip of coast) on the left-hand side at the entrance to Utorda Beach road, family-run Dom Pedro's is a lovely blue-and-white six-room affair with a Mediterranean feel. Upstairs is the popular Peter's Restaurant.

Royal Orchid Beach Resort HOTEL $$$
(☑ 0832-2884400; www.royalorchidhotels.com; d incl breakfast ₹12,000, ste ₹14,400; ❄ @ 🌐 ☀) Highly recommended by travellers with deep pockets, the Royal Orchid is a lush and plush place gracing Utorda's nice sands. Its Aristo Spa offers plenty of pampering, and a feature here is the Boat Quay Grill.

Kenilworth HOTEL $$$
(☑ 0832-6698888; www.kenilworthhotels.com; d from ₹8000; ❄ @ ☀) This ritzy resort is an upmarket affair backing onto the beach with all the standard five-star bells and whistles. Its Mallika restaurant offers 'Northern frontier' fine dining, with succulent kebabs, thick fluffy tandoori-oven breads, and other Punjabi and Kashmiri-inspired delights.

★ **Zeebop by the Sea** SEAFOOD $$$
(☑ 0832-2755333; www.zeebopgoa.com; mains ₹250-500; ☺ 10.30am-11pm) Renowned for its excellent seafood and party nights, stylish, award-winning Zeebop is set a little back from Utorda's main beach but still has a sandy floor. It a firm favourite with locals and is popular for weddings and parties so you might need to book ahead or miss out for dinner in season.

Majorda

Approached through pleasant, leafy Majorda village, Majorda Beach is a smarter, more organised option than neighbouring Utorda. A stream separates the laneways from the beach, forded by rickety bamboo bridges. The beach itself has about half a dozen Russian-oriented beach shacks, all serving up the standard beach fare with menu boards chalked up in Cyrillic.

🏃 Activities

Greenland Horse Riding HORSE RIDING
(☑ 9822586502; 10min ride ₹200) Majorda is currently the only place in Goa where you can ride a horse on the beach. Bookings with expat owner Frank are essential.

🛏 Sleeping

Rainbow's End GUESTHOUSE $
(☑ 0832-2881016; d from ₹1000) A good value place for those looking to stay for a while, these three simple self-contained units, situated in a characterful building amid a lovely garden, are on the corner as you turn down towards the beach road. They can sleep up to six; add another ₹500 per extra person – good for groups and families.

If there's no one around, the owner should be in the little store diagonally across the road.

★ **Vivenda Dos Palhacos** BOUTIQUE HOTEL $$$
(☑ 9881720221; www.vivendagoa.com; d ₹6750-11,750; ❄ @ ☀) This lovely boutique hotel, run by an Indian-born British brother-and-sister team, is a gem of the south Goan coast and strictly for seriously discerning travellers who value quality accommodation and privacy. It's back from the beach and the road, is unsignposted, and is an oasis of calm in a heavily touristed world.

Rooms inhabit an old Portuguese-era mansion and older Hindu house, with sparkling courtyard pool and resident basset hound. There's also a top-end tent and self-contained cottage on offer.

✖ Eating

Greenland Bar & Restaurant MULTICUISINE $
(mains from ₹120; ☺ 10am-10pm) On Majorda's southern 'Cabana Beach', across a little bamboo bridge, you'll find cute Greenland, run by a British couple. It serves up some great Goan specialities including *xacuti* and vindaloo, along with the usual beach-shack fare.

Raj's Pentagon Restaurant & Garden Pub INDIAN $$
(☑ 0832-2881402; www.goapentagon.com; mains ₹140-390; ☺ noon-midnight) Raj's is as much a place to come for the live music as to eat, though the food is pretty good and the ambience inviting. Decent garden setting, great seafood and regular musos in season.

SOUTH GOA BOGMALO TO BETALBATIM

Betalbatim

Though the beaches along this entire strip are really just different patches of one long and continuous stretch of sand, some places have more character than others. Betalbatim, just to the north of Colva, is a good example of what a difference a few hundred metres can make, as calm, quiet and pastoral as Colva is crowded and soulless. And even Betalbatim itself consists of several different smaller strips of beach – try **Sunset Beach** or the romantically named **Lovers Beach**.

🛌 Sleeping & Eating

Alila Diwa   HOTEL $$$
(📞 0832-2746800; www.alilahotels.com; r from ₹12,000; ❄ 🛜 ☀) The Alila is a standout boutique design hotel with an awesome infinity pool overlooking the rice paddies. Rooms are modern and minimalist and the excellent restaurants include Spice Studio. Naturally there's a spa.

Martin's Corner   GOAN $$$
(www.martinscornergoa.com;   mains ₹250-400; ⏲ 11.30am-2pm & 6.30-11pm) An award-winning local legend but now very much upmarket, Martin's Corner, near Sunset Beach, is a great place to sample Goan cuisine and seafood in a relaxed setting back from the beach. The *xacutis* and vindaloos are superb, and there are plenty of tasty vegetarian options on offer. Live music most nights from 8pm.

Colva

POP 10,200

Once a sleepy fishing village, and in the '60s a hang-out for hippies escaping the scene up at Anjuna, Colva is still the main town-resort along this stretch of coast, but these days it has lost any semblance of the beach paradise vibe.

A large concrete roundabout marks the end of the beach road and the entrance to the beach, filled with day-trippers, package tourists and listless hawkers. The main

---

COLVA'S MENINO JESUS

Colva's 18th-century **Our Lady of Mercy Church** is home to a little statue known as the 'Menino' (Baby) Jesus, which is said to miraculously heal the sick. Legend has it that the statue was discovered by a Jesuit priest named Father Bento Ferreira in the mid-17th century, after he was shipwrecked somewhere off the coast of Mozambique. The plucky missionary swam to shore, to see vultures circling a rocky spot. On closer inspection, he discovered the statue, apparently washed ashore after having been tossed overboard as worthless by Muslim pirates.

When he was posted to Colva in 1648, Father Ferreira took the Menino Jesus along with him, and had it installed on the high altar, where it promptly began to heal the sick. It wasn't long before it was worshipped with its own special **Fama de Menino Jesus festival**, which still occurs each year on the second Monday in October.

However, all was not smooth sailing for the Menino. When the Portuguese suppressed many religious orders in 1836, the Jesuits were forced to flee Colva, and took the Menino with them to their seminary in Rachol (p166). Colva's residents weren't pleased with the removal of their miracle-worker, and petitioned the head of the Jesuits in Rome, then the viceroy, then the king of Portugal himself for its return.

Finally they got the answer they hoped for – orders for the statue to go back to Colva. However, the Jesuits refused and finally the Colvan villagers clubbed together and had their own replica made, furnished with a diamond ring that had fallen off the finger of the original Menino during the move to Rachol. Meanwhile, in Rachol, the first statue slowly appeared to lose its healing powers, while the newcomer healed away merrily, prompting the delighted villagers to claim it had been the ring, and not the statue, that was the source of its miraculous powers all the while.

These days, the distinctly unmiraculous Menino is still kept at Rachol Seminary, while its more successful successor only sees the light of day during the annual Fama festival. Then, the little image is removed from deep within the church's vaults, paraded about town, dipped in the river, and installed in the church's high altar for pilgrims to pray to, hoping for their own personal miracle.

Colva

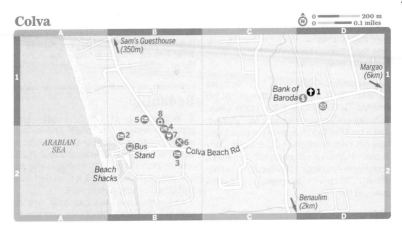

Colva

⊙ Sights
1 Our Lady of Mercy Church D1

🛏 Sleeping
2 Colmar Beach Resort.............................. B2
3 La Ben.. B2
4 Skylark Resort... B2
5 Soul Vacation B1

🍴 Eating
6 Sagar Kinara B2

🍸 Drinking & Nightlife
7 Leda Lounge & Restaurant B2

🛍 Shopping
8 Goa Animal Welfare Trust Shop............ B1

beach drag is lined with dreary stalls and shabby cafes. Travel a little way north or south, though, and you'll find some of the peace missing in central Colva.

⊙ Sights & Activities

Colva's beach entrance throngs with young men keen to sell you **parasailing** (per ride ₹800), **jet-skiing** (15 minutes single/double ₹300/500) and **dolphin-spotting trips** (per person around ₹300). Rates are fixed but ensure that life jackets are supplied.

🛏 Sleeping

Colva has a few budget guesthouses hidden in the wards north of the beach road, but overall good-value pickings are a little slim.

Sam's Guesthouse   HOTEL **$**
(📞 0832-2788753; r ₹650; 🛜) Away from the fray, north of Colva's main drag on the road running parallel to the beach, Sam's is a big, cheerful place with friendly owners and spacious rooms that are a steal at this price. Rooms are set around a pleasant garden courtyard and there's a good restaurant and whacky bar.

La Ben   HOTEL **$**
(📞 0832-2788040; www.laben.net; Colva Beach Rd; r without/with AC ₹1100/1400; ❄🛜) Neat, clean and not entirely devoid of atmosphere. If you're not desperately seeking anything with character, La Ben has decent, good-value rooms and has been around for ages. A great addition is the adjacent Garden Restaurant.

Colmar Beach Resort   RESORT **$**
(📞 022-67354666; www.colmarbeachresort.net; d without/with AC from ₹700/1100, poolside cottage ₹1500; ❄🛜🏊) Colmar Beach Resort is the closest budget place to Colva's beach and, provided you're not expecting too much, it can make a reasonable stay. The cottages around the small pool are the pick, while the ageing rooms at the back are cheaper and a bit grimy. The beach is right in front and the adjacent restaurant and bar is quite good.

★ Skylark Resort   HOTEL **$$**
(📞 0832-2788052; www.skylarkresortgoa.com; d with AC ₹2885-3639, f ₹4270; ❄🛜🏊) A serious step up from the budget places, Skylark's clean, fresh rooms are graced with bits and

pieces of locally made teak furniture and block-print bedspreads, while the lovely pool makes a pleasant place to lounge. The best (and more expensive) rooms are those facing the pool.

Soul Vacation   HOTEL $$$
(✆0832-2788147; www.soulvacation.in; d incl breakfast ₹6000-7000; ❄☎☲) Thirty sleek, white rooms arranged around nice gardens and a pool are the trademarks of Soul Vacation, set 400m back from Colva Beach. This is central Colva's most upmarket choice and, though pricey, there's a nice air of exclusivity about it. There's an ayurvedic spa, garden cafe and bar.

✗ Eating & Drinking

Numerous beach shacks line the Colvan sands between November and April, offering the standard range of fare and fresh seafood.

For simpler eating, head up to the roundabout just before the church, where tourist joints are replaced by simple chai shops, thali places and chicken kebab stands. At night, *bhelpuri* (crisp fried thin rounds of dough with lentils, puffed rice and onions) vendors also set up camp here, dishing up big portions of the fried noodle snack.

Sagar Kinara   INDIAN $
(Colva Beach Rd; mains ₹60-180; ☉7am-10.30pm) A pure-veg restaurant upstairs (nonveg is separate, downstairs) with tastes to please even committed carnivores, this place is clean, efficient and offers cheap and delicious North and South Indian cuisine all day.

Leda Lounge & Restaurant   BAR
(☉7.30am-midnight) Part sports bar, part music venue, part cocktail bar, Leda is Colva's best nightspot by a long shot. There's live music from Thursday to Sunday, fancy drinks (mojitos, Long Island iced teas) and good – but pricey – food (mains ₹270 to ₹600).

ⓘ Information

Colva has plenty of banks, ATM machines, the odd internet cafe and travel agents strung along Colva Beach Rd, and a post office on the lane that runs past the eastern end of the church.

ⓘ Getting There & Away

Buses from Colva to Margao run roughly every 15 minutes (₹15, 20 minutes) from 7.30am to about 7pm, departing from the parking area at the end of the beach road.

Benaulim

A long stretch of largely empty sand, peppered with a few beach shacks and water-sports enthusiasts, the beaches of Benaulim and nearby Sernabatim are much quieter than Colva, partly because the village is a good kilometre back from the beach and linked by several laneways.

Out of season it has a somewhat desolate feel, but the lack of traffic or any serious beachfront development is an obvious attraction to many travellers, some of whom rent houses in the village and stay for the season.

Benaulim also has a special place in Goan tradition: legend has it that it was here that the god Parasurama's arrow landed when he fired it into the sea to create Goa. Modern-day archers, however, might choose a prettier spot.

Most accommodation, eating options, grocery shops and pharmacies are concentrated along the Vasvaddo Beach Rd near the Maria Hall intersection.

ⓞ Sights & Activities

★ Goa Chitra   MUSEUM
(✆0832-6570877; www.goachitra.com; St John the Baptist Rd, Mondo Vaddo, Benaulim; admission ₹200; ☉9am-6pm Tue-Sun) Artist and restorer Victor Hugo Gomes first noticed the slow extinction of traditional objects – from farming tools to kitchen utensils to altarpieces – as a child in Benaulim. He created this ethnographic museum from the more than 4000 cast-off objects that he collected from across the state over 20 years (he often had to find elderly people to explain their uses). Admission to this fascinating museum is via a one-hour guided tour, held on the hour. Goa Chitra is 3km east of Maria Hall – ask locally for directions.

Pele's Water Sport   WATER SPORTS
(✆9822686011) Water sports in Benaulim are not as chaotic as in Colva, though some operators hang around the beach shacks. One of the best is Pele's Water Sport; jet skis cost ₹500 per 10 minutes, parasailing costs ₹800 per ride, and dolphin trips are ₹500 per person.

Benaulim

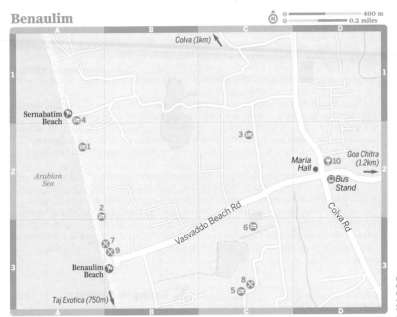

🛏 Sleeping

Lots of budget rooms for rent can be found along the roads towards Benaulim and Sernabatim Beach, while the big five-stars are further south. The best of the budget beachfront accommodation is at Sernabatim Beach, a few hundred metres north of Benaulim. Prices have slowly crept up, but there are still lots of family-run places with just a handful of rooms with bargain-basement prices.

Rosario's Inn　　　　　　　　GUESTHOUSE **$**
(📞 0832-2770636; r without/with AC ₹450/800; ❄) Across a football field flitting with young players and dragonflies, family-run Rosario's is a large establishment with very clean, simple rooms and a restaurant. Excellent value.

D'Souza Guest House　　　　GUESTHOUSE **$**
(📞 0832-2770583; d ₹600) With just three rooms, this traditional blue-painted house in the back lanes is run by a local Goan family and comes with bundles of homely atmosphere and a lovely garden. It's often full so book ahead.

Furtados　　　　　　　　　　GUESTHOUSE **$**
(📞 0832-2770396; www.furtadosbeachhouse.com; Sernabatim Beach; d ₹1000, with AC ₹1500; ❄)

Benaulim

At the end of the road to Sernabatim Beach, Furtado's has decent, clean and pretty good value rooms behind its restaurant.

Blue Corner　　　　　　　　　　HUT **$$**
(📞 9850455770; www.bluecornergoa.com; huts ₹1600) Behind the beach shack restaurant a short walk north of the main beach entrance is this group of sturdy cocohuts – not so common around here – with fan and verandah. The restaurant gets good reviews from guests.

GOA'S FORTS

Goa has several surviving colonial forts that have stood watch for several centuries over strategically important estuaries. Built by the Portuguese (but frequently on the sites of older defensive structures) soon after their 16th-century arrival into Goa, the forts were made of locally mined laterite, a red and porous stone that proved, in most instances, a good match for the forces pitted against it.

Under the supervision of Italian architect Fillipo Terzi, the Portuguese developed their Goan bastions to be able to withstand the forces of gunpowder and cannonballs. Inside the strong fort walls, the buildings were often carved directly out of the stone itself, with storerooms for supplies and weaponry connected by a maze of subterranean tunnels. Sometimes these tunnels led down as far as to the sea itself to supply the forts during any lengthy times of siege.

Though the forts were made to withstand attacks from the sea by Portugal's main trade rivals, the Dutch and the British, they were never the sites of full-scale warfare, and as the threat of maritime invasion slowly faded during the 18th and 19th centuries, most forts fell into disrepair. Some, such as Cabo da Rama, Reis Magos and Fort Aguada, found favour as prisons, while others became army garrisons or plundering sites for building materials. Today they're atmospheric relics of a bygone age, with the advantage of some picture-perfect views down over the coast they once guarded so closely.

Anthy's Guesthouse   GUESTHOUSE $
(☑0832-2771680; anthysguesthouse@rediffmail.com; Sernabatim Beach; d ₹1300, with AC ₹1700; ❋) One of a handful of places lining Sernabatim Beach itself, Anthy's is a firm favourite with travellers for its good restaurant, book exchange, and well-kept chalet-style rooms, which stretch back from the beach surrounded by a garden. Ayurvedic massage is available here.

Palm Grove Cottages   HOTEL $$
(☑0832-2770059; www.palmgrovegoa.com; Vaswado; d incl breakfast ₹2020-3700; ❋🛜) Old-fashioned, secluded charm and Benaulim's leafiest garden welcomes you at Palm Grove Cottages, a great midrange choice. The quiet air-con rooms, some with balcony, all have a nice feel, but the best are the spacious deluxe rooms in a separate Portuguese-style building. The **Palm Garden Restaurant** here is exceptionally good.

Taj Exotica   HOTEL $$$
(☑0832-6683333; www.tajhotels.com; d from ₹30,000; ❋@🛜) Bollywood stars, sheiks and other celebs are known to stay at the Taj Exotica, one of Goa's plushest resorts. Set in 23 hectares of tropical gardens 2km south of Benaulim, it has all the facilities you would expect, including spas, restaurants, buffet breakfast and pool. Most travellers will be content to visit its excellent restaurants, including the Goan cuisine of Allegria and the beachfront Lobster Shack.

🍴 Eating & Drinking

The beach is lined with restaurant shacks north and south in season, so you won't have trouble finding a place for a sunset drink or seafood dinner. Benaulim isn't known for its nightlife, but there's a new club in town and live music on weekends at Sernabatim Beach.

Pedro's Bar & Restaurant   GOAN, MULTICUISINE $$
(Vasvaddo Beach Rd; mains ₹110-350; ⊙7am-midnight) Set amid a large, shady garden on the beachfront and popular with local and international travellers, Pedro's offers standard Indian, Chinese and Italian dishes, as well as Goan choices and 'sizzlers'.

Johncy Restaurant   GOAN, MULTICUISINE $$
(Vasvaddo Beach Rd; mains ₹110-350; ⊙7am-midnight) Unlike most beach shacks, Johncy has been around forever, dispensing standard Goan, Indian and Western favourites from its location just back from the sand.

Malibu Restaurant   INDIAN, ITALIAN $$
(mains ₹120-450; ⊙8.30am-11pm) The chairs are white plastic and the tablecloths cheesy checks, but Malibu offers a nice dining experience in its secluded garden setting on a back lane a short walk back from the beach. It does reasonable renditions of Italian favourites and has occasional live music.

Club Zoya CLUB
(☑ 9822661388; www.clubzoya.com; ☺ 8pm-late)
The party scene has hit sleepy little Benaulim in the form of barn-sized Club Zoya, with international DJs, big light shows and a cocktail bar featuring speciality flavoured and infused vodka drinks. Something's on most nights here in season but check the website for upcoming events and DJs.

❶ Getting There & Around

Buses from Margao to Benaulim are frequent (₹15, 15 minutes); some continue on south to Varca and Cavelossim. Buses stop at the Maria Hall crossroads, or at the junctions to Sernabatim or Taj Exotica – just ask to be let off. From Maria Hall an autorickshaw costs around ₹60 for the five-minute ride to the beach.

Varca, Cavelossim & Mobor

Heading south from Benaulim, you'll travel a road lined with beautiful Portuguese-era relics, paddy fields, whitewashed churches and farmland, encountering first the town of Varca – a sleepy village near where several five-star resorts occupy space along the beach. Next up is Cavelossim, a burgeoning strip of stalls, malls, and midrange to top-end hotels running parallel to the beach. Finally, where the Sal River meets the Arabian Sea, you'll find little Mobor, dominated by the presence of the Leela, one of Goa's biggest and swankiest hotels, and the peninsula tipped by a tiny fishing settlement of poor migrant fishers from Orissa state.

These three village resorts back a 10km stretch of lovely beach, where it's little effort to find a comfy sun lounge or a deserted patch of virgin sands, depending on your preference. The presence of luxury residences (and the high precedent set for the price of sea-facing real estate here) seems to have saved this swathe of sands from tacky, midrange development. Even if you're not staying at one of the swanky addresses along it, the beaches are open to everyone; many resorts employ their own staff to keep the beachfront litter-free.

Regular buses serve the main coastal road from Margao, via Colva or Benaulim, all the way down to Mobor. They run daily, every few minutes between around 8am and 10pm, and can be flagged down along the road. The furthest stop south drops you out-side the grounds of the Leela, from which it's an easy walk to the beach.

🏃 Activities

Betty's Place Boat Trips BOAT TOUR
(☑ 0832-2871456, 9226424717; www.bettysgoa.com; Mobor Beach) A decent restaurant by night, Betty's offers a wide range of boat cruises by day, including a full-day combined dolphin-watching and birdwatching trip (₹1000 including lunch and drinks), fishing trips, sunset boat rides (₹350), and a two-hour birdwatching trip on the River Sal (₹400; departs daily at 4pm). Located opposite the Holiday Inn.

🛏 Sleeping & Eating

★ **Bamboo House Goa** HUT $$
(☑ 9766649369; www.bamboohousegoa.com; hut from ₹3000) The 10 bamboo and thatch cottages here, at the end of the Mobor peninsula road, are well crafted and way better than any other hut operation on this stretch of coast. It's a peaceful place set in a neat gardenlike block within easy reach of the beach. The huts have comfy beds, large bathrooms and safe lockers. With its eco-credentials (composting, solar energy, innovative sewage treatment) and its total separation from the rather hectic pace of Cavelossim, this is a breath of fresh Mobor air.

Leela Goa HOTEL $$$
(☑ 0832-6621234; www.theleela.com; r from ₹16,000; ❄ @ 🛜 ⛱) Goa's largest and most luxurious resort, the opulent Leela is the place to indulge your five-star fantasies. Set amid 30 hectares of land, this enormous expanse of manicured Goan perfection has its own 12-hole golf course, and various rooms of varying degrees of decadence. Go for upmarket Indian and Goan cuisine at its signature Jamavar restaurant, or alfresco at Riverside, on the banks of the River Sal, which serves delicious Italian dishes along with a good dollop of *la dolce vita*.

★ **Blue Whale** INDIAN, MULTICUISINE $$
(mains ₹100-350) Near where the tip of the Mobor peninsula meets the Sal River, Blue Whale is a classic seasonal beach shack with an extensive all-day menu, run by friendly and knowledgeable local Roque Coutinho. The food is good, the welcome equally so, and it's a world away from the five stars that dominate the coast around here.

❶ Getting There & Away

To the south of Mobor is the mouth of the Sal River. To continue down along the coast of South Goa, take the backcountry roads and the brand new bridge spanning the Sal River to Assolna, then continue on towards Betul.

Assolna to Agonda

One of the most beautiful roads in Goa is the coastal stretch between Assolna, on the south side of the Sal River, and the village of Agonda, some 20km south – perfect on a scooter or Enfield. Hilly, winding and highly scenic, the road takes you into tiny , through thick patches of coconut grove, and up to some stunning vistas out over the sea. Take a detour out to windswept Cabo da Rama fort and Cola Beach along the way.

Betul

Continuing southwards from Assolna, opposite the narrow Mobor peninsula, is the ramshackle fishing village of Betul. Few foreign tourists stay here and, apart from getting local boatmen to take you out on the river or watching the fishermen unload their catch at the harbour, there's not much to do. But it's an interesting place to wander past the tangle of fishing huts and boats of the bay and estuary. When the tide's in, you'll see seabirds diving for fish; when it's out, you'll see locals in the mud searching for crabs and other seafood.

Cabo da Rama

The laterite spurs along the coastline of Goa, providing both high ground and ready-made supplies of building stone, were natural sites for fortresses, and there was thus a **fortress** at Cabo da Rama long before the Portuguese ever reached Goa.

Named after Rama of the Hindu Ramayana epic, who was said to have spent time in exile here with his wife Sita, the original fortress was held by various rulers for many years. It wasn't until 1763 that it was obtained by the Portuguese from the Hindu Raja of Sonda and was subsequently rebuilt; what remains today, including the rusty cannons, is entirely Portuguese.

Although the fort saw no real action after the rebuild, it was briefly occupied by British troops between 1797 and 1802 and again between 1803 and 1813, when the threat of

French invasion troubled the British enough to move in. Parts were used as a prison until 1955, before the whole thing was allowed to fall into ruin.

There is little to see of the old structure except for the front wall, with its dry moat and unimposing main gate, and the small church that stands just inside the walls, but the views north and south are worth coming for. Services are still held in the chapel every Sunday morning.

To get to the fort from the coast road between Betul and Agonda, turn west at the red-and-green signposted turn-off about 10km south of Betul. The road dips into a lush valley then winds steeply up to a barren plateau punctuated by farmhouses and wandering stock. The fort is at the end of this road, about 3km from the turn-off.

Local buses come here from Margao or Betul (₹15, around 40 minutes) several times daily but check times for returning buses as you might get stuck. A couple of simple cafes outside the fort entrance serve snacks and ice-cold drinks.

A return taxi to Cabo da Rama costs around ₹800 from Palolem, including waiting time. With your own transport it's an excellent ride from Palolem, Agonda or elsewhere along the south coast.

Cola Beach

Cola Beach was, for a long time, one of those hidden gems of the south coast – a relatively hard-to-reach crescent of sand enclosed by forested cliffs and with a gorgeous emerald lagoon stretching back from the beach.

It's still all of those things, except for the hidden part. Between November and April several hut and tent villages set up here, but it's still a beautiful place and popular with day-trippers from Agonda and Palolem.

Further north around the headland is an even more remote beach known as **Khancola**, or Kakolem, with one small resort reached via a steep set of jungly laterite steps from the clifftop above.

🛏 Sleeping

Palm Discoveries HUT **$$**
(☏ 9820991637; www.palmdiscoveries.com; Khancola Beach; hut ₹2000) The six huts here are very simple and wonderfully isolated. It's a steep walk down laterite steps through the jungle to get here and at the bottom you're greeted with the secluded covelike

Khancola Beach and the smiling staff at the small restaurant-bar. Even if you don't stay it's worth hiking down for a few hours on the beach.

★ **Blue Lagoon** HUT, TENT **$$**
(www.bluelagooncola.com; Cola Beach; tent ₹3000, cottage ₹4000) These sweet timber cottages and Rajasthani-style tents overlook either the beach or the lagoon at Cola and are the first place you'll find on the walk down from the parking area.

Cola Beach Resort TENT RESORT **$$$**
(✆ 9822061223; www.colabeach.com; Cola Beach; tent ₹6500) A short walk north of the lagoon, and fronting a quieter stretch of beach, the safari tents here are spacious and comfortable enough but way overpriced.

Agonda

Agonda Beach is a fine 2km stretch of white sand framed between two forested headlands. Travellers have been drifting here for years and seasonal hut villages – some very luxurious – now occupy almost all available beachfront space, but it's still much more low-key than Palolem and a good choice if you're after some relaxation.

The coast road between Betul and Palolem passes through Agonda village, while the main traveller centre is a single road running parallel behind the beach.

Agonda is not without things to do. Lots of foreigner-run yoga, meditation and ayurve-da courses and classes set up in season, and local boats can take you on trips to other beaches or to spot dolphins. The surf can be a bit fierce and swimming is not as safe as Palolem, but lifeguards are on patrol. Olive ridley marine turtles nest at the northern end of the beach in winter. They're protected courtesy of a forestry department-staffed beach shack, and the buried eggs are cordoned off for their safety.

Lots of shops and useful travel agents are along the beach road, and a HDFC ATM is just beside the church crossroads.

🛏 Sleeping

Agonda has gone seriously upmarket in its beach-hut operations in recent years, with the best resorts offering air-con, TV and giant open-sky bathrooms, and all with a restaurant and bar, usually beachfacing. As with any seasonal accommodation, standards and ownership can change. Back from the beach on the parallel road are a few cheaper guesthouses and rooms to let.

Fatima Guesthouse GUESTHOUSE **$**
(✆ 0832-2647477; d ₹600-700, with AC ₹800; ❄ 🛜) An ever-popular two-storey guesthouse with clean rooms, a good restaurant and highly obliging staff, on the southern stretch of Agonda's beach road. The rooftop yoga classes and extended courses (and the budget price) mean it's often full. Owner Steve is behind the other Fatima ventures in town.

SOUTH GOA AGONDA

THE LOST JUNGLE HOTEL

Tucked away in the jungle beyond the southern end of Agonda Beach, and just visible above the tree line, is the eerie concrete shell of the abandoned Seema Hotel. In the early 1980s, so the story goes, a handful of absentee landlords sold the palm groves in the southern portion of the beach to a hotel consortium, allegedly backed by the former PM Rajiv Gandhi, who was later assassinated in 1991.

Agonda's toddy tappers, however, angered by the destruction of their livelihood, refused to move as building work got under way for a luxury hotel, with helipad, golf course and luxe swimming pool. The toddy tappers remained adamant, threatening to use force if necessary, and painting a rock in the bay with the ominous slogan, 'Your tourists will never be safe here'.

The project collapsed soon after. Some claim it was this local pressure that caused the building work to be abandoned, others that one of Gandhi's business partners was involved in some dodgy dealings and ran out of funds, others still that the partners quarrelled to the point of no return.

Today the partly constructed site remains in the hands of receivers, looking very forlorn. There's usually a caretaker on-site who won't mind you looking around. It's tricky to get to but take the dirt road at the sign for Rama Resort and follow the jungle-strewn path in the direction of the hotel.

Abba's Gloryland GUESTHOUSE $

(✉9404312232, 0832-2647822; www.abbasgloryland.com; hut/r ₹1000/1200; ☎) On the backside of the road at the northern end of the
beach, this friendly, family-run place offers
cool, tiled rooms in a pink building, and
neat bamboo huts with slate floors. A good
budget option with no sea views, but only a
short walk from the beach.

Hangout Agonda HUT $

(✉9930048185; d ₹1200) At the far northern end of Agonda Beach, this is one of the
cheaper beachfront options with decent
palm-thatch huts with fan and bathroom in
a neat garden.

Agonda White Sand HUT $$

(✉9823548277; www.agondawhitesand.com; hut
from ₹3800; ☎) Beautifully designed and
constructed cottages with open-air bathrooms and spring mattresses surround a
central bar and restaurant at this stylish
beachfront place. Less than 100m away the
same owners have a pair of amazing five-
star sea-facing villas (₹7000 to ₹9000) with
enormous beds and cavernous bathrooms
large enough to contain a garden and fish
pond!

Chattai HUT $$

(✉9423812287; www.chattai.co.in; hut ₹2100)
Towards the north end of the beach, Chattai offers lovely, airy huts on the sands, and
popular yoga classes under its secluded Yoga
Dome.

★H2O Agonda HUT $$$

(✉9423836994; www.h2oagonda.com; d incl
breakfast ₹4500-6500; ❋☎) With its purple
and mauve muslin curtains and Arabian
nights ambience, H2O is among the most
impressive of Agonda's luxury cottage set-
ups. From the hotel-style reception, walk
through a leafy garden to the spacious
cottages with air-con, TV and enormous
open-air bathrooms. The more expensive sea-facing cottages, with zebra print
spreads on king-size beds, are worth paying extra for.

Cuba Agonda COTTAGE $$$

(✉0832-2645775; www.cubagoa.com; Agonda Beach; d ₹5500; ❋) These blue-and-
white sea-facing cottages look a bit like
fancy English bathing boxes but they're
well-appointed inside with air-con, TV
and comfy beds, and verandahs with steps
straight to the beach.

✕ Eating

★Fatima Thali Shop SOUTH INDIAN $

(veg/fish thali ₹80/100) Beloved by locals and
visitors, tiny Fatima, with just four tables,
is an Agonda institution, with filling South
Indian thalis whipped up inside its improbably small kitchen. It's also a cosy spot for
breakfast, salads and chai.

La Dolce Vita ITALIAN $$

(mains ₹250-370; ⏱from 6.30pm) Excellent
Italian food is dished out at Dolce Vita, an
Italian place with gingham tablecloths, a
long, sprawling blackboard menu, and plenty of passionate yelling and gesturing when
the place gets busy. Wood-fired pizzas are
authentic, the range of pastas will satisfy
most tastes and the tiramisu is well worth
saving space for. It's at the southern end of
the beach road.

Fatima's Corner SEAFOOD $$

(mains ₹80-250; ⏱7.30am-11pm) Fatima's latest
hotspot, this corner restaurant specialises in
beautifully prepared fresh local seafood and
tandoori dishes.

❶ Getting There & Away

Scooters and motorbikes can be rented from
lots of places on the beach road for around ₹250
and ₹350 respectively. Autorickshaws depart
from the main T-junction near Agonda's church
to Palolem (₹250) and Patnem (₹300). Taxis are
around ₹50 more.

Local buses run from Chaudi sporadically
throughout the day (₹12), but make sure you get
one to Agonda Beach, otherwise you'll be let off
in the village about 1km away.

Chaudi

Also known as Canacona, the bustling small
town of Chaudi, with all its essential services along its single main street (which is also
the NH17 highway), is the place to come to
get things done if you're staying in Palolem,
Agonda, Patnem or around. Here you'll find
several banks and ATM machines, pharmacies, doctors, a supermarket of sorts, a
post office, a stationery and toy shop, mobile-phone vendors, and a good fruit and
vegetable market and bakeries for stocking
up on self-catering essentials.

Chaudi also has the south's biggest train
station (Canacona), about 1.5km northeast of town and is the gateway, by rail, to
Palolem.

Palolem

Palolem is undoubtedly one of Goa's most postcard-perfect beaches: a gentle curve of palm-fringed sand facing a calm bay. But in season it's bursting at the seams.

If you want to see what Palolem looked like 10 or 15 years ago, turn up in September or early October, before the beach huts start to go up. Once the hammering and sawing begins, the beachfront is transformed into a toy-town of colourful and increasingly sophisticated timber and bamboo huts fronted by palm-thatch restaurants. As busy as Palolem is in season though, it's still a great place to be and is popular with backpackers, long-stayers and families. The atmosphere is vibrant and there's plenty to do. As a protected bay Palolem is one of the safest swimming spots in Goa and you can comfortably kayak and paddleboard for hours here.

Away from the beach you can learn to cook, drop in to yoga classes or hire a motorbike and cruise to surrounding beaches, waterfalls and wildlife parks. At night you can listen to live reggae as the sun sets or dance in silence at a headphone party.

Palolem lulls you into a sense of peace but keeps you active and excited. This is Goa's best beach, so find your hut, order a Kingfisher or cocktail, and enjoy.

🏃 Activities

Palolem is an active sort of place and although the yoga and spirituality outfits aren't as comprehensive as in the north, there's no shortage of yoga, reiki and meditation classes in season. Locations and teachers tend to change seasonally. Massage and ayurvedic treatments are also advertised – ask around locally to see whose hands-on healing powers are hot this season.

Palolem's calm waters are perfect for **kayaking** and **stand-up paddleboarding**. Kayaks are available for hire for around ₹150 per hour (with optional life vest), paddleboards for ₹500. **Mountain bikes** (₹100 per day) can be hired from **Seema Bike Hire** (Ourem Rd).

Space Goa YOGA
(📞 80063283333; www.thespacegoa.com) Space Goa is part cafe, part wellness centre offering reiki, reflexology and kids' activities. Drop-in morning yoga classes are ₹500.

Aranya Yoga YOGA
(📞 9341738801; Palolem Beach Rd; ⊙ classes 8.30am & 4pm) Daily yoga classes (₹300) are arranged at the Butterfly Bookshop.

Bhakti Kutir YOGA, MEDITATION
(www.bhaktikutir.com; Colomb Bay) This rustic jungle hut-resort is a long-standing spiritual retreat for yoga and meditation. Daily morning and afternoon drop-in yoga classes and extended courses, as well as an ayurveda centre.

Humming Bird Spa SPA
(Ciaran's; 1hr massage from ₹1900) For sheer pampering, Palolem's best all-round spa is at Ciaran's. Choose from ayurvedic, Swedish, Balinese, Thai or aroma massage, waxing or even a full-body chocolate wrap.

🎓 Courses

Rahul's Cooking Class COOKING
(📞 07875990647; www.rahulcookeryclass.com; Palolem Beach Rd; per person ₹1400; ⊙ 11am & 6pm) Rahul's is one of the original cooking schools with three-hour morning and afternoon classes each day. Prepare five dishes including chapati and coconut curry. Minimum two people; book at least one day in advance.

Masala Kitchen COOKING
(per person ₹1200) Well-established cooking classes; enquire at the Butterfly Book Shop (p188) and book a day in advance.

👉 Tours

You'll find plenty of local fishermen keen to take you out on dolphin-spotting and fishing expeditions on their outrigger boats. They charge a minimum of ₹1200, or ₹1600 for four or more people, for a one-hour trip. They also do trips to nearby Butterfly and Honeymoon Beaches, or up to Agonda and Cola beaches.

Goa Jungle Adventure OUTDOORS
(📞 9850485641; www.goajungle.com; trekking & canyoning trips ₹1890-3590) This adventure company, run by an experienced French guide, will take you out for thrilling trekking and canyoning trips in the Netravali area at the base of the Western Ghats, where you climb, jump and abseil into remote water-filled plunges. Trips run from a half-day to several days, and extended rafting trips into Karnataka are also sometimes offered.

Palolem

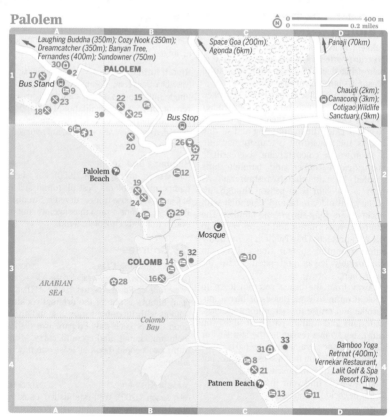

Laughing Buddha (350m); Cozy Nook (350m);
Dreamcatcher (350m); Banyan Tree,
Fernandes (400m); Sundowner (750m)

Space Goa (200m);
Agonda (6km)

Panaji (70km)

PALOLEM

Bus Stand

Chaudi (2km);
Canacona (3km);
Cotigao Wildlife
Sanctuary (9km)

Bus Stop

Palolem
Beach

*ARABIAN
SEA*

COLOMB

Mosque

*Colomb
Bay*

Bamboo Yoga
Retreat (400m);
Vernekar Restaurant,
Lalit Golf & Spa
Resort (1km)

Patnem Beach

SOUTH GOA PALOLEM

Shoes can be rented for ₹190 per day. Call to arrange a meeting with Manu; he's at Crunch Restaurant each evening.

🛏 Sleeping

Most of Palolem's accommodation is of the seasonal beach-hut variety, though there are plenty of old-fashioned guesthouses or family homes with rooms to rent back from the beach for ₹600 to ₹1000. It's still possible to find a basic palm-thatch hut or plywood cottage somewhere near the beach for as little ₹500, but many of the huts these days are more thoughtfully designed using quality materials – the very best have air-con, flat-screen TV and sea-facing balcony. These rooms can cost ₹3000 to ₹5000 a night but the beauty of Palolem is that you can park your bags in a beachfront cafe and easily hunt around for

a room that suits your budget; book ahead for peak season, though.

The main access points for the beach are Ourem Rd for the south, the main Palolem Beach road for the central and northern sections, and the Patnem road for Colomb Bay. A useful resource for checking out or booking beach huts in Palolem and surrounding beaches is www.beachhutbooking.com.

Huts start to go up in November and are dismantled in April; standards and operations can vary from one year to the next.

My Soulmate   GUESTHOUSE **$**
(☎ 9823785250; mysolmte@gmail.com; d ₹1000, with AC ₹1500; ❄) This friendly and spotless two-storey guesthouse in a good location just off the main Palolem Beach road is a good nonbeach bet. Neat rooms come with TV and hot water and the newer ones have sexy circular beds. Good cafe, nice staff.

Palolem

Sevas HUT $
(☑9422065437; www.sevaspalolemgoa.com; s/d hut ₹600/800, family cottage ₹1600; @ 🛜) Hidden in the jungle on the Colomb Bay side of Palolem, Sevas has a range of simple palm-thatch huts with open-air bathrooms and larger family huts and rooms set in a lovely shaded garden area. Wi-fi is ₹100 per day.

⭐**Ciaran's** HUT $$
(☑0832-2643477; www.ciarans.com; hut incl breakfast ₹3000-4000, r with AC ₹4500; ❄🛜) Ciaran's has some of the most impressive huts on the beachfront. Affable owner John has worked hard over the years to maintain a high standard and his beautifully designed cottages around a plant-filled garden and pond are top-notch. The sea-view cottages are the more expensive and there are some air-con rooms – including a Jacuzzi room. There's a popular multicuisine restaurant, tapas restaurant and quality massage and spa centre. Eco-credentials are also good here: Ciaran's has a sewerage treatment plant, solar hot water and solar lighting.

⭐**Art Resort** HUT $$
(☑9665982344; www.art-resort-goa.com; Ourem Rd; hut ₹1500-2500; 🛜) The nicely designed cottages behind an excellent beachfront restaurant have a Bedouin camp feel with

screened sit-outs and modern art works sprinkled around. The resort hosts art exhibitions and has regular live music.

Kate's Cottages GUESTHOUSE $$
(☑9822165261; www.katescottagesgoa.com; Ourem Rd; d ₹3000-5000; ❄🛜) The two stunning rooms above Fern's restaurant are beautifully designed with heavy timber finishes, huge four-poster beds, TV, modern bathrooms and views to the ocean from the balcony. There are also a couple of cheaper ground-floor cottages.

Dreamcatcher HUT $$
(☑0832-2644873; www.dreamcatcher.in; hut ₹1750-2500) Probably the largest resort in Palolem, Dreamcatcher's 60 sturdy huts are nevertheless secluded, set in a coconut grove just back from the far northern end of the beach. One of the highlights here is the riverside restaurant and cocktail bar, and the wide range of holistic treatments, massage and yoga on offer, with daily drop-in yoga and reiki courses available. Access it from the back road running parallel to the beach.

Fernandes HUT $$
(☑9637398149; www.fernandeswoodencottages.com; hut ₹1800-2500; 🛜) This smart wooden beach hut operation located towards the northern end of the beach has a set of neat

huts behind its restaurant and the premium sea-facing cottages above it. A very mellow option on an otherwise quite busy stretch of sand.

Cozy Nook
HUT $$

($\mathbb{Z}$ 0832-2643550, 9822584760; www.cozynook-goa.com; hut ₹2500-3500) This long-running operation at the northern end of the beach has well-designed cottages, including some treehouses, more pedestrian rooms, and a funky bar.

Bhakti Kutir
COTTAGE $$

($\mathbb{Z}$ 0832-2643469, 9823627258; www.bhaktiku-tir.com; Colomb Bay; cottage ₹2200-3300; @) Ensconced in a thick wooded grove in the Colomb Bay area south of Palolem, Bhakti's well-equipped rustic cottages are a little worn and you might find yourself sharing with local wildlife but this is still a popular eco and spiritual retreat with an ayurvedic massage centre and daily drop-in yoga classes.

Palolem Guest House
HOTEL $$

($\mathbb{Z}$ 0832-2644879; www.palolemguesthouse.com; Ourem Rd; d from ₹1600, with AC ₹2100; ▒) Set back from the beach on Ourem Rd, this place offers a range of plain but comfortable rooms ranged around a nice leafy garden.

Village Guesthouse
GUESTHOUSE $$

($\mathbb{Z}$ 9960487627, 0832-2645767; www.villageguest housegoa.com; d incl breakfast ₹3400-4300; ▒ 🛜) The Village is a lovely expat-run boutique hotel with eight spotless and spacious air-con rooms that are a cut above most Palolem hotels. Nicely furnished with sparkling bathrooms, four-poster beds, TV and homely touches, it makes a good base if you value peace more than being on the beach. Breakfast is served in the rear garden.

Oceanic Hotel
HOTEL $$

($\mathbb{Z}$ 0832-2643059; www.hotel-oceanic.com; d ₹3500, deluxe ₹5500; ▒ @ ▒) This neat white building, set a fair distance from the beach on the road between Palolem and Patnem, is a popular six-room place, made particularly appealing by its swimming pool and patio restaurant. The standard rooms are compact, the upstairs deluxe ones bigger. Add ₹350 for air-conditioning.

✕ Eating

Palolem's beach doesn't have the sort of beach-shack restaurants you'll find further north – there's simply not enough room on

the beach – but in season every hut operation lining the beach perimeter has its own restaurant, often with tables and umbrellas plonked down on the sand. They all serve fresh seafood and largely indistinguishable menus, so just check out a few and find the ambience that suits.

Little World Cafe
CAFE $

(chai ₹10, snacks ₹70-120; ⊙ 8am-6pm) This shanti little cafe serves up Palolem's best masala chai, along with healthy juices and a warm welcome.

Shiv Sai
INDIAN $

(thalis ₹70-90, mains ₹60-150; ⊙ 9am-11pm) A thoroughly local lunch joint on the parallel beach road, Shiv Sai serves tasty thalis of the vegie, fish and Gujarati kinds.

Hira Bar & Restaurant
INDIAN $

(breakfast from ₹20; ⊙ breakfast & lunch) It looks like something from a Mumbai slum but with a simple *bhaji-pau* and a glass of chai, it's not a bad way to start the day and budget-minded long-termers know it.

Boom Shankar
SEAFOOD, MULTICUISINE $

(mains ₹100-250; ⊙ 8.30am-3.30pm & 5.30-10.30pm) As popular for its view over the bay as for its cuisine; the Indian, Goan, Chinese, Thai and Western food here is good value, but it's the sunset cocktails, and attendant happy hour, that draw regulars.

★ Space Goa
CAFE $$

($\mathbb{Z}$ 80063283333; www.thespacegoa.com; mains ₹90-250; ⊙ 8.30am-5pm) On the Agonda road, Space Goa combines an excellent organic whole-food cafe with a gourmet deli, craft shop and a wellness centre offering reiki and reflexology. The food is fresh and delicious, with fabulous salads, paninis and meze, and the desserts – such as chocolate beetroot cake – are divine. Drop-in morning yoga classes are ₹500.

★ Café Inn
CAFE $$

(Palolem Beach Rd; meals ₹150-550; ⊙ 10am-11pm; 🛜) If you're craving a cappuccino, semi-open-air Café Inn, which grinds its own blend of beans to perfection, is one of Palolem's favourite hang-outs – and it's not even on the beach. Its breakfasts are immense, and comfort-food burgers and panini sandwiches hit the spot. From 6pm there's an excellent barbecue. Free wi-fi.

SILENT HEADPHONE PARTIES

Neatly sidestepping Goa's statewide ban on loud music in open spaces after 10pm, Palolem's 'silent parties' are the way to dance the night away without upsetting the neighbours. Turn up around 10pm, don your headphones with a choice of two or three channels featuring Goan and international DJs playing trance, house, hip hop, electro and funk, and then party the night away in inner bliss but outer silence. At the time of writing there were four headphone parties in Palolem, all operating on different nights:

Silent Noise @ Alpha Bar (www.silentnoise.in; cover charge ₹500; ⊘9pm-4am Thu Nov-Apr)

Neptune Point (www.neptunepoint.com; Neptune's Point, Colomb Bay; cover charge ₹600; ⊘9pm-4am Sat Nov-Apr)

Deafbeat (Cleopatra's, Palolem Beach Rd; cover charge before 11pm free; ⊘from 9pm Wed)

Laughing Buddha (cover charge ₹400; ⊘from 10pm Tue)

Banyan Tree   THAI, MULTICUISINE $$
(mains ₹140-200; ⊘8am-10pm) The best place on Palolem Beach for Thai curries, soups and noodle dishes, the simple Banyan Tree does Thai food pretty well but also has the usual gamut of Indian, European and seafood dishes.

Fern's By Kate's   GOAN $$
(☑9822165261; mains ₹200-450; ⊘8.30am-10.30pm; 🐾) Back from the beach, this solid timber place with a vague nautical feel serves up excellent authentic Goan food such as local sausages, fish curry rice and shark *ambot tik*.

Dropadi   INDIAN, SEAFOOD $$
(mains ₹180-300; ⊘9am-10pm) Ask locals for their favourite beach restaurant and many will say Dropadi, an ordinary-looking place at the main beach entrance. The speciality here is fresh seafood and pan-Indian cuisine. It's been around long enough to justify its reputation for well-prepared food.

German Bakery   BAKERY, MULTICUISINE $$
(Ourem Rd; pastries ₹25-80, mains ₹80-210; ⊘7am-10pm) Tasty baked treats are the stars at the Nepali-run German Bakery, but there is also an excellent range of set breakfasts and things like yak-cheese croissants. It's set in a peaceful garden festooned with flags.

Magic Italy   ITALIAN $$
(☑88057 67705; Palolem Beach Rd; mains ₹180-460; ⊘5pm-midnight) On the main beach road, Magic Italy has been around for a while and the quality of its pizza and pasta remains high, with imported Italian ingredients like ham, salami, cheese and olive oil, imaginative wood-fired pizzas and home-made pasta. Sit at tables, or Arabian-style on floor cushions. The atmosphere is busy but chilled.

★ Ourem 88   FUSION $$$
(☑8698827679; mains ₹440-650; ⊘6-10pm Tue-Sat) Big things come in small packages at British-run Ourem 88, a gastro sensation with just a handful of tables and a small but masterful menu. Try tender calamari stuffed with Goan sausage, slow-roasted pork belly, fluffy souffle or fillet steak with Béarnaise sauce. Worth a splurge.

🍷 Drinking & Nightlife

Palolem doesn't party like the northern beaches, but it's certainly not devoid of nightlife. Some of the beach bars stay open 24 hours in season, there are silent headphone parties four nights a week, and there's a huge new club on the road to Agonda.

Leopard Valley   CLUB
(www.leopardvalley.com; Palolem-Agonda Rd; admission from ₹600; ⊘9pm-4.30am Fri) South Goa's biggest new outdoor dance club is a sight (and sound) to behold, with 3D laser light shows, pyrotechnics and state-of-the-art sound systems blasting local and international DJs. It's in an isolated but easily reached location between Palolem and Agonda, but given noise restrictions we don't know if it will endure. Held on Friday night at the time of writing but possibly Sunday too.

Cleopatra's   BAR, CLUB
(www.cleopatraresorts.com; Palolem Beach Rd) Cleo's is a late-night hotspot back from the beach with headphone parties on Wednesday and live music Sunday afternoon.

WORTH A TRIP

TANSHIKAR SPICE FARM

One of the best day trips you can make away from the coast in Goa's far south is the winding 35km drive to the village of Netravali in search of an excellent spice farm, the mysterious bubble lake and jungle treks to hidden waterfalls. The ride out from Palolem alone makes this trip worthwhile, passing farms then the hilly forest of the Netravali Protected Area.

Tanshikar Spice Farm (☑0832-2608358, 9421184114; www.tanshikarspicefarm.com; Netravali; spice tour incl lunch ₹450; ☺10am-4pm) is a working, family-run organic spice farm with crops including vanilla, cashews, pepper, nutmeg and chillies, as well as bee-keeping. There are no tour buses out here and the amiable young owners give you a personalised tours of the plantation and nearby bubble lake. They can also offer guided jungle treks to nearby waterfalls. If you really want to feel the serenity, book into one of the excellent mud-walled eco-cottages (₹1500) with bamboo sit-outs, or a room in the Hindu-style house.

Near the spice farm (about 500m before the T-junction), the **Netravali 'Bubble Lake'** is actually the bathing tank of the small Hindu Gopinath temple. Tiny streams of bubbles constantly bob up to the lake's surface, appearing to get faster if you clap your hands close to the lake's surface. The cause is trapped methane gas escaping from the sandy bottom.

The other highlight of a day trip out here is the series of **waterfalls** that can be reached by jungle hikes. Treks to the falls vary from 45 minute to three hours. Ask directions at Tanshikar Spice Farm.

From Palolem or Chaudi on the NH17, turn off at the Forest Checkpoint on the left-hand side (before Cotiago Sanctuary) and follow the road for about 30km to the T-junction, turn right and look out for the signs to Tanshikar.

Sundowner   BAR
(☺9am-11pm) At the far northern end of the beach, across the narrow estuary, Sundowner is indeed a cool place to watch the sun set. The rickety bamboo bar is nicely isolated and you can wander across the rocks to forested Canacona Island.

 Shopping

The main Palolem Beach Rd is lined with rows of shops and stalls selling jewellery, textiles, clothing, carvings and the like from all over India. Bargaining is expected in most places.

Butterfly Book Shop   BOOKS
(☑9341738801; ☺9am-10.30pm) The best of several good bookshops in town, this cute and cosy place stocks best sellers, classics, and a good range of books on yoga, meditation and spirituality. This is also the base for yoga classes and cooking courses.

 Information

Palolem's beach road is lined with travel agencies, internet cafes and places to change money. The nearest ATM is on the road to Chaudi about 1km from the beach entrance and there are several in Chaudi itself. An autorickshaw from Palolem to Chaudi costs ₹100.

 Getting There & Away

Frequent buses run to nearby Chaudi (₹7) from the bus stop on the corner of the road down to the beach. Hourly buses to Margao (₹40, one hour) depart from the same place, though these usually go via Chaudi anyway. From Chaudi you can pick up regular buses to Margao, from where you can change for Panaji, or head south to Polem Beach and Karwar in Karnataka.

The closest train station is Canacona, 2km from Palolem's beach entrance.

An autorickshaw from Palolem to Patnem should cost ₹80, or ₹120 to Chaudi. A taxi to Dabolim Airport is around ₹1200.

Patnem

Smaller and less crowded than neighbouring Palolem, pretty Patnem makes a much quieter and more family-friendly alternative. The waters aren't as calm and protected as at Palolem, but the beach is patrolled by lifeguards and it's safe for paddling.

The beach is, naturally, lined with shack restaurants and beach-hut operations in season but it has an altogether relaxed vibe where lazing on the sand or sipping a cocktail is the order of the day. It's easy enough to walk around the northern headland to Colomb Bay and on to Palolem.

🛏 Sleeping & Eating

Long-stayers will revel in Patnem's choice of village homes and apartments available for rent. A very basic house can cost ₹10,000 per month, while a fully equipped apartment will go for ₹40,000 or more. There are a dozen or so beach-hut operations (all with attached beachfront restaurants) lining the sands; many change annually, so walk along to find your perfect spot.

Micky's   HUT $

(☎ 9850484884; www.mickyhuts.com; Patnem Beach; hut & hut with bathroom ₹800-1500; ☎) If you don't mind huts so basic they don't even have electricity, you can sleep cheap here. Fear not: there are also better huts with power and attached bathroom; rooms are available most of the year (closed only August and September). It's run by a friendly family at the northern end of the beach. Micky's Naughty Corner is a cruisy beachfront cafe in front of the accommodation.

Papaya's   COTTAGE $$

(☎ 9923079447; www.papayasgoa.com; hut ₹3000, with AC ₹4000; ❄☎) Solid huts constructed with natural materials head back into the palm grove from Papaya's popular restaurant, which does great versions of all the beachfront classics. Each hut is lovingly built, with lots of wood, four-poster beds and floating muslin.

Palm Trees   COTTAGES $$

(☎ 9673178731; www.thepalmtreesgoa.com; Patnem Beach Rd; cottage incl breakfast ₹3000-4500; ☎) The Keralan-style cottages here are a step up from most beach-hut accommodation, with bamboo and palm-thatch materials imported from Kerala and thoughtful furniture and artworks.

Bamboo Yoga Retreat   YOGA RETREAT $$$

(☎ 9765379887; www.bamboo-yoga-retreat.com; Patnam Beach; s/d from ₹5300/7400; ☎) This laid-back yoga retreat, with classes and treatments exclusive to guests, has a wonderful open-sided shala facing the ocean at the southern end of Patnem Beach, and

comfortable thatched huts in a garden at the rear. Yoga holiday rates include breakfast, brunch and two daily yoga classes, but there are also training courses and ayurvedic spa treatments.

★Home   CONTINENTAL $$

(☎ 0832-2643916; www.homeispatnem.com; Patnem Beach; mains ₹180-290; ☺8.30am-9.30pm; ☎) Standing out from the beach shacks like a beacon, this bright white, relaxed vegetarian restaurant is run by a British couple and serves up Patnem's best breakfasts, pastas, risotto and salads, continental-style. A highlight here is the dessert menu – awesome chocolate brownies, apple tart and cheesecake. Home also rents out eight nicely decorated, light rooms (from ₹1500). Email to book or ask at the restaurant.

🛍 Shopping

Jaali   HANDICRAFTS

(☺9.30am-6.30pm) This small boutique shop back from Patnem Beach stocks handicrafts, textiles, antiques and clothing sourced from all over India by the expat owner. Individual, hand-picked and interesting stuff.

❶ Getting There & Away

The main entrance to Patnem Beach is reached from the country lane running south from Palolem (past the Oceanic Hotel), then turning right at the yellow Hotel Sea View. Alternatively, walk about 20 minutes along the path from Palolem via Colomb Bay, or catch a bus heading south (₹5). An autorickshaw charges around ₹100 from Palolem.

Rajbag

Quiet little Rajbag is a small sandy cove, one beach south from Patnem and accessible by road or via a nice short walk around the headland from Patnem Beach, clambering across the rocks along the way. The beach lacks any real character since the perimeter of the five-star Lalit takes up part of it, and treacherous undertows can make swimming dangerous.

Though dominated by the resort, Rajbag is a nice enough place to linger on the sands, and is usually quite quiet (unless said five-star happens to be hosting a massive wedding or providing backdrop for a Bollywood blockbuster-in-the-making). In the village back from the beach are some decent local restaurants.

SOUTH GOA RAJBAG

Sleeping & Eating

A number of locals have apartments and houses geared to long-stayers up for grabs in Rajbag; ask around for leads. Meanwhile, venture down to the end of the main Rajbag road, which ends abruptly at the banks of the Talpona River, to get your feni fix from one of the local bars.

Lalit Golf & Spa Resort   HOTEL **$$$**
(☑0832-2667777; www.thelalit.com; Rajbag Beach; d from ₹10,500, ste from ₹12,500; ❋@☎☒) Rajbag is dominated by the presence of this 85-acre five-star property. The hotel is particularly popular with well-heeled domestic and Russian tourists, and is notable for having Goa's only championship nine-hole golf course, a helipad and the Rejuve Spa. The lagoon swimming pool will probably make you forget there's an ocean outside.

Look out for the small Hindu temple to the left of the entrance – local pressure forced the developers to build around it rather than move it.

Vernekar Restaurant   INDIAN **$**
(☑0832-2644649; mains from ₹50; ⊙11am-3pm & 7-11pm) Sometimes you need to search a bit to find great local restaurants. Vernekar doesn't look like much, but it serves up quailty food at local prices, including a mean tandoori chicken and fine *aloo gobi* for less than the price of a Coke at the nearby five-star Lalit Resort. To find it, take the lane directly opposite the Lalit main gates and continue about 200m.

Cotigao Wildlife Sanctuary

About 9km southeast of Palolem, and a good day trip, is the beautiful, remote-feeling **Cotigao Wildlife Sanctuary** (☑0832-2965601; adult/child ₹20/10, camera/video ₹30/150; ⊙7am-5.30pm). Stretching inland, this is Goa's second-largest sanctuary but also its most accessible, if you have your own transport. Don't expect to bump into its more exotic residents (including gaurs, sambars, leopards and spotted deer), but frogs, snakes, monkeys, insects and blazingly plumed birds are in no short supply.

Trails are hikable; set off early morning for the best sighting prospects from one of the two forest watchtowers, 7km and 12km from the park entrance.

If you're serious about spotting wildlife, it might be worth staying a night in one of the forest department **cottages** (₹500-1500), right behind the reception at the park entrance. They're no frills but clean, and meals can be arranged. From here you can make a start before the park even opens.

Galgibag & Talpona

Galgibag and Talpona form another of south Goa's beach gems – a broad stretch of hardly touched sand framed by the Talpona River in the north and the Galgibag River to the south, all backed by swaying pines and palms.

Near the southern end, 'Turtle Beach' is where rare, long-lived olive ridley marine turtles come to nest on the beach between November and March. This is a protected area: a Forest Department information hut here should be staffed during nesting season. Undertows and currents can be strong here, so although lifeguards are stationed at either end, swimming out of your depth is not recommended.

With your own transport, getting to Talpona and Galgibag is half the fun. From Palolem or Chaudi, a wonderfully scenic back road follows the Talpona River then skirts behind the beach to Galgibag. From here you can continue along the Galgibag River to join up with NH17 at Poinguinum.

There are a handful of low-key beach shacks at Talpona and a pair of excellent cafes and a few beach huts at Galgibag.

Surya Beach Café (Galgibag Beach; mains ₹90-250; ⊙9am-10pm), nestled at Galgibag's southern end in the pine trees, specialises in fresh oysters, clams, mussels and crabs caught from the Galgibag River. Surya himself will show you the live catch and prepare it *rava* (semolina) fried or spicy Goan-style. Delicious. It's a simple place with plastic chairs on the sand, but they make much of the claim that celebrity chef Gordon Ramsay has dined here and recommended it. Surya also has two timber beach bungalows (₹3500) for rent.

Next door, **Santosh Family Restaurant** does much the same thing but claims to have been recommended by Jamie Oliver!

Polem

In the very far south of the state, 25km south of Palolem and a couple of kilometres from the Karnataka border, Polem is Goa's southernmost beach, set around a small bay on the seafront of the small village of the same name. With no beach shacks or development of note, it has a real castaway feel, pristine, litter-free sand and a beautiful view of a cluster of rocky islands out towards the horizon. There's one family-run place to stay and eat on the beach, but otherwise it retains a local feel, with a few fishermen bringing in their catch to the northern end and nothing much else to keep you company except scuttling crabs and circling seabirds.

Kamaxi Beach Resort (☑9141615846, 9341367429; www.kamaxibeachresort.com; huts from ₹600, d without/with bathroom ₹900/1200, d with AC 2500; ☀), the sole place to stay, has some pretty earthy rooms for this price but you're paying for the seclusion and the friendly brothers work hard at keeping the place very low key. At the time of our visit there were two candle-powered dirt-floor huts at the southern end of the beach and simple rooms in a pair of buildings at the northern beach entrance. A restaurant serves fresh seafood and cold drinks.

To get to Polem, take a bus from Chaudi (₹20, 50 minutes) and get off at the bus stop, around 3km after the petrol station. The stop is directly opposite the turn-off to the beach, then it's a 1km walk to the village and beach. There's an ATM in nearby Majali.

BEYOND GOA

The most popular interstate excursion from South Goa is into Karnataka and south to the holy town and hippie beaches of Gokarna, around 50km from the border. Another interesting trip is to Jog Falls, the highest in India.

Gokarna

☑ 08386

A regular nominee among travellers' favourite beaches in India, Gokarna is a more laid-back and less-commercialised version of Goa. It attracts a crowd for a low-key, chilled-out beach holiday and not for full-scale parties. Most accommodation is in thatched bamboo huts along its several stretches of blissful coast.

In fact there are two Gokarnas; adjacent to the beaches is the sacred Hindu pilgrim town of Gokarna, full of ancient temples that come to life during important festivals such as **Shivaratri** (☺Feb/Mar) and **Ganesh Chaturthi** (☺Sep). While its lively bazaar is an interesting place to visit, most foreign tourists don't hang around overnight, instead making a beeline straight to the adjoining beaches.

Note that bag searches and passport checks by police are common upon arrival.

◎ Sights & Activities

Temples

Foreigners and non-Hindus are not allowed inside Gokarna's temples. However, there are plenty of colourful rituals to be witnessed around town. At the western end of Car St is the **Mahabaleshwara Temple**, home to a revered lingam. Nearby is the **Ganapati Temple**, while at the other end of the street is the **Venkataraman Temple**. About 100m further south is **Koorti Teertha**, the large temple tank where locals, pilgrims and immaculately dressed Brahmins perform their ablutions.

Beaches

The best beaches are due south of Gokarna town, with Om Beach and Kudle Beach being the most popular.

Don't walk around the paths after dark, and not alone at any time – it's easy to slip or get lost, and muggings have occurred.

Om Beach   BEACH

Gokarna's most famous beach twists and turns over several kilometres in a way that's said to resemble the outline of an Om symbol. It's a great mix of lovely long beach and smaller shady patches of sand, perfect for sunbathing and swimming.

It's a 20-minute walk to Kudle Beach; an autorickhaw to Gokarna town is about ₹150.

Kudle Beach   BEACH

Lined with rows of restaurants and guest-houses, Kudle Beach has emerged as a popular alternative to Om Beach. It's one of Gokarna's longest and widest beaches, with room to stretch out on its attractive sands.

It's a 20-minute hike from both Gokarna town or Om Beach along a path that heads up along the barren headland with expansive sea views. Otherwise it's a ₹60 autorickshaw ride to town.

Gokarna Beach
BEACH

While Gokarna's main town beach isn't meant for casual bathing, and is more popular with domestic tourists, walk up a bit and you'll find a long stretch of pristine sand that seems to go forever – perfect for those seeking isolation.

Half Moon & Paradise Beach
BEACH

Well hidden away south of Om Beach lie the small sandy coves of Half Moon Beach and Paradise Beach. Half Moon is the more attractive, with a lovely sweep of powdery sand and basic hut accommodation. Paradise Beach is a mix of sand and rocks, and a haven with the long-term 'turn-on-tune-in-drop-out' crowd; unfortunately the government routinely destroys all the huts out this way, leaving it in a ramshackle state – hence it's BYO everything here.

From Om Beach, these beaches are a 30-minute and one-hour walk, respectively. Watch out for snakes along the path and don't walk it after dark. A fishing boat from Om Beach will cost around ₹700, which can fit 10 people. For Paradise Beach you can also grab a bus to Velikom from Gokarna (₹12, 20 minutes), from where it's a 15-minute walk.

Cocopelli Surf School
SURFING

(☑8105764969; www.cocopelli.org; Gokarna Beach; lesson per person ₹2000, 2hr board rental ₹750; ☺Oct-May) Offers lessons by internationally certified instructors and rents boards. Has accommodation along here too.

🛏 Sleeping & Eating

With a few exceptions, the choice here is from basic, but perfectly comfortable, beach shacks, most of which serve food. Most close from May to August.

Om Beach

Om Shree Ganesh
BUNGALOW $

(☑08386-257310; www.omshreeganesh.com; hut ₹500, without bathroom ₹300) A winning combination of cheap bungalows, friendly management and beachside location makes this place justifiably popular. Its atmospheric double-storey restaurant rocks at night and does tasty dishes such as tandoori prawns, mushroom tikka and *momos* (Tibetan dumplings).

Sangham
BUNGALOW $

(☑9448101099; r without/with bathroom ₹300/500,) A blissful spot overlooking the water with a sandy path leading to the bungalows out back among banana trees; life's definitely a beach at Sangham.

Moksha Cafe
BUNGALOW $

(☑9741358997; Om Beach; r shared/private bathroom ₹300/600) In the middle of Om Beach, these graffiti-splashed bungalows are as good as any with private porches, hammocks and a sandy garden full of coconut palms.

Dolphin Bay Cafe
BUNGALOW $

(☑9742440708; r from ₹200; ☺8am-10pm) Literally plonked on the beach, Dolphin Bay is your classic chilled-out shack restaurant (mains ₹80 to ₹180) that makes Gokarna so great. It has a choice of sandy-floor huts or sturdier concrete rooms.

Dolphin Shanti
GUESTHOUSE $

(☑9740930133; r from ₹200) Occupying the last plot of land on Om Beach (heading towards Half Moon beach), this mellow guesthouse sits perched upon the rocks with fantastic ocean views, and lives up to its name with dolphins often spotted. Rooms are ultrabasic yet appealing.

Nirvana Café
GUESTHOUSE $

(☑08386-329851; d ₹250, cottage ₹400-600; @) Towards the southern end of Om, Nirvana has popular el cheapo huts and spacious cottages set among a shady landscaped garden. Internet costs ₹60 per hour and hammocks are for sale if you need one.

Namaste Café
GUESTHOUSE $

(☑08386-257141; www.namastegokarna.com; Om Beach; r with fan/AC from ₹800/1500; ❄🕸) Situated at the beginning of Om, this long-standing guesthouse has a very different vibe to the others, with a more proper resort feel. It's an excellent choice, especially if you're after the comforts of air-con, wi-fi, hot water, cold beer and romantic open-air restaurant with dreamy sea views. These days it's more popular with domestic travellers.

SwaSwara
HOTEL $$$

(☑08386-257132; www.swaswara.com; Om Beach; s/d 5 nights €1730/2300; ❄@🕸☀) One of South India's finest retreats, this health resort offers a holiday based around yoga and ayurveda. No short stays are possible, but once you've set eyes upon its elegant private villas – some with forest views, others with river – you'll be happy to stay put. All have small garden courtyards full of basil and lemongrass, open-air showers and lovely sitting areas.

Kudle Beach

Sea Rock Cafe   GUESTHOUSE $
(☑7829486382; Kudle Beach; r from ₹300) Yet more chilled-out bungalows, with an option of more comfortable rooms and a beachside restaurant where the good times roll.

Ganga View   GUESTHOUSE $
(☑9591978042; Kudle Beach; r from ₹250; ☎) At the end of Kudle, relaxed Ganga is a perennial favourite. Also has rooms up the hill with soaring views. Wi-fi costs ₹50 per hour.

Goutami Prasad   GUESTHOUSE $
(☑9972382302; Kudle Beach; hut from ₹200, r from ₹500) Relaxed, family-run guesthouse with a prime spot in the centre of Kudle Beach. Choose between basic huts with sandy floors or more comfortable, spotless rooms.

Uma Garden   GUESTHOUSE $
(☑9916720728; Kudle Beach; r without bathroom ₹250) Tucked around the corner at the beginning of Kudle, this bucolic guesthouse has a laid-back owner and a sea-facing vegetarian restaurant.

Strawberry Farmhouse   GUESTHOUSE $$
(☑7829367584; Kudle Beach; r from ₹700; ❋) A kitschy guesthouse at the northern section of Kudle with over-the-top bright cottages (some with AC) and prime position looking out to the water.

Half Moon Beach

Half Moon Garden Cafe   BUNGALOW $
(☑9743615820; Half Moon Beach; hut ₹200) A throwback to the hippie days, this hideaway has a blissful beach and bare-bones huts without electricity.

Gokarna Beach

This seemingly endless stretch of beach is the place for a more isolated relaxed beachside hang out.

Hema Shree Garden   BUNGALOW $
(☑9845983223; Gokarna Beach; r from ₹250) A super-chilled beach guesthouse that's a 20-minute walk along Gokarna Beach with a variety of rooms around its tropical garden, plus some bungalows looking directly to the ocean.

Namaste Garden   BUNGALOW $
(☑9448906436; Gokarna Beach; r ₹500) Delightfully simple huts with hammocks, beachside tables and umbrellas. It's in the middle of Gokarna Beach, 10 minutes from town.

Gokarna Town

Shree Shakti Hotel   HOTEL $
(☑9036043088; Gokarna Beach Rd; s/d ₹300/600) On Gokarna's main strip, this friendly hotel is excellent value with immaculate lime-green rooms above a restaurant that does excellent food, including homemade ice cream.

Greenland Guesthouse   GUESHTOUSE $
(☑9019651420; www.gokarnagreenland.in; Gokarna Town; r from ₹200) Hidden down a jungle path outside town, this mellow family-run guesthouse has clean rooms in vibrant colours. Will suit those not wanting a beach shack, but somewhere with character.

Hotel Gokarna International   HOTEL $
(☑9739629390; Main Rd; r with fan/AC ₹450/1000; @) This typical institutional Indian hotel is worth a look if you want large air-con rooms with TV and balcony.

🛍 Shopping

Shree Radhakrishna Bookstore   BOOKS
(Car St, Gokarna Town; ☺10am-6pm) Second-hand novels, postcards and maps.

ℹ Information

Axis Bank (Main St, Gokarna Town)
SBI (Main St, Gokarna Town)
Shama Internet Centre (Car St, Gokarna Town; per hr ₹40; ☺10am-11pm)
Sub Post Office (1st fl, cnr Car & Main Sts, Gokarna Town; ☺10am-4pm Mon-Sat)

ℹ Getting There & Away

BUS

A mix of local and private buses depart daily to Bengaluru (₹509, 12 hours) and Mysore (from ₹550, 12 hours), as well as Mangalore (₹240, 6½ hours) and Hubli (₹190, four hours), mostly transferring at Kumta (₹34, one hour), or Honnavar (₹55, two hours) for Jog Falls.

For Hampi, **Paolo Travels** (☑ 0832-6637777; www.phmgoa.com) is a popular choice that heads via Hospet (fan/AC ₹1100/1600, seven hours). Note that if you're coming from Hampi, you'll be dropped at Ankola from where there's a free transfer for the 26km journey to Gokarna.

There's also regular buses to Panaji (₹116, four hours) and Mumbai (₹900, 12 hours).

TRAIN

Many express train services stop at Gokarna Road station, situated 9km from town; however, double check your ticket as some stop at Ankola, 26km away. Many of the hotels and small travel agencies in Gokarna can book tickets.

The 3am Matsyagandha Express goes to Mangalore (sleeper ₹235, 4½ hours); the return train leaves Kumta around 6.30pm for Madgaon (sleeper ₹170, 2½ hours) and Mumbai (sleeper/2AC ₹465/1735, 12 hours).

Autorickshaws charge ₹200 to go to Gokarna Road station (or ₹500 to Ankola); a bus from Gokarna town charges ₹40 and leaves every 30 minutes.

Jog Falls

Nominally the highest waterfalls in India, Jog Falls only really come to life during the monsoon or immediately afterwards. The tallest of the four falls is the Raja, which drops 293m. In order to get a good view of the falls, bypass the area close to the bus stand and hike to the foot of the falls down a 1200-plus-step path. Watch out for leeches during the wet season.

Hotel Mayura Gerusoppa (☑ 08186-244732; d with fan/AC from ₹1800/2200; ❄), which is located near the car park, has a few enormous, musty double rooms. Stalls near the bus stand serve thalis and noodle dishes.

Jog Falls isn't the easiest place to reach without a car, so most people hire a taxi; a return trip from Gokarna costs around ₹2000. Otherwise you can get a string of buses that head via Kumta and turn off at Honavar (₹66); or Shimoga (Shivamogga) if coming via Bengaluru (₹468, nine hours).

Understand
Goa &
Mumbai

Goa Today

Goa joined the rest of India more than 50 years ago, but it has continued to dance to the beat of its own drum – socially, musically, economically and politically. It might still be considered small fry by more powerful Indian states, but Goa's tourism rupee – both foreign and domestic – should never be underestimated and, for better or worse, much of Goa's population relies more than ever on the annual influx of holidaying visitors.

Best in Print

Maximum City: Bombay Lost and Found (Suketu Mehta) Mumbai in all its gritty glory.

Shantaram (Gregory David Roberts; 2003) Gripping tale of a fugitive in Mumbai, with Goa featuring.

Goa and the Blue Mountains (Richard Burton) Classic account of Goa, written in 1851.

Goa Traffic (Marissa de Luna) Thriller set in Goa's party scene.

Reflected in Water: Writings on Goa (Jerry Pinto) Collected writings by literary luminaries.

Houses of Goa (Pandit/Mascarenhas) Beautifully illustrated book on Goa's mansions.

Goa Freaks: My Hippie Years in India (Cleo Odzer) A disturbing tale of the drug-crazed, hippie 'freak' days of the 1960s and '70s, by one who lived it.

Goan Music

Goa Trance (www.goatranceradio.com) Goan psy-trance.

Goan Fusion (www.remomusic.com) Legend Remo Fernandes.

Goa Freaks (www.goa-freaks.com) Social network of psychedelic trance with streaming.

Konkani radio (www.live365.com/stations/61664) Traditional Goan music of all kinds.

Paradise Found

Goa was a solitary Portuguese outpost in India for almost 500 years and the influence of colonial rule can still be seen everywhere: in the exquisite, crumbling architecture; in the East-meets-West cuisine; and in the siesta-saturated *joie de vivre* that Goans themselves call *susegad*.

Little wonder with all these charms that just about everybody wants – or has wanted at some point in history – to come here. The growth in tourism in the past two decades has surprised even the locals. From the hippies and euro charter tourists to the Israeli ravers, passing backpackers and interstate holidaymakers, Goa's tourist scene has changed over time but rarely waned. In 1985, total tourist arrivals were just a tick over 775,000; in 2013 it was over 3.12 million – almost doubling in the last 10 years alone.

Russians now make up the bulk of the overseas holiday crowd – almost 40% of foreign visitors – but that's nothing compared with the visitor numbers from interstate. Young Indian tourists, singles, couples and families, often middle-class with disposable incomes, are making Goa their holiday destination of choice. While most tourism operators rely on the brief November to February tourist trade, domestic tourists are increasingly visiting in the summer (monsoon) season.

All of this is generally good news for those involved in a saturated tourist trade and for the state's GDP, but a little bemusing for the rest of the population who deal with the annual invasion and the overstretching of precious resources.

Still, Goa enjoys one of India's highest per-capita incomes and comparatively high health and literacy rates, factors which attract migrants and traders from other parts of India who arrive looking for work and that magical *susegad* they've heard so much about.

The Darker Side

Despite its charms Goa is not a perfect paradise. The state's large homeless population is mostly made up of migrants from Karnataka and Maharashtra, driven from their homes by water shortages and lured to Goa's coast hoping life will treat them more kindly. Almost inevitably, it doesn't. Locals also complain of uncontrolled foreign investment with wealthy buyers snapping up prime real estate, and 'mafia-run' businesses paying off corrupt authorities.

Meanwhile Goa suffers from a sorely stressed environment, burdened by the effects of logging, iron-ore mining, relentlessly expanding tourism and uncontrolled industrial growth. Rare turtle eggs have traditionally been considered a delicacy but are now precariously protected on increasingly busy beaches, plastic bottles pile up, and vagrant cows feast on refuse from noisome rubbish bins.

Poverty, prostitution, a shady underworld drugs trade, violent crime and police corruption also remain pressing problems. Animal shelters overflow with unwanted domestic creatures and children's homes struggle to provide shelter, safety and education for the state's disturbingly large population of at-risk and orphaned children. A number of charities address some of these issues; though, as they'll attest, their level best is seldom enough.

A Better Future?

If a healthy economy is any indication of a state's ability to weather the storm, then the picture isn't all bleak. Goa's active economy has given rise to a healthy Gross Domestic Product of around US$3 billion annually, about 2.5 times India's national average.

In 2008 and 2009, tourism to Goa plummeted due to the global economic downturn along with fears of terrorism spawned by the 2008 Mumbai (Bombay) attacks, but locals held on tight, and by 2012 tourism appeared to have recovered. In 2014 the biggest concern was the falling Russian rouble and trade sanctions, and a corresponding drop in charter visitors.

Meanwhile, enterprising locals slowly lead the way towards a cleaner, more sustainable future, instigating local recycling initiatives, volunteering on turtle-egg protection duties, or working with local green organisations, such as the Goa Foundation and Green Goa Works on campaigns such as stopping illegal mining. Such efforts, along with luck, persistence and political will, may ensure Goa's charms retain their place on travel itineraries for centuries to come.

POPULATION: **1.8 MILLION**

AREA: **3700 SQ KM**

TOURIST ARRIVALS 2013:
**TOTAL 3.12 MILLION;
FOREIGNERS 492,322**

LITERACY RATE: **87%;
NATIONAL AVERAGE: 74%**

if 100 people visited Goa

83 would be Indian

belief systems
(% of population)

64 Hindu
30 Christian
5 Muslim
1 Other

population per sq km

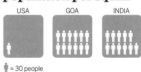

USA GOA INDIA

≈ 30 people

History

A 100,000-year look back through the history of Goa offers you a keen insight into some of the region's most mysterious and alluring archaeological and historic remains, and into the Goan psyche itself. Archaeologists believe even Goa's earliest inhabitants were settlers from elsewhere, but the state's story in the past millennium is one of conflicts and conquests – from the Hindu Kadambas and Muslim Bahmanis to the Portuguese, whose 450-year rule left the greatest lasting influence.

Prehistoric Beginnings

Head out to remote Usgalimal in South Goa to examine the petroglyphs (rock art), including images of a peacock and a dancing woman inscribed into the laterite river rocks by the earliest Goans.

According to Hindu legend, Goa was created by Parasurama, the sixth incarnation of the Hindu god Vishnu, who shot an arrow into the Arabian Sea and commanded the tide to retreat, to create a peaceful spot for his Brahmin caste to live.

A trip out into the Goan hinterland, however, to the riverside rock carvings of Usgalimal offers an alternative picture of the first Goans, hunter-gatherer tribes who inhabited the hinterland sometime between 100,000 BC and 10,000 BC. No one really knows where they originally came from; some believe they were migrants from Africa, others that they hailed from eastern Asia, or were a northern tribe forced southwards by instability in their homeland.

Early Trading

In the 3rd century BC Goa became part of the mighty Buddhist Mauryan empire. Ashoka, probably the greatest, sent a Buddhist missionary to convert the locals; the monk set up shop in a rock-cut cave near modern-day Zambaulim, preaching nonviolence and urging the tribes to give up their nasty habit of blood sacrifice. Though he had some success, introducing the plough and spreading literacy, his liturgy fell largely on deaf ears, and following the rapid demise of the Mauryans after the death of Ashoka in 232 BC, Goa turned to Hinduism, commingled with its old tribal practices.

The next seven centuries saw Goa ruled from afar by a succession of powerful Hindu trading dynasties, which sent Goan goods and spices to

TIMELINE	100,000–10,000 BC	2400–700 BC	AD 420
	Hunter-gatherer tribes inhabit the Goan interior, evidenced by the impressive rock carvings at Usgalimal and stone implements discovered at the Zuari River, near Dudhsagar Falls.	Goa experiences at least two waves of Aryan immigration from the north, bringing with them improved farming techniques and the first elements of what would become Hinduism.	Goa's home-grown Hindu rulers, the Kadambas, rise to power over their distant overlords, and install their own royal family, ushering in a period of religious tolerance, prosperity and innovation.

Africa, the Middle East and Rome. However, continued wrangling between these dynasties offered the opportunity for a homespun dynasty to quietly emerge: in AD 420 the local Kadamba clan declared independence, and created their very own 'royal family'.

Kadamba Prosperity

Under the Kadamba royal family, Goa finally had some stability. By the late 6th century, the Kadambas had found their stride, and in contrast with what was to come, the Kadamba rule was a period of tolerance. Muslim merchants from Arabia and East Africa were encouraged to settle, Hindu temples were constructed statewide and prestigious academic institutions were inaugurated.

Yet, like all good things, it was not to last. The success of the Kadambas signalled their own downfall, as Muslim Bahmani sultans from the Deccan in South India, keen on getting their hands on Kadamba wealth, began pouring into Goa from the 10th century onwards. Today, the sole Kadamba structure to survive the troubled years to follow is the melancholy Tambdi Surla Shri Mahadeva Temple, saved from a grisly fate only by its remote jungle location.

In 1352 the Muslim Bahmanis triumphed, and years of religious tolerance were brought to an abrupt and painful end. The new rulers immediately set about a harsh regime of Hindu persecution, destroying the grand Kadamba temples and killing their priests. They reigned intermittently, ousted by rival kingdoms from time to time, until the late 1400s, when a force far bigger than their own was to sail merrily over the horizon.

Portuguese Arrive

In 1498 Vasco da Gama, a Portuguese sea captain, landed south of Goa at Calicut (present-day Kozhikode) on the Malabar Coast, 'seeking Christians and spices', with a view to superseding the Arab monopoly of the overland spice trade. He didn't have much luck finding Christians, but there were certainly spices in abundance.

However, it was to take 50 years of Muslim–Christian fighting before Portugal was able to claim those spices as its own, establishing firm territorial borders in Goa – now known as the Velhas Conquistas (Old Conquests) – that stretched from Chapora Fort in the north to Cabo da Rama Fort in the south.

The Inquisition

Initially, Portugal's approach to its new subjects was relatively enlightened: Hindus were considered friends against Portugal's Muslim foe, and 'conversion' was largely confined to allowing Portuguese soldiers to marry local women, so that their children would be raised Christian.

A Hindu legend relates that Goa's name came from Lord Krishna, who was so enchanted by the place that he named it after the cows ('Go' in Sanskrit) belonging to the charming milkmaids he encountered here – for whom Krishna had quite the famous predilection.

HISTORY KADAMBA PROSPERITY

1054	1352	1498	1534
Goa's capital shifts from Chandrapur (modern-day Chandor) to Govepuri (now Goa Velha). Wealth and trade skyrocket, with locals building vast homes and places of worship with the profits from the spice trade.	After suffering three centuries of Muslim raids, Goa comes under the rule of Muslim Bahmanis and almost all trace of the Kadambas' Hindu legacy is quickly destroyed, except for the Tambdi Surla Shri Mahadeva Temple.	Portuguese captain Vasco da Gama arrives in Goa, making him the first European to reach India via the Cape of Good Hope. The Portuguese hope this will allow them to dominate Eastern trade routes.	Portugal gains the islands that form modern-day Mumbai from the Muslim sultans of Gujarat. They name the area 'Bom Bahia'. A century later, the British government takes possession.

GOAN HOUSE OF HORRORS

Of all Portugal's alleged abuses of its Goan subjects, the terrors to which the population was subjected to under the iron rule of the Inquisition – also known as the Holy Office or Santo Officio – were undoubtedly the worst.

The Inquisition was dispatched to Goa on royal command, originally conceived to target 'New Christians' (Cristianos Nuevos), the forcibly converted Jews and Muslims of Portugal who had fled to the country's colonies and 'lapsed' back to their original faiths. By the time the Inquisition arrived, life was already becoming increasingly difficult for the region's Hindus, who for some years had been enduring a slowly eroding official toler-ance to their faith. Idols had already been banned, temples closed and priests banished. Now, with the arrival of the Inquisitors, matters went from bad to worse: refusing to eat pork became a crime punishable by imprisonment, as was possession of turmeric, in-cense and other items used in traditional Hindu worship.

Though the genuinely louche and licentious Portuguese gentry were generally above the law, the lower, indigenous classes soon found themselves at risk of imprisonment in the fearsome dungeons of the Palace of the Inquisition, the *orlem ghor* (big house) of Old Goa, with tortures such as the rack, flesh-eroding quicklime, burning sulphur and thumb-screws awaiting their arrival.

Once a 'confession' of heresy had been extracted, the prisoner then languished in a windowless cell, awaiting one of the Inquisition's famous *autos-da-fé* (trials of faith). Dur-ing these morbidly theatrical 'trials', dozens of prisoners, dressed in tall mitres and robes emblazoned with macabre images of human beings engulfed in flames, would be marched across the city of Old Goa, from the Palace of the Inquisition to the Church of St Francis of Assisi, amid crowds of onlookers and to the solemn tolling of the Sé Cathedral bell.

Inside the church, following a lengthy sermon, the judgements were read to the accused.

The luckiest ones were to endure slavery abroad. Victims who refused to recant their 'heresy' were usually burned at the stake; those willing to admit to it were thoughtfully strangled before the pyre was lit.

In the period between 1560 and 1774 (after which records become sketchy) a total of 16,176 people were arrested by the Inquisition, mostly Hindus, though more than two-thirds of those burned alive were Jews who had been forcibly converted as Cristianos Nuevos. In 1814 the Inquisition was finally repealed, as part of an Anglo-Portuguese trea-ty, and most of its later records destroyed.

But in 1532 Goa's first Vicar General arrived, and the age of tolerance was over. Increasingly stringent laws were passed to forbid Hindu wor-ship, and to allow only Christians rights to land. Then, in 1560, the ter-rifying Portuguese Tribunal of the Holy Office – otherwise known as the Goan Inquisition – came to Goa.

1543	1560	1612	1664
Goa's Muslim sultan cedes areas of Goa to Portugal, to stop it from supporting a rival contender for the throne. Portugal now owns land from Chapo-ra Fort in the north to Cabo da Rama Fort in the south.	Portugal's Tribunal of the Holy Office (the Goan Inquisition) arrives in Goa to begin its brutal 200 years of suppression of religious freedoms, executing hundreds of 'heretics', and instilling fear into Goan hearts.	British East India Company ships defeat a Portuguese fleet off the coast of Western Gujarat, starting the end of Portuguese hold. The Dutch soon outmanoeuvre Portu-guese ships with their superior technology.	The Hindu Marathas, under the leadership of legendary, fearsome warrior Shivaji, tempo-rarily take parts of Goa, alerting the Portuguese to the dangers lurking in Eastern, as well as Western, powers.

Establishing itself at the old sultan's palace in what is now Old Goa, the tribunal soon began flexing its ecclesiastical muscles. But astonishingly, the subsequent two centuries of Portuguese religious terrorism failed to completely eradicate Hinduism from Goa. Many Hindus fled across the Mandovi River, into the region around modern-day Ponda, smuggling their religious statuaries to safety and secretly building temples to house them.

Goa's Golden Age

Not all religious orders, however, came tarred with the same cruel and zealous brush as the Inquisitors. By the mid-16th century, Franciscan, Dominican and Augustinian missionaries, along with Jesuits and others, were present in Goa, establishing hospitals and schools, and teaching alternative methods of farming and forestry.

When they weren't busy converting the masses, they were masterminding much of Goa Dourada's (Golden Goa's) glorious ecclesiastical building boom. Levies from the lucrative international spice trade financed work on the Sé Cathedral and the Basilica of Bom Jesus, and soon Old Goa's population stood at 300,000, larger than London or Lisbon itself. Though life remained perilous – many would-be immigrants perished at sea en route, or succumbed to bouts of malaria, typhoid or cholera that swept the city – in Goa it seemed truly golden.

Portuguese Struggles

Just as 'Goa Dourada' and its magnificent edifices were in their ascendancy, Portugal's own fortunes were beginning to wane.

In 1580 bankrupted by a disastrous campaign in North Africa, Portugal was annexed by Spain, and it wasn't until 1640 that the Portuguese regained independence. Wranglings followed over Goa, both with Britain and with the last of the mighty Maratha Empire, led by Shivaji, whose homeland lay in the Western Ghats of southern Maharashtra. In 1739, following a two-year siege, a treaty between the Portuguese and the Marathas forced the Portuguese to hand over large tracts of their northern territory, near Mumbai (Bombay), in exchange for a full Maratha withdrawal from Goa.

And though Portugal succeeded in adding more territory to Goa during the 18th century – four *talukas* (districts), including Ponda, Quepem and Canacona, known as the Novas Conquistas, or New Conquests – the grand age of Portuguese Goa was on the decline. The effects of the Inquisition, coupled with plague after horrendous plague sweeping Old Goa, meant that by 1822 Old Goa had been completely abandoned, its monuments lost in a tangle of jungle. The senate moved to Panjim (present-day Panaji) in 1835, which soon after became Goa's official capital.

The 'Inquisition Table', around which sat its dreaded interrogators, is now housed at the Goa State Museum in Panaji (Panjim). A crucifix that once stared down, with open eyes, at the Inquisitors' victims, now also lives in Panaji, at the Chapel of St Sebastian.

1739	1781–88	1787	1835
The Portuguese sign a treaty with the Marathas, handing over large tracts of their northern territory near Mumbai (Bombay) in exchange for full Maratha withdrawal from Goa.	The Novas Conquistas (New Conquests) sees Portugal add to its Goan territory, delineating, by 1788, the confines of the state as we know it today.	The first serious local attempt to overthrow the Portuguese, the Pinto Revolt, is attempted; it's unsuccessful and its leaders are either tortured and executed, or shipped to Portugal.	Goa's senate moves from Old Goa to a healthier capital at Panjim (today's Panaji). Goa's viceroy, Dom Manuel de Portugal e Castro, levels the dunes and drains the swamps to make it a habitable alternative.

INCORRUPTIBLE OLD ST FRANCIS

Goa's patron saint, Francis Xavier, was born in Spain in 1506. A founding member of the Society of Jesus (the Jesuits), he embarked on a number of missionary voyages from Goa between 1542 and 1552, before dying off the coast of China just before Christmas in 1552.

After his death (so the story goes) several sackfuls of quicklime were emptied into his coffin, to consume Xavier's flesh in preparation for the return of the mortal remains to Goa. Yet, two months later, the body remained in perfect condition – 'incorrupt' despite all that quicklime. The following year, it arrived back in Goa, where its preservation was declared a miracle.

The church, however, wanted proof. In 1554 the viceroy's physician performed a medical examination, and declared all internal organs intact and that no preservatives had been used. He then asked two Jesuits in attendance to insert their fingers into a small wound in Xavier's body. 'When they withdrew them,' he noted, 'they were covered with the blood which I smelt and found to be absolutely untainted.'

It took until 1622 for Francis Xavier to be canonised for his posthumous efforts. But by then, holy relic hunters had corrupted the incorruptible: his right arm had been removed and divided between Jesuits in Japan and Rome (where it could allegedly still sign its name), and by 1636 parts of one shoulder blade and internal organs had been scattered throughout Southeast Asia. Even his diamond-encrusted fingernail was removed, and is now squirrelled away at the Pereira-Braganza house in Chandor.

At last, at the end of the 17th century, the body reached an advanced state of desiccation and the miracle appeared to be over. Nowadays the parched remains of Francis Xavier are kept in a glass coffin in the Basilica of Bom Jesus in Old Goa. But once every decade on Xavier's feast day, 3 December, the coffin is paraded through Old Goa for closer examination by the masses.

Meanwhile Portugal continued to struggle with troublemakers within and without. In 1787 the short-lived Pinto Revolt (p125), whose conspirators were largely Goan clerics, sought to overturn their overlords' rule. The revolt was discovered while it was still in the planning, and several of the leaders were tortured and put to death, while others were imprisoned or shipped off to Portugal.

End of an Empire

The 19th century saw increasing calls for Goan freedom from Lisbon. Uprisings and rebellions became common, and by the 1940s the Goan leaders were taking their example from the Independence movement across the border in British India. But despite widespread demonstrations, on 10 June 1947 the Portuguese Minister of Colonies, Captain Teofilo

1843	1926	1940s	1955
Panjim becomes Goa's new capital, and Old Goa is left almost uninhabited. British adventurer Richard Burton soon describes Old Goa as a place of 'utter devastation'.	Portugal declares itself a republic, and dictator Dr Antonio de Oliveira Salazar takes the helm, refusing to relinquish control over the country's colonies.	Goa's independence movement gains ground. On 18 June 1946, a demonstration in Margao leads to the arrest of independence activist Dr Ram Manohar Lohla. In the aftermath, 1500 campaigners are jailed.	On 15 August a huge satyagraha (nonviolent protest) is called. Portuguese troops open fire on protesters; many are arrested, beaten, imprisoned and exiled to Africa.

Duarte, warned that the 'Portuguese flag will not fall down in India without some thousands of Portuguese, white and coloured, shedding their blood in its defence'.

The March to Independence

When overtures by the newly independent Indian government were made to the Portuguese in 1953, it became clear that the Portuguese had no intention of withdrawing. On 11 June 1953 diplomatic relations between the two countries were broken off.

Within Goa, protests continued, often met with violent retaliation from Portuguese forces. Meanwhile India manoeuvred for international support. However, Indian Prime Minister Jawaharlal Nehru found himself pushed to the brink when, in November 1961, Portuguese troops stationed 10km south of Goa opened fire on Indian fishing boats. On the night of 17 December 1961 Operation Vijay saw Indian troops crossing the border. They were met with little resistance and by evening of the following day the troops reached Panaji.

At 8.30am on 19 December, troops of the Punjab Regiment occupied the Panaji Secretariat Building and unfurled the Indian flag, signifying the end of the 450-year Portuguese occupation of Goa. The Portuguese left quietly shortly afterwards.

Post-Independence

Initially, India's self-proclaimed 'liberation' of Goa was met with a lukewarm response from Goans themselves. Some feared a drop in their relatively high standard of living, and saw in themselves few similarities with their Indian neighbours. Others feared the loss of their cultural identity, and that Portuguese plutocrats would simply be replaced by an army of Indian bureaucrats.

Nevertheless, the first full state government was operating in Goa by the end of December 1962. On 31 May 1987 Goa was officially recognised as the 25th state of the Indian Union, and in 1992, its native tongue, Konkani, was recognised as one of India's official languages.

For most of the 1990s political instability plagued the young state: between 1990 and 2005, Goa had no fewer than 14 governments. Corruption became rife, and policy-making impossible. One of the parties to benefit from the chaos was the right-wing Hindu nationalist Bharatiya Janata Party (BJP). In March 2006 communal riots between Muslims and Hindus broke out in Sanvordem, in the interior of Goa, threatening the very religious tolerance Goans themselves are famous for.

Away from the political machinations, from the 1960s Goa began to experience a new wave of visitors – travellers on the hippie trail setting up camp and dancing on the beaches. This naturally developed into

On encountering Francis Xavier's 'incorrupt' body in 1634, a Portuguese noblewoman named Dona Isabel de Caron was allegedly so anxious to obtain a relic that she bit off the dead saint's little toe... and it gushed fresh blood into her mouth.

Portugal's dictator Dr Antonio de Oliveira Salazar attempted to lobby world leaders into condemning India's claims over Goa: he even managed to persuade John F Kennedy to write to Nehru, advising him against the use of force on the issue.

1961	1987	1996	2008
On 17 December, Indian troops cross the border into Goa; by 19 December, an Indian flag flies atop Panaji's Secretariat Building.	On 31 May, Goa is officially declared India's 25th state by Prime Minister Rajiv Gandhi, in a landmark ruling for the state's generations of armed supporters.	Bombay's name is officially changed to Mumbai, the name derived from the goddess Mumba who was worshipped by early Koli fisherfolk in the area.	A series of coordinated terrorist attacks by Pakistani militants rocks Mumbai in November (known as '26/11'), leaving 164 people dead, including 10 in the Leopold Cafe.

mainstream tourism, from the trance parties of the 1980s to package and charter tourists of the 1990s onwards. Over time, Goan entrepreneurs took to tourism-related industries – hotels, restaurants, beach shacks, travel agents and boat tours – and the economy naturally shifted from mainly agriculture, fishing and commerce to seasonal tourism. Heavy industry in the form of controversial iron-ore mining and the manufacture of petrochemicals followed, forever changing the face of Goa.

Modern Goa

In an age of extremists, Goa has remained relatively unscathed. In 2009 a Hindu group publicly threatened to attack Western women seen drinking alcohol in pubs, though this was roundly condemned within Goa. Violent crime frequently makes newspaper headlines, police corruption is still considered a problem, and the November 2008 terrorist attacks on Mumbai's hotels and restaurants rattled Goans, who feared they'd be the next hard hit.

But things have calmed considerably since, tourist numbers are steadily increasing and even the political landscape has settled. After seven years of power the Indian National Congress party was soundly defeated by the BJP in State Assembly elections in 2012, returning popular former Chief Minister Manohar Parrikar to the top job (he was previously Chief Minister twice between 2000 and 2005).

Parrikar had campaigned strongly for zero tolerance on corruption, stopping illegal mining and cleaning up industry and tourism practices (including moving the floating casinos out of the Mandovi River). His star was clearly on the rise, and in 2014 he was hand-picked by new Indian Prime Minister Narendra Modi to take on the important defence ministry portfolio in the central government.

A small faction within Goa still advocates independence from India; learn more at www.freegoa.com.

2009	2012	2014	2014
India takes to the polls in countrywide elections. On 22 May the new government is sworn in, with the Indian National Congress party's Prime Minister Manmohan Singh in for a second consecutive term.	Iron-ore mining in Goa is suspended by the Supreme Court following investigations into illegal and corrupt operations.	A change of government for India as Narendra Modi, leader of the Hindu nationalist BJP party, is sworn in as India's 15th prime minister.	Goa's popular Chief Minister Manohar Parrikar is appointed Minister of Defence in the Central Government. He is replaced as party leader by Laxmikant Parsekar.

The Way of Life

Goa's compact coastal geography and four centuries of Portuguese rule have imbued in its people a uniquely independent spirit and culture that's undeniably Indian, but unmistakeably Goan. Whether Goan are working in farming, fishing or the tourist industry, life here changes with the seasons, family is all-important and festivals are celebrated with gusto.

Goan Identity

With the frequent comings and goings of the sultans, kings, governors and colonising cultures over the last several thousand years, Goans have grown adept at clinging tight to their indigenous traditions while blending in the most appealing elements of each successive visitation. Goans today take substantial pride in their Portuguese heritage – evident in their names, music, food and architecture – combining this seamlessly with Hindu festivals, Konkani chatter, Christmas parties, a keen interest in the English football leagues and, with the influx of Russian travellers, an uncanny ability to read Cyrillic and rustle up a good bowl of borscht.

Whether Catholic Goan, Hindu Goan, Muslim Goan or 'new' Goan, some things unite everyone native to this eclectic state. Everyone has a strong opinion about the constantly changing face of Goa, and of what it means, in essence, to be Goan. Everyone possesses a set of nostalgic memories of 'the way things used to be', whether this means the opulent landowning days of Portuguese dependence, the trippy free-love '60s, the calm before the package-holiday storm or before the damage of heavy industry. Above all, Goans across the state are eager to ensure, each in their own individual way, that Goa doesn't lose its alluring, endearing, ever-evolving distinctiveness in the decades to come.

Lifestyle

Compared with the rest of the country, Goa is blessed with a relatively high standard of living, with healthcare, schooling, wages and literacy levels all far exceeding the national average. Its population of somewhere around 1.8 million is divided roughly down the middle between rural and urban populations, and many people continue to make their living from tilling the land, fishing or raising livestock.

However, there are still those who fall desperately far below the poverty line. You may notice slums surrounding the heavy industry installations as

SUSEGAD

You won't get far in Goa without hearing references to *susegad* or *sossegado*, a *joie de vivre* attitude summed up along the lines of 'relax and enjoy life while you can'. Originating from the Portuguese word *sossegado* (literally meaning 'quiet'), it's a philosophy of afternoon siestas, and long, lazy evenings filled with feni and song. On the 25th anniversary of Goan Independence, even Prime Minister Rajiv Gandhi described how 'an inherent non-acquisitiveness and contentment with what one has, described by that uniquely Goan word *sossegado*, has been an enduring strength of Goan character'.

GOA'S CASTE SYSTEM: HINDU & CHRISTIAN ALIKE

Every Hindu is born into an unchangeable social class, a caste or varna, of which there are four distinct tiers, each with its own rules of conduct and behaviour.

These four castes, in hierarchical order, are the Brahmins (Bamons in Konkani; priests and teachers), Kshatriyas (Chardos in Konkani; warriors and rulers), Vaisyas (merchants and farmers) and Sudras (peasants and menial workers). Beneath the four main castes is a fifth group, the Untouchables (Chamars in Konkani; formerly known as 'Harijan', but now officially 'Dalits' or 'Scheduled Castes'). These people traditionally performed 'polluting' jobs, including undertaking, street sweeping and leather working. Though discrimination against them is now a criminal offence in India, it's nevertheless still an unfortunate part of life.

While the caste system doesn't play as crucial a part of life in Goa as elsewhere in India, it's still recognised and treated in a uniquely Goan way, and holders of public office remain largely of the Bamon or Chardo castes.

The Christian community also quietly adheres to the caste system, a situation that can be traced back to Portuguese rule since, as an incentive to convert to Catholicism, high-caste Goan families were able to keep their caste privileges, money and land. Even today, in village churches, high-caste Christians tend to dominate the front pews and the lower castes the back of the congregation, and both Hindus and Christians carefully consider questions of caste when selecting candidates for a suitable marriage match.

you drive south on the national highway from Dabolim Airport. Many migrant workers, attracted to Goa by the hopes of benefiting from its tourist trade, end up begging on its beaches, and hundreds of homeless children from surrounding states are supported by local and international charities.

Another acute social problem, linked both to poverty and Goa's liberal attitude to drinking, is alcoholism, though it's a problem shared with other South Indian states.

Traditional Culture

Though many cultural traditions overlap and mingle, particularly within Goa's Christian and Hindu communities, you'll find some traditional practices still going strong in Goa.

Marriage

Embracing the digital age, Goans, like almost everyone else, are taking to the internet in search of love. Popular sites – allowing would-be brides and grooms (and their parents) to scour the whole of India for suitable matches include www.bharatmatrimony.com and www.shaadi.com.

Though 'love matches' are increasingly in vogue in Goa in Christian and Hindu circles alike, both communities still frequently use a matchmaker or local contacts to procure a suitable partner for a son or daughter. If all else fails, you'll find scores of ads listed in the newspaper classifieds or online sites, emphasising the professional qualifications, physical attributes and 'wheatish' complexion of the young, eligible individual.

Following Hindu marriages, generally the young wife will leave her family home to live with her husband's family. However, this is not always the case, and many young couples today are choosing to branch off to begin their own family home. Dowries are usually still required by the groom's family in both Christian and Hindu weddings, either helping facilitate a match or hindering it; a mixed-caste marriage will become much more acceptable if there's a good dowry, but a high-caste girl from a poor family can find it very difficult to secure a partner of a similar 'status'.

Hindu weddings in Goa are lengthy, gleeful and colourful, while Christian wedding ceremonies are more sombre (though the party afterwards usually kicks up a storm) and similar to those in the West, with some elements, such as the ritual bathing of the bride, borrowed from Hinduism. *Chudas,* green bracelets traditionally worn by married women, are donned by both Hindu and Christian brides, and tradition dictates that, should her husband die before her, the widow must break the bangles on his coffin.

Death

Death, as everywhere, is big business in Goa, and you'll spot plenty of coffin makers, headstone carvers and hearse services on your travels. In the Christian community, personal items are placed with the deceased in the grave, including (depending on the habits of the deceased) cigarettes and a bottle of feni, while most Hindus are cremated. Annual memorials, wakes and services for the dead are honoured by Christians and Hindus alike.

There are numerous superstitions in the Hindu and Christian communities about restless spirits – particularly of those who committed suicide or died before being given last rites – and a number of measures are undertaken at the funeral to discourage the spirit from returning. The clothing and funeral shroud are cut, and a needle and thread are placed in the coffin. The spirit of the deceased who wishes to come back must first repair its torn clothing, a task that takes until daylight, at which time departure from the grave is impossible.

At the Church of Our Lady of Miracles in Mapusa, which was built on the site of an ancient Hindu temple, the church's annual feast day, held 16 days after Easter, is celebrated by Christians and Hindus together.

Contemporary Issues
Women in Goan Society

Generally, the position of women in Goa is better than that elsewhere in India, with women possessing property rights, education options and career prospects not shared by their sisters in other states. The result of Goa's progressive policies today is that women are far better represented than elsewhere in professions and positions of influence. While men undoubtedly still predominate and many women still choose to fulfil traditional household roles, around 15% of the state's workforce are women, many of whom fill roles as doctors, dentists, teachers, solicitors and university lecturers, and 30% of panchayat (local government council) seats are reserved for women.

Religion

On paper, at least, it's clear: roughly 30% of Goa's population is Christian, 65% Hindu and 5% Muslim. But statistics alone don't reveal the complex, compelling religious concoction that typifies the population's belief.

Religious Hybrids

During the fierce, Inquisition-led imposition of Christianity by the Portuguese, many Hindus fled to parts of the state still considered safe, while others converted to the new faith and remained in Portuguese territory. Thus, for generations, many Goan families have contained both Catholics and Hindus.

The distinction was further blurred by the ways in which Christianity was adapted to appeal to the local population. As early as 1616 the Bible was translated into Konkani, while in 1623 Pope Gregory permitted Brahmin families to retain their high-caste status after converting to Catholicism, and allowed the continuance of a number of local festivals and traditions.

Today this fusion of these religions is still extremely evident. In Goa's numerous whitewashed churches, Christ and the Virgin Mary are often adorned with Hindu flower garlands, and Mass is said in Konkani. Christians and Hindus frequently pay respects to festivals of the others' faith, with both Christmas and Diwali being a source of celebration and *mithai*-giving (sweet-giving) for all.

But that's not to say that Goa is free from religious tensions. In 2006 anti-Muslim riots, beginning with the destruction of a makeshift village mosque in Sanvordem, shook Goa's religiously tolerant to the core.

Goan Hindu homes are identifiable by the multicoloured *vrindavan* (ornamental container) that stands in front of the house. Growing inside it is the twiggy tulsi plant, sacred to Hindus as in mythology the tulsi is identified as one of the god Vishnu's lovers, whom his consort, Lashmet, turned into a shrub in a fit of jealousy.

Hinduism

Though Hinduism encompasses a huge range of personal beliefs, the essential Hindu belief is in Brahman, an infinite being, or supreme spirit,

DO & DON'TS

Do...

Refill plastic water bottles with filtered water.

Consider buying souvenirs from cooperatives or charity concerns.

Cover shoulders and legs in churches and cathedrals.

Use shower water sparingly to avoid shortages affecting locals.

Don't...

Sunbathe nude or topless; it's illegal and unwelcome in Goa.

Wear shoes inside local Goan houses.

Dress in bikinis and swimwear outside beach resorts; they're not considered appropriate.

FOOTBALL

from which everything derives and to which everything will return. Hindus believe that life is cyclical and subject to reincarnations *(avatars)*, eventually leading to moksha, spiritual release. An individual's progression towards that point is governed by the law of karma (cause and effect): good karma (through positive actions such as charity and worship) may result in being reborn into a higher caste and better circumstances, and bad karma (accumulated through bad deeds) may result in reincarnation in animal form. It's only as a human that one can finally acquire sufficient self-knowledge to achieve liberation from the cycle of reincarnation.

Hindus have long worshipped animals, particularly snakes and cows, for their symbolism. The cow represents fertility and nurturing, while snakes are associated with fertility and welfare. Cows take full advantage of their special status in Goa, lazing in the middle of even chaotic highways, seemingly without a care on this mortal coil.

Islam

Brought to Goa in the 11th century by wealthy Arab merchants, who were encouraged by local rulers to settle here for reasons of commerce, Islamic rule predominated in the region for large chunks of medieval Goan history.

The official soccer season runs from January to May; tickets to the matches generally cost less than ₹30 and can be bought at the ticket kiosks outside the Jawaharlal Nehru Stadium (Fatorda Stadium) in Margao on match days.

With the arrival of the Portuguese, Islam all but disappeared from Goa, and now remains only in small communities. Most Goan Muslims today live in Goa's green heartland, around Ponda, in the vicinity of the state's biggest mosque, the Safa Masjid.

Christianity

Christianity (Catholicism) has been present in Goa since the arrival of the Portuguese in the 16th century, who enforced their faith on Goa's Muslim and Hindu populations by way of the Goan Inquisition. By the time Hindus and Muslims were once again able to practise freely, Catholicism had taken root and was here to stay.

For the last 30 years or so, a form of faith known as 'Charismatic Christianity' has being gaining ground in Goa. Worship involves lots of dancing, singing and sometimes 'speaking in tongues', with readings from the New Testament allegedly used to harness the power of the Holy Spirit, heal the sick and banish evil forces. Unlike mainstream Catholicism, Charismatic Christianity's services are usually in the open air, and its priests reject all notions of caste, understandably making the movement particularly popular among Goa's lower castes.

Sport

Most people know how seriously Indians take the pursuit of cricket, but it may come as a surprise to learn that Goa's top sport is football (soccer), another legacy left over from the days of Portuguese rule. Every village has at least one football team, and sometimes several – one team for each *waddo* (ward) of the village – and league games are fiercely contested.

This has seen the creation of several teams that regularly perform at National Football League (NFL) level. The main Goan teams to watch are Salgaonkar SC from Vasco da Gama, Dempo SC from Panaji (Panjim), and Churchill Brothers SC from Margao (Madgaon). The big matches are played out at the Jawaharlal Nehru Stadium (known locally as Fatorda Stadium) in Margao, regularly attracting up to 35,000 fans.

Goans are also keen cricketers and you'll see plenty of dusty playing fields being used for local matches. The state team plays at Margao's Dr Rajendra Prasad Stadium. Volleyball, too, is a firm local favourite, with regular matches played at sunset on beaches and on almost every village green.

Delicious India

Goan cuisine, with its piquant combinations of coconut, chillies, vinegar, rice and spice, is one of the world's original fusion foods, rich in Portuguese and South Indian heritage. 'Prodham bhookt, magi mookt', say the locals in Konkani; 'You can't think until you've eaten well', and Goans take the sating of their appetites extremely seriously.

Goan Cookbooks

Great Goan Cooking: 100 Easy Recipes – Maria Teresa Menezes

Savour the Flavour of India – Edna Fernandes

Goan Recipes and More – Odette Mascarenhas

According to linguists, there's no such thing as an Indian 'curry' – the word, an Anglicised derivative of the Tamil word *kari* (black pepper), was used by the British as a term for any dish including spices.

Staples & Specialities

Given Goa's seaside location, it's little wonder that the local lunchtime staple is 'fish-curry-rice', crisp fried mackerel steeped in a thin coconut, tamarind and red chilli sauce and served with rice; you'll find it on any 'nonveg' restaurant's menu, and it's a cheap and tasty way to fill up for lunch.

Aside from seafood, chicken and pork are popular meat dishes in Goa, and the latter makes for a local lunchtime favourite, served up in the form of a piled plate of Goan *chouriços*. These air-dried, spicy red pork sausages (similar to Spanish chorizo) are flavoured with feni (liquor distilled from cashew fruit or palm sap), toddy (palm sap) vinegar and chillies, and strung in desiccated garlands from streetside stalls.

Another delicacy you won't find anywhere else in India is pork *sorpotel*, a spicy masala dish combining chillies, ginger, garlic, cinnamon, cloves and a dash of feni; it's often served at Christmas.

Sauces

Uniquely Goan preparations include *xacuti* (pronounced *sha-coo-tee*), a spicy sauce combining coconut milk, freshly ground spices and red chillies. Chicken and seafood are frequently served basted with *rechead*, a spicy marinating paste. Dry-fried chicken might otherwise be served spicy *cafrial* style, marinated in a green masala paste and sprinkled with toddy vinegar. Meanwhile, the original *vindalho* is a uniquely Goan derivative of Portuguese pork stew that traditionally combines *vinho* (wine vinegar) with *ahlo* (garlic) and spices.

Spices

Head to one of Goa's divinely scented spice farms to find evidence of the sought-after spices that kept conquerors coming back to Goa for centuries. South India still produces the very best of the world's black-pepper crop, an essential ingredient in savoury dishes worldwide, while locally produced turmeric, coriander and cumin, combined with garlic, chillies, tamarind and *kokum* (a dried fruit used as a spice) form the basis of many a Goan curry. Other locally-grown spices include cardamom, vanilla, cinnamon, cloves, curry leaves, ginger and nutmeg.

Rice

Rice is by far the most important staple in southern India, providing most meals for most people throughout most of their lives, and India is one of the world's largest rice producers. Apart from being boiled or steamed, rice is cooked up to make *pulao* (pilau; aromatic rice casserole), or a Muslim biryani, with a layer of vegetable, chicken or mutton curry. Naturally it forms the basis of the Goan staple 'fish-curry-rice'.

Dhal

Vegetarian or omnivorous, Christian, Hindu or Muslim, India is united in its love for dhal (lentils or pulses). In Goa, you'll find three types of dhal: thin, spicy *sambar*, served with many breakfast dishes; dhal fry, which is yellow and mild with the consistency of a thick soup; and dhal makhani, richer and darker, spiked with *rajma* (kidney beans), onions and another handful or two of some of the 60 types of pulses grown in the country. Various other pulses, including *kabuli chana* (chickpeas) and *lobhia* (black-eyed beans), also turn up regularly in that delicious Goan breakfast staple, *bhaji-pau.*

Seafood

Seafood is plentiful, fresh and delicious in Goa, though not cheap compared with other dishes. Among the most famous Goan fish dishes are *ambot tik*, a slightly sour curry usually accompanied by shark; *caldeirada*, a mild seafood stew with vegetables flavoured with wine; and the Portuguese-inflected *recheiado* which sees a whole fish, usually a mackerel or pomfret, slit down the centre, stuffed with a spicy red sauce, and fried up in hot oil. Another regular on Goan menus is *balchao*, a rich, tangy tomato and chilli sauce, often cooked with tiger prawns or fish.

Sweets

Look out for bebinca, the most famous of Goan sweets, a rich 16-layer coconut pancake-type cake, whipped up with sugar, nutmeg, cardamom and egg yolks. Also be sure to sample *batica,* a squidgy coconut cake best served piping hot from the oven; *doce,* made with chickpeas and coconut; and *dodol,* a gooey fudgelike treat, made from litres of fresh coconut milk, mixed with rice flour and jaggery.

In typical South Indian restaurants, rice and curry dishes are often eaten with the hands. Try to eat only with your right hand; the left is considered unclean and for the purposes of ablution only. If you're invited to dine with a family, always take off your shoes and wash your hands before dining.

Drinks

Nonalcoholic Drinks

Chai (tea) is the national drink, boiled for hours with milk, sugar and masala spices, and served piping hot, sweet and frothy.

Coffee is less widely consumed by Goans, but you'll have no problem finding Indian-style coffee, and espresso machines are becoming common in upmarket cafes that cater to international tastes.

Fizzy drinks, fresh lime soda, lassis and shakes are standard fare at cafes and shacks. Look out for coconut street vendors – for ₹30 they'll chop the top off and poke a straw in for a refreshing, natural drink.

Cooking classes (p32) are gaining popularity in Goa. You'll find them at Anjuna, Palolem, Patnem and Siolim.

Alcoholic Drinks

Goans love to drink and low taxes mean alcohol is cheaper here than elsewhere in India. Beer is king (when it's cold), and Kingfisher and Kings are the two local brands, though Tuborg, Heineken and others are often available. The fiery local liquor is feni, made either from fermented cashew fruit or palm sap (toddy), which is distilled to around 30% to 35% proof. Feni first-timers mix it with a soft drink, soda water, or just close your eyes and take your medicine.

CLASSIC COCONUTS

Coconut palms are thick in Goa and a vital part of the local diet. Coconut flesh, known as copra, gives flavour and substance to almost every Goan speciality dish, savoury and sweet alike, as well as providing oil for use in other sorts of cooking, soap manufacture, hair oil and cosmetics. The hairy outer shell of the coconut is spun into water-resistant coir rope, and used by Goan fishermen to secure their boats.

Coconut sap, known as toddy, is collected by toddy tappers, who shinny up their swaying trees two or three times daily. It's fermented and made into that killer liquor, feni.

DELICIOUS INDIA DRINKS

Hard liquor, known in India as IMFL – Indian-made foreign liquor – is very cheap (if purchased at a liquor store) and the rum, brandy and whiskey versions are reasonably palatable.

Wine, though not India's strong point, is slowly gaining ground, but you'll pay dearly for choosing the grape over the grain: bought at a liquor store, even a mediocre bottle of local wine costs around ₹500 (safe bets are Sula, Chateau Indage and Grover).

Celebrations

Cooking Online

www.goanfood recipes.com

www.hildastouch ofspice.com

www.rice-n-curry. com

www.goafoodguide. com

Goan festivals and celebrations are synonymous with feasting. Weddings are occasions to indulge gastronomic fantasies, and often include dishes such as *sorpotel,* a combination of meat, organs and blood, diced and cooked in a thick, spicy sauce flavoured with feni. Seafood also features at feasts. Desserts might include bebinca and *leitria* (an elaborate coconut covered by a lacy filigree of egg yolks and sugar syrup).

Hindu festivals, too, are big food affairs. *Karanjis,* crescent-shaped flour parcels stuffed with sweet *khoya* (milk solids) and nuts, are synonymous with Holi, the most boisterous Hindu festival, as are *malpuas* (wheat pancakes dipped in syrup), *barfis* (fudgelike sweets) and *pedas* (multicoloured pieces of *khoya* and sugar). Pongal (Tamil for 'overflowing'), the south's major harvest festival, produces a dish of the same name, made with the season's first rice along with jaggery, nuts, raisins and spices.

Where to Eat & Drink

Goa's eating-out options are divided into the 'local' and 'nonlocal' varieties: the local serving up Indian or Goan cuisine of one sort or another, and the nonlocal encompassing everything from Tibetan kitchens and pizza restaurants to French fine dining.

The simplest local restaurants, often known as 'hotels' come either in 'veg' or 'nonveg' varieties, and are the best places for a cheap breakfast or a filling lunch.

Midrange Indian restaurants generally serve one of two basic genres of Indian food: South Indian (the vegetarian food of Tamil Nadu and Karnataka) and North Indian (richer, and often meatier, Punjabi-Mughlai food). The final (and rarest) type of local restaurant is that serving Goan cuisine itself.

Street Food

In Mumbai (Bombay) you'll encounter roadside carts cooking up samosas (deep-fried pyramid-shaped pastries filled with spiced vegetables and sometimes meat) and *aloo tikka* (mashed potato patties), along with *puri* (also spelt *poori*; thin, puffed-up, deep-fried breads) and *bhelpuri,* an addictive Mumbai snack made from thin rounds of dough, with rice, lentils, lemon juice, onion, herbs and chutney.

Street-food carts are not as common in Goa, but you will find them at Miramar Beach in Panaji (Panjim) and at the main beach entrances to Calangute and Colva. A good rule of thumb is that if locals are eating at a streetside stand, it's a pretty safe bet, but make sure it's freshly cooked – don't eat anything that looks like it has been sitting around for a while.

Vegetarians & Vegans

South Indian cuisine is some of the best in the world for those who abstain from fish, flesh and fowl. Vegans might face some challenges, since it's sometimes hard to work out whether food has been cooked in ghee (clarified butter) but look out for the words 'pure veg'.

Markets & Shopping

Shopping is a big part of any exotic holiday and India is a shoppers' paradise. From colourful markets to traditional handicrafts, in Goa and Mumbai (Bombay) you'll find souvenirs, textiles, jewellery, carpets and one-off bargains from all over India.

Where to Shop

Mumbai is one of the most exciting places in India to start shopping. Handicraft emporia, antique shops, designer boutiques and gritty, grimy markets are all part of the retail landscape in the nation's biggest city. Set aside at least an afternoon, if not a day, to devote to the fine art of Mumbai shopping – you'll undoubtedly leave heavier of suitcase and lighter of wallet.

Although Goa can't compete in terms of the range of goods available, there's still plenty on offer, with tourism luring market traders from all over India. While this means that you're unlikely to take home much that is genuinely Goan – apart from decorative bottles of cashew feni, packets of locally grown spices and perhaps hand-painted tiles – it also means that you can find almost anything from Kashmiri carpets to Karnatakan carvings.

Panaji (Panjim) has a growing number of upscale 'lifestyle boutiques' vending high-end household goods and gorgeous Goan coffee-table books. Craft shops, department stores and clothes shops line the 18th June Rd and MG Rd, while Caculo Mall is a modern multistorey department store. Calangute and Candolim, too, host a selection of sleek boutiques, souvenir shops and big-name brands. Most stores are situated on the roads leading down its beaches, and on the main Fort Aguada road.

Markets

Mumbai's markets are manifold, as you'll find if you walk into the labyrinthine bazaars just north of the Chhatrapati Shivaji Terminus (Victoria Terminus). Shop alongside locals at Crawford Market or Bhuleshwar Market, both vending foodstuffs and household goods, or trawl Mangaldas Market for silks and fabrics. For clothing, try the stalls on MG Rd between Azad and Cross maidans, and for Indian jewellery, including thousands of glass bangles, go to Zaveri Bazaar.

In Goa, the markets are either aimed specifically at tourists or specifically at locals. For local shopping, try the municipal markets in Panaji and Margao (Madgaon), with plenty of colour and a good line in spices, bangles and posters of Indian gods, or head to Mapusa, where the daily morning market is busiest and most vibrant on Fridays.

Anjuna's Wednesday flea market, though somewhat commercialised, is still a major weekly attraction and good fun to wander around. The two Saturday night markets – Mackie's in Baga and the Saturday Nite Market (formerly Ingo's) in Arpora – are also good fun, with food stalls, entertainment, neon-lit stalls and lots of flashing jewellery. The three tourist markets operate only during the high season from November to the end of March.

The roads leading to the beach in Palolem and Arambol are packed with stalls selling silver jewellery, drums, hammocks, embroidered bedsheets, sandals, and all the usual lines in Indian souvenirs. But if you

Best Bookshops

Golden Heart Emporium, Margao (p165)

Other India Bookstore, Mapusa (p143)

Singbal's, Panaji (p91)

Rainbow Bookshop, Vagator (p148)

Butterfly Book Shop, Palolem (p188)

Broadway Book Centre, Candolim (p126)

THE ART OF HAGGLING

The friendly art of haggling is an absolute must in most parts of Goa and Mumbai, unless you don't mind paying above market value. Traders in towns and markets are accustomed to tourists who have lots of money and little time to spend it, meaning that a shopkeeper's 'very good price' might in fact be a rather bad one.

If you have absolutely no idea what something should really cost, a good rule of thumb is to bank on paying half of what you're originally quoted. The vendor will probably look aghast and tell you that this is impossible, as it's the very price they had to pay for the item themselves. This is when the battle for a bargain begins and it's up to you and the salesperson to negotiate a price. You'll find that many shopkeepers lower their so-called final price if you head out of the shop and tell them that you'll think about it.

Don't lose your sense of humour and sense of fairness while haggling – it's not a battle to squeeze every last rupee out of a poor trader, and not all vendors are out to make a fool of you. In essence, the haggle itself is often the very spirit, and the fun, of the Indian shopping experience. Don't forget to smile – and never get angry.

prefer the goods to come to you, never fear: sit for 15 minutes on almost any stretch of beach, and migrant vendors will appear bearing jewellery, fabrics, and an excellent line in well-practised hard-sell.

What to Buy

Antiques

You'll find a concentration of antiques on Mutton St in Mumbai, though you'll need to determine the real from the reproduction. For genuine antiques at genuine antique prices, try Phillips in Colaba, a Mumbai institution that's been around for the last century and a half.

In Goa you'll find a couple of knick-knack–style antique shops in Mapusa, near the Municipal Gardens, along with antique-furniture shops scattered here and there across the state. Most shops can organise shipping.

Be aware that antiques more than 100 years old are not permitted to be exported from India without an export clearance certificate.

Carpets

It may not surprise you that India produces and exports more hand-crafted carpets than Iran, but it probably comes as more of a surprise to find that some of them are of virtually equal quality. India's best carpets come from Kashmir, and can be found in usually Kashmiri-run shops throughout Goa.

Leatherwork

Indian leatherwork is not made from cowhide but from buffalo, camel, goat or some other form of animal. *Chappals,* the basic sandals found all over India, are the most popular buy.

Papier-Mâché

Probably the most characteristic Kashmiri craft, papier-mâché items are made in a mould, then painted and polished in layers until the final intricate design is produced. Items include bowls, jewellery boxes, tables and lamps.

Textiles

This is still India's major industry and 40% of the total production is at village level, where it is known as *khadi* (homespun cloth). Bedspreads, tablecloths, cushion covers or fabric for clothing are popular *khadi* purchases. In Gujarat and Rajasthan heavy material is embroidered with tiny mirrors and beads to produce everything from dresses to stuffed toys to wall hangings; tie-dye work is popular in Rajasthan and Kerala; and in Kashmir embroidered materials are turned into shirts and dresses.

For an unusual gift for that budding Houdini, or to provide means to pass time on a long bus journey, seek out rabbits in hats and enchanted handkerchiefs at Shamin Khan's Star Magic Shop (p134) in Baga, which also has a weekly stall at the Anjuna Flea Market.

Arts & Architecture

Goa's traditional art forms, much of its architecture, and even its sporting passions are strongly influenced by its colonial legacy. Goans display an infectious love of music, festivals, dance, poetry, literature and a rich artistic and cultural heritage, seamlessly blending Indian and Portuguese elements.

Music & Dance

Listen carefully beyond the Bob Marley, lounge and techno jumble of the beach shacks, and you'll hear Goa's own melodies, a heady concoction of East and West.

The most famous kind of Goan folk song is the *mando,* also known as 'the love song of Goa', a slow melody with accompanying dance, which sees its largely Catholic participants dance in parallel lines, flourishing paper fans and handkerchiefs. You might catch a glimpse of this if you pass a Christian wedding or feast day in progress.

Though increasingly rare, the melancholy, haunting fado can still be heard here and there in Goa, whose songs lament lost love, or the longing for a Portuguese home that most singers, in fact, have never seen. Listen out for the late, great folk singer Lucio de Miranda, or Oslando, another local folk and fado favourite.

Local Konkani pop is a strange and sometimes wonderful combination of tinny, trilly musical influences – African rhythms and Portuguese tunes, with a bit of calypso thrown in. You'll catch its twangy melodies from passing cars, buses and taxis, and in local Goan lunch spots. A classic, old-school performer to look out for, who has influenced a whole new generation of local musicians, is the much-loved Lorna, 'the Goan nightingale'.

Aside from local celebrations (to which tourists are often extended a warm welcome), the best place to find traditional music and dance performances is at Panaji's Kala Academy (p90).

Goa Trance

The Western electronic music scene in Goa still thumps – albeit less incessantly than in past years – to the hypnotic rhythms of Goa trance and psy-trance, a uniquely Goan sound that came to prevalence on the beaches of Anjuna in the early 1990s.

Its most famous exponent is Goa Gil, who still DJs trance parties worldwide. Go to www.goagil.com to see where he's next appearing – the schedule usually includes gigs in Goa or elsewhere in India. Other well-known artists include Hallucigen, Astral Projection and Cosmosis. You can pick up Goa trance CDs at the Anjuna flea market.

For an especially good selection of the most up-to-date local Goan literary releases, drop in to Margao's Golden Heart Emporium (p165), Mapusa's Other India Bookstore (p143), or the numerous book stores around Panaji's Municipal Gardens.

Literature

Although it can be difficult to get hold of Goan literature (books go out of print very quickly), a decent amount of Konkani literature is available in English translation.

Some mainstays of Goan literature include *Angela's Goan Identity,* a 1994 fictional work by Carmo D'Souza, which offers a fascinating insight into a girl's struggle to define her Goan identity towards the final years of the Portuguese era in Goa, while Frank Simoes' engaging *Glad Seasons in Goa* offers an affectionate account of Goan life.

Perhaps the greatest classic of Goan literature, though, is *Sorrowing Lies My Land,* by Lambert Mascarenhas, first published in 1955, which deals with the struggle for Goan Independence launched in Margao in 1946. Meanwhile, Victor Rangel Ribeiro weaves together Goan vignettes in his award-winning first novel *Tivolem.* Mario Cabral E Sa's *Legends of Goa,* illustrated by one of Goa's best-known artists, Mario de Miranda, is a colourful reworking of some of Goa's best folk tales and historical titbits.

Mumbai (Bombay) is an architectural paradise filled with Victorian Gothic fantasies, including the High Court, Chhatrapati Shivaji railway station, and the Taj Mahal Palace hotel. Don't miss, too, the modern engineering of the Global Pagoda, and the serene spirituality of Haji Ali Mosque.

Architecture

Goa's most iconic architectural form is likely the slowly crumbling bungalow mansion, with its wrought-iron balconies, shady front *balcãos* (pillared porches), oyster-shell windows and central *saquãos* (inner courtyards), around which family life traditionally revolved.

Most were built in the early 18th century, as rewards to wealthy Goan merchants and officials for their services to the Portuguese. The architecture was inspired by European tastes, but the materials – red laterite stone, wood, terracotta, and oyster shells used instead of glass for windows – were all local. The wealthiest of these homes also contained a locally crafted wooden chapel or oratory, which housed gilded and golden relics, altars and images of Catholic saints as the focal point for family prayers.

Churches, too, bear the hallmark of Portugal, many of them cruciform and constructed of whitewashed laterite stone. Even village churches usually sport a sumptuous interior, with an elaborate gilt *reredos* (ornamental altarpiece or screen), and lots of carving, painting and chandeliers.

Goan temples are yet another form of architectural hybrid, enfolding both Muslim and Christian elements into traditional Hindu designs. Domed roofs, for example, are a Muslim trait, while balustraded facades and octagonal towers are borrowed from Portuguese church architecture. Their most unusual and distinctive features, however, are their 'light towers', known as *deepastambhas,* which look a little like Chinese pagodas and are atmospherically decorated with oil lamps during festival periods.

Painting

Although there's no painting style particular to Goa, some of the state's most historically significant artistic output can be seen in the murals at Rachol Seminary, in the ornately decorated churches across Goa, and adorning the portraiture-heavy walls of Goa's grand mansion homes.

Internationally, one of Goa's best-known artists is Francis Newton Souza (1924–2002), whose expressionist paintings can be found in galleries

REMO FERNANDES

Goan singer, musician and producer Remo Fernandes is famous in India for his ability to fuse cultural influences in both his music and his image.

Remo was born in Siolim in 1953. After studying architecture in Bombay (Mumbai) and hitchhiking around Europe and Africa (busking along the way), he returned to Goa. Several rejections from Indian labels made him record his first (and arguably one of his best) albums, *Goan Crazy,* at home in Siolim. From there, Remo shot to success with more hit albums, film-score offers, awards, product endorsements and titles such as 'the Freddie Mercury of India'.

Remo is loved in Goa, not only for the versatility of his talent but also for never cutting his Goan roots along his path to fame. When Remo turned 50 in May 2003, he celebrated with a free 4½-hour concert in Goa.

Look out for *Old Goan Gold* as well as *Forwards into the Past,* which has arrangements by Remo and vocals by the late, fado-famed Lucio de Miranda. Remo lives and records in Siolim. You can follow him online at www.remofernandes.com.

GOA ON FILM

Goa is becoming an increasingly popular shooting location for Indian films (Bollywood, Tamil, Konkani, Telugu and Malayalam), either as a beach backdrop or with Goa providing an integral setting in the film's plot. Films to look out for:

Finding Fanny (2014; director Homi Adajania) Comedy road trip set in a fictional Goan village. In English and Hindi.

Baga Beach (2013; Laxmikant Shetgaonkar) This award-winning Konkani film tackles tricky subjects such as the seedy side of tourism, migrants in Goa and child sexual abuse.

Dum Maaro Dum (2011; Rohan Sippy) This hit crime-thriller proved controversial in Goa for the line: 'Over here, liquor is cheap but women are even cheaper.'

Husbands in Goa (2012; Saji Surendran) For something different this Malayalam (Keralan) comedy follows three men travelling to Goa to escape from their domineering wives.

My Brother...Nikhil (2005) Set in Goa in the late 1980s this film explores the sensitive themes of HIV and homosexuality.

Bourne Supremacy (2004) This Hollywood action film is worth a look just to see Matt Damon jogging on Palolem Beach and out-driving the baddies (miraculously emerging in Panaji in the very same scene).

Last Hippie Standing (2001; Marcus Robbin) This short documentary (find it on YouTube) traces the history of the hippie days of the 1960s and '70s, with interviews and some original Super 8 footage.

worldwide. Out and about in Goa, the two artists you're most likely to come across are installation artist Dr Subodh Kerkar, and the late, much-loved artist and illustrator Mario de Miranda, who died in 2011 but whose distinctive style continues to adorn everything from books to billboards to the walls of Café Mondegar in Mumbai (Bombay). You can see his work at the Mario Gallery (p156) in Torda.

Cinema

The Indian film industry is the largest on the planet, with around 800 movies produced annually, most of them elaborate, formulaic, melodramatic Bollywood montages that celebrate romance, violence and music, with saccharine lip-synced duets and fantastic dance routines, all performed by Indian megastars who are worshipped like deities countrywide. While in Goa or Mumbai, you must see at least one of these incredible creations of high camp. In Panaji, head to the comfortable INOX Cinema or the far more gritty Cine Nacional. In Mumbai there are many classic art-deco cinemas, including the Regal.

The INOX plays host to Goa's grand and glittering annual **International Film Festival of India** (IFFI; www.iffi.gov.in), the country's largest festival, which sees Bollywood's greatest and most glorious jetting in for preening and partying all along the red carpet.

Theatre

Goa's theatre scene is dominated by the unique local street plays known as *tiatr* and *khell tiatr* (a longer form of *tiatr* performed only during festivals such as Carnival and Easter). The *tiatrs,* almost all of which are in Konkani, provide a platform for satire on politics, current affairs and day-to-day domestic issues.

Since 1974 Panaji's Kala Academy (p90) has held an annual festival (performed in Konkani) each November, showcasing the work of well-known *tiatr* writers. Throughout the year, this is also the venue for arts, drama and folk theatre.

Stroll the lanes of Chandor, Siolim or the coastal villages between Velsao and Mobor for a treasure trove of Portuguese-era mansions in various stages of decay. Visit the Houses of Goa Museum (p156) at Torda to get up to speed on Goa's architectural heritage.

Wildlife & the Environment

Goa may be tiny but it possesses a surprising diversity of landscape and environment. In the five decades since the Portuese left its shores, Goa has experienced phenomenal growth in tourism, industry and population, sometimes taxing to the limit this beautiful yet fragile ecosystem.

The Land

Goa – A View from the Heavens, by aerial photographer Gopal Bodhe, is a beautifully photographed book dedicated to Goa's environment and heritage.

Goa occupies a narrow strip of the western Indian coastline, approximately 105km long and 65km wide, but within this relatively tiny area exists an incredibly diverse mixture of landscapes, flora and fauna.

To the east of the state lie the gorgeous green Western Ghats, whose name derives from the Sanskrit for 'sacred steps'. This mountain range runs along India's entire west coast, but in Goa is made up of the Sahyadri Range, comprising around one-sixth of the state's total area. The ghats are the source of all seven of Goa's main rivers, the longest of which, the Mandovi, meanders for 77km to the Arabian Sea at Panaji (Panjim).

Goa's grassy hinterland is made up mostly of laterite plateaux, with thin soil covering rich sources of iron and manganese ore. The midland has thus suffered from large-scale open-cast mining, evident in the red gashes in Goan hillsides.

Spice, fruit, cashew and areca-nut plantations predominate commercially, while terraced orchards make efficient use of limited water sources to support coconut, jackfruit, pineapple and mango groves.

Though just a fraction of the state's total area, Goa's coast is its crowning glory. Mangroves line tidal rivers, providing shelter for birds, marine animals and crocodiles, while paddy fields, coconut groves, and the seas and estuaries provide the majority of the population's food.

The beaches and marine waters have suffered from unfettered tourist development, overfishing, untreated sewage, pollution from sea tankers and iron-ore mining.

Wildlife

Seven great rivers flow from the Western Ghats to Goa's coast. From north to south: Terekhol (Tiracol), Chapora, Mandovi, Zuari, Sal, Talpona and Galgibag.

Despite Goa's diminutive size, the state is home to a surprising array of fauna and some spectacular birdlife. The most impressive mammalian species, such as wild elephants and leopards, occur only in small numbers, are incredibly shy, and thus hard to spot. Tigers have been recorded by the forest department in Mhadei Wildlife Sanctuary.

Mammals

The wild animals you'll most likely encounter in Goa are the state's mischievous monkeys: most visible are smallish, scavenging bonnet macaques, and larger, black-faced, long-limbed Hanuman langurs.

Other inhabitants include common mongooses, smooth Indian otters, giant squirrels, slender lorises and shaggy sloth bears.

In Goa's wildlife sanctuaries, you may come across gaur (Indian bison), porcupines, sambars (buff-coloured deer), chitals (spotted deer) and barking deer. One of the rarer animals inhabiting Goa's forests is the nocturnal pangolin (scaly anteater). The 'mini-leopard' (known as the *vagati* in Konkani), a greyish fluffy-tailed creature about the size of a domestic cat, is also sometimes seen, along with the Indian civet.

Common dolphins can often be found frolicking offshore or in estuaries, while fruit bats and Malay fox vampire bats come out in force as the Goan sun goes down.

Reptiles, Snakes & Amphibians

Snakes are common, though reclusive, with 23 species of which eight are venomous. You're most likely to see nonvenomous green whip snakes, golden tree snakes, rat snakes, cat snakes, wolf snakes and Russel sand boas. *Kusadas* (sea snakes) are common along the coastline, but generally live in deep waters, far off the coast.

Goa is also home to chameleons, monitor lizards, turtles and two species of crocodile. Flap-shell turtles and black-pond turtles are freshwater species plentiful during the monsoon, while a third species, the olive ridley marine turtle, is in grave danger of extinction (p150). There are protected nesting sites on Mandrem, Morjim and Agonda beaches.

Though crocs are also threatened, you can spot the saltwater variety in the Mandovi and Zuari estuaries, along with the less aggressive 'Mandovi mugger' which mostly inhabits Mandovi River waters around Divar and Chorao Islands.

Birds

Goa is big news for visiting birdwatchers. Top birdwatching spots include Dr Salim Ali Bird Sanctuary on Chorao Island, Bondla Wildlife Sanctuary (p107) and Mayem Lake (p158).

In open spaces, a flash of colour may turn out to be an Indian roller, identified by its brilliant blue flight feathers. Drongos are common, while pipits and wagtails strut in large flocks among the harvest stubble. Common hoopoes are often seen (or heard) in open country, while birds of prey such as harriers and buzzards soar overhead. Kites and vultures can wheel on thermals for hours; ospreys, another large hawk, patrol reservoirs and waterways for fish suppers.

Stalking long-legged at the shallow edges of ponds are various species of egret. Indian pond herons, also known as paddy birds, are small and well camouflaged in greys and browns.

Colourful kingfishers, Goa's unofficial mascot, patiently await their prey on overhanging branches. Species include black-and-white pied kingfishers, colourful common kingfishers (also known as river kingfishers) and stork-billed kingfishers, sporting massive red bills.

In the forest, woodpeckers are more often heard than seen as they chisel grubs from the bark of trees. Their colourful relatives include barbets and Indian koels, whose loud, piercing cry can be relentless in spring. Hill mynahs are an all-black bird with a distinctive yellow 'wattle' about the face.

The jewels in Goa's avian crown must be its three magnificent species of hornbill, resembling South American toucans. At the other end of the size spectrum, the iridescent, nectar-feeding purple sunbird is equally brilliant. A host of smaller birds, such as flycatchers, warblers, babblers and little tailorbirds forage for insects in every layer of vegetation.

Wildlife Sanctuaries

Roughly 12%, or 455 sq km, of Goa's total area is given over to wildlife sanctuaries and reserves.

The best time for wildlife watching is as soon after the monsoon as possible. October is perfect, when tourist numbers and temperatures are low and animals are attracted to still-verdant watering holes.

Birds of Southern India, by Richard Grimmet and Tim Inskipp, is a comprehensive birdwatching field guide, considered by many to be the must-have guide to the region. More focussed is *Birds of Goa*, by local naturalist Rahul Alvares and Heinz Lainer. Online, check out www.birdsofgoa. com.

The three main wildlife sanctuaries were created in the late 1960s: Bondla (p107), the smallest at just 8 sq km; Bhagwan Mahavir (p108), which also contains Molem National Park and is the largest at 240 sq km; and Cotigao (p190) in the south (86 sq km). In 1999 Madei (208 sq km) in Satari *taluka* (district) and Netravali (211 sq km) in Sanguem *taluka* were declared protected areas.

S Prater's *The Book of Indian Animals* and Romulus Whitaker's *Common Indian Snakes* are two reliable guides to the nonhuman residents of Goa.

Plants

Flowering plants, grasses, brackens and ferns all play their part in Goa's ecology, and the Western Ghats comprise some of Asia's densest rainforest. On their lower slopes, thinner, drier soil supports semievergreen forest; in other places the arid landscape leads to savannah-like vegetation.

The coastal region has a wide range of flora, with saline conditions supporting mangrove swamps. In villages, banyan and peepul trees provide shade for the Hindu and Buddhist shrines that are often beneath them.

Environmental Issues

Deforestation

Over-cutting of the forested Western Ghats began at the start of the 20th century, and environmental groups estimate that more than 500 hectares of Goa's forests continue to disappear every year.

The damage caused by deforestation is far-reaching. Animal habitats are diminishing, as are the homelands of the tribal Dhangar, Kunbi and Velip peoples. In an effort to curb the damage, the government has stepped up its efforts to protect Goa's forests: felling fees now apply, licences must be issued, and reforestation projects are under way.

Mining

In past decades nearly half the iron ore exported annually from India has come from Goa, with huge barges ferrying the ore along the Zuari and Mandovi Rivers to waiting ships.

Of the 80 million tonnes of rock and soil extracted annually, only 13 million tonnes are saleable ore. Surplus is dumped on spoil tips and is washed away come the monsoon, smothering both river and marine life. Other side effects of mining include the disruption of local water tables and pollution of air and drinking water.

In 2010 the Shah Commission report into illegal mining – lobbied for by environmental groups such as the Goa Foundation – revealed corruptions, scams and unlicensed mining which led to the Supreme Court suspending all mining activities in 2012.

The Goa Foundation described this victory as 'suspending more than a decade of senseless extraction and looting which irreversibly brutalised the natural environment, destroyed the peace of village communities and damaged public health.'

By 2014 the Goan government had renewed a limited number of mining licences, paving the way for at least partial resumption of an industry that has provided some 10% of the state's GDP.

Online Resources

Goa Foundation (www.goafoundation.org)

Green Goa Foundation (www.greengoafoundation.org)

Green Goa Works (www.greengoaworks.in)

World Wildlife Fund (www.wwfindia.org)

Tourism

While bringing countless jobs and raising standards of living for many in Goa, unchecked hotel building, inadequate sewage facilities, water-guzzling swimming pools and landscaped golf courses have all taken their toll on the environment. Count up the plastic water bottles you might use during your visit, multiply this figure by two million, then refill your own with filtered water to do your bit towards saving Goa from an avalanche of nonbiodegradable plastic.

Survival Guide

Scams

India has a deserved reputation for scams. Of course, most can be easily avoided with a little common sense and an appropriate amount of caution. Scams tend to be more of a problem in the big cities of arrival (such as Delhi or Mumbai), or very touristy spots (such as Rajasthan), though in Goa and Kerala they are rare. Chat with fellow travellers to keep abreast of the latest cons. Look at the India branch of Lonely Planet's Thorn Tree Travel Forum (www.lonelyplanet.com/thorntree), where travellers post warnings about problems they have encountered on the road.

Contaminated Food & Drink

➡ The late 1990s saw a scam in North India where travellers died after consuming food laced with dangerous bacteria from restaurants linked to dodgy medical clinics; we've heard no recent reports but the scam could resurface. In unrelated incidents, some clinics have also given more treatment than necessary to procure larger payments.

➡ Most bottled water is legit, but ensure the seal is intact and the bottom of the bottle hasn't been tampered with. While in transit, try to carry packed food. If you eat at bus or train stations, buy cooked food only from fast-moving places.

Credit-Card Con

Be careful when paying for souvenirs with a credit card. While government shops are usually legitimate, private souvenir shops have been known to run off extra copies of the credit-card imprint slip and use them for phoney transactions later. Ask the trader to process the transaction in front of you. Memorising the CVV/CVC2 number and scratching it off the card is also a good idea, to avoid misuse. In some restaurants, waiters will ask you for your PIN with the intention of taking your credit card to the machine – never give your PIN to anyone, and ask to use the machine in person.

Druggings

Occasionally, tourists (especially solo travellers) are drugged and robbed during train or bus journeys. A spiked drink is the most commonly used method for sending them off to sleep – chocolates, chai from a co-conspiring vendor and 'homemade' Indian food are also known to be used. Use your instincts, and if you're unsure, politely decline drinks or food offered by strangers.

Gem Scams

This classic scam involves charming con artists who promise foolproof 'get rich quick' schemes. Travellers are asked to carry or mail gems home and then sell them to the trader's (nonexistent) overseas representatives at a profit. Without exception, the goods – if they arrive at all – are worth a fraction of what you paid, and the 'representatives' never materialise.

KEEPING SAFE

➡ A good travel-insurance policy is essential.

➡ Email copies of your passport identity page, visa and airline tickets to yourself, and keep copies on you.

➡ Keep your money and passport in a concealed money belt or a secure place under your shirt.

➡ Store at least US$100 separately from your main stash.

➡ Don't publicly display large wads of cash when paying for services or checking into hotels.

➡ If you can't lock your hotel room securely from the inside, stay somewhere else.

Don't believe hard-luck stories about an inability to obtain an export licence, or the testimonials they show you from other travellers – they are fake. Travellers have reported this con happening in Agra, Delhi, and Jaisalmer among other places, but it's particularly prevalent in Jaipur. Carpets, curios and *pashminas* are other favourites for this con.

Overpricing

Always agree on prices beforehand while availing services that don't have regulated tariffs. This particularly applies to friendly neighbourhood guides, snack bars at places of touristy interest, and autorickshaws and taxis without meters.

Photography

Use your instincts (better still, ask for permission) while photographing people. The common argument – sometimes voiced after you've snapped your photos – is you're going to sell them to glossy international magazines, so it's only fair that you pay a fee.

Theft

Theft is a risk in India, as anywhere else. Keep luggage locked and chained on buses and trains. Remember that snatchings often occur when a train is pulling out of the station, as it's too late for you to give chase.

Touts & Commission Agents

➡ Touts come in many avatars and operate in mysterious ways. Cabbies and autorickshaw drivers will often try to coerce you to stay at a budget hotel of their choice, only to collect a commission (included within your room tariff) from the receptionists afterward.

➡ Wherever possible, arrange hotel bookings (if only for

OTHER TOP SCAMS

➡ Gunk (dirt, paint, poo) suddenly appears on your shoes, only for a shoe cleaner to magically appear and offer to clean it off – for a price.

➡ Some shops are selling overpriced SIM cards and not activating them; it's best to buy your SIM from an official shop (Airtel, Vodafone etc) and check it works before leaving the area (activation can take 24 hours).

➡ Shops and restaurants 'borrow' the name of their more successful and popular competitor.

➡ Touts claim to be 'government-approved' guides or agents, and sting you for large sums of cash. Enquire at the local tourist office about licensed guides and ask to see identification from guides themselves.

➡ Artificial 'tourist offices' that are actually dodgy travel agencies whose aim is to sell you overpriced tours, tickets and tourist services.

the first night), and request a hotel pick-up. You'll often hear stories about hotels of your choice being 'full' or 'closed' – check things out yourself. Reconfirm and double-check your booking the day before you arrive.

➡ Be very sceptical of phrases like 'my brother's shop' and 'special deal at my friend's place'. Many fraudsters operate in collusion with souvenir stalls, so be careful while making expensive purchases in private stores.

➡ Avoid friendly people and 'officials' in train and bus stations who offer unsolicited help, then guide you to a commission-paying travel agent. Look confident, and if anyone asks if this is your first trip to India, say you've been here several times, even if you haven't. Telling touts that you have already prepaid your transfer/tour/onward journey may help dissuade them.

Transport Scams

➡ Upon arriving at train stations and airports, if you haven't prearranged pick-up, book transport from government-approved booths. All major airports now have radio cab, prepaid taxi and

airport shuttle bus counters in the arrival lounge. Never go with a loitering cabbie who offers you a cheap ride into town, especially at night.

➡ While booking multiday sightseeing tours, stick to itineraries offered by tourism departments, or those that come recommended either in this guidebook or by friends who've personally used them. Be extremely wary of anyone in Delhi offering houseboat tours to Kashmir – we've received many complaints over the years about dodgy deals.

➡ When buying a bus, train or plane ticket anywhere other than the registered office of the transport company, make sure you're getting the ticket class you paid for. Use official online booking facilities where possible.

➡ Some tricksters pose as Indian Railways officials and insist you pay to have your e-ticket validated on the platform; ignore them.

➡ Train station touts (even in uniform or with 'official' badges) may tell you that your intended train is cancelled/ flooded/broken down or that your ticket is invalid. Do not respond to any 'official' approaches at train stations.

Women & Solo Travellers

There are extra considerations for women and solo travellers when visiting India – from cost to safety. As with anywhere else in the world, it pays to be prepared.

Women Travellers

Although Bollywood might suggest otherwise, India remains a conservative society. Female travellers should be aware that their behaviour and attire choice are likely to be under constant scrutiny.

Unwanted Attention

Unwanted attention from men is a common problem.

➡ Be prepared to be stared at; it's something you'll simply have to live with, so don't allow it to get the better of you.

➡ Refrain from returning male stares; this can be considered encouragement.

➡ Dark glasses, phones, books or electronic tablets are useful props for averting unwanted conversations.

Clothing

Avoiding culturally inappropriate clothing will help avert undesirable attention.

➡ Steer clear of sleeveless tops, shorts, short skirts (ankle-length skirts are recommended) and anything else that's skimpy, see-through or tight-fitting.

➡ Wearing Indian-style clothes is viewed favourably.

➡ Draping a dupatta (long scarf) over T-shirts is another good way to avoid stares – it's shorthand for modesty, and also handy if you visit a shrine that requires your head to be covered.

➡ Wearing a *salwar kameez* (traditional dresslike tunic and trousers) will help you blend in; a smart alternative is a kurta (long shirt) worn over jeans or trousers.

➡ Avoid going out in public wearing a choli (sari blouse) or a sari petticoat (which some foreign women mistake for a skirt); it's like strutting around half-dressed.

➡ Aside from at pools, many Indian women wear long shorts and a T-shirt when swimming in public view; it's wise to wear a sarong from the beach to your hotel.

Health & Hygiene

➡ Sanitary pads are widely available but tampons are usually restricted to pharmacies in big cities and tourist towns (even then, the choice may be limited). Carry additional stocks for travel off the beaten track.

Sexual Harassment

Many female travellers have reported some form of sexual harassment while in India, such as lewd comments, invasion of privacy and even groping. Serious sexual assaults do happen but are rare; follow similar safety precautions as you would at home.

➡ Women travellers have experienced provocative gestures, jeering, getting 'accidentally' bumped into on the street and being followed.

➡ Incidents are common at exuberant (and crowded) public events such as the Holi festival. If a crowd is gathering, make yourself scarce or find a safer place overlooking the event so that you're away from wandering hands.

➡ Women travelling with a male partner will receive far less hassle.

Staying Safe

The following tips will help you avoid uncomfortable or dangerous situations during your journey:

➡ Always be aware of your surroundings. If it feels wrong, trust your instincts. Tread with care. Don't be scared, but don't be reckless either.

➡ If travelling after 9pm, use a recommended, registered taxi service.

➡ Don't organise your travel in such a way that means you're hanging out at bus/train stations or arriving late at night. Arrive in towns before dark.

➡ Keep conversations with unknown men short – getting involved in an inane conversation with someone you barely know can be misinterpreted as a sign of sexual interest.

→ Some women wear a pseudo wedding ring, or announce early on in the conversation that they're married or engaged (regardless of the reality).

→ If you feel that a guy is encroaching on your space, he probably is. A firm request to keep away usually does the trick, especially if your tone is loud and curt enough to draw the attention of passers-by.

→ The silent treatment can also be very effective.

→ Follow local women's cues and instead of shaking hands say namaste – the traditional, respectful Hindu greeting.

→ Avoid wearing expensive-looking jewellery and carrying flashy accessories.

→ Check the reputation of any teacher or therapist before going to a solo session (get recommendations from travellers). Some women have reported being molested by masseurs and other therapists. If you feel uneasy at any time, leave.

→ Female filmgoers may attract less attention and lessen the chances of harassment by going to the cinema with a companion.

→ Lone women may want to invest in a good-quality hotel in a better neighbourhood.

→ At hotels keep your door locked, as staff (particularly at budget and midrange places) can knock and walk in without waiting for your permission.

→ Avoid wandering alone in isolated areas even during daylight. Steer clear of gallis (narrow lanes) and deserted roads.

→ When on rickshaws alone, call/text someone, or pretend to, to indicate someone knows where you are.

→ Act confidently in public; to avoid looking lost (and thus more vulnerable) consult maps at your hotel (or at a restaurant) rather than on the street.

Taxis & Public Transport

Being female has some advantages; women can usually queue-jump for buses and trains without consequence and on trains there are special ladies-only carriages. There are also women-only waiting rooms at some stations.

→ Solo women should prearrange an airport pick-up from their hotel, especially if their flight is scheduled to arrive after dark.

→ Delhi and some other cities have licensed prepaid radio cab services such as Easycabs – they're more expensive than the regular prepaid taxis, but promote themselves as being safe, with drivers who have been vetted as part of their recruitment.

→ If you do catch a regular prepaid taxi, make a point of writing down the registration and driver's name – in front of the driver – and giving it to one of the airport police.

→ Avoid taking taxis alone late at night and never agree to have more than one man (the driver) in the car – ignore claims that this is 'just my brother' etc.

→ Solo women have reported less hassle by choosing more expensive classes on trains.

→ If you're travelling overnight in a three-tier carriage, try to get the uppermost berth, which will give you more privacy (and distance from potential gropers).

→ On public transport, don't hesitate to return any errant limbs, put an item of luggage between you and others, be vocal (attracting public attention, thus shaming the pest), or simply find a new spot.

Solo Travellers

One of the joys of travelling solo in India is that you're more likely to be 'adopted' by families, especially if you're commuting together on a long rail journey. It's a great opportunity to make friends and get a deeper understanding of local culture. If you're keen to hook up with fellow travellers, tourist hubs such as Goa, Rajasthan, Kerala, Manali, McLeod Ganj, Leh, Agra and Varanasi are some popular places to do so. You may also be able to find travel companions on Lonely Planet's **Thorn Tree Travel Forum** (www.lonelyplanet.com/thorntree).

Cost

The most significant issue facing solo travellers is cost.

→ Single-room accommodation rates are sometimes not much lower than double rates.

→ Some midrange and top-end places don't even offer a single tariff.

→ It's always worth trying to negotiate a lower rate for single occupancy.

Safety

Most solo travellers experience no major problems in India but, like anywhere else, it's wise to stay on your toes in unfamiliar surroundings.

→ Some less honourable souls (locals and travellers alike) view lone tourists as an easy target for theft and sexual assault.

→ Single men wandering around isolated areas have been mugged, even during the day.

Transport

→ You'll save money if you find others to share taxis and autorickshaws, as well as when hiring a car for longer trips.

→ Solo bus travellers may be able to get the 'co-pilot' (near the driver) seat on buses, which not only has a good view out front, but is also handy if you've got a big bag.

Directory A–Z

Accommodation

Goa's accommodation ranges from basic beach huts to opulent five-star resorts and boutique-hotel havens.

Budget

➡ **Beach Huts** The quintessential Goan accommodation experience is the beach hut, also sometimes known locally as 'coco-huts' or 'treehouses' (if on stilts). These range from basic bamboo and palm thatch to more sophisticated midrange and even top-end versions. They're most commonly found at Arambol, Mandrem, Aswem, Agonda, Palolem and Patnem.

➡ Costs vary widely from ₹600 to ₹6000 a night: the better it looks, the further away from the neighbours it is, and the closer to the beach, the more it costs. Most have a verandah or balcony, fan and private bathroom with sit-down toilet and cold-water shower.

➡ To browse and book beach huts in South Goa, see www. beachhutbookings.com

➡ **Budget Guesthouses** No-frills, fan-cooled rooms set back from the beach, found all along the coast and in cities such as Panaji and Margao. Only the very cheapest places have shared bathroom.

➡ **Hostels** These are a small but growing option and a good deal for solo travellers. Clean dorms with free wi-fi, lockers, bed lights, breakfast, fully-equipped kitchen and a good chance of meeting other travellers. The best are found in Anjuna, Vagator, Panaji and Morjim.

➡ **Rooms & Houses to Let** Those staying in one place from a week to six months should consider renting a local house or room(s) in a house. These can start at ₹1000 to ₹3000 per week depending on condition, length of rental, location and time of year. Signs (with a phone number) are common around places such as Anjuna, Chapora and Benaulim but there are rooms available all along the coastal belt. Get in early (before November) for the best deals.

Midrange

➡ **Hotels & Guesthouses** In the midrange category hotels will come with TV, private bathroom, balcony or verandah, optional air-conditioning, free wi-fi, usually an attached restaurant and services such as travel desk, housekeeping etc.

➡ **Apartments** A more upmarket version of local houses to let, modern serviced and unserviced apartments are available for stays from a week to several months. Some include swimming pool and security. Check sites such as www. goaholidayhomes.com, or www.goarooms.in

Top End

➡ **Heritage & Boutique Hotels** The stand-out accommodation option in Goa is the range of heritage properties, often housed in restored Portuguese homes. In a similar category are boutique hotels and luxury high-class places, often with just a few rooms.

➡ **Resorts** These include four- or five-star beachfront

ACCOMMODATION PRICE RANGES

The following price ranges refer to a double room with bathroom in high (November to February) but not peak (Christmas and New Year) season. In this guide, we've listed reviews from budget to top end and by author preference within each category.

	Goa	Mumbai
$	<₹1200	<₹2500
$$	₹1200–5000	₹2500–6000
$$$	>₹5000	>₹6000

BOOK YOUR STAY ONLINE

For more accommodation reviews by Lonely Planet authors, check out www.lonelyplanet.com/hotels. You'll find independent reviews, as well as recommendations on the best places to stay. Best of all, you can book online.

properties with swimming pools, spas, high-end restaurants, first-class service and sometimes tennis courts or golf courses. You will also find the occasional luxury tent encampment or fabulously equipped private villa in this price range.

Costs & Taxes

➡ Unless otherwise stated, prices are for the high season (mid-October to February) but not the peak (between Christmas and New Year) season.

➡ Outside high season, count on discounts of between 25% and 60% on hotels and guesthouses that remain open.

➡ During the peak Christmas season expect high-season prices to double or even triple.

➡ There's a government 'luxury' tax of 5% on rooms over ₹500, 8% on rooms over ₹2000 and 12% for rooms over ₹5000. For most budget places, the quoted prices include this tax, but at midrange and top-end hotels, expect the tax to be added to the quoted rates.

➡ Many midrange and top-end hotels add their own additional 10% 'service tax' and sometimes even more – up to 20% in the fanciest five-star places.

Customs Regulations

➡ Duty-free allowance is 2L of wine or spirits and 200 cigarettes (or 50 cigars, or 250g of tobacco) per person.

➡ Foreign currency totalling more than US$10,000 must be declared.

➡ It's illegal to take Indian rupees out of the country. This is rarely, if ever, policed but exchange bureaux at the airport like to exploit this law.

➡ Antiques more than 100 years old are not permitted to be exported from India without an export clearance certificate. See the Central Board of Excise and Customs website (www.cbec.gov.in) for more information.

Electricity

➡ There are two sizes of electricity socket in Goa: one large, one small (the small is more common).

➡ European round-pin plugs will loosely go into the smaller sockets.

➡ Universal adaptors are widely available at electrical shops in Goa.

➡ Electricity in Goa can be unpredictable and power cuts are frequent.

230V/50Hz

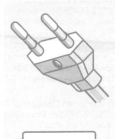

230V/50Hz

Embassies & Consulates

Australian Consulate (10th fl, A Wing, Crescenzo Bldg, G Block, Plot C 38-39, Bandra Kurla Complex, Mumbai)

British Deputy High Commission (☑022-66502222; Naman Chambers, C/32 G Block Bandra Kurla Complex, Bandra East, Mumbai)

Canadian Consulate (☑022-67494444; 6th fl, Fort House, 221 Dr DN Rd, Mumbai)

French Consulate (☑022-66694000; 7th fl, Hoechst House, Nariman Point, Mumbai)

German Consulate (Map p82;☑0832-2235526; Ourem Rd, Panaji) German consulate in Goa's capital. There's also a consulate in Mumbai (☑022-22832422; 10th fl, Hoechst House, Nariman Point, Mumbai).

Israeli Consulate (☑022-61600500; Marathon Futurex, 1301, A Wing, N M Joshi Marg, Lower Parel, Mumbai)

Italian Consulate (☑022-23804071; Kanchanjunga, 1st fl, 72G Deshmukh Marg, Kemp's Corner, Mumbai)

Japanese Consulate (☑022-23517101; 1 ML Dahanukar Marg, Cumballa Hill, Mumbai)

Malaysian Consulate
(☑022-26455751/2; Notan Plaza, 4th fl, Turner Rd, Bandra West, Mumbai)

Maldivian Honorary Consulate (☑022-22078041; 212A Maker Bhawan No 3, New Marine Lines, Churchgate, Mumbai)

Netherlands Consulate (☑022-22194200; Forbes Bldg, Home St, Fort, Mumbai)

New Zealand Consulate (☑022-61316666; Level 2, Maker Maxity, 3 North Ave, Bandra Kurla Complex, Mumbai)

Russian Consulate (☑022-23633627; www.russiaconsulmumbai.mid.ru; 42 L Jagmohandas Marg, Mumbai)

Singapore Consulate (☑022-22043205; Maker Chambers IV, 10th fl, 222 Jamnalal Bajaj Rd, Nariman Point, Mumbai)

South African Consulate (☑022-23513725; Gandhi Mansion, 20 Altamount Rd, Cumballa Hill, Mumbai)

Sri Lankan Consulate (☑022-22045861; Mulla House, 34 Homi Modi St, Fort, Mumbai)

Swiss Consulate (☑022-22884563-65; 102 Maker Chambers IV, 10th fl, 222 Jamnalal Bajaj Marg, Nariman Point, Mumbai)

Thai Consulate (☑022-22823535; Dalamal House, 1st fl, Jamnalal Bajaj Marg, Nariman Point, Mumbai)

US Consulate (☑022-26724000; C49, G Block, Bandra Kurla Complex, Mumbai)

FOOD PRICE RANGES

The following price ranges refer to a standard main course.

$ less than ₹150

$$ ₹150–250

$$$ more than ₹250

Gay & Lesbian Travellers

➤ Homosexuality was ruled illegal by India's Supreme Court in 2013, overturning a previous decision to decriminalise it in 2009.

➤ Gay and lesbian visitors should be discreet. Public displays of affection are frowned upon for both homosexual and heterosexual couples.

➤ Goa's liberal reputation draws gay men, and there's a discreet scene, mainly around the Calangute/Baga and Candolim area.

➤ Mumbai's LGBTQ scene is understandably underground, but it's gaining momentum.

Publications & Websites

➤ *Time Out Mumbai* (₹50) Gay events in Mumbai.

➤ **Humsafar Trust** (☑022-26673800; www.humsafar.org; 3rd fl, Manthan Plaza Nehru Rd, Vakola, Santa Cruz East) Gay and transgender advocacy, support groups and events in Mumbai.

➤ **Gay Bombay** (www.gaybombay.org) Lists gay events and offers support and advice.

➤ **Queer Azaadi Mumbai** (www.queerazaadi.wordpress.com)

Insurance

Comprehensive travel insurance to cover theft, loss and medical problems (as well as air evacuation) is strongly recommended.

➤ Some policies exclude potentially dangerous activities such as scuba diving, motorcycling, paragliding and even trekking: read the fine print.

➤ If you plan to hire a motorcycle in India, make sure the rental policy includes at least third-party insurance.

➤ Check in advance whether your insurance policy will pay doctors and hospitals directly or reimburse you later.

➤ It's crucial to get a police report in India as soon as possible if you've had anything stolen; insurance companies may refuse to reimburse you without one.

➤ Worldwide travel insurance is available at www.lonelyplanet.com/bookings. You can buy, extend and claim online anytime – even if you're already on the road.

Internet Access

➤ Internet and email services in Goa are reasonably plentiful, reliable and relatively cheap. Internet charges are around ₹40 per hour, usually with a minimum of 15 minutes (₹10 to ₹15).

➤ Free wi-fi is becoming common in cafes, beach shacks and accommodation; ask before booking.

➤ USB dongles (modems) for 2G/3G internet connections direct to your laptop are available at mobile-phone shops.

➤ If you have a smart phone with a local SIM and data plan, you can use this as a personal hotspot modem with your laptop computer or tablet.

Legal Matters

It's important to realise what your own embassy can and can't do to help you if you get into trouble. Generally it won't be much help if the trouble you're in is your own fault. Your embassy will not be sympathetic if you end up in jail after committing a crime locally, even if such actions are legal in your own country.

PRACTICALITIES

Newspapers & Magazines Goa has three English-language dailies: the *Herald* (www.oheraldo.in), the *Navhind Times* (www.navhindtimes.in) and the local version of the *Times of India* (http://timesofindia.indiatimes.com), along with the weekly *Goan on Saturday* (www.thegoan.net). Local magazines include *Planet Goa* (www.planetgoaonline.com), lifestyle mag *Viva Goa* (www.vivagoamagazine.com) and *Goa Streets* (www.goastreets.com).

Radio All India Radio (AIR; www.airpanaji.gov.in) transmits local and international news. There are several private FM broadcasters and music stations.

TV The government TV broadcaster is Doordarshan. Satellite TV, which has BBC World, CNN, Star World and Star Movies, MTV, VH1 and HBO, is widely available at hotels.

Weights & Measures Although India officially uses the metric system, imperial weights and measures are still sometimes used. You may hear the term lakh (100,000) and crore (10 million) referring to rupees, people or anything else in large numbers.

Drugs

Drugs of various types are still readily available in Goa, but drug laws in India are among the toughest in the world; possession of even a relatively small amount of *charas* (hashish; 10g or so) can lead to a *minimum* 10 years in jail and a ₹100,000 fine. Fort Aguada jail houses a number of prisoners, including Westerners, who are serving drug-related sentences. Be aware that you may be held in jail (without the possibility of bail) on drug-related charges before going to trial. These pretrial stays can be lengthy.

Police

Police corruption can be a problem in Goa, with drug use among travellers giving some poorly paid police officers opportunities for extortion, but the local Goan government has worked hard at stamping out this practice in recent years.

Probably the best way to deal with police extortion, should it happen to you, is through polite, respectful persuasion. If that fails, attempt to bargain down the 'fine' before paying up, and try to establish the identity (or at least a good mental image) of the police officer.

In practical terms, the most contact the average traveller is likely to have with the law will be on the road. You may be unlucky enough to be flagged down for not wearing a helmet on certain parts of the NH66, or checked for papers by an opportunistic police officer who is hoping to extract a 'fine'. If this happens, keep your cool and you may be able to negotiate the fine down to zero.

Smoking & Spitting

On 1 January 2000, a law came into force in Goa banning smoking, spitting and chewing tobacco in all public places. It was a welcome move, but has proven impossible to enforce except in government buildings and places such as railway stations, where transgressors face a ₹1000 fine. Smoking is banned in many, but not all, restaurants; open-air beach shacks are okay with (cigarette) smoking.

Money

The Indian rupee (₹) is divided into 100 paise but you'll rarely see a paise coin. Coins come in denominations of ₹1, ₹2, ₹5 and ₹10; notes come in denominations of ₹10, ₹20, ₹50, ₹100, ₹500 and ₹1000.

ATMs

➡ There are many 24-hour ATMs in Goa, particularly in the cities of Panaji, Margao and Mapusa, but also in villages and smaller beach resorts such as Agonda, Palolem and Arambol.

➡ ATMs linked to Axis Bank, Citibank, HDFC, HSBC, ICICI and State Bank of India recognise foreign cards (Cirrus and Maestro). Other banks may accept major cards (Visa, MasterCard etc).

➡ Check with your home bank about foreign ATM charges. You'll often be charged for transactions at both ends, so it pays to withdraw as much cash as possible, rather than making lots of small withdrawals.

➡ ATMs dispense mostly ₹500 and ₹1000 notes, which can be difficult to change for small purchases. Most banks have a limit of ₹10,000 to ₹15,000 per transaction.

➡ Some 'remote' beach or inland destinations still require a trek to find an ATM, so you'll need to bring cash along with you.

Cash

➡ It pays to carry some US dollars, pounds sterling or euros tucked away for emergencies or for times when you can't find an ATM.

➡ The best exchange rates are usually at Thomas Cook and the State Bank of India, while next best are private moneychangers. Hotels offer the least attractive rates.

AN IMPORTANT NOTE ON COSTS

With an inflation rate running at around 11% annually – slightly above the national average – costs in Goa are rising quickly. Accommodation prices in Goa fluctuate with supply and demand but expect them to rise year on year. Food, transport and petrol prices are also subject to inflation.

Credit Cards

➡ Credit cards are accepted only in upmarket hotels and restaurants, most travel agencies and higher-end stores.

➡ MasterCard and Visa are the most widely accepted credit cards.

Encashment Certificates

➡ With every exchange transaction you are supposed to be provided with an encashment certificate, which can be useful if you want to change excess rupees back to hard currency, buy a tourist-quota train ticket or if you need to show a tax clearance certificate.

➡ ATM receipts serve the same purpose, so hold on to them.

International Transfers

International money transfers can be arranged through Thomas Cook or Western Union; both have branches in Panaji and some of the larger towns in Goa. Western Union transfers can also frequently be made at post offices.

Tipping

➡ There's no official policy on tipping in India, though it's always appreciated: 10% of a bill is acceptable.

➡ In five-star international hotels, tipping hotel porters and maids is the norm (at least ₹50).

➡ Low-paid hospitality staff, including waiters and bar staff, expect a tip from tourists more so than elsewhere in India, even at beach shacks.

➡ Taxi drivers don't need to be tipped for short trips, but if you've hired the driver for the day, adding 10% is fair.

➡ Baksheesh is a form of tipping in India, generally defined as a small gratuity paid to someone in order to have a little extra service delivered, or to pay someone off for turning a blind eye (authorities, guards etc).

Post

The Indian postal service (www.indiapost.gov.in), though massive, is pretty good. Letters sent from Goa and Mumbai almost invariably reach their destination.

It costs ₹12 to send a small postcard anywhere in the world from India, and ₹25 for a large postcard or a standard letter (up to 20g).

Sending Parcels

➡ All parcels sent through the government postal service must be packed up in white linen and the seams sealed with wax – agents outside the post office will offer this tailoring service for a small fee.

➡ Customs declaration forms, available from the post office, must be stitched or pasted to the parcel. No duty is payable by the recipient for gifts under the value of ₹1000.

➡ Book packages (up to 5kg) can be sent without a customs form for ₹350. They will need to be wrapped in a manner that allows the contents to be seen by postal inspectors.

➡ Parcel post has a maximum of 20kg to 30kg depending on the destination. Airmail takes one to three weeks, sea mail two to four months and Surface Air-Lifted (SAL) – a curious hybrid where parcels travel by both air and sea – around one month.

Public Holidays

In addition to the public holidays listed below, a number of festivals and events (p18) are celebrated throughout the region at various times of year.

Republic Day 26 January

Good Friday (Easter) March/April

Buddha Jayanti April/May

May Day 1 May

Independence Day 15 August

Gandhi Jayanti 2 October

Guru Nanak Jayanti November

Feast of St Francis Xavier 3 December

Goa Liberation Day 19 December

Christmas 25 December

Safe Travel

Goa is generally a safe place to travel but it is not without its dangers, including swimming in the Arabian Sea and riding a motorcycle on pot-holed roads.

From time to time there are reports of 'date rape' or theft-related druggings, usually in busy, trendy tourist bars. Be wary, though not terrified, of accepting food or drinks from strangers or even new friends.

There have also been incidents of attacks on women. See p224. Some measures have been introduced, such as limited street lighting and security patrols on some beaches, but it's still not a good idea for women – or men, for that matter – to wander alone at night, especially on the beach or quiet backstreets.

Goa is not as bad for traveller-oriented scams as

many places in India (hello Agra and Varanasi!), but they do exist. See p222.

Tips for Safe Travel

While the majority of travellers in Goa will have no serious problems, tourists have occasionally been the target of theft or assault. There are some common-sense steps you can take to minimise the risk:

➡ Don't open the door to someone you don't know. Leave windows and doors locked when you're sleeping and when you're out.

➡ Don't leave valuables – cameras, phones, passports, cash etc – in your room. If you're staying in a hotel, guesthouse, beach hut or rented home where there is a safe or similar lockable facility, use it.

➡ Avoid quiet, poorly lit streets or lanes – take the longer way if it's brighter and more populated, and walk with confidence and purpose. Better still, catch a taxi or autorickshaw after dark.

➡ If you are being sexually harassed on public transport, embarrass the culprit by loudly complaining, and report them to the conductor or driver.

➡ As tempting as it is to stare someone down, women should just ignore stares. Dark or reflective glasses can help.

Telephone

Local and long-distance telephone calls can be made from private call offices (labelled PCO/ISD/STD) or from internet cafes using Skype, VOIP or similar, but most travellers take their mobile phone and get hooked up to a local network.

Mobile Phones

Any unlocked GSM phone will work fine in Goa and most parts of India but expensive international roaming charges (for making and receiving

calls) mean a better option is to buy a local SIM card and connect to a local carrier.

➡ Popular and reliable prepaid carriers in Goa include Airtel and Vodafone, though you'll also find !dea, Tata Docomo, Aircel and BSNL.

➡ To buy a SIM card go to any shop or travel agent advertising your preferred carrier (they're everywhere) and look at the prepaid call and data plans on offer.

➡ Foreigners need two passport photos, photocopies of passport identity and visa pages and preferrably a copy of a driving licence or similar with your home address (the phone shop can sometimes do the photocopies for you).

➡ You must also supply a residential address, which can be the address of your hotel or a local friend. Usually the phone company will call your hotel (notify reception in advance) any time up to 24 hours after your application to verify that you are staying there.

➡ At some outlets tourists can pay extra (around ₹700) and bypass the paperwork and activation period but the validation is usually limited to 30 days.

➡ Prepaid mobile-phone kits (SIM card and phone number, plus an allocation of calls) are available from about ₹200, while internet data allowance costs around ₹300 for 1GB. Once activated, you can easily top up talk-time and data at any store advertising your carrier.

➡ Local (India-wide) call costs from Goa are less than ₹1 a minute, and international calls are less than ₹10 a minute.

Time

India is 5½ hours ahead of GMT/UTC, 4½ hours behind Australia (EST) and 10½ hours ahead of the USA

(EST). It is officially known as IST – Indian Standard Time, although many Indians prefer to think it stands for Indian Stretchable Time. There's no daylight saving time.

Tourist Information

Goa Tourism Development Corporation (Goa Tourism, GTDC; Map p82; ☎0832-2437132; www.goa-tourism.com; Paryatan Bhavan, Dr Alvaro Costa Rd, Panaji; ⏱9.30am-5.45pm Mon-Sat) State government tourism body.

Government of India Tourist Office (Map p82; ☎0832-2223412; www.incredibleindia.com; Communidade Bldg, Church Sq, Panaji; ⏱9.30am-1.30pm & 2.30-6pm Mon-Fri, 10am-1pm Sat) Office of India Tourism.

Travellers with Disabilities

There are few provisions for travellers with disabilities in Goa outside of the most top-end hotels, and thus the mobility-impaired traveller will face a number of challenges. Few older buildings have wheelchair access; toilets have certainly not been designed to accommodate wheelchairs; and footpaths are often riddled with potholes and crevices. If your mobility is restricted you will need an able-bodied companion to accompany you, and you'd be well-advised to hire a private vehicle with a driver.

Resources

Disability Rights Association of Goa (DRAG; Map p82; ☎0832-2427160; www.disabilitygoa.org; Opp Head Post Office, Panaji, c/o Star Investments) This Panaji-based rights and advocacy group is a useful resource for people with disabilities.

Disability Rights UK (☎+44 (0)20-7250 8181; www.disabilityrightsuk.org; 49-51

East Rd, London N1 6AH) Travel information and support group.

Mobility International USA (MIUSA; ☑541-3431284; www.miusa.org; Ste 343, 132 E Broadway, Eugene, OR 97440, USA) Disbility information and support for travellers.

Visas

Almost everyone, except nationals of Nepal and Bhutan, needs a visa before arriving in India. Note that your passport should be valid for at least six months beyond your intended stay, and have two blank pages.

Visa on Arrival

Citizens of more than 70 countries are currently able to apply for a 30-day single-entry visa on arrival (VOA) at Bengaluru (Bangalore), Chennai (Madras), Kochi (Cochin), Delhi, Goa, Hyderabad, Kolkata, Mumbai (Bombay) and Trivandrum airports.

These countries include: Australia, Brazil, Cambodia, Cook Islands, Djibouti, Fiji, Finland, Germany, Guyana, Indonesia, Israel, Japan, Jordan, Kenya, Kiribati, Laos, Luxembourg, Marshall Islands, Mauritius, Mexico, Micronesia, Myanmar, Nauru, New Zealand, Niue Island, Norway, Oman, Palau, Palestinian Territories, Papua New Guinea, Philippines, Republic of Korea, Russia, Samoa, Singapore, Solomon Islands, Thailand, Tonga, Tuvalu, UAE, Ukraine, USA, Vanuatu, and Vietnam. It's intended that the scheme will be rolled out to 180 nations, including the UK and China, so check online for any updates.

To participate in the scheme, you need to apply online at https://indian-visaonline.gov.in for an Electronic Travel Authority (ETA), a minimum/maximum four/30 days before you are due to travel. The fee is US$60, and you have to upload a photograph as well

as a copy of your passport. Travellers have reported being asked for documentation showing their hotel confirmation at the airport, though this is not specified on the VOA website. The VOA is valid from the date of arrival.

Other Visa Types

If you want to stay longer than 30 days, or are not covered by the VOA scheme, you must obtain a visa before arriving in India (apart from Nepali or Bhutanese citizens). Visas are available at Indian missions worldwide, though in many countries, applications are processed by a separate private company. In some countries, including the UK, you must apply in person at the designated office as well as filing an application online.

Note that your passport needs to be valid for at least six months beyond your intended stay in India, with at least two blank pages. Most people are issued with a standard six-month tourist visa, which for most nationalities permits multiple entry. Tourist visas are valid from the date of issue, not the date you arrive in India. Student and business visas have strict conditions (consult the Indian embassy for details).

Five- and 10-year tourist visas are available to US citizens only under a bilateral arrangement; however, you can still only stay in the country for up to 180 days continuously. Currently you are required to submit two passport photographs with your visa application; these must be in colour and must be 5.08cm by 5.08 cm (2in by 2in; larger than regular passport photos). An onward travel ticket is a requirement for some visas, but this isn't always enforced (check in advance).

Additional restrictions apply to travellers from Bangladesh and Pakistan, as well as certain Eastern European, African and Central Asian

countries. Check any special conditions for your nationality with the Indian embassy in your country. Visas are priced in the local currency and may have an added service fee. Extended visas are possible for people of Indian origin (excluding those in Pakistan and Bangladesh) who hold a non-Indian passport and live abroad.

For visas lasting more than six months, you're supposed to register at the **Foreigners' Regional Registration Office** (FRRO; ☑011-26711443; frrodil@nic.in; Level 2, East Block 8, Sector 1, Rama Krishna (RK) Puram, Delhi; h9.30am-3pm Mon-Fri) in Delhi within 14 days of arriving in India; enquire about these special conditions when you apply for your visa.

Visa Extensions

Officially, you can only get another six-month tourist visa by leaving the country and coming back in on a new visa, and many long-term travellers head off on a quick 'visa run' to Sri Lanka, Nepal or home, to replenish their tourist visa. Business and employment visas can be extended in Goa, but not tourist visas.

Visa Registration

People travelling on tourist visas are not required to register with the Foreigners' Regional Registration Office (FRRO); the form that you fill out each time you check into a hotel, beach hut or guest house takes the place of this. Only foreigners with visas valid for longer than 180 days are officially required to register, as are nationals of Pakistan and Afghanistan. For more information, see the Bureau of Immigration website at http://boi.gov.in.

FRRO Goa (Map p82; ☑0832-2428623; Police Headquarters Bldg, opp Azad Maidan, Panaji; ⏱9.30am-1pm & 2-5.30pm) Register here if your visa is for longer than 180 days.

Transport

GETTING THERE & AWAY

Entering Goa

Unless you're on a charter flight, getting to Goa requires flying in to one of India's major international gateways – Mumbai (Bombay), Chennai or Delhi – and taking a connecting flight or overland transport from there. Once in India, you can enter Goa with no border restrictions.

Air

Airports & Airlines

INTERNATIONAL FLIGHTS

➡ Mumbai's **Chhatrapati Shivaji International Airport** (☎022-66851010; www.csia.in) is India's second busiest after Delhi and the usual entry point for noncharter flight passengers coming to Goa. If you're flying in from the east (Southeast Asia or Australasia), Chennai and Kochi are good entry points.

➡ Goa's only airport is the small and newly refurbished **Dabolim Airport** (DABOLIM, Goa International Airport; ☎0832-2540806), around 30km from Goa's capital, Panaji. Somewhat controversial plans are under consideration to build a second airport at Mopa in the state's north.

➡ A handful of charter companies operate seasonal international flights directly into Dabolim Airport, most from the UK, Germany and Russia. Aeroflot, Finnair, Etihad, Air Arabia and Novair also fly in Russian and Scandinavian package holidaymakers who make up some 40% of Goa's annual international visitors.

DOMESTIC FLIGHTS

Several budget airlines, along with the national carrier **Air India** (☎27580777, airport 28318666; www.airindia.com; Air India Bldg, cnr Marine Dr & Madame Cama Rd, Nariman Point; ⊙9.30am-6.30pm Mon-Fri, to 5.15pm Sat & Sun), operate direct daily flights between Goa and Mumbai, Chennai, Delhi, Bangalore, Hyderabad and several other cities. A return flight to Mumbai with a low-cost carrier such as SpiceJet can cost as little as US$70 if booked a few weeks in advance. You can book online directly with the airline or through a booking site.

Dabolim's arrivals hall has currency exchange, ATMs and a prepaid taxi counter.

Domestic airlines flying into and out of Goa:

GoAir (☎092-23222111; www.goair.in)

Indigo (☎call centre 0 99 10383838; book.goindigo.in)

Jet Airways (☎022-39893333; www.jetairways.com; B1, Amarchand Mansion, Madam Cama Rd, Colaba; ⊙9am-6pm Mon-Sat)

SpiceJet (☎airport 0987-1803333; www.spicejet.com)

CLIMATE CHANGE & TRAVEL

Every form of transport that relies on carbon-based fuel generates CO_2, the main cause of human-induced climate change. Modern travel is dependent on aeroplanes, which might use less fuel per kilometre per person than most cars but travel much greater distances. The altitude at which aircraft emit gases (including CO_2) and particles also contributes to their climate change impact. Many websites offer 'carbon calculators' that allow people to estimate the carbon emissions generated by their journey and, for those who wish to do so, to offset the impact of the greenhouse gases emitted with contributions to portfolios of climate-friendly initiatives throughout the world. Lonely Planet offsets the carbon footprint of all staff and author travel.

CHARTER FLIGHTS TO GOA

Reliable charter flights into Goa from the UK or Germany:

Thomson Airlines (☑0203-4512688; www.thomsonfly.com)

Monarch Airlines (☑0333-0030100; www.monarch.co.uk)

Condor Airlines (www.condor.com)

Thomas Cook Airlines (www.thomascookairlines.com)

Land

Car

Hiring a self-drive car in any major Indian city and driving to Goa is possible, but given the dangers of the roads and the high cost, this sort of a rental isn't particularly recommended.

A better choice is to make your way to the nearest taxi rank and start bargaining. Most drivers will happily charter their services for a day or even longer. The 600km trip from Mumbai to Goa takes about 14 hours; many drivers will happily do this in one stretch. You'll have to pay for the taxi's return trip, so the cost will be at least ₹15,000. Even if you're part of a group, it's quicker, cheaper and less stressful to fly or take the train in to Goa from any other city.

Bus

➡ Private and state-run long-distance buses run to and from Goa daily, and in many cases you can simply turn up at the bus station and jump on the next available bus.

➡ For more comfortable VIP, air-con or sleeper buses you may need to book ahead, especially in peak season. You can do this directly at the bus station, through a travel agent or online through a booking agency.

➡ State-run and private companies offer 'ordinary', 'deluxe', 'superfast' and VIP services, but definitions are flexible. The most comfortable are the Volvo buses with reclining seating and air-conditioning.

➡ Many long-distance buses travel overnight – bring earplugs if you want to block out the Bollywood movies on the video screens.

➡ On some routes such as Goa–Mumbai and Goa–Hampi, flat-berth sleeper buses are available. While these can be comfortable, bus travel is not like train travel – you might wake to find yourself flying out of bed on the first sharp corner.

➡ Travel into and out of Mumbai's city traffic is interminably slow.

➡ Online booking agencies include **Kadamba** (www.goakadamba.com), **Make My Trip** (www.makemytrip.com), **Paulo Travels** (☑0832-6637777; www.phmgoa.com), **Red Bus** (www.redbus.in).

INTERSTATE BUSES

Buses for Mumbai and other cities depart from Panaji, Margao and Mapusa daily.

Mumbai (₹350 to ₹1100, 12 to 14 hours)

Bengaluru (₹600 to ₹1200, 14 to 15 hours)

Hampi (private sleeper; ₹900 to ₹1100, 10 to 11 hours)

Pune (₹325 to ₹1000, 11 hours)

Train

The 760km-long **Konkan Railway**, completed in 1998, is the main train line running through the state, connecting Goa with Mumbai to the north, and Mangaluru (Mangalore) to the south.

➡ For services, fares and bookings check **Konkan Railway** (www.konkanrailway.com), **Indian Railways** (www.indianrail.gov.in; www.erail.in),

Cleartrip (www.cleartrip.com/trains) or **Makemytrip** (www.makemytrip.com/railways)

➡ Children under the age of five travel for free; those between five and 12 are charged half price.

➡ The main train stations in Goa are Madgaon station in Margao; Vasco da Gama; and Karmali station near Old Goa, 12km from Panaji.

➡ In-person train bookings are best made at Margao's station, at the train reservation office at Panaji's Kadamba bus stand or at any travel agent selling train tickets.

➡ Book as far in advance as possible for sleepers, as they fill up quickly, though a limited number of tickets go on sale the day before travel, so it's always worth checking. Reservation fees generally range from ₹40 to ₹60, or slightly more if booking through a travel agent.

➡ Even if there are no seats, passengers cancel and there are regular no-shows. Buying a ticket on the waiting list or as a 'Reservation Against Cancellation' (RAC) will usually get you a seat or sleeper berth.

➡ Other useful Goan railway stations (which not all interstate trains stop at) include Pernem for Arambol, Thivim for Mapusa, and Canacona for Palolem.

TRAIN CLASSES

There are several different classes, but not all are available on all trains. Sleeper berths are converted to bench seats by day.

AC First Class (1A) Air-con accommodation in simple two-berth or four-berth lockable compartments. Bedclothes and meals are provided.

AC 2 Tier (2AC) Two-tier berths arranged in groups of two and four-berth curtained compartments in an air-conditioned, open-plan carriage.

AC 3 Tier (3AC) Three-tier berths arranged in groups of six in an open-plan air-con carriage.

MAJOR TRAINS FROM MARGAO (MADGAON)

DESTINATION	TRAIN NO & NAME	FARE	DURATION (HOURS)	DEPARTURES
Mumbai (CST)	10112 Konkan Kanya Express	sleeper ₹390, 3AC ₹1055, 2AC ₹1250	12	6pm
	10104 Mandovi Express	sleeper ₹390, 3AC ₹1055, 2AC ₹1520	12	9.15am
Mumbai (Dadar)	12052 Jan Shatabdi Express	second sitting ₹197, AC chair ₹700	8½	2.50pm
Bangalore	02779 Vasco da Gama-SBC Link	sleeper ₹360, 3AC ₹970	15	3.50pm
Ernakulum (Kochi)	12618 Lakshadweep Express	sleeper ₹445, 3AC ₹1165, 2AC ₹1665	14½	7.20pm
Mangalore	12133 Mangalore Express	sleeper ₹290, 3AC ₹735, 2AC ₹1035	5½	7.10am
Pune	12779 Goa Express	sleeper ₹335, 3AC ₹930, 2AC ₹1315	12	3.50pm

First Class (FC) A non-AC version of AC First Class (1A).

AC Chair Car (CC) Air-con carriage with reclining seats.

Sleeper (SL) Similar to AC 3 Tier but without air-conditioning. Instead there are fans and open windows.

Second Sitting (2S) Unreserved second-class seating on plastic chairs or wooden benches.

GETTING AROUND

Bicycle

Goa offers plenty of variety for cycling, certainly in the village back lanes. A bicycle can also be a convenient and ecofriendly way of getting around beach towns.

➡ At most beach resorts in Goa you'll find people who will rent out a local, Indian-made, single-gear rattler, though mountain bikes are sometimes also available. Expect to pay around ₹50 to ₹100 per day.

➡ For a longer stay of three months or more in Goa, consider buying a bicycle locally. Basic Indian road bikes (including Hero, Atlas, BSA and Raleigh) are available at bicycle shops in cities from ₹3500 and mountain bikes from ₹4000. You should be able to pick up a second-hand bike for ₹1000 to ₹1500.

➡ If you want a quality machine for serious touring, bring your own, along with spare parts and accessories and a very strong bike lock.

Bus

➡ An extensive network of buses shuttle to and from almost every tiny town and village, though the main hubs are Panaji, Margao and Mapusa. Travelling between north and south Goa you'll need to change buses at Margao, Panaji or both.

➡ There are no timetables, but buses are frequent and usually have the destination posted (in English and Konkani) in the front window. Fares range from ₹5 to ₹40.

➡ Local buses are mostly old rustbuckets and can be slow – stopping frequently to drop off or pick up passengers. Avoid bus travel on the busy, congested road between Candolim and Baga. Between Panaji and Margao or Mapusa, look for the 'express' buses.

Car

➡ It's easy in Goa to organise a private car with a driver (or simply a taxi) for long-distance day trips. Expect to pay from ₹2000 for a full day out on the road (usually defined as eight hours and 80km).

➡ Self-drive hire cars start from ₹900 to ₹1200 per day for a small Maruti to upwards of ₹2000 for a large 4WD, excluding fuel and usually with a per kilometre limit. Your best bet for rental is online at sites such as www.goa2u.com and www.mygoatour.com.

➡ Familiarise yourself with road signs: on Goa's major NH66 national highway there are different speed limits for different types of vehicle.

Local Transport

Autorickshaw

An autorickshaw (also called an auto, three-wheeler or, outside of India, a tuk-tuk) is the quintessential Indian short-hop form of transport, a yellow-and-black three-wheeled contraption powered by a noisy two-stroke motorcycle engine. It's about a third cheaper than a taxi and generally a better option for short trips – count on a minimum ₹50 for a short journey and ₹100 for a slightly longer one.

Flag down an autorickshaw and negotiate the fare before you jump in; if the driver is charging too much, try another.

Motorcycle Taxi

Goa is the only state in India where motorcycles are a licensed form of taxi. You can tell the motorcycle taxis (or 'pilots') by the yellow front mudguard. They're not as common these days but you might see them gathering with taxis in towns and beach resorts. They cost half the equivalent taxi fare.

Taxi

➡ Taxis, ranging from old Ford Ambassadors to slick air-conditioned Maruti vans, are widely available for hopping town-to-town.

➡ A full day's sightseeing, depending on the distance, is likely to be around ₹1500 to ₹2000.

➡ Agree on a price before you agree to be a passenger. The exception is in Mumbai, where newer taxis have functioning meters.

Motorcycle

Getting around Goa by scooter or motorcycle is the most popular form of private transport, both for locals and tourists. It's easy to hire one but riding is not without its perils

and inexperienced (especially first-time) riders should give it careful consideration.

Driving Licence

An international driving permit is not technically mandatory, but it's useful to bring one. The first thing a policeman will want to see if he stops you is your licence, and an international permit is incontrovertible. Permits are available from your home automobile association. In any case, carry your home driving licence.

Fuel

➡ Though subject to change, at the time of research unleaded petrol cost around ₹70 per litre.

➡ Distances are generally short and small bikes (such as the Honda Kinetic or Activa) are very economical – at least 30km per litre.

➡ There are increasing numbers of petrol stations in main towns including Panaji, Margao, Mapusa, Ponda and Vasco da Gama. There are busy pumps near Vagator, Palolem and Arambol.

➡ Where there are no petrol pumps, general stores sell petrol by the litre (usually in recycled water bottles at ₹80 to ₹100); beware that sometimes petrol in plastic bottles has been diluted.

➡ Before hiring, ensure that the fuel gauge works.

Hire

Hiring a motorcycle in Goa is easy and cheap enough.

Owners will probably find you, and are more often than not decent locals who are just looking to make a bit of cash on the side. Another option is to ask at your hotel or guesthouse.

➡ Private bike owners are not technically allowed to rent out a machine, so if you are stopped by the police for any reason, your hirer would prefer that you say you have borrowed it from a 'friend'.

➡ Make sure registration papers are in the bike – it gives the police one less argument against you.

WHICH MOTORBIKE?

➡ At the base of the scale are the most popular rental bikes – gearless scooters such as the 100cc Honda Kinetics, Activa or Bajaj scooters. They are extremely practical and easy to ride. You only need a car driving licence to ride these bikes.

➡ Next up are the 100cc and 135cc bikes – Yamaha being the most common. Fuel economy is good, they go faster than a Kinetic, and are more comfortable over long distances. You'll need a motorcycle licence and some riding experience.

➡ At the top of the pile are the classic thumping Enfield Bullets, made in India since the 1950s. They are far less fuel-friendly, require more maintenance than the others, are heavy and take a little getting used to – but they provide the ultimate street cred. Most Enfields available for hire are 350cc, but there are also some 500cc models around.

COSTS & PRACTICALITIES

➡ Outside of the high season you can get a scooter for as little as ₹150 per day. During high season (December to February) the standard rate is ₹250 to ₹350 (up to double that over Christmas peak).

➡ Expect to pay ₹400 for a 100cc bike and up to ₹700 for an Enfield.

WOMEN'S TAXI SERVICE

Women's Taxi Service (☎0832-2437437) This excellent Goa Tourism initiative has put female drivers behind the wheel of modern, metered air-con taxis. They can only be booked in advance by phone and only females, couples or families are accepted as passengers. The female drivers are trained in first aid, customer service and even self-defence, while the vehicles are fitted with GPS monitoring and a panic button for ultimate peace of mind. Fares can even be paid with a credit card.

➡ The longer you hire a bike (and the older it is), the cheaper it becomes.

➡ Make absolutely sure that you agree with the owner about the price. Clarify whether one day is 24 hours, and that you won't be asked to pay extra for keeping it overnight.

➡ You may be asked to pay cash up front; get a written receipt.

➡ Always get the mobile phone number of the owner in case something goes wrong with the bike; this works both ways.

➡ Take note of any damage, dings or scratches when you hire and write them down or take a snapshot of the bike so the owner won't accuse you of causing it. Conversely, you'll be expected to pay up for any damage.

On the Road
ROAD CONDITIONS & SAFETY

Goan roads can be treacherous, filled with human, bovine, canine, feline, mechanical and avian obstacles, as well as a good sprinkling of potholes and hairpin bends.

➡ Be on the lookout for 'speed breakers'. Speed humps are stand-alone back breakers or come in triplets.

➡ Take it slowly, try not to drive at night (country lanes are poorly lit), and don't attempt a north–south day trip on a 50cc bike.

➡ Goa's main NH66 is a highway in name only: aside from a multilane stretch between Panaji and Margao, it's single-lane each way and consequently can be a little congested.

ROAD RULES
➡ Driving is on the left, vehicles give way to the right and road signs are universal pictorial signs.

➡ Helmets are mandatory for two-wheelers in Goa though most riders continue

GOA'S FERRIES

One of the joys of day tripping in Goa is a short ride on one of the state's few remaining vehicle/passenger ferries, which, until the recent addition of road bridges spanning Goa's wide and wonderful rivers, formed a crucial means of transport for locals. Most ferries run every half hour or so (busy routes run nonstop) from around 7am to 10pm. The ferries are free to pedestrians and two-wheelers.

Panaji to Betim (p92) The most popular ferry and a useful short cut to the northern beaches.

Ribandar to Chorao Island (p93) For Dr Salim Ali Bird Sanctuary.

Old Goa to Divar Island (p101)

Divar Island to Naroa (p158)

Querim (Keri) to Terekhol Fort (p154)

to ignore this. In theory you can be pulled over and fined for not wearing one and the safety implications are obvious.

➡ At busy intersections, traffic police are often on hand to reduce the chaos. Otherwise, make good use of your horn.

➡ Speed limits range from 30kmh to 60kmh. The blood alcohol limit is 0.03% – which equals one standard drink for most people.

➡ The highway code in India can be reduced to one essential truth – 'Might is Right' – meaning the bigger the vehicle, the more priority you're accorded. Motorbikes sit only above bicycles and pedestrians on the food chain!

Organised Tours
Classic Bike Adventure (www.classic-bike-india.com; Assagao) This well-established Goan company organises motorbike tours on Enfields through the Himalaya, Nepal, South India and Goa.

Enfield Riders (☑9821688770; www.enfiel-driders.com) Mumbai-based outfit that has a fleet of Royal Enfield motorcycles and organises tours around Goa and further afield.

➡ **Live India** (☑0845-2241917; www.liveindia.co.uk) UK-based outfit offering all-inclusive tours of Goa on Enfield Bullets.

Train

Goa's rail services, though great for getting to and from the state, aren't particularly useful for getting around it. It's usually quicker and more convenient to travel by bus, taxi or under your own steam. An exception is travelling the length of the state, say from Arambol or Mapusa to Palolem, which would otherwise require several bus changes.

➡ There are two railways in Goa: the South Central Railway runs east from Vasco da Gama, through Margao and into Karnataka. This line is most useful for day tripping to Dudhsagar Falls via Colem station.

➡ The interstate Konkan Railway train line passes through Goa: stations from north to south in Goa are: Pernem (for Arambol), Thivim (for Mapusa), Karmali (for Old Goa and Panaji), Verna, Margao (for Colva and Benaulim), Bali, Barcem and Canacona (for Palolem).

Health

Hygiene is generally poor in most regions so food and water-borne illnesses are fairly common. A number of insect-borne diseases are present, particularly in tropical areas. Medical care is basic in various areas (especially beyond the larger cities) so it's essential to be well prepared.

Pre-existing medical conditions and accidental injury (especially traffic accidents) account for most that are life-threatening. Becoming ill in some way, however, is common. Fortunately, most travellers' illnesses can be prevented with some common-sense behaviour or treated with a well-stocked travellers' medical kit – however, never hesitate to consult a doctor while on the road, as self-diagnosis can be hazardous.

The following information is a general guide only and certainly does not replace the advice of a doctor trained in travel medicine.

BEFORE YOU GO

You can buy many medications over the counter in India without a doctor's prescription, but it can be difficult to find some of the newer drugs, particularly the latest antidepressant drugs, blood-pressure medications and contraceptive pills. Bring the following:

➡ medications in their original, labelled containers

➡ a signed, dated letter from your doctor describing your medical conditions and medications, including generic names

➡ a doctor's letter documenting the necessity of any syringes you bring

➡ if you have a heart condition, a copy of your ECG taken just prior to travelling

➡ any regular medication (double your ordinary needs)

Insurance

Don't travel without health insurance. Emergency evacuation is expensive. Consider the following when buying insurance:

➡ You may require extra cover for adventure activities such as rock climbing.

➡ In India, doctors usually require immediate payment in cash. Your insurance plan may make payments directly to providers or it will reimburse you later for overseas health expenditures. If you do have to claim later, make sure you keep all relevant documentation.

➡ Some policies ask that you telephone back (reverse charges) to a centre in your home country where an immediate assessment of your problem will be made.

Vaccinations

Specialised travel-medicine clinics are your best source of up-to-date information; they stock all available vaccines and can give specific recommendations for your trip. Most vaccines don't give immunity until *at least* two weeks after they're given, so visit a doctor well before departure. Ask your doctor for an International Certificate of Vaccination (sometimes known as the 'yellow booklet'), which will list all the vaccinations you've received.

Medical Checklist

Recommended items for a personal medical kit:

➡ Antifungal cream, eg clotrimazole

➡ Antibacterial cream, eg mupirocin

➡ Antibiotic for skin infections, eg amoxicillin/clavulanate or cephalexin

➡ Antihistamine – there are many options, eg cetrizine for daytime and promethazine for night

➡ Antiseptic, eg Betadine

➡ Antispasmodic for stomach cramps, eg Buscopam

➡ Contraceptive

➡ Decongestant, eg pseudoephedrine

➡ DEET-based insect repellent

➡ Diarrhoea medication – consider an oral rehydration solution (eg Gastrolyte), diarrhoea 'stopper' (eg loperamide) and antinausea medication (eg prochlorperazine). Antibiotics for diarrhoea include ciprofloxacin; for bacterial diarrhoea azithromycin; for giardia or amoebic dysentery tinidazole

➡ First-aid items such as elastoplasts, bandages, gauze, thermometer (but not mercury), sterile needles and syringes, and tweezers

➡ Ibuprofen or another anti-inflammatory

➡ Iodine tablets (unless you're pregnant or have a thyroid problem) to purify water

➡ Migraine medication if you suffer from migraines

➡ Paracetamol

➡ Pyrethrin to impregnate clothing and mosquito nets

➡ Steroid cream for allergic or itchy rashes, eg 1% to 2% hydrocortisone

➡ High-factor sunscreen

➡ Throat lozenges

➡ Thrush (vaginal yeast infection) treatment, eg clotrimazole pessaries or Diflucan tablet

➡ Ural or equivalent if prone to urine infections

Websites

There is lots of travel-health advice on the internet; www.lonelyplanet.com is a good place to start. Other options:

Centers for Disease Control and Prevention (CDC; www.cdc.gov) Travel health advice.

MD Travel Health (www.mdtravelhealth.com) Travel-health recommendations for every country, updated daily.

World Health Organization (WHO; www.who.int/ith) Its helpful book *International Travel & Health* is revised annually and is available online.

Further Reading

Lonely Planet's *Healthy Travel – Asia & India* is pocket sized with useful information, including pre-trip planning, first aid, immunisation

REQUIRED & RECOMMENDED VACCINATIONS

The only vaccine required by international regulations is **yellow fever**. Proof of vaccination will only be required if you have visited a country in the yellow-fever zone within the six days prior to entering India. If you are travelling to India from Africa or South America, you should check to see if you require proof of vaccination.

The World Health Organization (WHO) recommends the following vaccinations for travellers to India (as well as being up to date with measles, mumps and rubella vaccinations):

Adult diphtheria & tetanus Single booster recommended if none in the previous 10 years. Side effects include sore arm and fever.

Hepatitis A Provides almost 100% protection for up to a year; a booster after 12 months provides at least another 20 years' protection. Mild side effects such as headache and sore arm occur in 5% to 10% of people.

Hepatitis B Now considered routine for most travellers. Given as three shots over six months. A rapid schedule is also available, as is a combined vaccination with Hepatitis A. Side effects are mild and uncommon, usually headache and sore arm. In 95% of people lifetime protection results.

Polio Only one booster is required as an adult for lifetime protection. Inactivated polio vaccine is safe during pregnancy.

Typhoid Recommended for all travellers to India, even those only visiting urban areas. The vaccine offers around 70% protection, lasts for two to three years and comes as a single shot. Tablets are also available, but the injection is usually recommended as it has fewer side effects. Sore arm and fever may occur.

Varicella If you haven't had chickenpox, discuss this vaccination with your doctor.

These immunisations are recommended for long-term travellers (more than one month) or those at special risk (seek further advice from your doctor):

Japanese B Encephalitis Three injections in all. Booster recommended after two years. Sore arm and headache are the most common side effects. In rare cases, an allergic reaction comprising hives and swelling can occur up to 10 days after any of the three doses.

Meningitis Single injection. There are two types of vaccination: the quadravalent vaccine gives two to three years' protection; meningitis group C vaccine gives around 10 years' protection. Recommended for long-term backpackers aged under 25.

Rabies Three injections in all. A booster after one year will then provide 10 years' protection. Side effects are rare – occasionally headache and sore arm.

Tuberculosis (TB) Adult long-term travellers are usually recommended to have a TB skin test before and after travel, rather than vaccination. Only one vaccine given in a lifetime.

information, and what to do if you get sick on the road. Other good references include *Travellers' Health* by Dr Richard Dawood and *Travelling Well* by Dr Deborah Mills – check out the website (www.travellingwell.com.au) too.

IN INDIA

Availability of Health Care

Medical care is hugely variable in India. Some cities now have clinics catering specifically to travellers and expatriates; these clinics are usually more expensive than local medical facilities, and offer a higher standard of care. Additionally, they know the local system, including reputable local hospitals and specialists. They may also liaise with insurance companies should you require evacuation. It is usually difficult to find reliable medical care in rural areas.

Self-treatment may be appropriate if your problem is minor (eg traveller's diarrhoea), you are carrying the relevant medication, and you cannot attend a recommended clinic. If you suspect a serious disease, especially malaria, travel to the nearest quality facility.

Before buying medication over the counter, check the use-by date, and ensure the packet is sealed and properly stored (eg not exposed to the sunshine).

Infectious Diseases

Malaria

This is a potentially deadly disease. Before you travel, seek expert advice according to your itinerary (rural areas are especially risky) and on medication and side effects.

Malaria is caused by a parasite transmitted by the bite of an infected mosquito. The most important symptom of malaria is fever, but general symptoms, such as headache, diarrhoea, cough or chills, may also occur. Diagnosis can only be properly made by taking a blood sample.

Two strategies should be combined to prevent malaria: mosquito avoidance and antimalarial medications. Most people who catch malaria are taking inadequate or no antimalarial medication.

Travellers are advised to prevent mosquito bites by taking these steps:

➡ Use a DEET-based insect repellent on exposed skin. Wash this off at night – as long as you are sleeping under a mosquito net. Natural repellents such as citronella can be effective, but must be applied more frequently than products containing DEET.

➡ Sleep under a mosquito net impregnated with pyrethrin.

➡ Choose accommodation with proper screens and fans (if not air-conditioned).

➡ Impregnate clothing with pyrethrin in high-risk areas.

➡ Wear long sleeves and trousers in light colours.

➡ Use mosquito coils.

➡ Spray your room with insect repellent before going out for your evening meal.

There are a variety of medications available:

Chloroquine & Paludrine combination Limited effectiveness in many parts of South Asia. Common side effects include nausea (40% of people) and mouth ulcers.

Doxycycline (daily tablet) A broad-spectrum antibiotic that helps prevent a variety of tropical diseases, including leptospirosis, tick-borne disease and typhus. Potential side effects include photosensitivity (a tendency to sunburn), thrush (in women), indigestion, heartburn, nausea and interference with the contraceptive pill. More serious side effects include ulceration of the oesophagus – take your tablet with a meal and a large glass of water, and never lie down within half an hour of taking it. It must be taken for four weeks after leaving the risk area.

Lariam (mefloquine) This weekly tablet suits many people. Serious side effects are rare but include depression, anxiety, psychosis and seizures. Anyone with a history of depression, anxiety, other psychological disorders or epilepsy should not take Lariam. It is considered safe in the second and third trimesters of pregnancy. Tablets must be taken for four weeks after leaving the risk area.

Malarone A combination of atovaquone and proguanil. Side effects are uncommon and mild, most commonly nausea and headache. It is the best tablet for scuba divers and for those on short trips to high-risk areas. It must be taken for one week after leaving the risk area.

Other diseases

Avian Flu 'Bird flu' or Influenza A (H5N1) is a subtype of the type A influenza virus. Contact with dead or sick birds is the principal source of infection and bird-to-human transmission does not easily occur. Symptoms include high fever and flu-like symptoms with rapid deterioration, leading to respiratory failure and death in many cases. Immediate medical care should be sought if bird flu is suspected. Check www.who.int/en/or www.avianinfluenza.com.au.

Dengue Fever This mosquito-borne disease is becomingly increasingly problematic, especially in the cities. As there is no vaccine available it can only be prevented by avoiding mosquito bites at all times. Symptoms include high fever, severe headache and body ache and sometimes a rash and diarrhoea. Treatment is rest and paracetamol – do not take aspirin or ibuprofen as it increases the likelihood of haemorrhaging. Make sure you see a doctor to be diagnosed and monitored.

Hepatitis A This food- and water-borne virus infects the liver, causing jaundice (yellow skin and eyes), nausea and lethargy. There is no specific treatment for hepatitis A; just allow time for the liver to heal. All travellers to India should be vaccinated against hepatitis A.

Hepatitis B This sexually transmitted disease is spread by body fluids and can be prevented by vaccination. The long-term consequences can include liver cancer and cirrhosis.

Hepatitis E Transmitted through contaminated food and water, hepatitis E has similar symptoms to hepatitis A, but is far less common. It is a severe problem in pregnant women and can result in the death of both mother and baby. There is no commercially available vaccine, and prevention is by following safe eating and drinking guidelines.

HIV Spread via contaminated body fluids. Avoid unsafe sex, unsterile needles (including in medical facilities) and procedures such as tattoos. The growth rate of HIV in India is one of the highest in the world.

Influenza Present year-round in the tropics, influenza (flu) symptoms include fever, muscle aches, a runny nose, cough and sore throat. It can be severe in people over the age of 65 or in those with medical conditions such as heart disease or diabetes – vaccination is recommended for these individuals. There is no specific treatment, just rest and paracetamol.

Japanese B Encephalitis This viral disease is transmitted by mosquitoes and is rare in travellers. Most cases occur in rural areas and vaccination is recommended for travellers spending more than one month outside of cities. There is no treatment, and it may result in permanent brain damage or death. Ask your doctor for further details.

Rabies This fatal disease is spread by the bite or possibly even the lick of an infected animal – most commonly a dog or monkey. You should seek medical advice immediately after any animal bite and commence postexposure treatment. Having pretravel vaccination means the postbite treatment is greatly simplified. If an animal bites you, gently wash the wound with soap and water, and apply iodine-based antiseptic. If you are not prevaccinated you will need to receive rabies immunoglobulin as soon as possible, and this is very difficult to obtain in much of India.

Tuberculosis While TB is rare in travellers, those who have significant contact with the local population (such as medical and aid workers and long-term travellers) should take precautions. Vaccination is usually only given to children under the age of five, but adults at risk are recommended to have pre- and post-travel TB testing. The main symptoms are fever, cough, weight loss, night sweats and fatigue.

Typhoid This bacterial infection is also spread via food and water. It gives a high and progressive fever and headache, and may be accompanied by a dry cough and stomach pain. It is diagnosed by blood tests and treated with antibiotics. Vaccination is recommended for all travellers who are spending more than a week in India. Be aware that vaccination is not 100% effective, so you must still be careful with what you eat and drink.

Travellers' Diarrhoea

This is by far the most common problem affecting travellers in India – between 30% and 70% of people will suffer from it within two weeks of starting their trip. It's usually caused by a bacteria, and thus responds promptly to treatment with antibiotics.

Travellers' diarrhoea is defined as the passage of more than three watery bowel actions within 24 hours, plus at least one other symptom, such as fever, cramps, nausea, vomiting or feeling generally unwell.

Treatment consists of staying well hydrated; rehydration solutions like Gastrolyte are the best for this. Antibiotics such as ciprofloxacin or azithromycin should kill the bacteria quickly. Seek medical attention quickly if you do not respond to an appropriate antibiotic.

Loperamide is just a 'stopper' and doesn't get to the cause of the problem. It can be helpful, though (eg if you have to go on a long bus ride). Don't take loperamide if you have a fever or blood in your stools.

Amoebic Dysentery Amoebic dysentery is very rare in travellers but is quite often misdiagnosed by poor-quality labs. Symptoms are similar to bacterial diarrhoea: fever, bloody diarrhoea and generally feeling unwell. You should always seek reliable medical care if you have blood in your diarrhoea. Treatment involves two drugs: tinidazole or metronidazole to kill the parasite in your gut and then a second drug to kill the cysts. If left untreated complications such as liver or gut abscesses can occur.

Giardiasis Giardia is a parasite that is relatively common in travellers. Symptoms include nausea, bloating, excess gas, fatigue and intermittent diarrhoea. The parasite will eventually go away if left untreated but this can take months; the best advice is to seek medical treatment. The treatment of choice is tinidazole, with metronidazole being a second-line option.

Environmental Hazards

Air Pollution

Air pollution, particularly vehicle pollution, is an increasing problem in most of India's urban hubs. If you have severe respiratory problems, speak with your doctor before travelling to India.

Diving & Surfing

Divers and surfers should seek specialised advice before they travel to ensure their medical kit contains treatment for coral cuts and tropical ear infections. Divers should ensure their insurance covers them for decompression illness – get specialised dive insurance through an organisation such as Divers Alert Network (www.danasiapacific.org). Certain medical conditions are incompatible with diving; check with your doctor.

Food

Dining out brings with it the possibility of contracting diarrhoea. Ways to help avoid food-related illness:

➧ eat only freshly cooked food

➧ avoid shellfish and buffets

➧ peel fruit

➧ cook vegetables

➧ soak salads in iodine water for at least 20 minutes

➧ eat in busy restaurants with a high turnover of customers

Heat

Many parts of India, especially down south, are hot and humid throughout the year. For most visitors it takes around two weeks to comfortably adapt to the hot climate. Swelling of the feet and ankles is common, as are muscle cramps caused by excessive sweating. Prevent these by avoiding dehydration and excessive activity in the heat. Don't eat salt tablets (they aggravate the gut); drinking rehydration solution or eating salty food helps. Treat cramps by resting, rehydrating with double-strength rehydration solution and gently stretching.

Dehydration is the main contributor to heat exhaustion. Recovery is usually rapid and it is common to feel weak for some days afterwards. Symptoms include:

➧ feeling weak

➧ headache

➧ irritability

➧ nausea or vomiting

➧ sweaty skin

➧ a fast, weak pulse

➧ normal or slightly elevated body temperature.

Treatment:

➧ get out of the heat

➧ fan the sufferer

➧ apply cool, wet cloths to the skin

➧ lay the sufferer flat with their legs raised

➧ rehydrate with water containing one-quarter teaspoon of salt per litre.

Heat stroke is a serious medical emergency. Symptoms include:

➧ weakness

➧ nausea

➧ a hot dry body

➧ temperature of over 41°C

➧ dizziness

➧ confusion

➧ loss of coordination

➧ seizures

➧ eventual collapse.

Treatment:

➧ get out of the heat

➧ fan the sufferer

➧ apply wet cloths to the skin or ice to the body, especially to the groin and armpits.

Prickly heat is a common skin rash in the tropics, caused by sweat trapped under the skin. Treat it by moving out of the heat for a few hours and by having cool showers. Creams and ointments clog the skin so they should be avoided. Locally bought prickly-heat powder can be helpful.

Altitude Sickness

If you are going to altitudes above 3000m, Acute Mountain Sickness (AMS) is an issue. The biggest risk factor is going too high too quickly – follow a conservative acclimatisation schedule found in good trekking guides, and *never* go to a higher altitude when you have any symptoms that could be altitude related. There is no way to

---

DRINKING WATER

➧ Never drink tap water.

➧ Bottled water is generally safe – check the seal is intact at purchase.

➧ Avoid ice unless you know it has been made hygienically.

➧ Be careful of fresh juices served at street stalls in particular – they may have been watered down or may be served in unhygienic jugs/glasses.

➧ Boiling water is the most efficient method of purifying it.

➧ The best chemical purifier is iodine. It should not be used by pregnant women or those with thyroid problems.

➧ Water filters should also filter out most viruses. Ensure your filter has a chemical barrier such as iodine and a small pore size (less than four microns).

predict who will get altitude sickness and it is quite often the younger, fitter members of a group who succumb.

Symptoms usually develop during the first 24 hours at altitude but may be delayed up to three weeks. Mild symptoms include:

→ headache

→ lethargy

→ dizziness

→ difficulty sleeping

→ loss of appetite.

AMS may become more severe without warning and can be fatal. Severe symptoms include:

→ breathlessness

→ a dry, irritative cough (which may progress to the production of pink, frothy sputum)

→ severe headache

→ lack of coordination and balance

→ confusion

→ irrational behaviour

→ vomiting

→ drowsiness

→ unconsciousness.

Treat mild symptoms by resting at the same altitude until recovery, which usually takes a day or two. Paracetamol or aspirin can be taken for headaches. If symptoms persist or become worse, immediate descent is necessary; even 500m can help. Drug treatments should never be used to avoid descent or to enable further ascent.

The drugs acetazolamide and dexamethasone are recommended by some doctors for the prevention of AMS; however, their use is controversial. They can reduce the symptoms, but they may also mask warning signs; severe and fatal AMS has occurred in people taking these drugs.

To prevent acute mountain sickness:

→ ascend slowly – have frequent rest days, spending

CARBON-MONOXIDE POISONING

Some mountain areas rely on charcoal burners for warmth, but these should be avoided due to the risk of fatal carbon-monoxide poisoning. The thick, mattress-like blankets used in many mountain areas are amazingly warm once you get beneath the covers. If you're still cold, improvise a hot-water bottle by filling your drinking-water bottle with boiled water and covering it with a sock.

two to three nights at each rise of 1000m

→ sleep at a lower altitude than the greatest height reached during the day, if possible. Above 3000m, don't increase sleeping altitude by more than 300m daily

→ drink extra fluids

→ eat light, high-carbohydrate meals

→ avoid alcohol and sedatives

Insect Bites & Stings

Bedbugs Don't carry disease but their bites can be very itchy. They usually live in furniture and walls and then migrate to the bed at night. You can treat the itch with an antihistamine.

Lice Most commonly appear on the head and pubic areas. You may need numerous applications of an antilice shampoo such as pyrethrin. Pubic lice are usually contracted from sexual contact.

Ticks Contracted walking in rural areas. Ticks are commonly found behind the ears, on the belly and in armpits. If you have had a tick bite and have a rash at the site of the bite or elsewhere, fever or muscle aches, you should see a doctor. Doxycycline prevents tick-borne diseases.

Leeches Found in humid rainforest areas. They do not transmit any disease but their bites are often intensely itchy for weeks and can easily become infected. Apply an iodine-based antiseptic to any leech bite to help prevent infection.

Bee and wasp stings Anyone with a serious bee or wasp allergy should carry an injection of adrenalin (eg an Epipen). For others pain is the main problem –

apply ice to the sting and take painkillers.

Skin Problems

Fungal rashes There are two common fungal rashes that affect travellers. The first occurs in moist areas, such as the groin, armpits and between the toes. It starts as a red patch that slowly spreads and is usually itchy. Treatment involves keeping the skin dry, avoiding chafing and using an antifungal cream such as clotrimazole or Lamisil. The second, *Tinea versicolor,* causes light-coloured patches, most commonly on the back, chest and shoulders. Consult a doctor.

Cuts and scratches These become easily infected in humid climates. Immediately wash all wounds in clean water and apply antiseptic. If you develop signs of infection (increasing pain and redness), see a doctor.

Women's Health

For gynaecological health issues, seek out a female doctor.

Birth control Bring adequate supplies of your own form of contraception.

Sanitary products Pads, rarely tampons, are readily available.

Thrush Heat, humidity and antibiotics can all contribute to thrush. Treatment is with antifungal creams and pessaries such as clotrimazole. A practical alternative is a single tablet of fluconazole (Diflucan).

Urinary-tract infections These can be precipitated by dehydration or long bus journeys without toilet stops; bring suitable antibiotics.

Language

WANT MORE?

For in-depth language information and handy phrases, check out Lonely Planet's *India Phrasebook*. You'll find it at **shop .lonelyplanet.com**, or you can buy Lonely Planet's iPhone phrasebooks at the Apple App Store.

Thanks to its unusual colonial history, Goa has inherited a mixture of languages. Portuguese is still spoken as a second language by a few Goans, although it is gradually dying out. Konkani is the official language of Goa, whereas Marathi is taught as a standard subject in the state, as well as being the main language of Mumbai. Children in Goa are obliged to learn Hindi in school, and the primary language used in many schools is actually English, since both Hindi and English have official status in India. English is widely spoken in tourist areas in Goa and Mumbai.

HINDI

Hindi has about 600 million speakers worldwide, of which 180 million are in India. It developed from Classical Sanskrit, and is written in the Devanagari script. In 1947 it was granted official status along with English.

Most Hindi sounds are similar to their English counterparts. The main difference is that Hindi has both 'aspirated' consonants (pronounced with a puff of air, like saying 'h' after the sound) and unaspirated ones, as well as 'retroflex' (pronounced with the tongue bent backwards) and nonretroflex consonants. Our simplified pronunciation guides don't include these distinctions – if you read them as if they were English, you'll be understood just fine.

The pronunciation of vowels is important, especially their length (eg a and aa). The consonant combination ng after a vowel indicates nasalisation (ie the vowel is pronounced 'through the nose'). Note also that au is pronounced as the 'ow' in 'how'.

Word stress in Hindi is very light; we've indicated the stressed syllables with italics.

Basics

Hindi verbs change form depending on the gender of the speaker (or the subject of the sentence in general) – meaning it's the verbs, not the pronouns 'he' or 'she', which show whether the subject of the sentence is masculine or feminine. In these phrases we include the options for male and female speakers, marked 'm' and 'f' respectively.

Hello./Goodbye.	नमस्ते ।	na·ma·*ste*
Yes.	जी हाँ ।	jee haang
No.	जी नहीं ।	jee na·*heeng*
Excuse me.	सुनिये ।	su·ni·ye
Sorry.	माफ़ कीजिये ।	maaf *kee*·ji·ye
Please ...	कृपया ...	kri·pa·*yaa* ...
Thank you.	थैंक्यू ।	*thayn*·kyoo
You're welcome.	कोई बात नहीं ।	*ko*·ee baat na·*heeng*

How are you?
आप कैसे/कैसी हैं?
aap *kay*·se/*kay*·see hayng (m/f)

Fine. And you?
मैं ठीक हूँ ।
आप सुनाइये ।
mayng teek hoong
aap su·*naa*·i·ye

What's your name?
आप का नाम क्या है?
aap kaa naam kyaa hay

My name is ...
मेरा नाम ... है ।
me·raa naam ... hay

Do you speak English?

क्या आपको अंग्रेज़ी   kyaa aap ko an·*gre*·zee
आती है?   *aa*·tee hay

I don't understand.

मैं नहीं समझा/   mayng na·*heeng* sam·jaa/
समझी।   *sam*·jee (m/f)

Accommodation

Where's a ...?	... कहाँ है?	... ka·*haang* hay
guesthouse	गेस्ट हाउस	gest *haa*·us
hotel	होटल	*ho*·tal
youth hostel	यूथ हास्टल	yoot *haas*·tal

Do you have a ... room?	क्या ... कमरा है?	kyaa ... *kam*·raa hay
single	सिंगल	*sin*·gal
double	डबल	da·*bal*

How much is it per ...?	... के लिये कितने पैसे लगते हैं?	... ke li·*ye* *kit*·ne *pay*·se *lag*·te hayng
night	एक रात	ek raat
person	हर व्यक्ति	har *vyak*·ti

Numbers – Hindi

1	१	एक	ek
2	२	दो	do
3	३	तीन	teen
4	४	चार	chaar
5	५	पाँच	paanch
6	६	छह	chay
7	७	सात	saat
8	८	आठ	aat
9	९	नौ	nau
10	१०	दस	das
20	२०	बीस	bees
30	३०	तीस	tees
40	४०	चालीस	*chaa*·lees
50	५०	पचास	pa·*chaas*
60	६०	साठ	saat
70	७०	सत्तर	*sat*·tar
80	८०	अस्सी	*as*·see
90	९०	नब्बे	*nab*·be
100	१००	सौ	sau
1000	१०००	एक हज़ार	ek ha·*zaar*

Eating & Drinking

What would you recommend?

आपके ख़्याल में   aap ke kyaal meng
क्या अच्छा होगा?   kyaa *ach*·chaa ho·gaa

Do you have vegetarian food?

क्या आप का खाना   kyaa aap kaa *kaa*·naa
शाकाहारी है?   shaa·kaa·*haa*·ree hay

I don't eat (meat).

मैं (गोश्त) नहीं   mayng (gosht) na·*heeng*
खाता/खाती।   *kaa*·taa/*kaa*·tee (m/f)

I'll have ...

मुझे ... दीजिये।   mu·*je* ... *dee*·ji·ye

That was delicious.

बहुत मज़ेदार हुआ।   ba·*hut* ma·ze·*daar* hu·*aa*

Please bring the menu/bill.

मेन्यू/बिल लाइये।   *men*·yoo/bil *laa*·i·ye

Emergencies

Help!

मदद कीजिये!   ma·*dad kee*·ji·ye

Go away!

जाओ!   *jaa*·o

I'm lost.

मैं रास्ता भूल   mayng *raas*·taa bool
गया/गयी हूँ।   ga·*yaa*/ga·*yee* hoong (m/f)

Call a doctor!

डॉक्टर को बुलाओ!   *daak*·tar ko bu·*laa*·o

Call the police!

पुलिस को बुलाओ!   pu·*lis* ko bu·*laa*·o

I'm ill.

मैं बीमार हूँ।   mayng *bee*·maar hoong

I'm allergic to (antibiotics).

मुझे (एंटीबायोटिकिस)   mu·*je* (en·tee·baa·*yo*·tiks)
की एलरजी है।   kee e·*lar*·jee hay

Where's the toilet?

टॉइलेट कहाँ है?   *taa*·i·let ka·*haang* hay

Shopping & Services

I'd like to buy ...

मुझे ... चाहिये।   mu·*je* ... *chaa*·hi·ye

I'm just looking.

सिर्फ़ देखने आया/   sirf *dek*·ne *aa*·yaa/
आयी हूँ।   *aa*·yee hoong (m/f)

Can I look at it?

दिखाइये।   di·*kaa*·i·ye

Do you have any others?

दूसरा है?   *doos*·raa hay

How much is it?
कितने का है?   *kit*·ne kaa hay

It's too expensive.
यह बहुत महंगा/   yeh ba·*hut* ma·*han*·gaa/
महंगी है ।   ma·*han*·gee hay (m/f)

Can you lower the price?
क्या आप दाम   kyaa aap daam
कम करेंगे?   kam ka·*reng*·ge

There's a mistake in the bill.
बिल में गलती है ।   bil meng *gal*·tee hay

Transport & Directions

When's the **... (bus)?**	... (बस) कब जाती है?	... (bas) kab *jaa*·tee hay
first	पहली	*peh*·lee
next	अगली	*ag*·lee
last	आख़िरी	*aa*·ki·ree
bicycle **rickshaw**	साइकिल रिक्शा	*saa*·i·kil *rik*·shaa
boat	जहाज़	ja·*haaz*
bus	बस	bas
plane	हवाई जहाज़	ha·*vaa*·ee ja·*haaz*
train	ट्रेन	tren
a ... ticket	के लिये ... टिकट दीजिये ।	ke li·*ye* ... ti·*kat* dee·ji·ye
1st-class	फ़र्स्ट क्लास	farst klaas
2nd-class	सेकंड क्लास	se·*kand* klaas
one-way	एक तरफ़ा	ek ta·ra·*faa*
return	आने जाने का	*aa*·ne *jaa*·ne kaa
I'd like to **hire a ...**	मुझे ... किराये पर लेना है।	mu·*je* ... ki·*raa*·ye par le·naa hay
4WD	फ़ोर व्हील ड्राइव	for vheel *draa*·iv
bicycle	साइकिल	*saa*·i·kil
car	कार	kaar
motorbike	मोटर साइकिल	*mo*·tar *saa*·i·kil

Where's ...?
... कहाँ है?   ... ka·*haang* hay

How far is it?
वह कितनी दूर है?   voh *kit*·nee door hay

What's the address?
पता क्या है?   pa·*taa* kyaa hay

Can you write it down, please?
कृपया यह लिखिये?   kri·pa·*yaa* yeh li·*ki*·ye

Can you show me (on the map)?
(नक्शे में) दिखा   (*nak*·she meng) di·*kaa*
सकते है?   *sak*·te hayng

KONKANI

After a long and hard-fought battle, Konkani was recognised as the official language of Goa in 1987, becoming a national language in 1992. Before that, argument had raged that Konkani was actually no more than a dialect of Marathi, the official language of the much larger Maharashtra. Konkani is an Indo-Aryan language and has 2.5 million speakers. The Devanagari script (also used to write Hindi and Marathi) is the official writing system for Konkani in Goa. However, Konkani speakers also use the Kannada script, as given here.

A few pronunciation tips: ai is pronounced as in 'aisle', eu as the 'u' in 'nurse' (a short sound), oh as the 'o' in 'note' and ts as in 'hats'. The symbol ng (as in 'sing') indicates the nasalisation of the preceding consonant, meaning that the consonant sound is pronounced 'through the nose'.

Basics

Hello.	ಹಲ್ಲೋ.	*hal*·lo
Goodbye.	ಮೆಳ್ಯಾಂ.	*mel*·yaang
How are you?	ಕಸೊ/ಕಶಿ ಆಸಾಯ್?	*keu*·so/*keu*·shi aa·saay (m/f)
Fine, thanks.	ಹಾಂವ್ ಬರೊ ಆಸಾಂ.	*haang*·ung *beu*·rong aa·saang
Yes.	ವ್ಹಯ್.	*weu*·i
No.	ನಾ.	naang
Please.	ಉಪ್ಕಾರ್ ಕರ್ನ್.	*up*·kaar keurn
Thank you.	ದೇವ್ ಬರೆಂ ಕರುಂ.	*day*·u bo·reng ko·roong
Excuse me.	ಉಪ್ಕಾರ್ ಕರ್ನ್.	*up*·kaar keurn
Sorry.	ಚೂಕ್ ಜ್ಹಾಲಿ, ಮಾಫ್ ಕರ್.	tsook *zaa*·li maaf keur

What's your name?
ತುಜೆಂ ನಾಂವ್ ಕಿತೆಂ?   *tu*·jeng *naang*·ung ki·teng

My name is ...
ಮ್ಹಜೆಂ ನಾಂವ್ ...   *meu*·jeng *naang*·ung ...

Do you speak English?
ಇಂಗ್ಲಿಶ್ ಉಲೆಯ್ತಾಯ್ಗೀ?   *ing*·leesh u·*leuy*·taay·gee

I don't understand.
ನಾ, ಸಮ್ಜೊಂಕ್–ನಾ.   naang *som*·zonk·naang

Numbers – Konkani		
1	ಏಕ್	ayk
2	ದೋನ್	dohn
3	ತೀನ್	teen
4	ಚಾರ್	chaar
5	ಪಾಂಚ್	paants
6	ಸೊ	so
7	ಸಾತ್	saat
8	ಆಟ್	aat
9	ನೋವ್	nohw
10	ಧಾ	daa
20	ವೀಸ್	wees
30	ತೀಸ್	tees
40	ಚಾಳೀಸ್	tsaa·lees
50	ಪನ್ನಾಸ್	pon·naas
60	ಸಾಟ್	saat
70	ಸತ್ತರ್	seut·teur
80	ಐಂಶಿಂ	euyng·shing
90	ನೊವೋದ್	no·wod
100	ಶೆಂಭರ್	shem·bor
1000	ಹಜಾರ್	ha·zaar

Accommodation

Do you have a single/double room?
ಸಿಂಗಲ್/ಡಬಲ್ ರೂಮ್
ಮೆಳಾತ್ಗೀ?
sin·gal/da·bal room
me·laat·gee

How much is it per night?
ಏಕಾ ರಾತೀಚೆಂ
ಭಾಡೆಂ ಕಿತ್ಲೆಂ?
e·kaa raa·ti·cheng
baa·deng kit·leng

How much is it per person?
ಏಕ್ಲ್ಯಾಕ್ ಭಾಡೆಂ ಕಿತ್ಲೆಂ?
ek·lyaak baa·deng kit·leng

Eating & Drinking

Can you recommend a dish?
ಬರೆಂ ಏಕ್ ನಿಸ್ತೆಂ
ಜ್ಞಾಲ್ಯಾರ್ ಖೈಂಚೆಂ?
beu·reng ayk nis·teng
zaa·lyaar keu·ing·cheng

I'd like the menu, please.
ಮೆನೂ ಜ್ಞಾಯ್ ಆಸ್–ಲ್ಲೊ. me·noo zaay aa·sul·lo

I'd like the bill, please.
ಬಿಲ್ಲ್ ಜ್ಞಾಯ್ ಆಸ್–ಲ್ಲೆಂ. bil zaay aa·sul·leng

Emergencies

Help! | ಮ್ಹಾಕಾ | maa·kaa
| ಕುಮೆಕ್ ಕರ್! | ku·meuk keur
Go away! | ವಸ್! | weuts

Call ...! | ... ಆಪೈ! | ... aa·pai
 a doctor | ದಾಕ್ತೆರಾಕ್ | daak·te·raak
 the police | ಪೊಲಿಸಾಂಕ್ | po·li·saank

I'm lost.
ಮ್ಹಜೀ ವಾಟ್ ಚುಕ್ಲ್ಯಾ. meu·ji waat tsuk·lyaa

Where are the toilets?
ಟೊಯ್ಲೆಟ್ ಖೈಂಚೆರ್
ಆಸಾತ್?
toy·let keu·ing·tseur
aa·saat

Shopping

Can I look at it?
ಪಳಯಿತ್ಗೀ? peu·leu·yet·gee

How much is it?
ತಾಕಾ ಕಿತ್ಲೆ ಪೈಶೆ? taa·kaa kit·le peuy·she

That's too expensive.
ತೆಂ ಏಕ್ದಮ್ ಮ್ಹಾರಗ್. teng ayk·dam maa·reug

Transport & Directions

Where's the ...?
... ಖೈಂ ಆಸಾ? ... keuyng aa·saa

Can you show me (on the map)?
(ಮೇಪಾಚೆರ್)
ದಾಕೈಶಿಗೀ?
(mae·paa·cher)
daa·keuy·shi·gee

What time's the first/last bus?
ಪಯ್ಲೆಂ/ಆಖ್ರೇಚೆಂ
ಬಸ್ ಕಿತ್ಲ್ಯಾ ವೆಳಾರ್
ಯೆತಾ?
peuy·leng/ak·ray·cheng
bas kit·lyaa we·laar
ye·taa

One ... ticket | (ಪೆರ್ಮುದೆ) ... | (per·mu·de) ...
to (Permude), | ಮ್ಹಾ ಕಾ ಏಕ್ | maa·kaa ayk
please. | ಟಿಕೇಟ್ ಜ್ಞಾಯ್. | ti·kayt zaay
 one-way | ವಚೊಂಕ್ | wo·tsonk
 | ಮಾತ್ರ್ | maatr
 return | ವಚೊಂಕ್ | wo·tsonk
 | ಆನಿಂ ಪಾಟಿಂ | aan·ing paa·ting
 | ಯೆಂವ್ಕ್ | ayng·wuk

GLOSSARY

auto-da-fé – trial of faith

ayurveda – ancient study of healing arts and herbal medicine

baksheesh – tip, bribe or donation

balcão – shady porch at front of traditional Goan house, usually with benches built into the walls

betel – nut of the areca palm; the nut is mildly intoxicating and is chewed with *paan* as a stimulant and digestive

caste – four classes into which Hindu society is divided; one's hereditary station in life

charas – resin of the cannabis plant; also referred to as hashish

crore – 10 million

Dalit – preferred term for India's casteless class; see *Untouchable*

dhaba – basic restaurant or snack bar

Dhangars – tribe of Goa's indigenous people

dharma – Hindu and Buddhist moral code of behaviour; natural law

Dravidian – general term for the cultures and languages of the south of India, including Tamil, Malayalam, Telugu and Kannada

fado – melancholy song of longing, popular in Portuguese colonial era

garbhagriha – inner sanctum of a Hindu temple

ghat – steps or landing on a river; range of hills, or road up hills; the Western Ghats are the range of mountains that run along India's west coast, effectively forming the eastern border of Goa

GTDC – Goa Tourism Development Corporation

Harijan – name given by Gandhi to India's *Untouchables*; the term is no longer considered acceptable; see also *Dalit* and *Untouchable*

Jainism – religion and philosophy founded by Mahavira in the 6th century BC in India; its fundamental tenet is nonviolence

khadi – homespun cloth

Kshatriya – Hindu *caste* of warriors and administrators

KTC – Kadamba Transport Corporation; Goa's state bus company

Kunbis – Descendants of Goa's first inhabitants; among the state's poorest groups

lakh – 100,000

lingam – phallic symbol representing the god *Shiva*

maidan – open grassed area in a city

mandapa – pillared pavilion of a temple

mando – famous song and dance form, introduced originally by the Goan Catholic community

Manueline – style of architecture typical of that built by the Portuguese during the reign of Manuel I (r 1495-1521)

marg – major road

masjid – mosque

monsoon – rainy season between June and October

paan – mixture of betel nut and various spices, chewed for its mildly intoxicating effect, and as a digestive after meals

panchayat – local government; a panchayat area typically consists of two to three villages, from which volunteers are elected to represent the interests of the local people (the elected representative is called the panch; the elected leader is the sarpanch)

pousada – Portuguese for hostel

prasad – food offering

puja – offerings or prayers; literally 'respect'

raj – rule or sovereignty

raja, rana – king

ramponkar – traditional Goan fisherman; fishes the coastal waters from a wooden boat, using a hand-hauled net (rampon)

reredos – ornamental screen behind the altar in Goan churches

saquão – central courtyard in traditional Goan houses

satyagraha – literally 'insistence on truth'; non-violent protest involving a fast, popularised by Gandhi; protesters are *satyagrahis*

shri – honorific; these days the Indian equivalent of Mr or Mrs; also spelt sri, sree, shree

sitar – Indian stringed instrument

sossegado – see susegad

Sudra – caste of labourers

susegad – Goan expression meaning relaxed or laid-back

taluka – administrative district or region

tank – reservoir

tiatr – locally written and produced drama in the Konkani language

tikka – mark devout Hindus put on their foreheads with *tikka* powder

toddy tapper – one who extracts toddy (palm sap) from palm trees

Untouchable – lowest *caste* or 'casteless' for whom the most menial tasks are reserved; name derives from the belief that higher castes risk defilement if they touch one (formerly known as *Harijan*, now *Dalit* or *Scheduled Castes*)

varna – concept of *caste*

veda – knowledge

waddo – section or ward of a village; also known as a vaddo

wallah – man or person; can be added onto almost anything to denote an occupation, thus dhobi-wallah, taxi-wallah, chai-wallah

Behind the Scenes

SEND US YOUR FEEDBACK

We love to hear from travellers – your comments keep us on our toes and help make our books better. Our well-travelled team reads every word on what you loved or loathed about this book. Although we cannot reply individually to your submissions, we always guarantee that your feedback goes straight to the appropriate authors, in time for the next edition. Each person who sends us information is thanked in the next edition – the most useful submissions are rewarded with a selection of digital PDF chapters.

Visit **lonelyplanet.com/contact** to submit your updates and suggestions or to ask for help. Our award-winning website also features inspirational travel stories, news and discussions.

Note: We may edit, reproduce and incorporate your comments in Lonely Planet products such as guidebooks, websites and digital products, so let us know if you don't want your comments reproduced or your name acknowledged. For a copy of our privacy policy visit lonelyplanet.com/privacy.

OUR READERS

Many thanks to the travellers who used the last edition and wrote to us with helpful hints, useful advice and interesting anecdotes:

Clive & Sheila Robinson, Jenny & David Thomas, Lelena Pierce, Remo Klinger, Tiago Raimundo

AUTHOR THANKS

Paul Harding

Thanks to Hannah and Layla for accompanying me to Goa and putting up with my absence while in Kerala. Cheers to Joe for entrusting me with such a great part of India. In India, thanks to all who offered advice and company but especially to all the new friends I met in Goa and mostly to the old friends I already knew – you all know who you are!

Abigail Blasi

Thank you Joe Bindloss and Sarina Singh, DE and CA supreme, and to my wonderful co--authors. Thanks in Delhi to Sarah Fothering-ham, to Nicolas Thompson and Danish Abbas, to Dilliwala Mayank Austen Soofi, to Rajinder and Surinder Budhraja, to Nirinjan and Jyoti Desai, my Delhi family, and to Luca for holding the fort.

Trent Holden

Thanks first up to Joe Bindloss for giving me the opportunity again to work again on India – a seriously dream gig. As well as to my co-authors, especially Sarina for all the help and tips along the way. A shout out to all the good folk I met along the road and shared a beer with. But as always my biggest thanks goes to my beautiful girlfriend Kate, and my family and friends who I all miss back home in Melbourne.

Iain Stewart

It was great to hang with Laksh in Bandra and have a virtual beer with Paul Harding by the sea. Thanks to the good folk at the MTDC all over the state, particularly Mr Shaker and Mrs Singh in Mumbai. I'm also very grateful to Aditya in Nagpur and Tadoba, Maria in Matheran and the merry musicians of Kolhapur.

ACKNOWLEDGMENTS

Climate map data adapted from Peel MC, Finlayson BL & McMahon TA (2007) 'Updated World Map of the Köppen-Geiger Climate Classification', Hydrology and Earth System Sciences, 11, 163344.

Cover photograph:Anjuna Beach, Goa/ Kimberley Coole/Getty

THIS BOOK

This 7th edition of Lonely Planet's *Goa & Mumbai* guidebook was researched and written by Paul Harding, Abigail Blasi, Trent Holden and Iain Stewart.

This guidebook was produced by the following:

Destination Editor
Joe Bindloss

Product Editors
Kate Mathews, Alison Ridgway

Book Designer
Clara Monitto

Assisting Editors Imogen Bannister, Kate Chapman, Kate Evans, Samantha Forge, Paul Harding, Gabrielle Innes, Katie O'Connell, Lauren O'Connell, Kathryn Rowan, Saralinda Turner

Cover Researcher
Naomi Parker

Thanks to Lonely Planet Cartography, Ellie Simpson

Index

Map Pages **000**
Photo Pages **000**

Map Legend

Sights
- Beach
- Bird Sanctuary
- Buddhist
- Castle/Palace
- Christian
- Confucian
- Hindu
- Islamic
- Jain
- Jewish
- Monument
- Museum/Gallery/Historic Building
- Ruin
- Shinto
- Sikh
- Taoist
- Winery/Vineyard
- Zoo/Wildlife Sanctuary
- Other Sight

Activities, Courses & Tours
- Bodysurfing
- Diving
- Canoeing/Kayaking
- Course/Tour
- Sento Hot Baths/Onsen
- Skiing
- Snorkelling
- Surfing
- Swimming/Pool
- Walking
- Windsurfing
- Other Activity

Sleeping
- Sleeping
- Camping

Eating
- Eating

Drinking & Nightlife
- Drinking & Nightlife
- Cafe

Entertainment
- Entertainment

Shopping
- Shopping

Information
- Bank
- Embassy/Consulate
- Hospital/Medical
- Internet
- Police
- Post Office
- Telephone
- Toilet
- Tourist Information
- Other Information

Geographic
- Beach
- Hut/Shelter
- Lighthouse
- Lookout
- Mountain/Volcano
- Oasis
- Park
- Pass
- Picnic Area
- Waterfall

Population
- Capital (National)
- Capital (State/Province)
- City/Large Town
- Town/Village

Transport
- Airport
- Border crossing
- Bus
- Cable car/Funicular
- Cycling
- Ferry
- Metro station
- Monorail
- Parking
- Petrol station
- Subway station
- Taxi
- Train station/Railway
- Tram
- Underground station
- Other Transport

Routes
- Tollway
- Freeway
- Primary
- Secondary
- Tertiary
- Lane
- Unsealed road
- Road under construction
- Plaza/Mall
- Steps
- Tunnel
- Pedestrian overpass
- Walking Tour
- Walking Tour detour
- Path/Walking Trail

Boundaries
- International
- State/Province
- Disputed
- Regional/Suburb
- Marine Park
- Cliff
- Wall

Hydrography
- River, Creek
- Intermittent River
- Canal
- Water
- Dry/Salt/Intermittent Lake
- Reef

Areas
- Airport/Runway
- Beach/Desert
- Cemetery (Christian)
- Cemetery (Other)
- Glacier
- Mudflat
- Park/Forest
- Sight (Building)
- Sportsground
- Swamp/Mangrove

Note: Not all symbols displayed above appear on the maps in this book

OUR STORY

A beat-up old car, a few dollars in the pocket and a sense of adventure. In 1972 that's all Tony and Maureen Wheeler needed for the trip of a lifetime – across Europe and Asia overland to Australia. It took several months, and at the end – broke but inspired – they sat at their kitchen table writing and stapling together their first travel guide, *Across Asia on the Cheap*. Within a week they'd sold 1500 copies. Lonely Planet was born.

Today, Lonely Planet has offices in Franklin, London, Melbourne, Oakland, Beijing and Delhi, with more than 600 staff and writers. We share Tony's belief that 'a great guidebook should do three things: inform, educate and amuse'.

OUR WRITERS

Paul Harding

Coordinating Author; Goa Paul first landed in India in the mid-'90s looking for adventure and soon found himself in Goa looking for a decent beach hut. After many return visits to India as a traveller, writer and photographer, he keeps landing back in Goa, where the pace of life is a little slower but the wit of the people is often quicker. During his travels Paul worked on Lonely Planet's *Goa* guidebook in the 2000s and was fortunate enough to be drawn back for this edition, where he sampled seafood and beaches, sunsets and *susegad* and chose to ride a Honda Kinetic over an Enfield. Contributor to more than 40 Lonely Planet titles, this was Paul's 9th assignment on India and the second time with his intrepid young daughter, Layla.

Iain Stewart

Mumbai Iain grew up in Leicester, a very Indian town transplanted to the Midlands, UK (complete with its own curry mile). He first visited India in 1991 and explored the sights at totally the wrong time of year, with temperatures approaching 50°C in parts. For this trip he wised up and travelled post-monsoon: bar-hopping in Mumbai, meandering down the Konkan coast and having several near-misses with tigers in Tadoba.

Abigail Blasi

Abigail fell in love with India on her first visit in 1994, and since then she's explored and written about the country from north to south and back again. She's covered plenty of other places for Lonely Planet too, from Mauritania and Mali to Rome and Lisbon. Abigail wrote the Scams, Women & Solo Travellers and Health chapters.

Trent Holden

Beyond Goa On his third time authoring in India, Trent checked out Hampi's ruins before hitting the beaches in Gokarna. A freelance travel writer based in London, Trent also covers destinations such as Nepal, Zimbabwe and Japan. In between travels he writes about food and music. You can catch him on Twitter @hombreholden.

Published by Lonely Planet Publications Pty Ltd
ABN 36 005 607 983
7th edition – October 2015
ISBN 978 1 74220 803 9
© Lonely Planet 2015   Photographs © as indicated 2015
10 9 8 7 6 5 4 3 2 1
Printed in China